C000002587

BRASSEY'S
BOOK OF
SIEGES

BRASSEY'S
BOOK OF
SIEGES

WILLIAM SEYMOUR

WITH MAPS AND ILLUSTRATIONS BY
W.F.N. WATSON

BRASSEYS

This edition 2002

Brassey's
A member of Chrysalis Books plc
64 Brewery Road
London N7 9NT

Library of Congress Cataloguing in Publication Data available

British Library Cataloguing in Publication Data
A catalogue for this book is available
from the British Library

ISBN 1 85753 375 5

Printed in Great Britain by The Bath Press

To
CAROLYN
Who seems to have been forgotten —
but is never chippy!

Contents

List of Maps and Illustrations

Glossary

Abatis: A defence usually consisting of felled trees.

Banquette: An infantry fire-step built behind a parapet.

Bastion: A work with two front faces forming a salient angle, and two flanks, projecting from the curtain wall so as to allow flanking fire along it.

Berm: (1) A horizontal ledge between two slopes, e.g. the upper and lower sections of a rampart.

(2) A space 3 ft to 8 ft wide sometimes left between the ditch and the base of the parapet.

Camouflet: A mine calculated to shatter an underground gallery, usually without cratering the surface.

Caponier: A powerful casemated work sunk into the bank of the ditch, and projecting perpendicularly above ground level with overhead cover. Used for observation and to deliver flanking fire.

Cavalier: A raised artillery platform sited within the main enceinte usually in the centre of a bastion. Also occasionally constructed by the besiegers for the same purpose.

Cheval-de-Frise: A portable obstruction equipped with wooden stakes, sword blades etc, and used for blocking breaches.

Circumvallation: A line of siege works facing the open country so as to hold off a relieving force.

Counterguard: A narrow detached rampart placed immediately in front of an important work to protect it from being breached.

Counterscarp: The vertical face of the ditch on the outer side.

Countervallation: An entrenchment made at the beginning of a siege and facing the place of attack.

Covered Way: A path running along the rim of the counterscarp, sunk below the crest of the glacis to afford protection.

Crownwork: An outwork with a front face consisting of a central salient bastion and two flanking demi-bastions, and thus in plan resembling a crown.

Cunette, or Cuvette: A narrow trench dug in the bottom of the ditch and often flooded.

Curtain: A length of rampart between two bastions.

Demi-bastion: A half bastion of one face and one flank.

Demi-lune, Half-moon or Mezzalune: An outwork similar to a ravelin (qv), but constructed in front of a bastion, and having a crescent-shaped gorge.

Embrasure: An opening made through a parapet or wall to allow a cannon to fire through the thickness.

Enceinte: The principal continuous perimeter of a fort.

Enfilade: Firing coming from the flank in such a way that the effect is felt along the length of a fortification.

Fascines: Bundles of long sticks used in the construction and revetment of earthworks.

Fausse-braye: A parapet built between the base of the rampart and the ditch. Sometimes replaced by more modern counterguard. In earlier use a covered way.

Forlorn Hope: A small party of soldiers under a junior officer preceding an assault to draw fire, and induce the enemy to fire his mines.

Gabion: A basket about 3 ft deep and 2 ft diameter of woven brushwood, which is filled with earth. Used to provide rapid cover.

Glacis: The slope between the covered way and open country, designed to afford the attacker no cover.

Gorge: The rear of an outwork, usually only protected by palisades and a ditch so, when captured, untenable due to fire from the rear.

Hornwork: An outwork, generally rectangular, with a demi-bastion at each forward angle having a re-entrant angle between them. This giving a horned effect.

Lunette: A small outwork in the form of a little detached bastion. Or a small work at the side of a ravelin.

Palisade: A fence of close-set stakes used to hinder attackers generally, and especially to close the gorge of an outwork.

Parados: The earth bank at the rear of a trench.

Parapet: A wall placed along the forward edge of fortifications, especially on a rampart, to afford protection to the defenders.

Petard: A bell-like device, used for blowing in a gate.

Platform: A level site for mounting an artillery battery.

Rampart: A thick wall of earth, stone or masonry revetted on the front face, which forms the main defence of a fortress. It is normally supported by a terreplein at the rear.

Ravelin: A detached outwork placed in front of a curtain, usually triangular with two faces.

Redan: A V-shaped work, open to the rear.

Redoubt: (1) An outpost wall in front of the main enceinte, enclosed on all sides.

(2) A small fort placed at a strategic site.

Retrenchment: An interior defence constructed by besieged to cut off a breach.

Revetting: The shoring-up of vertical or near vertical earth banks with timber, turf, fascines or masonry to prevent crumbling.

Salient Angle: In a defensive work, an angle having its apex facing outward. In a re-entrant angle, the apex faces inward.

Sally Port: A small gate, usually set in a curtain, which permits troops to leave on a sortie.

Sap: A narrow trench, designed to make rapid progress forward.

Sap-roller: Used to protect workmen from enfilading fire during the opening of each section of the sap. A wicker casing compactly filled with cotton.

Scarp: The side of the ditch nearer the fort.

Tenaille: A detached oblong outwork in the ditch usually in front of, and parallel to, a curtain.

Terreplein: The backing behind a rampart.

Traverse: A bank or wall; usually at right angles to the main alignment of the work, which protects defenders from enfilade.

Zig-zags: Approach trenches.

Introduction

SIEGES are among the oldest operations of warfare, and because they come in so many different forms and usually contain a number of exciting, heroic, and even amusing incidents they are perhaps the best of all military reading. Man has besieged his fellow either singly or collectively ever since the forces of light and darkness have wrestled for the capture of his soul. There have been sieges of very long and of very short duration; epic legendary sieges such as Troy; sieges in which chivalry, butchery and romance have played their part; sieges that have been turning points in history, and sordid little sieges of town houses.

Anyone attempting a short account of them is confronted with a wide and difficult choice, and inevitably many have to be discarded, as also have most of the often amusing anecdotal recollections and personal reminiscences. I have concentrated on those sieges which are for the most part well known, and which played a significant part in a campaign, or in some instances in world history. My choice has been as widely spread as possible, and in each case the hardship and horrors, as well as the nobilities and sacrifices of a siege are apparent, my object being to present the facts accurately and to tell the story simply and clearly.

I believe it to be important to give something of the historical and military background to each siege, and not to be too detailed or technical, for this book is not intended as a profound work. There is, however, a need for a short initial chapter outlining some of the principles, weapons and fortifications applicable to siege warfare throughout the area. A glossary is essential, but it has been purposely kept to a brief description of only those terms used in the text. It is not always easy to visualise some of the terms from the written word, and I owe a great debt to Colonel Watson for his admirable descriptive drawings. He has also advised me throughout, and embellished the whole work with his excellent maps in which we have endeavoured to show every place name mentioned in the text.

This book is concerned with sieges of the past, and cannot crystal gaze into the future, where it is tempting to think that command of the air would be a decisive factor. This, however, is not borne out in the case of three of the four recent sieges discussed. Nevertheless, the enormously increased power of modern weapons is likely to improve considerably the prospects of the besiegers, who may no longer require to fulfil Napoleon's dictum of a four to one superiority in numbers. But perhaps the old fashioned siege has gone for ever, to be replaced by the large-scale blockade. And history tells us that blockades are seldom successful.

A great many people from a wide range of countries have been very kind in giving me assistance either in correspondence or in person, and to all of them I am extremely grateful. In particular I would like to mention Dr John Adair; Brigadier General Graf Attems-Petzenstein; Mr Tom Cordery who gave me the benefit of his experiences in Tobruk; Mr Ercihan Düzgünoğlu who took time off from his studies to conduct me round the walls of Constantinople; Mr Anthony Malley, Colonel Michael McCorkell and Mrs Mary McLaughlin who greatly helped me during my tour of Londonderry; Mr DeWitt Nelson; Dr Hugh Purcell; Mrs Chagit Rifinski; Mr Alan Turton whose expert guidance round Basing House was much appreciated; Colonel N Uvarov of the USSR; Mr Terrence Winschel who drove me round Vicksburg National Military Park and explained the battle; and Professor Z A B Zeman.

My publishers' editor, Brigadier Bryan Watkins, gave me advice and encouragement throughout and, as always, the staffs of the London Library, the Ministry of Defence Library and the Public Record Office offered me every assistance in carrying out my research. Also, as always, I owe a special debt to my secretary for her constant cheerfulness during many trying hours on the typewriter treadmill, especially latterly when she had an arm down.

Note.   Until 1752 England used the 'Old Style' (Julian) calendar, which was eleven days behind the 'New Style' (Gregorian) one. In this book I have used the dates as they appeared to those living at the time, but I have ignored the English custom of starting the year on Lady Day.

CHAPTER 1

The Mechanics of a Siege

'THE operation of an army before or round a fortified place to compel surrender' is one dictionary's short and simple definition of a siege. Others are similar and, so far as they go, correct, but there is much more to it than that. A siege is hardly ever an isolated operation (only Malta of those described in this book could be considered a possible exception), and in early days it was often the culmination and greatest part of a battle. Whereas the actual battle may have lasted just a day or two the siege could go on for weeks or months.

A siege not infrequently denotes military failure, for it must be the object of every general to defeat his enemy in the open field, while he who allows himself to be bottled up forfeits that valuable principle of war, mobility, and relies on others to get him out of trouble. There are, of course, exceptions to the latter of which Tobruk is a good example. There the besieged had a role to play that was vital to the campaign, for if Rommel were to take Egypt he must first take Tobruk. But no commander willingly embarks upon a siege, for it is an operation of war that involves great hardships, often for civilians as well as for soldiers, and contrary to popular opinion these hardships can be as bad for the besiegers as for the besieged.

In all the sieges later described there was never any thought of surrendering the town or fortress without a fight, nor was there any hesitation by the commander of the attacking force, but it was not always that way. Where the besieged lacked the three essential requirements for withstanding a long and most unpleasant incarceration, namely a strong defence, a sound supply system and, as the natural concomitant of these, high morale, it was sometimes thought wiser to surrender on terms. Similarly, to bypass or detach a force of observation occasionally made better sense than to invest and assault.

Throughout the centuries fortresses have been built and towns fortified for a wide variety of reasons. Countries have encircled vulnerable frontiers or coasts with a ring of fortresses as an extra aid to defence, as a boost to the citizens' morale, as a launching pad to invasion or a refuge in retreat. They have been sited to seal off mountain paths, to guard river crossings and for many other purposes. But from the crusader's castle to the Maginot Line

1

they have been massive constructions in which the defenders, who were invariably outnumbered by the besiegers, bestowed a great deal of (often misplaced) confidence. The underlying principle of the castle or fortress remained much the same from the time of the Norman motte-and-bailey through the Middle Ages and well into the 17th century. As the years unfolded stone replaced wood, the keep became stronger, outer walls were added in which towers were placed at intervals, gateways were protected and machicolations (projecting parapets) made their appearance. Except where they could be mined, these formidable fortifications were virtually indestructible up to, and through, the early days of gunpowder. But with the advent of heavy siege guns, greater strength in depth and certain innovations became necessary.

Chief among these was the bastion – virtually a platform that juts out from the wall – a more aggressive fortification than the tower which, together with machicolations, it gradually replaced. Originally it was round, to deflect shot, but later it was more usually pentagonal with two faces meeting at the projecting angle, two flanks that bordered the wall, and a rearmost fifth side called the gorge which was the entrance. Bastions were linked to the curtain wall, and were the same height as the wall. Thus there became a completely encircling wall with bastions known as the *enceinte*, behind which it was comparatively easy to deploy artillery. In some cases a cavalier (raised artillery platform) was built on the bastion to give the defenders additional height.

Immediately in front of the curtain wall was the ditch, which might be wet or dry, with its retaining wall (known as the counterscarp) on its outer side. Behind this retaining wall, and protected by its parapet, was the covered way along which the forward troops could pass in comparative safety. Outworks of varying sorts (such as the *tenaille*, a low work in the ditch) had been in use for some years before the more ambitious *ravelin*, hornwork and crownwork types appeared in the late 16th and 17th centuries, and were placed beyond the ditch, which in that case would be dry. The ravelin was a massive free-standing fortification with two faces, usually placed between two bastions, thus enabling the defence to bring enfilading fire on the assault troops. The horn and crownworks had a similar purpose, but with two long rectangular sides, fronted by two demi-bastions (hornwork) and a bastion and two demi-bastions (crownwork). There is a good example of the horn and crownworks at Valletta.

There has always been a wide choice of weapons available to both besieged and besiegers. From earliest times, boiling pitch or quicklime were favourite deterrents to those who were over-rash with the scaling ladders. Until the introduction of gunpowder brought handguns, the sling, bow, crossbow, mace and lance were the principal arms; Greek fire was the precursor of the flame-thrower, and the heavy artillery included a number of cumbersome, unwieldy yet effective weapons such as the ram, mangonel,

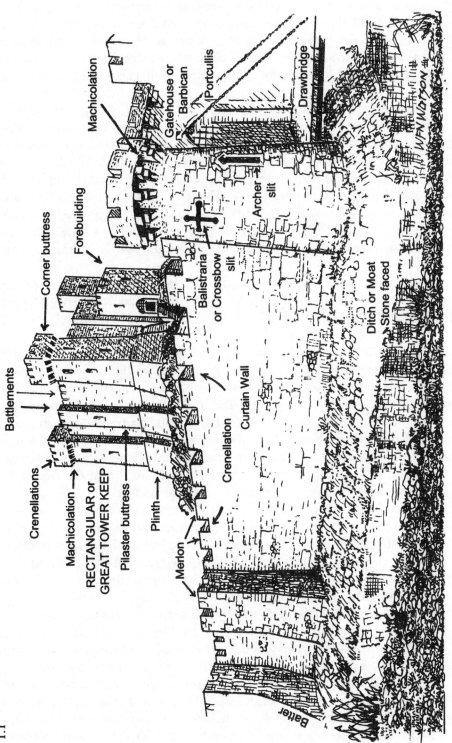

FIG 1.1

Medieval Castle

Machicolation

Gatehouse or
Barbican

Portcullis

Drawbridge

Archer
slit

Ballistraria
or Crossbow
slit

Corner buttress

Forebuilding

Battlements

Crenellations

Machicolation →

RECTANGULAR or
GREAT TOWER KEEP

Pilaster buttress

Plinth →

Merlon

Crenellation

Curtain Wall

Ditch or Moat
Stone faced

Batter

WFN WATSON

balista and trebuchet. As most of these weapons were used in the early sieges described, some of the more esoteric need a brief introduction.

The origins of the terrifying Greek fire are uncertain, but the weapon comprised a semi-liquid substance of sulphur, pitch and petroleum among other obscure materials. It was discharged from tubes and could burn on water, indeed it could only be extinguished by sand and vinegar – ingredients not always readily to hand. The ram was not strictly artillery, but was the earliest weapon used in an attempt to breach a wall. It was a stout tree trunk with a metal point, slung on a wooden frame mounted on wheels. It was surmounted by a cover of hides or turves, variously known as 'cat', 'rat', or 'sow', to protect the manipulators from descending missiles. It was surprisingly effective if the assault party (it needed about fifty men to swing it) were allowed uninterrupted action, which after the advent of machicolations was seldom the case. The bore, which burrowed into the wall rather than bashing it, was a somewhat lighter edition of the ram and less effective.

Early artillery, used for softening up the garrison, was based on the catapult and crossbow principle. The idea was copied from the Romans, and propelling power was produced by torsion (the mangonel), tension (the balista) and counterpoise (the trebuchet). The mangonel could hurl a heavy stone of about five hundredweight, but it was far from accurate. The two-armed balista looked and operated very much like a large crossbow, and might discharge either a stone ball, bolt or javelin, and was considerably more accurate than the mangonel. The trebuchet was cumbersome and difficult to move, but it was capable of discharging heavy weights in a high trajectory – the forerunner of the howitzer and mortar – and was also used to project combustible material. The 'gunners' had their lighter moments, for it was not unknown to lob very dead animals, and even the occasional herald whose message was unpalatable, over the walls.

In the early days of siege warfare when the artillery available was often unable to breach the walls the assault depended upon the use of scaling ladders and towers. Ladders, which were of wood or leather, were extended on arrival at the wall, placed against it and secured at the base. Archers would give covering fire during this hazardous operation, but it remained a chancy and costly manoeuvre.

Towers, nicknamed 'malvoisins', were cumbersome wooden contraptions three or four stories high. These top-heavy edifices crammed with troops had to be manipulated over filled ditches and inadequately smoothed ground often causing the towers to list if not collapse, while the defenders showered them with burning arrows, against which their protective cov-ering of skins was not always effective. Those towers that arrived at the wall were then subjected to a ration of Greek fire or burning pitch while they tried to fix their grappling irons and leap into the assault. Needless

F_{IG} 1.2

MANGONEL or ONAGER

A legacy from the Romans

1. A heavy skein of twisted rope or sinew was bound about the base of the throwing arm. (The Romans preferred human hair for its greater elasticity.)

2. The skein was winched forward until the arm was hard against the crossbar.

3. The arm was winched back against the torsion of the skein, and loaded with the missile.

4. When sprung, the arm shot forward against the crossbar and hurled the missile as much as a quarter of a mile (400 m).

5. In some cases a sling was fastened to the arm, which could increase the range by 30% to 50%. The sling had the added advantage of allowing range to be varied: shortening it sent the missile higher and shorter: lengthening lowered the angle and increased the range.

FIG 1.3

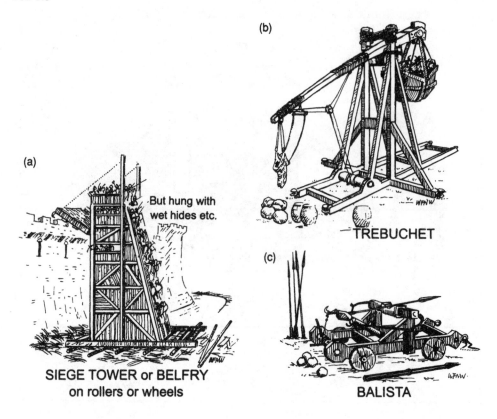

(b)

(a)

But hung with
wet hides etc.

TREBUCHET

(c)

SIEGE TOWER or BELFRY
on rollers or wheels

BALISTA

to say casualties were very high, and one can think of more pleasant ways of going to war.

Until the discovery of gunpowder, and the picaresque behaviour of early cannon had been improved upon, easily the most effective method of breaching the defence was by mining. Initially, this consisted of burrowing under a vulnerable corner or bastion, propping up the hole with wooden beams, which alone saved the foundations from collapse, and when all was ready, filling the chamber with straw and brushwood (King John used dead pigs at Rochester) and setting fire to the beams. Gunpowder made the business more effective, but mining was never an exact science, for it was difficult to estimate the depth and the correct location of the wall, and where the fortress was protected by water or built on solid rock mining was virtually impossible. The best defence against the mine was countermining. There were elementary ways of detecting a mining tunnel, and quite often the enemy engineers were discovered and driven out or killed.

By the middle of the 15th century cannon was taking over from earlier primitive propellants. At the siege of Constantinople in 1453, the Turks had one monster gun that was capable of piercing the city wall, and a whole range of lesser calibre pieces. Seventy years later, at Rhodes, they were using cannon that fired mammoth stone balls almost two feet in diameter. By the late 17th century, artillery, which by that time had become more mobile, was the dominant weapon of attack. A besieging army would be accompanied by a formidable artillery train of which heavy cannon (24-pounders) would form the greater part with smaller calibres (16 and 12-pounders) engaged in counter-battery work, and in discharging red-hot shot. There would also be a good number of howitzers and mortars.

A large artillery train could have well over a hundred cannon of various calibres, and the administrative requirements were frighteningly formidable. Huge numbers of horses and oxen were needed to drag the pieces over the appalling roads, and to transport the immense quantity of shot, fodder and baggage. Christopher Duffy in his excellent book *Fire and Stone* quotes a figure of 700,000 pounds of powder needed for a serious siege involving a large number of cannon and mortars.

This was the time of Marshal Sébastian Vauban (1633–1707), the man who made the greatest impact on all forms of siege warfare. He had the good fortune – denied to some of his nearly as brilliant contemporaries – to serve Louis XIV, a king quick to appreciate the importance of military engineering, and whose armies were the foremost in Europe. Vauban revolutionised siege warfare not only by the design and siting of the many fortresses he built, but also in the offensive by his improvements to trenching and sapping and the placing of his artillery.

Largely as a result of his work, the fortress was supreme on the battlefield during the late 17th and throughout the 18th century. But it was to be only a temporary pre-eminence, for with greatly improved artillery – particularly the rifled barrel – fortress engineers found it difficult to match concrete against cannonade. Nevertheless, the argument must remain an open one, for right up to the present time fortifications – often only of barbed wire, trenches, sandbags and mines – have beaten off superior numbers striving to overwhelm them.

The introduction of more powerful weapons necessitated a much lengthier and more cautious approach to the objective than a mad rush and the use of scaling ladders or towers. From at least the 16th century siege warfare assumed a pattern of investment, entrenching and assault which hardly varied over the succeeding centuries. Whenever possible investment needed to be total, and a large semicircular trench with salients and a protecting ditch, known as countervallation, was constructed beyond the range of defending artillery and served as a base. This trench would take a few days to dig, depending on what local labour could be impressed. Meanwhile the commander would select the point, or points, where he intended to open the siege. Once this decision was taken the siege parks, with all their massive materials, were laid out.

In a siege of some magnitude the approach to within assaulting distance

FIG 1.4

NOTIONAL PLAN OF 17th–18th CENTURY FORTRESS
to show various types of works and outworks used

Fire could no longer be brought down vertically upon attackers as previously from the machicolations and crenellations of medieval, above-ground walls, therefore the TRACE or ground-plan of fortifications was redesigned to allow fire to be brought from the FLANK as well as from the FACE, against attackers at any point.

RAVELIN:	An outwork consisting of two faces forming a salient angle constructed beyond the main ditch and in front of the CURTAIN.
CURTAIN:	The part of the wall which connects two bastions, gates, towers etc.
DEMI-LUNE or HALF-MOON:	An outwork similar to a RAVELIN but constructed in front of a BASTION, and having a crescent-shaped GORGE.
GORGE:	The neck of an outwork, or the entrance to it from the rear.
BASTION:	Projecting part of a fieldwork, in shape an irregular pentagon.
REDAN:	Simple form of fieldwork having two faces forming a salient angle.
ENCEINTE:	The main enclosure, or the main wall enclosing it.

Fig 1.5

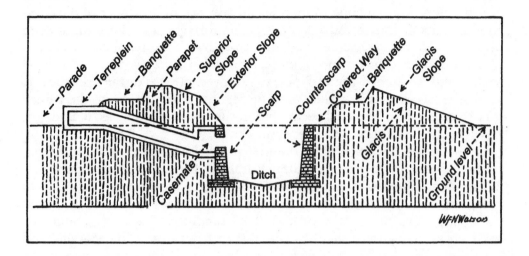

CROSS-SECTION of 17th–18th CENTURY FORTRESS

From the 16th Century, walls above ground could be breached by cannon-fire, therefore main defences were sunk below ground.

BANQUETTE: Firestep or firing position.

TERREPLEIN: Elevated emplacement behind parapet, for artillery.

CASEMATE: Fully protected firing position commanding the lower reaches of the DITCH.

PARADE: Assembly point for defending troops, from which they move to allotted posts.

GLACIS: Embankment built up beyond the ditch with the earth taken from it, gently sloped down to ground level, providing a clear field of fire, a shield to protect the ditch from direct observation, a banquette or firestep and a COVERED WAY.

COVERED WAY: A space about 30 ft wide between the COUNTER-SCARP and the GLACIS, extending all round the works of a fortification. It affords safe communication and movement all round the works and provides an assembly area for sorties.

was a major operation in itself, and carried out by the digging of parallel lines, with interconnecting trenches known as zigzags. The first parallel became the foundation of the siege, and was therefore a very important construction. A large body of men would advance under cover of darkness to within about four hundred yards of the fortress, and there dig a deep and wide trench which covered the objective. This parallel acted as a communication trench, and a place from where the troops could repel sorties and safeguard the engineers employed on the zigzag trenches. If sufficient labour was available, and the night was long enough, the trench was completed on the vital sector before dawn. But often, as at Badajoz, daylight came too soon and there was chaos.

In the following few nights, the first parallel was completed, and from it the zigzags (each arm extending to about forty yards) stretched out. When these approach trenches had made some headway it was time to bring up mortar and cannon batteries. These batteries needed to be placed on wooden platforms, and protected by sandbags, fascines, gabions, or earthworks. They were sited initially just in front of the first parallel and leapfrogged forward as the zigzag trenches inched their way towards the opening of the second and third parallels. It is easy to imagine the enormous task of bringing forward, each time the batteries were moved, planks, heavy cannonballs, mortar bombs and quantities of powder, and then constructing the platform.

From the third parallel, if it had been correctly sited, an assault could be made on the outer perimeter and covered way, and once this had been cleared of enemy the object of all the trenching and sapping had been achieved. The breaching batteries could come close enough to pound the ravelins or bastions, and open the way for an assault on the rampart. This was usually timed for first light, but the wall had to be sufficiently damaged for the rubble to form a gentle ramp, because only occasionally would it have completely collapsed, or a breach been made large enough for the assault troops to scramble through.

The besieging army had often to contend with a relieving force, and for many years it was the custom to construct lines of circumvallation on the open side as a means of protection. Unlike the line of countervallation this was a trench which might have to withstand a major attack, and so was more solidly built with redans sited between salients. During the 18th century lines of circumvallation began to lose favour, for they were too extensive for the troops available and, as Clausewitz points out, a circular position facing outward is awkward, and makes a successful sortie virtually impossible. This was borne out at the siege of Vienna. By the 19th century a separate corps of observation was greatly preferred, but this was not always possible, and as late as 1863 Grant's Federals had dug lines of circumvallation before Vicksburg.

Thus the weapons and manoeuvres of attack and defence; but the threat of starvation can be as potent a weapon as any of those described, and there have been numerous examples of garrisons being forced to surrender through lack of food and water. No one can foretell how long a siege will last, and if the troops cannot be resupplied morale declines in ratio to the daily ration until capitulation becomes inevitable. Command of the sea or air in more recent sieges did not always eliminate but greatly eased this problem. In times when roads were tracks and there were no railways the besieging army could also be afflicted by hunger, for the besieged would have thoroughly scorched the surrounding land and rounded up or killed the livestock. This gave the besiegers the additional hazard of having to bring in supplies over a long distance in hostile country, or raise the siege. The Christians before Acre had a desperate winter in 1190 when the besiegers were themselves besieged.

The three principles of strong defence, sound supply and high morale are interdependent, but when it comes to a long siege, heavy casualties and short rations, morale is pre-eminent. In a siege, to a far greater extent than in field operations, success or failure depends upon one man, the garrison commander. In almost all the epic sieges of history where the garrison has stood firm in the face of privation, carnage and destruction the men have found a sheet-anchor in the leader who has the ability to keep his head, rectify mistakes, improvise, encourage and above all endure. Joint leadership, or leadership through a council, usually brings divided loyalties and a crop of petty acerbities, for leadership cannot thrive on the principle of limited responsibility – Leningrad was an exception, Port Arthur and Dien Bien Phu were not.

The ingredients that make up a siege are a mix of boredom, discomfort, anxiety, courage, fear, hope, humiliation and hardship. The commander has to deal with them as they come. Boredom can be allayed by sorties, discomfort by ingenuity, anxiety by news from the home front, hope is helped by encouragement, humiliation is overcome by achievement, and hardship by little luxuries like tobacco, rum and brothels. But valour is the one thing that cannot be rationed in a siege.

As it was in the past so it will be in the future. No matter how advanced the weaponry or depleted the defences the moral factor is the one most likely to determine the holding or the losing of the fort. In the words of Sir George Macaulay Trevelyan:

> '. . . the real strength of a besieged place consists not on the scientific construction of its defences, nor in the multitude of the garrison, nor in abundant stores of provisions and ordnance, but in the spirit which is prepared to dare all and endure all, sooner than allow the assailants to set foot within the wall.'

CHAPTER 2

Acre 1189–91

IT is now exactly 800 years since King Richard I of England led his Crusaders out of Acre to meet the great Moslem Sultan who is known to the world as Saladin, to defeat him in the battle of Arsuf on 7 September 1191 and so bring down the curtain on what we now know as the Third Crusade. On 12 July, the Moslem garrison, after a gallant fight lasting two years, had surrendered the city to the Crusaders and so brought a period of savage and bloody fighting to a close. There is a good deal of mythology about the nature of the Crusades and a tendency to see the Crusaders themselves as knights in shining armour. As this chapter shows, they were as capable of brutality as their cruel enemy. However, the significance of the Siege of Acre is that it represents a classic example of early siege warfare, made all the more interesting by the fact that the besiegers were themselves besieged by a solid ring of Moslem troops, who thereby created some formidable logistic problems for the Christian army, in addition to keeping it involved in a prolonged fight on two fronts. Like many of the sieges considered in this book, the Siege of Acre is one in which almost all those threads which go to make up the warp and weft of human conflict can be found – courage and fortitude, determined leadership and craven incompetence and, above all, much suffering. Here we shall find too, that disease took an even greater toll of human life than the fighting – something that will be repeated time and again in later chapters.

* * *

Alexius I Comnensus won the Byzantine throne in 1081, but he soon realised that he had not the strength to defeat the encircling Turkish menace with his own military resources. He therefore appealed to Pope Urban II for mercenaries. The Pope was willing to oblige, and between the summer of 1096 and the spring of 1097 the First Crusaders arrived in large armies, each with their own leader. The achievements of these leaders demands considerable respect and admiration, for in many cases they had recruited, equipped and led a wild, undisciplined multi-racial body of men, who had received little training or battle experience. Nor were they themselves – except in one or two rare instances – competent generals, but they were courageous and resourceful.

The country in which they operated was varied. There was the coastal plain, often flanked by steep mountains; rivers and badly drained marsh-land; a number of forests (many more than today); and plenty of arid stretches of poor soil and rock. In Jerusalem, and on other high ground, the climate was reasonable, but in the plains it could be unpleasantly hot in the summer, and cold and wet in the winter. Moreover, the plains were insalubrious with stagnant water providing an ideal breeding ground for insects; malaria and dysentery were ever present, the plague and leprosy were endemic. It was a hard life with the ravages of disease more deadly than the arrows of the infidel.

In July 1099, Jerusalem was captured by the Crusaders, and the appalling massacre that followed was to send frissons of horror coursing through the civilised world. There followed more than a year of fierce arguments as to how it should be governed, by whom and with what powers. Eventually, on Christmas Day 1100, Baldwin of Edessa was crowned in the Church of the Nativity. Thus four and a half years after the armies of the First Crusade had arrived in Byzantium, they had achieved their ambition of founding the Kingdom of Jerusalem. In the course of the next 20 years or so they had, with the help of incoming pilgrims and some Genoese and Venetian sailors, carved out a sizeable kingdom in Palestine, along the Syrian coast (but never the inland towns) and in parts of Cilicia. The four principal states of the Kingdom were Jerusalem itself, Antioch, Tripoli and Edessa – although Edessa was lost in 1144.

Those who had taken the Crusader vows were certainly animated by a strong desire to liberate the Holy Places from the infidel, theirs was an act of devotion which was always uppermost in their minds. But as time went on, many who had settled in Syria and Palestine showed a tendency to divide their worship between Mammon and God. This regrettable lapse stimulated internal strife between the Crusader chiefs, alienated their cause from the rulers and magnates of Western Europe, and became a major reason for later disasters.

In 1104, five years after the capture of Jerusalem, King Baldwin took Acre with the help of a Genoese fleet after a brief siege and blockade lasting twenty days. In the summer of 1187, Joscelin of Courtenay surrendered the city without a fight. The great siege, which began in August 1189 under King Guy*, to recapture this important sea port and establish it as the capital of an attenuated kingdom lasted for a month under two years. On the Crusader side it was fought by those Franks who had already settled in Outremer† and by the newcomers of the Third Crusade, and on the

---

*Guy of Lusignan succeeded to the throne jointly with his wife Sibylla, the daughter of King Amalric, in 1185.
†Franks, together with Latins, was a name commonly given the Crusaders. Outremer referred to the collective Crusader states in the Near East.

MAP 2.1

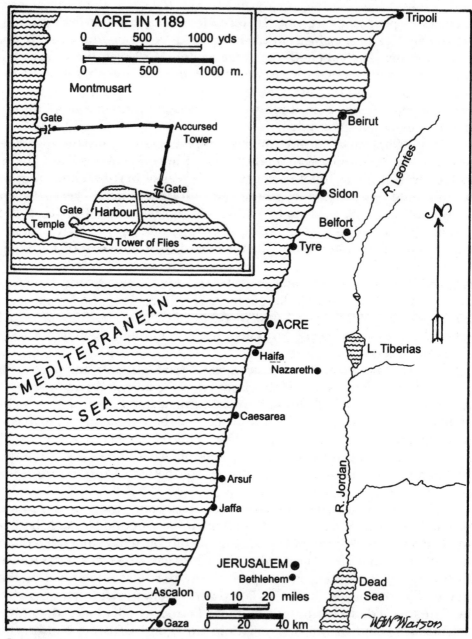

ACRE IN 1189

Montmusart

Gate

Accursed Tower

Gate

Gate   Harbour

Temple

Tower of Flies

MEDITERRANEAN

SEA

Tripoli

Beirut

Sidon

Belfort

Tyre

●ACRE

●Haifa

Nazareth●

R. Leontes

L. Tiberias

N

●Caesarea

●Arsuf

●Jaffa

R. Jordan

JERUSALEM●

Bethlehem●

Ascalon

●Gaza

Dead Sea

WGW Watson

Palestine

Moslem side by a variety of Turkomans, Kurds and Mamluks under their great Sultan, Salah ed-Din Yusuf ibn-Aiyub, a Kurd by birth and known to history as Saladin. It was a siege of particular interest, because the besiegers were themselves besieged and had to fight on two fronts for many months.

At the time of the siege of Acre the Latin kingdom was in disarray. Thanks mainly to the efforts of the Third Crusaders and the maritime interests of the great Italian republics, it was to survive for another hundred years, but the severe defeat inflicted on King Guy's army by Saladin at Hattin in July 1187, and the immediate aftermath (which included the loss of Acre) was a blow from which the kingdom never fully recovered. The King and many of his knights were in captivity, and Jerusalem and almost all the Crusader towns offered no resistance to the conqueror. The principal exceptions were Tyre and Tripoli. The former was saved by the fortuitous arrival from Constantinople, a few days after Hattin, of Conrad of Montserrat, who was a man made of sterner stuff than the demoralised commanders of Outremer, and Tripoli had been reinforced by ships and men recently dispatched by King William II of Sicily. It is possible that Saladin missed opportunities here, but he may have drawn some consolation from the immediate threat of a Crusader civil war.

In July 1188, Saladin released King Guy, and a number of his knights, having extorted a promise from Guy never to bear arms against him again – a promise that was immediately broken. But on arrival at Tyre, to resume responsibility for his greatly diminished kingdom, he found it barred against him with Conrad, whose popularity among the townspeople and Latin refugees now exceeded Guy's, determined to have nothing to do with him. Guy therefore retired to Tripoli, but returned in the spring of 1189 to force the issue with Conrad by blockade and siege. Civil war was imminent, but after four months Guy realised that he had neither the equipment nor the strength to take Tyre, and in August he raised the siege and – with considerable daring – marched on Acre. The number of men he had with him is not known (some accounts say 9,000 but it was probably less), for his march was more a gesture of defiance than a serious threat to Acre. However, he did have the Pisan fleet* whose commander had fallen out with Conrad.

The Crusaders brought to Outremer the feudal system, and their armies were made up of feudal tenants, pilgrims (often untrained and indifferently armed), native levies, mercenaries and the Military Orders, whose knights and sergeants formed the élite of the army. The Knights Hospitallers, who originated from a body of Benedictine monks running a hostel for pilgrims in Jerusalem in 1070, were given permission to form their own Order under the Pope in 1118, and some ten years later, a knight called Hugh of Payens persuaded the King of Jerusalem to allow him to form

---

*In the 11th century, Pisa, a part of the Etruscan Confederation, had become one of the greatest commercial and seafaring cities of the Mediterranean. During the first three Crusades their fleets were as important as those of Venice and Genoa.

another military and religious Order, which took the name of Knights Templar from their original headquarters in a wing of the royal palace close to Solomon's temple. Their Grand Master at this time was Gerard de Ridefort, who must bear much of the blame for Hattin. The Third Crusade (unlike most of the others) was also well served at sea by the Danes, Pisans, Venetians and Genoese.

Latin knights, who were usually of noble birth, were mounted on a weight-carrying charger that was sometimes armoured, and their bodies were well protected by a long mail shirt, a mail coif to guard neck and face, a shield and a conical helmet. They were armed with lance and sword. The foot soldiers also wore mail over well-padded gambesons*, and some form of hard cap. Their principal weapons were the bow, crossbow and spear. The major difference between the Latin troops and the Saracens was that the latter relied to a great extent on mounted archers, who were very much more mobile than the Latin knights.

Guy began his siege of Acre on 27 August 1189. He was short of men and without any siege engines. Saladin has been criticised for not mopping up his small force while it was on the march, but he was busy in the north and he knew Acre was well provisioned to withstand a siege, and he himself had supervised the strengthening of the walls during the previous year. Acre was built on a small peninsula, and to the south and west the town is protected by the sea, and there was a sea wall. There was an excellent harbour from which ran a mole south-east to a rock on which there stood a fortification known as the Tower of Flies. On the landward side there was a massive wall and ditch running north from the sea to a very strong tower called the Accursed Tower (legend has it associated with Judas Iscariot), and there it angled sharply to the west. This was a single wall, and the suburb of Montmusart was outside it. (After the earthquake of 1202, which did much damage to the fortifications, a double wall was built, and that did include Montmusart. Those walls were completed by 1212).

Guy took up a position about a mile east of Acre. Almost at once he attempted to assault the city, but without siege engines there was little chance of success. He therefore dug-in and awaited reinforcements, which by the beginning of September were arriving in welcome numbers. They were a mélange of races: Danes, Italians, French, Flemish and Germans. The Danes, who were good sailors, brought a fleet which was useful for blockading the harbour, although Moslem ships did get through quite often. The German contingent, commanded by Lewis IV, Margrave of Thuringia, were the forerunners of the large German force under the Emperor Frederick I, Barbarossa, forming part of the Third Crusade. The Margrave had come by sea, while the Emperor marched through

*Gambeson. A leather or quilted cloth padded and worn under mail, or as the principal garment.

Europe and Asia. Perhaps the most valuable reinforcements were the battle-hardened soldiers brought by Conrad, who had been persuaded to co-operate on the understanding he would not be required to serve under Guy.

Meanwhile, Saladin, who at first did not take Guy's threat too seriously, became alarmed when he learnt of the Christian reinforcements. Leaving a portion of his army to continue the siege of Beaufort Castle he hurried to Acre with the remainder. He established a rear base at Jebel el Kharruba, and then went forward to pitch his camp, as was his usual practice, in line of battle. His troops covered a semi-circle with their right on the sea north of the city, through El Aiyadiya, Tell Keisan to Tell Kurdana, where the left of his army rested on the river Belus (Nahr Namien). The line completely covered the smaller Christian army from a distance, in places, of more than two miles. The right of the line was held by the Sultan's best general (and nephew) Taqi ed-Din, the men from Mosul came next, and then the divisions of Saladin's two sons al-Afdal and az-Zahir. Saladin's command post was in the centre near El Aiyadiya, with the Kurds on his left, and on the extreme left was Asad ed-Din Shirkuh's Mamluks.

It is very difficult to estimate numbers in this long siege, for although both sides complained they lacked support both received reinforcements periodically, and in the Moslem camp contingents (which came from as far apart as Egypt and Kurdistan) were apt to withdraw, and either return in due course or be replaced. But the length of the respective lines (three and two miles) indicates very large numbers, and the Moslem army with perhaps 4,000 horse and 100,000 foot at this stage considerably outnumbered the Christians who, even with their recent reinforcements, probably had only about 2,000 horse and 30,000 foot. Guy commanded on the right of the line which rested on the Belus, about a mile downstream from Shirkuh's Mamluks, Conrad's men were on his left, then came the Margrave's Germans with the Templars holding the left. Here the line fell short of the sea ending in the region of Tell el Fukh-Khar, leaving much of the northern wall uncovered. Guy's brother, Geoffrey of Lusignan, commanded a reserve whose duty was to observe the garrison.

In the middle to late September there were a number of skirmishes by the advanced troops of both sides, but the fighting was very gentlemanly and in the intervals there was considerable fraternisation. But a sterner note was sounded when Taqi's men fought their way through to the city, and Saladin and his entourage were able to enter and inspect the fortifications. This stimulated the Franks to strengthen and, so far as possible, extend their line of circumvallation before the first major engagement began on 4 October.

This attack by the Franks on the Saracen line met with mixed fortunes. As they advanced across the open plain they needed to extend for a full frontal attack, and this resulted in their fighting the battle in three separate divisions. On the left the Templars either drove back Taqi's troops, or possibly the latter operated a feigned retreat, which was a part of Turkish battle drill. Either way Saladin sent men to reinforce his right, and the battle here remained, for the time being, in équipoise. But seeing that Saladin had weakened his centre the opposing Christian divisions advanced in a perfectly controlled attack with the infantry on close approach discharging their bows with deadly effect, and then opening up for the knights to ride through. The Mosul troops were routed, some not stopping short of Damascus, with the Franks in an uncontrolled pursuit. Thus the Moslem right and left still held in good order, but their centre was in complete disarray. It was now that Saladin fully recovered his initial error of weakening that part of his line, and showed the quality of his leadership.

By now the Christian centre was out of control. No effort had been made to recall the pursuit or stop the looting of the enemy camp. Saladin, by immense personal force, encouragement and exhortation, managed to rally a large portion of his beaten centre and hold them under strict control until the opportunity occurred for a surprise and devastatingly successful charge on the withdrawing Christian troops. The action on the Christian right had given no particular advantage to either side. Guy had held Shirkuh's men until the latter drove a wedge between him and the centre, when Guy was forced to withdraw covered by Count Geoffrey's reserve. On the left the Templars suffered very severely when the garrison sallied forth in support of Taqi, and came in on their flank.

When the Franks had regained their fortified lines, Saladin broke off the engagement. It might have been a decisive Christian victory had the centre, having won their battle, turned against the Moslem flanks, instead of wasting time in futile pursuit and looting in the company of Moslem camp followers. As it was, it had been a costly defeat. Beha ed-Din (p168) was told by a man who had helped to cast the dead into the river that on their left the Christians had lost 4,000 men. This may be an exaggeration, but certainly the Templars suffered very heavily, losing at least eighteen knights including the Grand Master, who was executed after capture.

There was little fighting – but occasionally friendly exchanges between the two camps – in the autumn and winter of 1189–90. Ramadhan* began in the middle of October, and the winter rain and cold made conditions unpleasant for fighting and almost unbearable for sitting in what were by now strongly fortified lines of circumvallation. The Franks received considerable reinforcements during this time, many European pilgrims, dissatisfied with the slow progress made by the leaders of the Third Crusade, took ship independently, and the Londoners' fleet arrived in

*The ninth month of the Mohammedan year in which the faithful must keep a strict fast, and so a period in which there is less inclination for warlike activity.

November. These extra men enabled the Franks to extend their line so that Acre became completely invested.

Saladin also received fresh troops, but not nearly so many as he had hoped for and expected, for virtually only those emirs who were his liege men were prompt to answer the call to Islam's holy war. Others made excuses, and some already in the camp took their men away, promising to return in the spring – a promise not always kept. Nevertheless, the Moslem camp remained strong, and more importantly for the garrison, the Sultan's sailors broke the blockade. At the end of October, fifty galleys got through, and three months later an Egyptian fleet succeeded in landing supplies.

In the stress of events, Guy and Conrad had temporarily shelved their enmity – the fact that Guy had saved Conrad's life when the latter had been cut off in the October battle may have helped. Now Conrad agreed to go to Tyre to fetch supplies. On his return, in March 1190, dented pride from failure to maintain the blockade was somewhat restored when his ships beat off a Moslem squadron, and brought in a valuable cargo. The Franks were fortunate in having a gently shelving beach near their camp which facilitated the landing of men and stores.

In the summer of 1190, both sides were looking for, and receiving, further reinforcements. Some of Saladin's emirs had returned to his camp, and in the north Beaufort Castle had been reduced, which relieved men for Acre. But against this, Saladin was anxious to intercept the ponderous march of the large German contingent and sent troops north for this purpose. The Christian camp was strengthened by the arrival of a force, said to number 10,000, under Henry of Troyes, Count of Champagne, and which included prominent prelates (the Archbishop of Besançon and the Bishops of Blois and Toul) and noblemen such as the Counts of Clermont and Blois. Count Henry, who was distinguished not only by his royal connections but also by his prowess in the field, was at once given overall command of the siege operations. These by now had assumed a regular pattern which was to last for the rest of the siege. The Franks, fighting on two fronts from their line of circumvallation, would attempt to assault the town and occasionally take the offensive against Saladin, while the latter would mount strong attacks on the Franks' position in order to relieve pressure on the garrison.

The first of these offensive-defensive battles took place at the beginning of May, by which time the Franks had constructed three very large towers from the timber brought by Conrad. Beha ed–Din tells us (p178) they were mounted on wheels, well protected with hides soaked in vinegar and capable of carrying five hundred men with a mangonel perched on their broad roofs. Obviously their first task must have been to protect labourers filling in the ditch to enable the towers to come close to the walls, which they overtopped. There was surprise and dismay among the garrison, for no amount of burning arrows or Greek fire immobilised them, but a young cauldron-maker from Damascus was in Saladin's camp, and he promised to destroy these monsters if he could be given certain materials, which he specified, and sent into the city. Somehow – one is not told any details – this was done, and with his third shot the first tower burst into flames, and the other two quickly suffered a similar fate. What alchemy he used is not related, but the results were spectacular and decisive in so far as that attempted assault was concerned.

A few days later, Saladin launched a full-scale attack on the Christian defences, but although he pressed it for eight days, his men could make no impression on what was now a strong defensive position. The only other major engagement of that summer was fought in July, shortly after Count Henry's force had arrived. Information indicated that the Saracen right wing had been weakened by the need to send men north and so, at midday on 25 July, the Franks initiated a major offensive against that sector. Initially this met with considerable success with a deep penetration, but no sooner had the enemy tents been reached than once again there was looting. This gave the Saracen centre divisions the chance to swing into the battle and take the Franks at considerable disadvantage. The fighting was savage and the slaughter heavy. Christian losses are not exactly known, but they were certainly more than a thousand, and among the dead the Moslems found four women in full chain mail.

In October, what was left of the once formidable German host arrived in the camp. The Emperor Frederick was 69 when he left Europe – a great age to undertake the rigours of a long march in appalling conditions through Europe and Asia Minor. The Byzantine Emperor (Isaac Angelus) was not friendly, indeed he had a treaty with Saladin, but the Sultan of Rum gave the Germans some assistance. Cilicia was reached after much hardship and loss of baggage, and here at the crossing of the river Calycadnus, near Selucia, Frederick's horse stumbled throwing him into the water. The Emperor was either drowned or died from the result of the fall. From then on, the force began to disintegrate; some men deserted, others were killed by Saladin's troops sent north to intercept them, and only about 5,000 reached the camp under Frederick's son the Duke of Swabia.

Nevertheless, every man was welcome and these were good fighters who were soon attempting to scale the walls. Furthermore, only a little behind them came Baldwin, Archbishop of Canterbury, at the head of a large English contingent. Almost at once he was expressing disgust at the fraternisation with the infidel enemy, and at the lax morals of the Christians. Three hundred 'lovely Frankish women' had recently arrived 'offering their bodies for sin'. The good Archbishop found it difficult to differentiate between morals and morale!

During the autumn, the Franks were constantly battering the city walls with their mangonels and a very powerful iron-headed ram; these made some impression, but the walls stood, and every attempt to scale them was

MAP 2.2

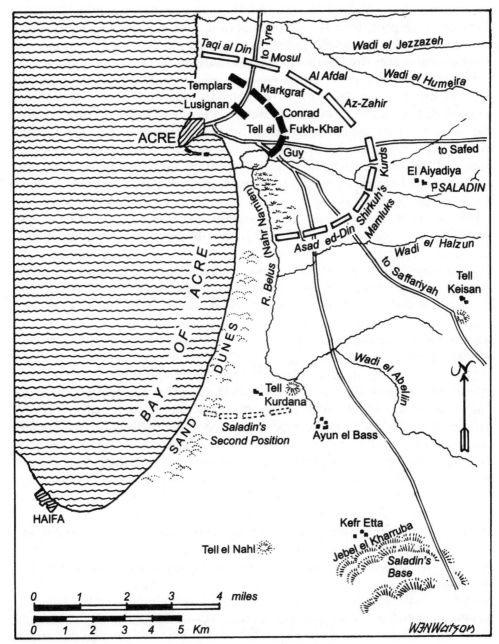

The Siege of Acre

repulsed. Moreover, the Governor of the city, Beha ed-Din Qaraqush, organised a number of sorties which destroyed many of the mangonels. By October, morale in the city had reached a low ebb, for food was in very short supply, although the situation was temporarily restored when some

Moslem sailors, disguised as Franks, ran the blockade to bring into the harbour much needed relief, and shortly afterwards an Egyptian fleet got through. This prompted the Christians to mount an attack with fire-ships on the Tower of Flies which guarded the entrance to the harbour, but the wind changed and the operation was a failure.

The Duke of Swabia strongly advocated an attack across the plain on the Saracen line. This was made in November with considerable success; Saladin was forced back some three miles after very heavy fighting. However, little was gained and the casualties had been heavy; Saladin re-established his line in a strong position in the Kharruba hills area, with his right near Ayun el Bass and his left on the sand dunes. This gave him free access to Haifa, which greatly helped his supply position in what was to be an exceptionally harsh winter for both sides.

Of the three contending forces Saladin's men fared the best in the winter of 1190–91. Troops arrived from the north which enabled the Sultan to strengthen his grip on the Latin lines, and yet allowed him to dismiss some emirs and their men until the new campaigning season. Moreover, on 13 February, he managed to relieve the garrison with a new commander and fresh troops, each of whom was ordered to carry a year's supply of hard rations. This was a great coup, for the existing garrison had become totally exhausted from continual bombardment and long bouts of near starvation.

The Franks were the most sorely tried of the three. Their only hope of provisions was from the sea, and the winter gales frequently prevented the ships from beaching. Hygiene was almost non-existent, and disease was rife and deadly throughout the camp. Duke Frederick of Swabia and Tibald, Count of Blois, died and Henry of Troyes very nearly did. Frederick's death left the Germans leaderless, but Leopold of Austria arrived shortly afterwards and took them over. In spite of their hardships, the Franks made two major attempts to storm the city. The first was timed to take advantage of an exodus to the harbour of much of the garrison to watch the death agonies of a stricken supply ship, and the second to take advantage of the collapse of a section of the wall – possibly by mining. But although both attempts were pressed resolutely the garrison threw them back in a welter of blood.

And so, with spring, the siege entered its twentieth month. With the coming of Richard I of England and Philip II of France, the two principals of the Third Crusade, the closing stages began. The news of the imminent arrival of one of these principals (Philip) was brought by a ship which, with the easing of the winter gales, reached harbour in the middle of March, laden with corn for an army that by then was reduced to eating its horses and even grass.

Philip II, along with Henry II of England, William II of Sicily and the Emperor Frederick Barbarossa, had been one of the architects of the Third

Crusade under the tutelage of Pope Gregory VIII. The Kings of England and France were constantly at war, but an uneasy peace had been agreed between Philip and Richard I (who had succeeded his father) whereby both kings would leave their kingdoms together. For many reasons there had been an unconscionable delay in their departure, but at last they set sail from Genoa (Philip) and Marseilles (Richard) in August 1190. Their progress, particularly that of Richard, was leisurely. The winter was spent in Sicily, but from Messina Philip sailed direct to the Holy Land arriving at Tyre on 20 April. The next day, together with Conrad, he landed at Acre.

He could not have brought many troops with him, for he had only six galleys, nor was he himself a courageous or inspiring soldier. He had no great enthusiasm for the Crusade and had come on it chiefly for political reasons. However, despite his unattractive demeanour and lack of charm, his was a name to conjure with and brought disquiet – although not to the extent that the name of Richard did – to the Moslem camp. More importantly, he had with him some competent engineers who built new siege engines and laid out a system of zig-zag trenching which enabled the Franks to launch their attacks from close to the wall. The ditch remained a constant obstacle, but large sections were now filled with any materials to hand, including dead horses and soldiers. Preparations for a major assault went ahead steadily, but it was decided to postpone it until Richard's arrival.

The King of England eventually reached Acre on 8 June 1191, four years after he had taken his Crusader vows. There were good reasons for the initial delay, because he was not crowned until September 1189, but there was little sense of urgency throughout his journey and much of his dalliance, and his behaviour in Sicily, were inexcusable. However, his capture of Cyprus from the breakaway self-styled Emperor Isaac Comnenus brought great riches to himself (and he was fond of gold) and, more usefully, enabled the Christians to keep a footing in the Holy Land for another hundred years. In Cyprus he was met by King Guy, and other Latin leaders opposed to Conrad, and on 12 May, in Limasol, he married Berengaria of Navarre. He left the island on 5 June, and arrived at Tyre on the 6th. Here Philip, at the instigation of his cousin Conrad, refused him admission, which proved fortunate, for sailing on to Acre he intercepted a large Moslem galley carrying weapons and 600 troops, which his ships sank after a brief engagement.

Men of the army readily forgave Richard for his dilatoriness, and there was much rejoicing at his arrival. And well there might be, for his 25 galleys were full of soldiers and war material, and his presence alone brought new life and hope to an army that was beginning to fall apart from sheer weariness. Indeed he was the archetypal Crusader: physically superb, handsome, courageous, gifted in the profession of arms, vital and adventurous. His quick temper could be as quickly assuaged, and there was much charm to counteract the arrogance. The fact that he was a bad king mattered little on the plains of Palestine. Very soon after he arrived Richard pressed for a meeting with Saladin, but the Sultan was disinclined to accept, believing kings should not meet without a peace treaty. Little could have been achieved except the romance behind a meeting of the two greatest captains of the age.

Throughout the siege Saladin had suffered bouts of illness which were never allowed to interfere with his control of operations. On more than one occasion when the fever was on him he had gripped a battle that was running his enemy's way, and turned defeat into victory. Now both Richard and Philip, who as yet had seen no action, were laid low by the current sickness. Richard's illness proved serious, but with the same indomitable spirit that had kept Saladin in action he insisted on being carried everywhere in a litter, overseeing the preparations for what proved to be the last stages of the siege. He had brought with him a number of siege engines including a giant catapult, and these kept up a steady bombardment of the wall throughout June and July without doing any damage that the garrison was not immediately able to repair. There appears to have been very little, if any, mining, but Richard supervised the building of a huge four-storey tower made of wood, lead, iron and copper which got to within about ten feet of the wall before being put out of action.

But it was in the defence, not the attack, that the siege would eventually be won. The two final assaults on the city, in June and July, lacked proper co-operation between the French and English commands, which rendered nugatory the valiant efforts of the soldiers. Saladin was well aware that unless he could break the ring of steel that surrounded the city soon, the garrison was doomed. He had received considerable reinforcements in June from the lords of Sinjar and Mosul, but during the winter and spring the Franks had put in much work to make the lines almost impregnable. Taqi nearly got through on the Saracen right, but Saladin's main attack on 2 and 3 July, which he led in person, was beaten back with heavy losses.

Meanwhile, the garrison had reached the end of its tether. Their defence had been heroic, but it could not go on. With the coming of the English and French fleets the Saracens could no longer get a ship through, and starvation was at hand. Moreover, there were insufficient fit men for the wall to be manned in shifts – it became a 24-hour duty under the greatest strain. A message was sent by swimmer (the only method of communication) to say they could hold out no longer. Saladin ordered them to break out, but the way was closely barred. There is contradiction in the contemporary accounts of the lead-up to the surrender, and the terms eventually agreed. But it seems the garrison first negotiated direct with the Franks, who rejected their conditions. Saladin, who learnt of this just after his last attack was beaten off, was then consulted by the Franks. Negotiations went on for several days during which there was sporadic fighting, but the emirs knew that the city was lost, and the troops proved unwilling to mount another attack on 5 July. Two days later, a second swimmer brought a final appeal to which Saladin had no answer, for his own negotiations had been equally unsuccessful. On 12 July the garrison agreed to surrender the city on Saladin's behalf, but without his consent.

Saladin was deeply distressed by the terms, but he had no choice other than to accept. The Governor, Qaraqush, had agreed on his behalf to surrender the city with all its contents, the ships in the harbour, 1,500 Frankish prisoners not of rank, and 100 nobles to be named by the Franks, and in addition 200,000 dinars would be paid and the Relic of the True Cross returned. Conrad, who had played an important part in arranging the treaty, was to receive a personal payment of 4,000 dinars. Thus the capture of Acre, which was soon to become the capital of the Latin kingdom. It had been won at an appalling cost: there are no reliable figures, but Sutherland (p132) says 'more than a hundred thousand Christians perished before the walls'. This figure must be too high, but in the course of the two years certainly half as many could have died in battle or from disease.

After the brave garrison had marched out of Acre, the Crusaders moved in. The friendship between their principal commanders was a very thin veneer, and an unseemly quarrel over accommodation quickly erupted, in the course of which the English insulted Leopold of Austria, which was to have unfortunate repercussions during Richard's return journey through his country. King Philip, who had never been well, sailed for home at the beginning of August, having promised not to attack Richard's French territory in his absence – a promise only partly kept. This left Richard in sole command of the Crusade and Conrad, who was no friend of Richard, made excuses to depart for Tyre.

Problems arose during August over Saracen compliance with the terms of the treaty, in particular the exchange of prisoners. Saladin's request for time was reasonable, but he baulked at the conditions imposed. Meanwhile, Richard was eager to leave Acre, and because he was unwilling to set free his 2,700 prisoners and could not take them with him he asserted, without any justification, that Saladin had broken the treaty. Thereupon he marched the prisoners on to the plain, and in front of the Saracen force his men butchered the lot. Some Saracens appalled at this sickening sight attempted to save their friends, but were driven back. Even allowing for the cold-blooded ferocity of the times this was a despicable and shameful act.

The Crusaders marched out of Acre on 22 August 1191, and on 7 September Richard met Saladin in open battle at Arsuf, and won a magnificent victory which enabled him to take the whole Palestinian coastland. But Saladin, although well beaten, was not a spent force, and throughout Richard's remaining months in the Holy Land, his Saracens continued to attack whenever opportunity occurred. In April 1192, Conrad, by a vote in Council, was given the kingdom, and Guy had to make do with Cyprus. But shortly afterwards Conrad was murdered by two of the Assassins (followers of Hassan el-Sabah, the Old Man of the Mountains), and Henry of Troyes was married into the crown, which had descended through the female line.

Richard had always hoped to take Jerusalem, but the energy he had expended in conquering the coastland and organising the kingdom had taken a heavy toll. By August he was a sick man, drawing on deep wells of stamina. Anyway, it would probably be true to say that Saladin's survival at Arsuf and quick recovery ensured his keeping Jerusalem. Richard was anxious to be away, and after some negotiating, a limited treaty (to last three years and eight months) was agreed with Saladin on 2 September. The Franks were to keep those towns they had won – except Ascalon which was to be demolished – and Christians were to have free access to Jerusalem. Saladin, if indeed he did possess the True Cross, was not prepared to surrender it. In fact at this time he even refused 200,000 dinars (which he badly needed) offered for it by Queen Tamara of Georgia.

Richard sailed from Acre on 9 October 1191. The Third Crusade, which has centred round his name, had failed to restore Outremer to its former glory, but at least it had saved it from almost certain oblivion. It was to survive for another hundred years. In the 13th century there were a number of Crusades, but very few permanent reinforcements. Many towns – including Jerusalem, which changed hands twice – that Saladin had taken were restored by treaty, but few were won by the sword, although there were some very fierce battles. With the coming of the Mamluk Sultans in the middle of the century the days of the Franks were numbered, for the Mamluk armies were strong and well led, and they were determined on total conquest. Had it not been for the inroad of the Tartars, who briefly kept the Moslems occupied, the Christians would have probably been swept out of Outremer before 1291.

It was Sultan Qalawun and his son al-Ashraf, who succeeded him in November of that year, who finally rang down the Christian curtain in the Holy land. The fortifications of Acre had been progressively strengthened since they had been rebuilt following the earthquake of 1202, but despite the strength of the double walls with their numerous towers, the Mamluks took the city on 31 July 1291 after a siege that had lasted only just over six weeks. Shortly afterwards, all the remaining Christian towns were lost.

There were to be other Crusades against the infidel and the heretic in Europe and Asia Minor (the last to be organised was in 1464), but the Holy Land was never retaken by a Christian army until 1917. What had these numerous Crusades achieved? The answer must be that with the exception of the First and, to a lesser extent, the Third virtually nothing.

The effort of raising, equipping, funding and organising each Crusade was stupendous, and very rarely did the achievement come near to matching the effort. At a time of European efflorescence nothing was contributed culturally or militarily, and only a little (castle building) architecturally by the Crusades. Perhaps the enduring work of the Hospitallers can be seen as a golden thread in an otherwise drab tapestry. Although even that is counteracted by the wanton cruelty and barbarism practised not only against the Moslems, but in their own countries and against the Jews, by many who took the Cross. It was a long tale of unfulfilled expectations.

CHAPTER 3

Constantinople 1453

BY the time of the birth of the Ottoman Empire in the 14th century, the power of Byzantium was beginning to wane although by no means altogether spent. The whole business of war was changing, not least through the advent of artillery, which profoundly affected the nature of siege warfare, putting a formidable new means of reducing fortifications into the hands of the besiegers. At the same time, the growth of large, powerful marauding fleets made possible the blockade and bombardment of great maritime cities like Constantinople. The Siege of Constantinople marked the end of an era, an era of great culture and learning in the Byzantine Empire. It also enabled the highly trained and well-led troops of Islam to establish a firm foothold in Europe, changing for ever the whole character of the Eastern Mediterranean. This is the story of a siege conducted by professionals, driven by the impetus of a common faith, against whom resistance, no matter how brave, was doomed to ultimate defeat though, as we shall see, that defeat was only gained at a formidable cost in human life. Yet, as we well know, even today the loss of life is regarded as of small consequence if given in the name of Islam – and the resources of Islam are almost limitless.

* * *

Since Constantine the Great had founded his city on the site of old Byzantium in AD 330, the Byzantine Empire, as it became known, had undergone many changes of fortune. There had been periods of greatness, expansion and consolidation as well as dark interludes of internal strife and external struggles for existence. On the road that led to the ultimate destruction of the Empire there were three important landmarks. The battle of Manzikert in 1071, the taking of Constantinople in 1204 by the Latins of the Fourth Crusade, and their occupation until 1261, and the rise to power of the Osmanli Turks in the first half of the 14th century.

When the Seljuk Sultan Alp Arslan defeated the Byzantine Emperor Romanus Diogenes he sounded the death knell of the Empire. Territorially there was to be some recovery, but the Byzantine army was never again the same formidable military machine capable of holding the frontiers of empire against Turkish inroads. Similarly, what had been the strongest and most civilised polity in Europe never really recovered from the fifty-seven muddled and miserable years of the Latin Empire, during which there was considerable in-fighting and two Greek empires were established, one at Trebizond and another at Nicaea. It was the troops of the Nicaean emperor, Michael VIII Palaeologus, that eventually retook the city, having gained entry through treachery. Thus, in 1261, there was once more a Byzantine Empire, and some of the mystique was restored. Constantinople remained the capital of Orthodox Christendom and the bulwark against paganism. But the loss of territory in Europe during the Latin occupation had been serious, and soon losses in Asia were to be much more so.

The third and, for a study of the siege of Constantinople the most immediate, of the three landmarks, was the beginnings of the Ottoman empire. Among the rise and fall of despotic Asian dynasties in the 13th and 14th centuries – Mongols, Seljuks and other Turkish tribes – and the constant forays of border barons known as *ghazis*, there came upon the scene a tribal leader called Ertoghrul, a *ghazi* somewhat above the common run who carved himself an emirate in Bithynia, bordering the shrinking boundaries of the Byzantine Empire. Here his people could improve upon a pastoral and nomadic economy by constant raids against the infidels. Before he died in 1281, his situation and rising authority had won him many followers, and his son, Osman, was to gain eponymous fame as the first of many great warrior despots who founded an empire.

Osman who, at the turn of the century styled himself Sultan, soon set about extending his territory, and before he died had captured Brusa which became the base for future operations in Europe, where Turkish raids had already begun. This once insignificant Turkish tribe under subsequent sultans, and through ceaseless blood-letting, raged through Anatolia like a flame through a field of corn, and then across the straits into Europe. In 1356, Adrianople was taken by Sultan Orchan and, although it was retaken, Murad I regained it and made it his capital. The Turks were now firmly established in Europe. Their progress and conquests in Asia and Europe were occasionally checked through internecine strife and, more seriously, by great leaders of men such as Timur the Tartar and John Hunyadi, later King of Hungary. But the Byzantine emperors made little impression, and the Western leaders appeared too preoccupied to help the sternly embattled Empire.

There were opportunities when the Byzantines might have rolled back the Turks, if not permanently, at least for many years. The best of these opportunities came directly after Timur and his Mongols had routed Bayazid, one of the most aggressive and dangerous of the Ottoman sultans, at Ankara in 1402. After his decisive victory, Timur ravaged much of Anatolia before returning to his native Samarkand, where Bayazid died in captivity. For ten years, the Osmanlis were in disarray while Bayazid's three sons strove for the succession. This was the Christians' chance at least to re-establish authority in Europe, but the Western kingdoms and principalities could spare no money nor troops for their Eastern co-religionists.

Eventually Mehmet I brought order out of chaos, and his son Murad II (1421–1451) straddled Asia and the Balkans as the champion of a militant, cruel and proselytising creed. In 1422, he besieged Constantinople, but he lacked the fire-power to breach the walls, and was anyway diverted in his purpose by an internal revolt. His was not an unrelieved success: the Hungarian, Hunyadi, inflicted two serious defeats on the Turks before being heavily outnumbered and defeated at Varna in 1444, and again at Kossovo in 1448. These two crushing defeats left the Turks almost unchallenged south of the Danube, and virtually supreme in Anatolia.

When Murad died in 1451, the Byzantine empire was in a profound decline with little left to it but Constantinople, and this his successor, Mehmet II, one of the greatest of the sultans, was determined to take. But some years before Murad died, the Emperor John VIII realised that without Western aid the Empire was doomed, and he reckoned the Pope was his principal hope. In order to gain papal support he was prepared to press for a union of the two Churches. To this end he headed a delegation that attended a council first in Ferrara and then in Florence, where in 1439 the Emperor on behalf of the Greek Church adopted certain doctrines of the Roman faith. The union of the two Churches was solemnly ratified, and proved a disaster. John got very little from the Pope who failed to honour most of his promises, and when the Union was reaffirmed in Constantinople, the city became divided with the Eastern Patriarchs and their acolytes refusing to be bound by it.

John died in 1449 and was succeeded by his son, Constantine XI, who was the last and one of the best in a long line of emperors. He proved to be a worthy opponent of his great rival Mehmet II. The two men had widely differing characters. Constantine, a strongly built man with well chiselled features, was 45 when he came to the throne. He had had plenty of administrative experience and had proved himself capable in that field and as a soldier. He was brave, honourable, generous and patient. Mehmet was 21 at the time of the siege, a handsome man of medium height with a hawk-like nose that overhung his upper lip. He was highly intelligent, a brave and excellent commander, capable of occasional generosity, but for the most part tyrannical, cruel and predatory.

He would not lay siege to Constantinople before he was completely ready. There was much preparation needed and time was on his side, for the Western powers showed little intention of heeding Constantine's appeals, although in this respect the Venetians and Genoese found themselves in difficulties. As part of his preparations the Sultan had constructed a new fort on the Bosphorus (now known as Rumeli Hisar) opposite one already built by Bayazid. This gave him command of the narrow waters, and from it he sank two Venetian ships. The Venetians had trade concessions with the Turks which they were not keen to lose, and the Genoese occupied Galata as an independent colony. The Venetians resolved the problem with a compromise, they agreed to give aid to the Christians, but refrained from provoking the Turks. The Genoese in Galata remained neutral in the forthcoming conflict.

In March 1453, Mehmet sailed his impressive fleet into the Sea of Marmora and thence to anchor at the Double Columns in the Bosphorus. There were some 140 vessels which included triremes, biremes, armed galleys, long boats (called *fustae*) and transport barges. Not surprisingly, this armada caused considerable disquiet to the inhabitants of Constantinople, who watched its progress from the walls powerless to interfere. By now Mehmet's preparations were almost complete. He had made treaties of peace, which he had no intention of keeping, with the Venetians and Hunyadi, his army had marched from Thrace and by 5 April was before the walls of Constantinople. All he now needed was an excuse to begin hostilities, and this was supplied by the Emperor's clumsy attempt at blackmail over the matter of a claimant to the Sultanate who was a pensioner residing in the city.

There are conflicting accounts of the number of soldiers Mehmet had for the siege, but what is certain is that it was a full mobilisation with only garrison and frontier troops excluded. He probably had about 150,000 combatants and a good many non-combatants and camp followers. Some of the Anatolian levies may have been mounted, but they would have fought on foot. They were not first class troops, but infinitely better material than the 25,000 irregulars known as Bashi-bazouks. The spearhead of the army was the tough and hardy Janissaries. They numbered no more than 12,000, but wrought by a lifetime of war they were the fiercest fighting men of their time. First formed by Sultan Orchan in 1326, as a bodyguard, they were reorganised by Murad I and II. They came from Christian families recruited between the ages of seven and twelve, forcibly converted to Mohammedanism and given the most rigorous training régime. Turkish troops mostly wore a long coat of mail, and were armed with sword, scimitar, bow or lance. It is probable that the Janissaries – somewhat ahead of their time – used handguns.

But Mehmet's most telling weapon was his artillery. In this arm he was well ahead of the Christians. The showpiece was a monster gun built by a Hungarian cannon-maker called Urban. This man had offered his services to the Emperor who could not afford his price, and so he transferred his allegiance to the Sultan, who immediately offered him a huge sum to cast large cannon. It was one of these guns, mounted on the new Bosphorus fort, that sank the Venetian ships. Thus encouraged, the Sultan urged him to make something bigger, and in due course a huge gun with a barrel length of over 26 feet encased in eight inches of bronze that was capable of

FIG 3.1

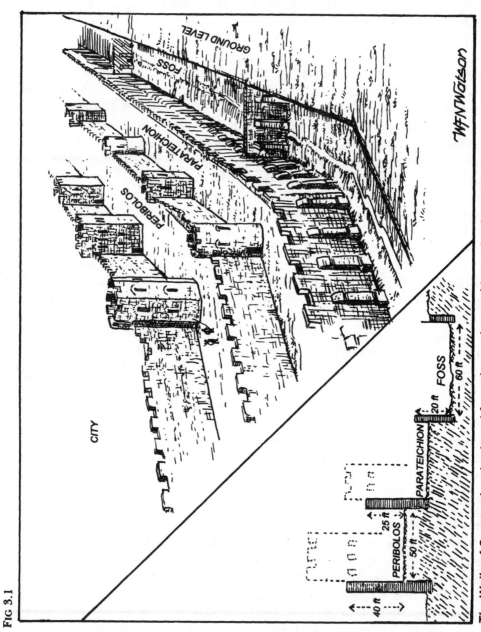

The Walls of Constantinople viewed from the north-west (the angle of attack)

firing a ball of twelve hundredweight* made its appearance at Adrianople. Its performance was most impressive, but was not maintained, for this vast, cumbersome piece of artillery, which had taken 200 men and 60 oxen to drag for days over specially prepared roads, did not stand up to the strain of seven shots a day – it took two hours to reload – and needed constant repair. However, the medium calibre pieces that Urban cast were a great success, and of these Mehmet had five batteries as well as a number of smaller guns.

The walls of Constantinople, against which, on 12 April, these guns began to hurl their shot, had for centuries withstood bombardment. They extended in all to thirteen miles and were in three parts. The landward side of four miles stretching from the Sea of Marmora to the Golden Horn; the shore wall along the Golden Horn to what is now Seraglio Point, which was three and a half miles in length; and the longest stretch of five and a half miles from Seraglio Point along the Sea of Marmora to Studion.

The sea walls were single, but on the landward side of the peninsula the wall was triple from the Marmora Sea to the Tekfur Serai (Imperial Palace), where it became single, protected at its lower end by a moat. The inner of these three walls was some 40 feet high, and was separated from the second, or outer wall (for the third one was only a strong seven-foot crenellated breastwork), by a covered way of about fifty feet known by the Greeks as the *peribolos* and this wall, which had strengthened in the time of the last emperor, was 25 feet high. Then there was another covered way known as the *parateichion* between the second wall and the breastwork that stood above the scarp of a formidable ditch over 60 feet wide and 20 feet deep, which at the time of the siege was dry. The inner and outer walls had 96 and 92 square or octagonal towers respectively, and those of the inner were echeloned to cover the unprotected parts of the outer curtain.

There were a number of gates on the landward side, some of which were reserved to the military. The wall along the Golden Horn, where the city's main harbour lay, could only be taken by an enemy having command of those waters, and, to prevent this, a massive chain-boom had been placed at the entrance to the Bosphorus, anchored from the Constantinople wall to a point on the neutral Galata shore. This not only gave the Christian fleet a safe anchorage, but meant that the eastern sea wall need only be lightly garrisoned.

To man these walls and carry out other duties, Constantine could muster only 5,000 Greek combatants out of about 20,000 male citizens of military age. This disappointingly small number of volunteers was supplemented by some 2,000 foreigners. The Pope had been prevailed upon to send 200

---

*This was the largest shot then known for a cannon, although machines had existed for some time that slung stones of up to 3,000 lbs.

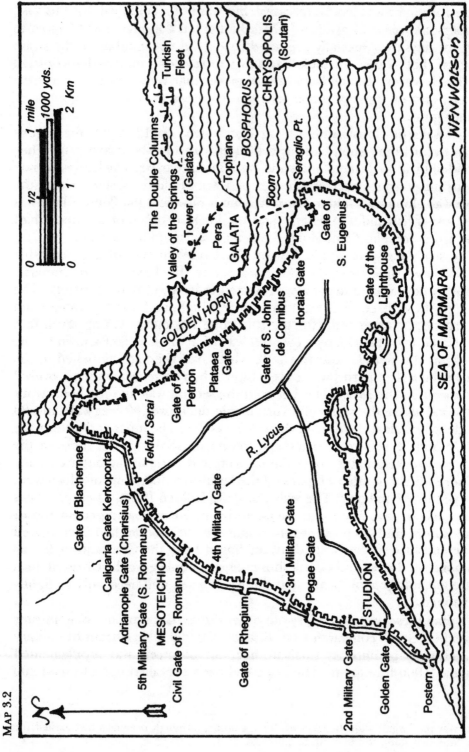

MAP 3.2

Byzantine Constantinople

Italians under his legate, Cardinal Isidore, and although the Venetians and Genoese (between whom no love was lost) could have done much more, there were one or two small bands of the latter financed and equipped by champions of Christendom, and there were a number of Venetians in the city when the siege began who were too ashamed not to offer their services. But the best of these auxiliaries were undoubtedly those that had arrived in January under the renowned Genoese captain, Giovanni Giustiniani. He had brought, in two galleys, seven hundred fully armed soldiers recruited in Genoa and the islands of Chios and Rhodes. These men were to bear the brunt of the fighting and to acquit themselves most bravely.

The Emperor's cannon played an insignificant part in the battle, for it comprised mostly small calibre and poor quality pieces. Moreover, their recoil was found to do damage to the walls and they were short of powder. But the defence had, in the words of a contemporary writer, 'a number of machines' which in this case probably meant mangonels, trebuchets and balistas. There was also a plentiful supply of arrows and bolts. The Christian fleet (supplied mainly by the Venetian colony in the city) comprised 26 well-found vessels, 10 of which were stationed at the boom, and 16 in reserve at the harbour.

There were not enough men to hold the inner land wall in strength and so the main defence was concentrated upon the second or outer wall. The Emperor had his headquarters where the landwalls crossed the Lycus valley, although he was always to be found where the fighting was heaviest. When he saw that Mehmet had chosen that area for his main attack, he ordered Giustiniani to bring his men to that point. On Giustiniani's right, near the Adrianople (Charisius) Gate, were the three Italian brothers, Antonio, Paolo and Troilo Bocchiardi with the troops they had raised, and farther up was Minotto, bailiff of the Venetian factory at Galata, whose sector was in the Blachernae quarter between the Tekfur Serai and the Caligaria Gate. On the Venetian's right, guarding the moat and single wall that ran to the Golden Horn, was another Italian contingent with Archbishop Leonard of Mitylene. South of, or below, Giustiniani the walls were manned by Greeks under Theophilus Palaeologus, and then Filippo Contarini's Venetians, with troops under Demetrius Cantacuzenus manning the wall from the Golden Gate to the Sea of Marmora.

The defence was as ready as it could be by the time the Sultan was before the walls, and the defenders could see how he deployed his large army for action. Zuganos Pasha, with a strong force, had already been sent to the northern shore of the Golden Horn with the task of guarding that shore and keeping watch on the neutral Genoese. The land rises fairly steeply from the Golden Horn to the Adrianople Gate and this sector was occupied by European troops under Karadja Pasha. The Pasha was allotted a number of heavy guns, for in the northern part of his sector the wall was single and vulnerable. The ground on Karadja's right slopes down to the

Lycus valley, before rising again to the Romanus Gate. The area between the Adrianople and Romanus Gates was known as the Mesoteichion, and was judged by Mehmet to be the most suitable for the main thrust. Here, about a quarter of a mile back, he pitched his splendid red and gold tent, and positioned the Janissaries and some of the heavier cannon – including the great gun.

The ground from the St Romanus Gate to the sea was given to the Anatolian division under the two pashas Ishak and Mahmud. The Bashi-bazouks were stationed in groups to the rear of the forward troops. In front of their position, and fairly close to the ditch, the Turks dug a line of countervallation along the whole front, with a wooden palisade on the rampart and a number of sally gates. The Marmora coast was the responsibility of Admiral Baltoghlu's fleet based on the Double Columns; his primary task was to prevent any supplies reaching the beleagured city, and to break through the boom.

In early April, Mehmet, as was customary, offered to spare the lives of the inhabitants if the city was surrendered. An offer that was unhesitatingly spurned. He then opened the battle on 6 April with a heavy bombardment in the area of the Adrianople Gate where the wall was soon severely damaged, but hastily repaired by the defenders that night. There was then a pause while the Sultan rearranged his batteries, and ordered his men to fill the ditch ready for immediate action when a breach was made. He also examined the possibilities of mining. During this short lull the Sultan occupied his troops in mopping up some outlying Greek posts, with great savagery.

It was on 12 April that his guns began their pounding in earnest. The noise was appalling: the beating of drums and cheers of the soldiers and camp followers were intermittently punctuated by the roar of Urban's cannon as the gunners, half-choked with smoke and acrid fumes of burning powder, strove to keep their pieces from sliding off the platforms into the mud. The Christians did what they could to protect the outer wall by hanging leather bundles and bales of wool over it, but the Turks had brought their siege batteries to the edge of the ditch and, from such close range, nothing could prevent the wall from crumbling little by little. Nevertheless, each night the Christians laboured, not unsuccessfully, to repair the damage.

Initially, the effect of cannonballs and heavy missiles (for the Turks combined ancient and modern with plenty of catapults) was not disastrous, but when a renegade Hungarian counselled the gunners to turn from random shots to pattern firing against the two opposite sides of the salient angles of the towers the damage became serious. By the sixth day the breastwork and outer wall in the Lycus valley were a shambles, and much of the rubble fell into the ditch making repairs difficult but assault easier. Giustiniani and his men had improvised a fairly stout stockade from which

MAP 3.3

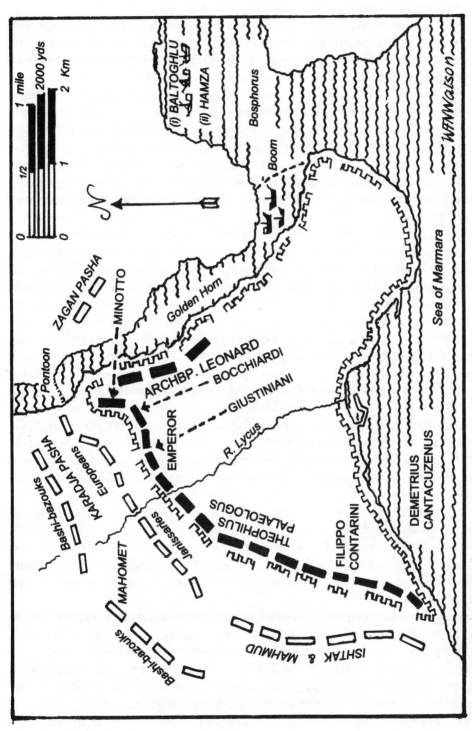

The Siege of Constantinople 1453: disposition of forces

they inflicted what damage they could when, on 18 April, two hours after sunset, Mehmet sent his men into the first assault.

As the sound of the cannonade echoed through the valley, the Janissaries and some of the Sultan's finest soldiers rushed towards the breaches to the accompaniment of drums and cymbals. Some had ladders and poles or lances with hooks to scale the unbroken parts of the wall. Once across the ditch, they were faced by a rugged defence from behind the stockade, where Giustiniani and his men, ably assisted by Greeks, resisted with spirit. After four hours of fierce close-quarter fighting, Mehmet called his men back. It had been a morale booster for the garrison but every day, at some part of the wall, the Turkish gunners would perform their remorseless task, and the soldiers would await their opportunity. The Emperor organised a sortie to silence some of the guns, but it was too expensive a failure ever to be repeated.

About the same time as this first major assault on the walls, Admiral Baltoghlu, who had received substantial reinforcements, was ordered to break the boom. Bringing into action some of his larger ships, he attempted to close with the Venetian ships that were stationed in line directly behind the boom. To this purpose he brought to bear arrow, cannon and, possibly, Greek fire before trying to grapple. But the Christian ships had the advantage of height and raked the Turkish decks with their stone-throwers and javelins. It became clear to Baltoghlu that the attack would not succeed, and when the Christians showed signs of passing through the boom to encircle his fleet, he ordered a withdrawal to the Double Columns.

This naval failure infuriated Mehmet, but soon it was to be repeated on a much more humiliating scale. Three Genoese galleys hired by Pope Nicholas V, and fully loaded with a wide variety of provisions and arms for the city, sailed in the middle of April from Chios where they had been held up waiting for a southerly wind. On their way they fell in with a large Imperial galley carrying corn from Sicily, and the four vessels were through the Dardanelles and into the Sea of Marmora by 20 April. Their progress was anxiously watched by the garrison and, with relish, by the Turks. This was Baltoghlu's chance. He at once led more than 100 craft powered by sail and oar to cut them off from the Horn. The Sultan had imperiously demanded a victory from his admiral, and came to the water's edge to watch the unequal contest.

However, once again the Christian vessels, having the advantage of height and better seamanship, were not to be taken easily. As they drove with the wind through the Turkish fleet, every attempt to board was sternly and successfully resisted with many kinds of weapon, and those Turks that did get aboard soon found their armour much inferior to that of the Christians. It looked as though the Christian ships would get through, when suddenly, just as they reached Seraglio Point, the wind dropped and they were becalmed. Cheered on by Mehmet, who in his excitement rode into the sea, the Turks closed in for the kill. The Christians were running short of powder, and although the Turkish cannon could not be elevated sufficiently, they had nevertheless done considerable damage. Then the miracle happened. As suddenly as it had dropped the wind blew up again from the same quarter, and bravely the hopelessly outnumbered galleys cut their way through the storm of shot. In the general turmoil and confusion, the Turkish oarsmen became intertwined and choked their art. Baltoghlu lost control and, as night fell, the boom was lifted, the trumpets rang and the galleys were home.

The Sultan was even more angry than on the previous failure of his ships, and only the pleas of some senior officers saved Baltoghlu, who had fought with exemplary courage, from immediate execution. The outcome of this debacle merely strengthened Mehmet's determination to put at least a part of his fleet into the Golden Horn, and to this end he devised an extraordinary – although not in fact original – plan. He would transport his ships overland.

Thousands of workmen were employed to level the ground from the shore at Tophane, up the Pera hill which rises to some 250 feet above sea level, and on to the ridge in the neighbourhood of the present Taksim Square, and from there down to what was called the Valley of the Springs (Kasimpasa) – a distance of about a mile. Planks had been laid and rollers and wheels prepared to carry the large wooden cradles into which the ships were floated before being 'landed' by the use of pulleys. All this activity had been concealed from prying eyes by a heavy bombardment on the boom from guns firing from the hill behind Galata. In an incredibly short time, all was ready, and on the night of 22 April some seventy vessels dragged by oxen began their strange procession up the hill. When they reached the top the whole operation became more bizarre as the sailors boarded their craft and went through the motions of rowing as they travelled downhill and into the water. All the ships had been safely transported and into the sea by the morning of the 23rd.

The Venetian fleet and the city's inhabitants were completely surprised and greatly dismayed, for now the Turks posed a threat to another wall, which meant a further dispersion of the garrison. There were hasty consultations in the Christian camp as to how the Turkish ships could be destroyed. There had not been time to pick them off singly as they were launched, and the idea of an all-out attack was discarded, for fear that the Genoese of Galata would join the Turks – indeed to keep an eye on the Genoese was one reason for Mehmet wanting his ships in the Horn. In the end, the plan of a Venetian sailor called Jacomo Coco, to set fire to the Turkish fleet in a surprise attack, was adopted and carried out with seven vessels, two of which – the fire ships – were laden with cotton and wool. But the plan was betrayed by the Genoese of Galata; surprise was lost and a brave sea fight ended in disaster with a barbaric aftermath.

While all this naval activity was happening, there had been no let-up against the landward walls. Now, with part of his fleet in the Horn, the Sultan could construct a substantial pontoon bridge (for which he used hundreds of wine barrels and planks) just above the harbour. The use of this bridge would enable Zuganos's men and cannon to exert pressure on the Blachernae part of the walls. By the beginning of May this additional threat, the loss of control in the Horn, the continued bombardment and, more particularly, the increasingly serious food situation were causing considerable despair in the city. Here matters were not improved by interdenominational bitterness over the Union, and scarcely suppressed rivalry between the Genoese and Venetians.

It had been suggested to the Emperor that he should leave the city to try to raise reinforcements, but this he absolutely refused to contemplate. However, there was reason to believe that a Venetian fleet with soldiers and supplies had been ordered to sail for the city, although details were lacking. It was therefore determined that a brigantine, flying the Turkish flag and with its sailors dressed in Turkish clothes, should slip through the boom to make contact with this eagerly sought Venetian fleet. The brigantine was safely through the boom and away by midnight on 3 May.

On 7 May the Sultan launched another major assault in the Mesoteichion area. An avalanche of men, unflinching and seemingly irresistible, rushed upon the walls with scaling ladders. For more than three hours, Greeks and Italians clashed with yelling Turks in the frenzied turmoil of battle. Scimitars flashed and fell and men fell with them, but all to no avail, the Turks were beaten back from stockade and wall. It was much the same five nights later. This time, Mehmet ordered an assault between the gates of Adrianople and Caligaria; here the walls had not been quite so badly damaged, and additional manpower from some ships inactive at safe anchorage was available. The failure of this second assault, and the poor impression made by Zuganos's guns in the Blachernae quarter, where the single wall had been more solidly constructed, decided Mehmet to move the guns to the Lycus valley where in future the major action would be.

It was at about this time too that he paid serious attention to mining. Previous attempts in the area of the Adrianople Gate had proved too difficult. Now, with the help of experienced miners from Zuganos's force, Mehmet switched to north of the Caligarian gate in the hope that mines would succeed on the single wall where shot had failed. But mining was still in its most elementary stage, and it was easier to detect an operation than to succeed in it. The Emperor had a German engineer in his pay called Johannes Grant, and this man detected almost every Turkish attempt. His skilful countermining caused them many casualties, and they had no noticeable success in this field – nor were they any more fortunate with their next stratagem.

At dawn on 18 May, the sentries on the walls were horrified to see a large wooden tower on wheels and full of troops immediately in front of the walls. Contemporary writers disagree over some of the details, but all are in unison as to its fate. It had been constructed in great secrecy, and appeared opposite the St Romanus Gate. Its primary purpose was to protect workmen filling the ditch. However, it was as high as the outer wall, and could have been used for an assault, a role for which it was supplied with hooks and ladders and framed with layers of animal skins as protection against fire. Turkish gunners had successfully bombarded a nearby turret, and while workmen laboured all day to fill the ditch with its rubble, the huge contraption towered above them as some tutelary deity. By night, much of the ditch had been filled, and the tower stood proudly upon it. But in the darkness Giustiniani, leading his men in almost the only successful sortie, destroyed it either by fire or gunpowder and dug out the ditch. Mehmet persevered with other towers, but none was successful.

The siege was now in its seventh week, and although it would be incorrect to say it had come to an equipoise, for the odds were still heavily in favour of the besiegers, both sides had become weary and the Turks were seriously considering departure. Food, powder and shot were all running short in the city, and while Christian casualties had so far been remarkably light there was sickness, superstition, dissension and despair. The latter was considerably increased when the brigantine, having failed to find any trace of the papal relief force, bravely returned to report and share the fate of the doomed city. Constantine was again urged to depart while there was still time. His answer was predictable and honourable to his name. His presence exercised a moral influence, for he was everywhere encouraging and exhorting. As the Christians prepared to face what they must have known would be the final assault, they saw every mishap as a divine portent; superstition coloured their thoughts and dictated their actions. But when the church services and orisons were over, they bent to their duties, determined to stand by their Emperor.

The Turks too had their problems. As more men joined the army, feeding it became increasingly difficult. Despite their wealth of siege machinery, which had done great damage, no Turk had lived long behind the wall. To a great extent, their navy had failed them, and their casualties had been extremely heavy. There was some unrest in the ranks, and division among the pashas. There were those, and chief among them was the Grand Vezir, Halil Pasha, who had never approved of the venture. He now spoke openly in council for raising the siege, stressing the difficulties and emphasising the failures, and he professed to know of an Italian fleet that was on its way. He found some support, but when Zuganos was called upon he spoke most persuasively in favour of a last supreme effort. This the council sensed was what Mehmet wanted to hear, and not only Mehmet but most of the troops. A major assault would be launched as soon as preparations were complete. Halil's days were numbered.

In accordance with tradition the Sultan made a final peace offer, but the terms were ludicrous and immediately rejected. Monday 28 May was spent by both sides in spiritual and physical preparation. The Turkish guns, which for weeks past had seldom ceased pounding the city walls, were strangely and eerily silent. The only activity in their camp was the bustle of huge fatigue parties labouring to fill the ditch. In the city, men and women attended services in the great church of St Sophia and in many other churches. Afterwards, they worked hard to repair the outer wall. When everyone had been given their allotted tasks, all gates in to the peribolos were locked to ensure that there could be no retreat. In the hour of greatest danger, internal dissensions had been put aside, and the whole garrison was uplifted by the courage and steely composure of the Emperor as he toured the defences and spoke encouragingly to the defenders.

The Sultan planned a simultaneous attack in three main areas. Zuganos, whose men were mostly already across the Horn, was to concentrate on the Blachernae quarter with Karadja on his right between the Tekfur Serai and Adrianople Gate; Mehmet would command the main thrust in the Lycus valley area; and Ishak would conduct the assault from the St Romanus Gate to the Marmora. Admiral Hamza (who had succeeded the luckless Baltoghlu) was ordered to keep the sea walls under fire. The essence of the plan was to maintain the momentum, for with his vastly superior numbers Mehmet hoped to wear down the Christians. To this end, he planned to use the Bashi-bazouks, his most expendable troops, first followed by the Anatolians, and then in the centre, where he felt the breakthrough would be most easily made, his élite troops, the Janissaries. When his orders had been given, the Sultan rode round his troops, and visited those ships in the Horn.

It was about 2 am on Tuesday 29 May when the long, uncanny silence was broken by the hideous din of wild yells, drums and cymbals as the Bashi-bazouks prepared to charge. These undisciplined, untrained men of mixed races were self-armed, mainly with shields and scimitars, but many carried bows and slings. As they neared the wall, the serried shields of the advancing thousands quivered beneath an avalanche of stones and other missiles. Ragged they may have been, but brave they certainly were, scrambling up and over the stockade, and throwing themselves against the wall, only to fall back in tangled heaps of death. After two hours they were withdrawn, having completed their task of blunting the defence.

The Christians scarcely had time to reform their ranks, and none to repair the stockade before the Anatolians were upon them. These men were better armed and better disciplined and all of one faith. Each attack was supported – probably at considerable risk – by the Sultan's cannon, and in the centre Urban's whimsical monster had been repaired and brought into action. Towards the end of the Anatolian attack it had a devastating effect on the stockade with a direct hit. The Anatolians, like the Bashi-bazouks before them, met with a stern and successful resistance. They flung themselves against the broken down walls and the Christians flung them back with severe losses. Some did manage to reach the peribolos, but it was in Giustiniani's sector and his Italians drove them out. Being better armoured, they suffered fewer casualties. In the northern sector, the defence, under the Venetian Minotto and the Bocchiardi brothers, proved too strong for Zuganos's and Karadja's troops. Thus the second wave was beaten back, and the defence still held.

It was about 5 am, as the stars disappeared, leaving a waning moon visible through a thin mizzle of rain, that the Janissaries were ordered forward. Mehmet himself led them as far as the ditch. Once across it, these splendid soldiers broke into a controlled double. All along the wall pressure was redoubled by supporting troops. Indeed there had been scarcely any pause between the withdrawal of the Anatolians and the advance of the Janissaries. The guns had ceased firing, but the yellow fog of powder smoke and dust blotted out everything. But nothing could drown the noise of cheering troops and pealing bells. The Christians had had virtually no time to repair the defences, and were becoming totally exhausted, but they fought on with great courage and patient endurance. The clash along the whole line was savage and the slaughter heavy. The fighting had lasted for more than an hour, with the Janissaries striving in vain to deliver the death punch, when a double disaster struck the Christians.

At the corner of the Blachernae wall there was, half concealed, a small sally-port known as Kerkoporta which was normally barred, but the Bocchiardis had opened it so as to conduct sorties against the flank of the attacking troops, and it had not been shut. A party of Turks, espying this, gained entrance to the outer wall and from that to the *peribolos* through a postern gate in the transverse wall. The Kerkoporta was quickly closed and it would not have been difficult to mop up the fifty or so enemy had it not been for the distraction of another even more unfortunate incident.

At about sunrise Giustiniani received a ball that pierced his breastplate, and he fell gravely wounded. In great pain he begged his men to carry him to the rear. Permission to unlock the gate was sought from the Emperor, who was fighting nearby. Hastening to the wounded man, he begged him to stay with his men. Giustiniani was a brave soldier, and it is possible that in his agony he did not fully appreciate the consequences of his insistence on being removed. The Emperor humanely, but perhaps unwisely, ordered the gate to be unlocked, and Giustiniani was carried into the city and on to a ship. His wound, which at first was thought to be not dangerous, proved mortal. His departure through the gate was fatal to the morale of his Genoese troops who, probably thinking the battle was lost and certainly dismayed by what they saw, panicked and made for the gate. Many got through before it could be closed, and the Emperor and his Greeks were left to hold back the Turkish hordes at the wall. This was, perhaps, the decisive event of the battle.

The end was very near. Everything seemed to happen at once. Mehmet could see that the defence was crumbling, and judged it the time to lead his Janissaries in person. Inspired by the presence of their Sultan, these, and many other troops, rolled forward unstoppable like the bore of a tidal river. The Emperor rallied what troops he could, fighting furiously in hand-to-hand grapple, and the Bocchiardi Italians were still giving cut and thrust near the fatal postern gate. But about this time, those Turks that had entered through the Kerkoporta captured a tower from which they lowered the Christian standard and hoisted their own, and the Turkish fleet landed men on the shore of the Horn who met with little resistance as they stormed that wall. The cry went up 'The city is taken', and so – but for a handful of Cretan sailors who held out in a tower for a further day – it proved to be. The Emperor, as soon as he knew the battle was lost, discarded his royal insignia and, with a few staunch companions, died fighting among the debris of wall and stockade. Later the Sultan sought his body, but it was never positively identified.

Before the siege began the Sultan had reminded his troops of the Islamic tradition that when a city is not surrendered the public buildings become the property of the victorious general, but the troops are given three days in which they may plunder at will. And so it was with Constantinople. The slaughter and atrocities committed against the survivors – soldiers and civilians, women and children – in the first few hours was indescribable, and when their blood lust was assuaged the troops ravaged the city in iconoclastic fury. Churches, and those inside them taking refuge, were ruthlessly destroyed, and many (but fortunately not all) of the most precious books, parchments, ikons and other treasures were looted or thrown to the flames. But these excesses were not more than normal for the times, and indeed there was soon some measure of discipline among the Sultan's troops. By the time he entered the city in the late afternoon, the soldiers' greed had mostly reached saturation point, and there was little trouble when he gave the order that looting was to cease.

There appears to have been no serious attempt to count the Turkish dead, but their casualties during the seven weeks of fighting must have been very heavy, running into thousands. Neither is there any reliable figure for Christian casualties, most of which took place during the sack. It is generally estimated that out of a probable figure of 50,000 inhabitants between three and four thousand were killed, and most of the rest were made captive, including 500 soldiers. Some were lucky enough to board ships and escape, for the Turkish sailors were too busy looting to guard the boom. Of the eminent Christians, the Grand Duke Lucas Notoras was at first spared but later, with his two sons, executed; Minotto, Paolo Bocchiardi, and indeed all the Italians captured, were put to death, but

Paolo's two brothers escaped. Archbishop Leonard was captured, but not recognised and later ransomed by the Genoese of Galata. Cardinal Isidore exchanged his clerical robes with a beggar and, being captured in them, was sold into slavery but almost immediately ransomed for a song. The beggar, however, was privileged after capture in having his head displayed as that of the cardinal!

When Mehmet rode into the city with his bodyguard of Janissaries, he went first to the Church of St Sophia, where he stopped the vandalism and at once decreed the building to be a mosque. But he was to be much more tolerant towards Christians than most of his successors. There were churches that had been spared in the sack, and these were allowed to continue their worship, and he appointed the scholar George Scholarius Gennadius to be Patriarch of the Greek Church. In the middle of June, the Sultan returned to his capital, Adrianople and, as he left, was said to have been greatly saddened at the damage done, although by no means all of the city was desolate. Soon he was to set about rebuilding and repairing the walls – although those of Galata, where neutrality had not saved the Genoese, were dismantled.

In 1456 Mehmet took Athens and shortly afterwards all Greece, and in 1461 Trebizond, the last Christian stronghold in the East, fell. By now he had determined to make Constantinople his capital. To re-populate it, he is said to have impressed 5,000 families from the conquered territories of Greece and Trebizond. They came from all walks of life – noblemen, craftsmen and merchants – and were allotted parcels of land and encouraged to beautify the city with their buildings.

Constantinople was ripe for plucking, its days of greatness had long gone. The Turks could have taken it, if not in 1453, then a few years later. Nevertheless, its fall came as an appalling shock to Western potentates. None of them had done much to save the city, now there was clamour for an immediate crusade against victorious Islam. But, once more, nothing was done. The importance of 29 May 1453 was that a great city of culture and learning had disappeared; its fall opened the gate for the all-conquering Turks to establish themselves permanently in Europe, and for centuries to cause a grave problem in the Balkans and even farther west; the schism between the two Churches would now be perpetual; and Levantine trade needed to be readjusted. It could be said that when he took Constantinople Mehmet II changed the spiritual, commercial and political axis of the Eastern Mediterranean.

CHAPTER 4

Malta 1565

ALTHOUGH more than a hundred years separated the sieges of Constantinople and Malta, the fundamental nature of the conflict remained the same – Christian against Turk. Once again, too, the sea was to play an important role, with assaults being launched from heavily armed ships. The Siege of Malta was to mark a high point in the history of the Knights of St John of Jerusalem. As a result, the island was to become their home for more than 200 years and a place in which they have a presence to this day. Unlike Constantinople, Malta was to prove a wonderful victory for the Knights, due not only to their superb skill and self-sacrifice but also to a series of gross errors by the Turkish command. The heroism of the people of Malta in the equally famous siege of the Second World War was to match that of the Knights, making it, perhaps, the only island in the world to have been successfully defended in two major sieges.

* * *

Every siege produces its own particular pattern of courage, endurance, heroism and recreancy. Writing of the siege of Malta, Jurien de la Gravière said, 'It was the greatest siege in history'. There have been longer sieges, and sieges of greater importance, but very seldom has there been displayed so much devotion to duty, self-sacrifice and comradeship in arms, regardless of rank or race, by every single member of the small Christian community that held Malta against 40,000 fanatical Turks in 1565.

The Knights of St John of Jerusalem (the Hospitallers) retained their headquarters in Acre until the Mamluks took that city, and indeed the whole of Outremer, in 1291. The Order had suffered grievous losses in the siege, but by then their reputation was well established and there were many new recruits eager to enlist. After a temporary sojourn in Cyprus, they cast their eye upon Rhodes, then governed as an independent state by a renegade Byzantine, which they took in 1307. From there, having become highly skilled seamen, they spent much of their time disrupting the maritime commerce of the enemies of their religion – principally the Ottoman Turks. The young Sultan, Suleiman I (the Magnificent), besieged the island in July 1522, and by December the Grand Master, de L'Isle Adam, was forced to accept terms which were very generous, although the Order had to quit Rhodes. In 1530, the Emperor Charles V offered to give the Maltese archipelago and Tripoli to the Knights which, after some hesitation, for it was a very different proposition to fertile Rhodes, they accepted.

At this time, the Order of St John was divided into three main groups of men, all of whom took religious vows and for whom Christianity was a shining beacon never absent from their daily lives. The group that dominated the Order was the Military Knights, men carefully selected from the most aristocratic Christian families of Europe, the second group was the Chaplains whose duties were in the Hospital and Conventual Church, and who in theory did not bear arms, and the third class were the serving brothers (sometimes referred to as servants-at-arms) who, like the Chaplains, were not required to be of noble birth but of good repute, and whose duties were military. These men elected their Grand Master who presided over the governing body, the Supreme Council, which owed allegiance only to the Pope. The Knights were divided into eight *langues* or tongues which, in order of seniority, were Provence, Auvergne, France, Italy, Aragon, England, Germany and Castile. After the Reformation, the English *langue* fell apart, and in 1565 consisted of only one Knight, Sir Oliver Starkey, Latin Secretary to the Grand Master.

On arrival in Malta, the Order found a somewhat inhospitable, soil-impoverished land with the sole merit of an excellent harbour. Previous Spanish occupants had sadly neglected the few fortifications, and materials such as wood and hard stone were very scarce. The capital, Mdina (known to the Knights as Città Notabile), situated on a hill in the centre of the island, was partially deserted and poorly protected. Moreover, until after the siege, the Order never gave up the hope of returning to Rhodes, and so there was little incentive for any major building projects. That is until the fall of Tripoli (the most dubious part of Charles's gift) in 1551, when the Turkish danger became very obvious. Some attention had already been paid to strengthening Fort St Angelo, at the tip of the Birgu peninsula, and there was much activity in improving the other island defences, including the Birgu fortifications where the Order had its headquarters. Fort St Michael was built at the neck of the Senglea peninsula, and on the sea point of Mount Sciberras construction started on the star-shaped Fort St Elmo.

In 1557, on the death of Grand Master La Sengle (after whom Senglea was called) the Order elected Jean Parisot de la Valette to succeed him. He was a man built upon a bigger scale than the common run, and the most illustrious Grand Master the Order ever had. He came from a distinguished Provencal family, and had joined the Hospitallers at the age of twenty. Now aged seventy-one, he had filled most of the important offices of the Order, and had recently been General of the Galleys. He had fought at Rhodes, and sailed with and against (for he had been captured and endured for a year the flail and torment of the galleys) such famous corsairs as Barbarossa

MAP 4.1

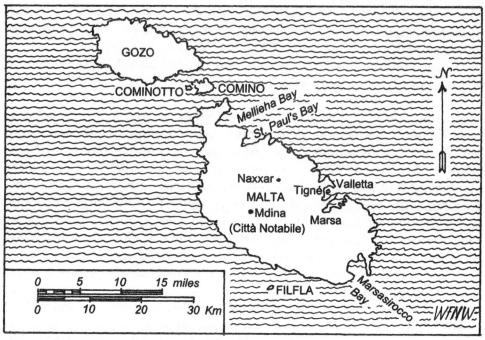

The Maltese Islands

and Dragut. He possessed a will of iron, unquestioned courage, and an enormous capacity for warfare both on land and sea. His faith was almost fanatical and he drew from it deep reserves of stamina.

No sooner had the Knights been established in Malta than they began their seafaring activities – for which purpose they had been given the island – against the Sultan's ships. Their fast and heavily armed galleys had swept the seas doing devastating damage to Moslem trade, while considerably enriching their Order. There had, of course, been reverses but the seamanship of the Knights was renowned throughout the Mediterranean and had evoked the furious fulminations of the Sultan. Suleiman's long and splendid reign had been the scarcely concealed envy of Europe, and ensured that his name be placed in the topmost rank of history. By 1565, he was seventy years old, but his ambitions remained unbounded and he looked upon Malta as the key to the Mediterranean and the gateway to further conquests in Europe. At the beginning of his reign, he had defeated the Knights and been magnanimous in victory, now in its closing years he would destroy them. In the autumn of 1564, the order went out for a full-scale attack to be launched on Malta in the spring of the following year. Shortly afterwards, Grand Master La Valette, who had his spies in the Grande Porte, was made aware of this decree.

There are contemporary reports which open for us a window on this siege; among them that of the Spaniard Francisco Balbi, who fought as an arquebusier and kept a day-to-day account. At the beginning of the siege, La Valette had under his command, in round figures, 600 Knights and servants-at-arms, and 8,500 soldiers, which included 3,000 Maltese who throughout fought most gallantly – although their nobility took no part. In addition, there were 1,000 slaves – mostly Moslems – who comprised a labour force. A wide assortment of weapons were used. The steel-clad Knights would wield a heavy two-handed sword, and there were pikes, spears, arquebuses, muskets and a variety of fireworks that included a combustible pot used as a sort of hand grenade-cum-flame thrower, something called a trump that was a refined form of Greek fire, and specially prepared flaming hoops. These latter were deadly, for they could encircle three or four Janissaries at a time and set alight their voluminous robes with an unquenchable flame. In the matter of cannon the Turks had the advantage in numbers and weight.

As soon as the Grand Master had positive information that an invasion was planned the whole island became a hive of activity. Time was short, but much was done. Ample provisions and supplies of powder and shot were brought in from Sicily for a siege which La Valette reckoned would not last beyond September. Each *langue* was allotted its defensive bastion, and the Birgu and Senglea fortifications were strengthened, and a chain stretched across the creek between St Angelo and the tip of Senglea. The ditch that separated St Angelo from the rest of the Birgu peninsula was deepened so that it could shelter galleys. That fort was garrisoned by fifty Knights and 500 men, and for the first part of the siege La Valette made his headquarters there. The garrison of Mdina was increased by six Knights and 150 men, and that of St Elmo by one Knight and 200 soldiers, but a further forty-six Knights volunteered for service there bringing the total to fifty-three Knights and 800 soldiers.

When the Viceroy of Sicily, Don Garcia de Toledo, visited the island shortly before the invasion, he recommended the building of a ravelin on the north-west side of St Elmo. This was completed in time, but proved an unfortunate error, for it was soon captured and used as an artillery platform against the fort, which was anyway overlooked by higher ground to the south. The Viceroy promised reinforcements by the end of June, which must have seemed a long way off to La Valette, and as we shall see his promises were unreliable. Beyond that there could be no expectations of help from Europe.

The vast Turkish armada was first sighted on the morning of 18 May. There were 130 royal galleys, 30 galleases, 11 barges and 50 vessels of lesser size, in which were packed over 30,000 fighting men of whom 6,300 were Janissaries (Suleiman had raised this élite corps to an establishment of 20,000) and 6,000 Spahis – expert bowmen. The command of this force was split, which proved fortunate for the Hospitallers. The army was to be commanded by Mustapha Pasha, who, like La Valette, had fought at Rhodes and was a very fit, and notoriously cruel, seventy. The fleet was entrusted to Piali, a younger man who had been born a Christian but abandoned by his parents and brought up in the Sultan's household. Both men were to heed the cogent advice of the redoubtable corsair, Dragut, and the Governor of Alexandria, al-Louk Ali, who were on their way to Malta independently. In the transport vessels was a vast quantity of stores – food, powder, shot, tents, clothing, as well as a number of horses to drag the heavy guns. It was a well executed logistic undertaking.

La Valette sent out his General of Galleys, the Chevalier Romegas, with four vessels to reconnoitre this fleet. Romegas was the most renowned Christian sailor of the time, whose exploits equalled those of Dragut, but even he refrained from interfering with the majestic progress of these great galleys, which having swept up the west coast of the island doubled back to anchor in Marsasirocco bay. The process of disembarking on the low-lying land of the Marsa, and establishing a base camp, began at once. The wells of the Marsa, which would be the army's only water supply, had been poisoned; nevertheless the Turks had to use them throughout the campaign, which may have contributed to the heavy incidence of dysentery and other illnesses they suffered.

Soon after they had landed, an argument developed between the two commanders. Mustapha was anxious to sweep north, take Mdina and occupy that part of the island so as to protect his rear while he attacked Birgu. Meanwhile, the fleet should seal off the Grand Harbour and patrol north-east to prevent reinforcements landing. He did not attach much importance to St Elmo. But Piali was adamant that the weather would not allow his fleet to remain in Marsasirocco, and that St Elmo must be taken first to enable the ships to use the greater safety of Marsamuscetto. Piali was wrong, but Mustapha could not overrule him, and it was the first and probably the most decisive mistake the Turks made.

La Valette was well aware that, with his small numbers, he could do nothing but meet the Turks behind his defences. He could not afford to waste men on sorties. But the sight of the enemy advancing towards Birgu with drums beating and banners flying in the wind, was too much for some of the young and eager Knights and, seeing them go forward, he felt he should support them with men and artillery fire. The engagement lasted six hours, before the Grand Master signalled the force to retire covered by the guns. Young Knights had been blooded, morale raised and only twenty-one Christians dead against two or three hundred Turks. But there were to be no more such actions. It had been noticeable in this engagement that the longer Turkish muskets had a greater range than the Christian ones, although being longer they were slower to load.

At intervals throughout the siege, renegade Christians from the Turkish army would make their escape, wanting to return to their faith and willing to give information. Two such, who had been present when the decision to attack St Elmo was made, were brought before the Grand Master who was thus able to hasten reinforcements and supplies (storage space at St Elmo was sadly lacking) to the garrison, and warn them that they would be first to bear the brunt.

The Turkish labour force was extremely efficient. In a remarkably short time, batteries of heavy guns were hauled four miles from Marsa and positioned on Mount Sciberras, and breastworks erected (the ground was too stony for digging) almost up to the St Elmo ditch. By 31 May the Turks had twenty-four guns aligned against the front of St Elmo ready to pummel the walls before the first major assault of 3 June. There were to be four of these large-scale attacks, and the pattern of each was very similar. Moreover, the garrison was kept busy every night trying to shore up the none too substantial walls of their fortress as they crumpled from the constant cannonade.

The day before the first attack, there was much jubilation in the Turkish camp when Dragut arrived with fifteen galleys. He brought reinforcements and supplies, but his presence alone was worth a division. He was the only one of the principals capable of conducting a siege, and he very quickly saw that Mustapha's strategy was the best, but he felt that to withdraw from St Elmo now would be bad for morale. However, he made a number of useful tactical suggestions, especially for the siting of the batteries, although it was not until the failure of the second attack, and shortly before he was mortally wounded, that his dispositions cut St Elmo's lifeline of reinforcements. La Valette knew that the longer St Elmo held out, the greater was the chance for the main fortifications. To this end, he was prepared to reinforce, frequently by night. However, the day that brought Dragut was not all Turkish delight. The Christian cavalry, which by now was based on Mdina, carried out a swift sortie on a raiding party in the west of the island, and killed or captured 400 Turkish soldiers.

Dawn came on 3 June in a pearly haze that foreshadowed another sizzling day, and with it came the Turkish advance. To supplement the heavy frontal bombardment, Dragut had sited a battery on the point of land* immediately north of Marsamascutto bay, from where fire could be brought to bear on the cavalier at the north-eastern end of the fort. Under cover of the guns, the Turks quickly gained the ravelin and the counterscarp. The ravelin – a great prize – unexpectedly fell into their hands. It has never been discovered why this outwork was totally unguarded, but as soon as a reconnoitring party had discovered the fact the Janissaries were ordered forward. With their scaling ladders, they were quickly over the top before resistance could be effective and the outwork was theirs. There then ensued

---

*Later named Tigné after the French engineer who advised the Knights on the fortifications in the early 18th century.

a furious fight for the bridge that connected the ravelin with the fort before the portcullis could be lowered.

This was the first of many full-scale attacks by the Janissaries during the siege. The furious advances of their phalanxes, scimitars gleaming, herons' plumes waving from their tall hats and their discipline born of professional pride, portrays the glamour and pageantry of war in all its beastliness, for in the space of minutes, hundreds were mown down, writhing and quivering in tangled heaps under the intensive fire of musket and cannon. The ditch was deep with their bodies as men, vainly endeavouring to scale the walls, were thrust back by the fury of the embattled defenders. The trumps and flaming hoops did terrible execution, human torches fell from the ladders and rushed madly for the sea. After about five hours of this carnage, Dragut, who was himself in the fore of the battle, sounded the retreat, for even with a covered way partially in his hands, the casualties kept mounting. In this savage assault, the Christians lost only ten Knights and seventy-three soldiers, while the Turks suffered nearly 2,000 casualties many of which were irreplaceable Janissaries. But possession of the counterscarp and ravelin amply repaid their losses.

In this first assault Christian losses, in proportion to those of their enemy, were not small, for each night La Valette was sending across the narrow waters more men than he could properly spare. The Viceroy in Sicily was not being helpful. He had promised a relief force by the end of June, but wanted the Order's galleys to transport them, which was a foolish demand. History has not been kind to Don Garcia over the way he procrastinated with reinforcements, but it has to be remembered that should Malta fall, and he had denuded Sicily of troops and ships, that island would become an easy prey. In the end, it is said that Philip II put pressure upon him, for although Europe was unwilling to give active assistance all realised what was at stake.

In the second assault, of 7 June, the Turks were again unable to scale the walls, and the fierce fighting round the temporary bridge they threw up was to no avail. Once again, they were forced back, chiefly through the use of the various flame-throwers. Their casualties were less than in the previous attack being estimated at around 500, again mostly Janissaries. The Christians had 40 soldiers killed. But the chief damage had been done by Turkish cannon, especially the battery on Tigné, which had rendered the cavalier useless. The walls were beginning to crumble under the continuous heavy pounding. Added to this Turkish engineers, unnoticed in the heat of the assault, were attempting to mine. However, there is no evidence they were successful on this stony ground, although later, at Birgu and Senglea, mines were used.

By now the garrison realised that it could not be long before the fort must fall, and many felt that their sacrifice was in vain and it would be better if everyone was evacuated to strengthen the main position. They sent the Chevalier de Medrano, well known to the Grand Master as a valiant Knight, to put their case. La Valette listened attentively, and consulted the Council many of which supported Medrano. But speaking most eloquently and putting all the facts before them, which included information that the Viceroy refused to hazard his fleet if St Elmo fell, he sent back orders to continue the struggle. He also commissioned a report to be made on the feasibility of further resistance, the findings of which did not satisfy some fifteen of the younger Knights, and La Valette had to use his authority to prevent them from sallying forth to die in the open rather than perish under the debris of the fort. St Elmo had to be held to the last man, and in the end this is what the Knights willingly did.

The third major assault, which came at dawn on 16 June, was a larger affair than either of its two predecessors, and Mustapha and Dragut confidently expected it to be the last. During the previous night, Piali had sailed his fleet round to stand off the point and add the weight of its guns to the general bombardment. There was now another battery firing from Gallows Point, and the Mount Sciberras guns were hurling shot of up to 160 lbs on the front of the rapidly disintegrating fortress. Moreover, on this day the hard pressed garrison became the victims of Fortune when the wind blew their flame-throwers into their faces, their fireworks magazine exploded causing many deaths, and a salvo from the guns of St Angelo was misdirected inflicting further casualties.

Nevertheless, once again the Hospitallers at bay showed such fury that the Turks were kept to the ditch. The initial advance by more than 4,000 men encompassed the entire front, but on this occasion the Janissaries were held back to administer the *coup de grâce*. These fine men, the pride of the Sultan's army, were animated by a desire for vengeance, for only two days back their much revered Lieutenant-Aga had been killed. Now they stormed into the ditch and on to the walls, eager to kill. A small party gained the ramparts, but not for long, and the process of death and mutilation was greater than ever. When Mustapha eventually gave the signal to retire the Turks had lost more than a thousand dead, and the Hospitallers 150 with many more wounded.

As a result of this third failure, a plan that Dragut had had in mind from his first inspection was at last put into execution. A formidable stone wall was constructed to extend the existing breastworks down to the sea on the fort's south-east front. Thus a covered way had been completed under the protection of which Turkish troops could be freely deployed, and could supplement their cannon with small arms fire against reinforcements being ferried to the fort. Failure to have done this from the beginning was the second major mistake made by the Turkish command.

This new fortification was carried out with the same skill and expedition that characterised the earlier earthworks, and was closely supervised by Mustapha and Dragut. It was to be the latter's last service to Islam, for on

18 June, while he was watching the work with some senior officers, a gunner at St Angelo let fire at them and a splinter of rock struck the corsair on the head. Until comparatively recently, in almost every army in the world, casualties to important and intrepid leaders had been disproportionately high on account of their fine plumage. Dragut was not the only one in this siege to be specially selected for death. The old warrior lived until 23 June, when news was brought to him of the fall of St Elmo. He would not have wished for a more fitting end to a distinguished career of princely piracy.

Just before the end, the Grand Master had made one last attempt to reinforce the fort, but it was no longer possible. The last battle began on Friday 22 June. This time the attack was launched on every part of the wall, and the garrison was assailed from behind when the Turks made a lodgement on the cavalier. On many occasions, the walls were scaled, or entered through the numerous breaches, and the action became close quarter grapple – pikes and swords supported by arquebusiers. The St Angelo guns could no longer give aid, and the garrison's most effective battery had been put out of action by the guns of the fleet, which was again in action. After some six hours of sustained slaughter, Mustapha called off the attack having lost perhaps as many as 2,000 men.

However, the garrison had also lost heavily, and now there were only about 150 fit for duty, and many of those were wounded. Even so, on the morning of the 23rd, they defied for one hour, with the utmost constancy and courage, another avalanche of battle-crazed fanatics. But they could do no more than die, and when the Sultan's standard replaced the flag of St John on what was left of St Elmo there were just nine wounded Knights alive. These escaped immediate death by falling into the hands of corsairs who hid them for their ransom. It is not known exactly how many Turks died in the taking of St Elmo, but probably around 8,000. The Order lost 1,500 men (including 89 Knights), but they had held the fort for three weeks instead of the Turkish expectancy of three days, and in doing so had saved Malta.

Sadly, in the aftermath of this great struggle there were two acts of barbarism. That committed by Mustapha sprang from fury and frustration, the other, by La Valette, from a desire for retaliation. When the nerves of commanders are stretched to breaking point these things can occur – and not only 400 years ago. Soon they were forgotten when the Turks began to withdraw their artillery from the Sciberras position and position batteries on the Coradin and Margarita heights in readiness for the next phase of the siege, for which the Hospitallers had been preparing during the three-week respite given them by the defenders of St Elmo.

A day or two after the fall of the fort, four galleys anchored off the north-east coast of the island bringing what became known as the 'Little Relief'. The Viceroy had instructed their captain not to land the troops had St Elmo fallen, but the news was kept from him and 734 fresh, experienced soldiers disembarked under the leadership of the Chevalier de Robles. Among them were forty-two Knights of the Order, two Englishmen (Edward Stanley and John Smith), and a number of Spaniards, French, Italians and some mercenary gunners. The force carried out a well-executed march down the west of the island, and did a wide detour of the newly formed Turkish lines to enter Birgu by the Kalkara Creek, which at the time was unguarded.

Thanks to La Valette's foresight, the Christian camp was still well provisioned, but information from the occasional deserter indicated that the Turks were becoming very anxious on this score, and that there was much disease in the camp. This may have been partly the reason why Mustapha now sent a Greek slave to the Christian lines with an offer of terms similar to those agreed at Rhodes. These were immediately rejected, and the Turks continued their laborious preparations, part of which was the transport of ships overland. As soon as St Elmo had been taken, Piali had gained his desired anchorage in the Marsamuscetto Bay and now, so as to be able to assist the coming offensive, he brought, in the course of a few days, eighty ships over the neck of land and into the Grand Harbour. This was a severe blow for the Hospitallers, and clearly indicated that the next attack would be against St Michael's fort and the Senglea peninsula, because the chain and the St Angelo guns would keep these ships from the Birgu peninsula.

This, and much else besides, was shortly confirmed by an important senior defector from the Turkish camp. Acting on his information, the Grand Master made further improvements to the defences of Senglea, chief among these being the erection of a stockade of stakes and chains a little way off shore along the whole western side of the peninsula. This was accomplished in nine nights of hard toil by the Maltese, for whom no labour was too hard nor danger too great. In addition, the St Michael fortifications were strengthened, and a floating bridge laid across the water dividing Birgu from Senglea.

For a whole week before the first major attack against Senglea on 15 July, the resounding thunder of iron shot rolled down from the surrounding hills as batteries on Sciberras, Coradin, and Margarita kept up their cannonade against the defences. This pounding was eased to enable a strange underwater fight to take place for possession of the stockade. Mustapha's swimmers tried hard to break the barrier, but the Maltese would not be denied and, when the battle started, the Turkish ships found it to be indestructible.

Mustapha had recently been joined by Dragut's son-in-law, Hassem the Governor of Algiers, who had not endeared himself to the Pasha by criticising the attack on St Elmo. And so Mustapha let him lead the land attack against St Michael's while his lieutenant commanded the ships, so as to cool his vain boasting. Francesco Balbi was quite overawed by the

MAP 4.2

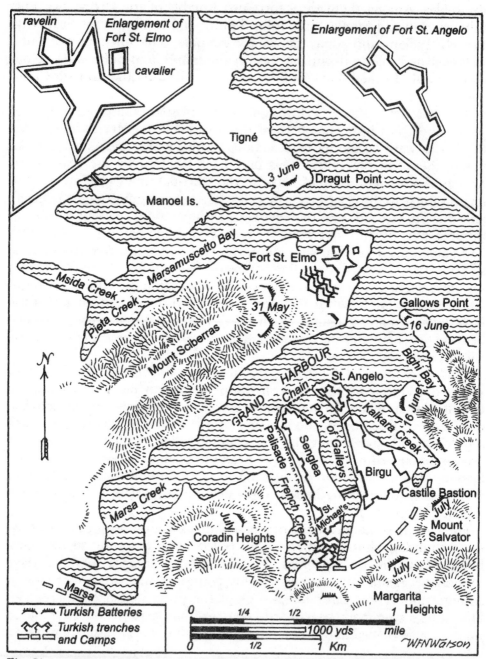

The Siege of Malta 1565

magnificence of the sea-borne invasion, and gives a vivid account of the
gorgeous clothes worn by the 3,000 troops as they sailed to assault the post
that his company was guarding. It is a pity that their 'cloth of gold, silver

and crimson damask' should so soon be spoilt, but the ships were quite unable to force the barricade and the soldiers had to scramble through it in water above their waists.

Somehow they managed to bring ladders ashore, and as two guns on the ramparts had been wrongly sited, they were able, in places, to reach the base of the bastions and there use their ladders. The garrison meted out the same treatment as their brothers had done at St Elmo. Pikes, engines of fire and heavy rocks were used to thrust these intrepid climbers back into the water. But an unfortunate explosion in the fireworks magazine, killing many of the defenders, enabled some Turks to gain the ramparts, and a very ugly situation was only saved by La Valette's foresight with the floating bridge, across which reinforcements were now sent. The fighting at the southern end of the peninsula was every bit as savage, but here Hassem's Algerians could not make a lodgement, and hundreds of his men were flung back into the ditch in maimed and dying heaps.

Mustapha had been waiting to judge the time for his master stroke, for he had ten large boats filled with 1,000 Janissaries ready to sail to the northern spur, where there was no barricade. With the battle finely balanced, he now gave the signal to dispatch these boats. It almost certainly would have been the end of Senglea had it not been for a battery of five guns at St Angelo sited for the very purpose of such an attack. Unnoticed until it was too late, these guns sent a hail of whistling metal against the boats, sinking most of them and killing some 800 of the Janissaries. The battle went on, but the Turks had been fought to a standstill in both sectors of the peninsula. After five hours, they retired, having lost 3,000 soldiers. The Hospitallers had lost only 250, but among the dead was the gallant commander of the spur and the Viceroy's son.

As a result of this battle, both sides made fresh dispositions. Mustapha resolved to attack the two peninsulas simultaneously after his usual bombardment, for which purpose he brought a number of heavy guns – one piece firing a ball of 300 lbs – to Mount Salvator, and he extended the Turkish entrenchments to reach round the foot of Salvator to Kalkara Creek thus, somewhat belatedly, closing the gap for any reinforcements. La Valette, realising from all this that the Castile bastion was to be attacked, ordered ships to be sunk in the Creek to form a blockade against a possible seaborne landing under cover of the recently positioned batteries. He also caused a number of houses in Birgu, which would have been blasted by gunfire, to be demolished and reduced to stones suitable for hurling – Balbi reported these as being invaluable – and the outer ditch of Castile, and the casemates, were to be quickly completed.

It was now the beginning of August and the heat had become bone-searing. Food was holding out but water had to be carefully preserved. The high temperatures were unpleasant enough for the soldiers in their leather jackets, but for the Knights in close-fitting armour, weighing perhaps 100 lbs, over a quilted jerkin, they must have been intolerable. Tradition forbade them to discard armour, and anyway it had saved many a life. These men had been scarcely off duty for several weeks, and no doubt had become emotionally and physically exhausted from long spells of bombardment and deadly grapple in the ramparts. But there was no sign of the promised relief, and all knew there was much fighting still to be done.

The first attack on both peninsulas was preceded by the heaviest bombardment so far. Twenty-six guns rained shot on the Castile bastion, St Angelo was under fire from two batteries, and those on Coradin took care of Senglea. The damage was considerable, but not nearly as great as Mustapha had hoped. At midday on 2 August, the cannonade ceased, and the Turkish warriors advanced against St Michael's and the Birgu bastions, but after more than five hours of desperate fighting – especially in the breaches made in St Michael – they were thrown back. For these joint attacks Mustapha had split the command, he took charge of that on Senglea while Piali commanded against Birgu. Under their distinguished and determined leaders the Turks had charged and countercharged, but to no avail, and so Mustapha decided to resume the softening-up process, and for five more days his batteries continued their relentless pounding.

Before the next assault began on 7 August, La Valette managed to get a Maltese messenger through the enemy lines with an urgent appeal to the Viceroy. These Maltese never failed the Grand Master in reaching the north of the island, and from there taking boat to Sicily. Balbi tells us that on this day 8,000 men were sent against St Michael's and 4,000 against Castile. It seems incredible that such weight of numbers should not prevail, and indeed they very nearly did at St Michael's. Piali's men in Birgu stormed over the partly filled ditch and through the outer wall which had been breached in many places, but La Valette had recently constructed an inner one which they were not able to scale, and they became trapped in a furious mêleé. For the garrison, seeing they had them at a disadvantage between the inner and outer walls, left their posts and took the offensive with some savage hand-to-hand fighting, until what had looked like becoming a Turkish triumph became a rout. In this comparatively short fight the Turks lost more than 200 men including al-Louk Ali, one of their most senior commanders.

At St Michael's it was a very much more dangerous affair. Here the Turks fought their way over the wall and up to the citadel. Turkish flags were on the ramparts, and the garrison was being forced farther and farther back, and this time no help was possible from Birgu. But then suddenly, as if by a miracle, the Turks withdrew and the position was saved. It was learnt later that, by a most fortunate chance, the Governor of Mdina, the Chevalier Mesquita, had chosen this time for a powerful sortie and finding the Turkish camp at the Marsa virtually undefended had destroyed it.

Mustapha, on getting reports of a 'large enemy force' had assumed the Viceroy had landed, and called off his attack to deal with this threat. On learning the truth, his rage was unbounded, but it was too late to return to St Michael's, where he had lost another thousand or more men.

There were to be two more major assaults on the garrisons, and the daily bombardment was timed to reach its apogee by 18 August, the day the troops would go in. La Valette had heard from Don Garcia that 14,000 men would arrive by the end of August, but as he said to his friend and confidant, Oliver Starkey, no longer could the Viceroy's word be relied upon. He summoned those Knights still standing, and told them they could only save Malta by their own efforts, and he was nearly right, for there was a faction in Sicily advocating no action to save the island. Fortunately its members were overruled.

For his attack on 18 August, Mustapha pinned great hopes on the mine his engineers had placed under the main wall of the Castile bastion. Only Senglea was to be attacked at first, in the hope that La Valette would reinforce from Birgu, leaving that peninsula to be overrun when the mine destroyed the wall. But La Valette was suspicious, and sent no troops to Senglea. The mine was not unexpected, although its exact position had not been located. Its explosion did much damage, enabling the Turks to make a firm lodgement and penetrate some distance. A minor panic ensued, and many favoured a retreat to St Angelo, but the Grand Master would not countenance that. Seizing his helm and pike he dashed into the fray, and his steadfastness set an example to all. Birgu survived this heavy attack. It was in this battle that the Turks first used a large tower, laden with troops and well protected. It posed a serious threat, but La Valette saw that its weakness lay in its base, and causing a hole to be made low down in the wall, chopped it with chain shot.

The fight for St Michael's had followed the usual fierce pattern, and once again the garrison had managed to hold on. No tower was used there, but instead a type of infernal machine in the form of a large cylinder filled with shot, stones and nails timed to explode when it had been manoeuvred among the debris of the wall and rampart. However, the fuse was mistimed and the troops were able to roll it back into the ditch, where it exploded among the Turks. On 19 and 20 August, the attacks were renewed, but much of the ardour had gone out of the Turkish troops. Nevertheless, three days later (the 23rd) they made one more supreme effort against the garrisons, now reduced to manning the fortifications with every man whose wounds would permit him to stand or sit, and with women and children bringing up the ammunition. It was a fight between two punch-drunk forces and, as before, Mustapha had to watch his men withdraw.

For the next week, the main activity was mining and countermining, with a few unsuccessful attempts to assault. By now Mustapha was deeply worried. He had lost around 15,000 soldiers, and he had almost as many sick with malaria and dysentery. The fleet had failed to protect supplies sent him from Africa, and he was getting short of powder, shot (the Turks fired some 70,000 cannonballs in the siege) and food. Moreover, the weather would soon be breaking. His abject failure would not be welcomed by Suleiman, and he seriously thought of wintering in Malta. For this purpose he led a force of 4,000 men against Mdina at the end of August, for the quick capture of the capital would give him a little prestige, some supplies and a winter base. But, at his approach, the Governor fooled him by dressing up the whole population, including women, to man the walls. Mustapha was so impressed by the apparent strength of this – in fact minute – garrison that he withdrew. Any further thoughts of wintering in Malta were dispelled when Piali, with whom by now he was on the worst of terms, adamantly refused to retain the fleet. As it happened, any such thoughts were soon nullified by the arrival of the long expected and long delayed relief force.

Unknown to the Hospitallers, who were still grimly embattled – there was another assault on 1 September, but it was a half-hearted affair by dispirited troops – help was on the way. Don Garcia had set sail in twenty-eight galleys on 25 August, bringing eight to ten thousand men under the command of Ascario de la Corna. There were 300 members of the Order in his force, and other trained soldiers from Italy, Germany and particularly Spain. Up to the very last, the Viceroy had been hesitant. One can appreciate his reasons, for he had charge of all Spanish possessions in the area, and he was unaware of the full situation in Malta, and in particular to what extent Mustapha's men had been depleted. Furthermore, he knew that he could be attacked by the largest fleet in the Mediterranean.

The Viceroy's fleet was forced to return to Sicily through bad weather but, after some hasty repairs, the galleys set sail again. There was more bad weather, which may have been the reason why the Turkish ships had ceased their patrol of the northern waters, although Piali's performance through-out the siege is open to censure. Whatever the reason, the relief force was unmolested, and the troops waded ashore in the shallow waters of Mellieha Bay on 7 September, after which Don Garcia, who had accompanied the force, returned to Sicily. The news reached the opposing commanders at much the same time. La Valette was fearful that so small a force might prove inadequate, and so he adopted a *ruse de guerre*. A captured Moslem slave was given his liberty as a gesture of thanksgiving for the safe arrival of 16,000 soldiers. The man was, as expected, questioned on his arrival in the camp and explained the reason for his freedom. The information was sufficient to determine Mustapha to be gone from the island, and be gone quickly.

That night the rumble of retreating artillery was clearly audible to the Christians, and on the morning of the 8th there was the joy of church bells ringing for High Mass, where for the past three months they had been rung only for an alarm. The immediate landscape was now silent, and the Turkish trenches held only dead men. All around the carnage was very evident; broken bodies, many of them putrid, lay among stones and earth reddened by their blood as terrible evidence of the hard won freedom now manifest by the open gates. Some Knights rode round to St Elmo, and above the ruins proudly hoisted the flag of the Order. Seeing from the point small boats crammed with Turkish soldiers being rowed out to the galleys, they sent back for some light cannon with which to hasten the embarkation.

But all was not quite over, for Mustapha had sent out patrols which reported the true size of the relief force. He was a man who did not bear adversity with composure, and at once ordered the men to disembark. This produced another confrontation with Piali who was anxious to get his fleet under sail, and it says much for Turkish discipline that, despite considerable grumbling, the exhausted and dejected soldiers were prevailed upon to leave their boats and once more form up for battle. Throughout the siege, Mustapha had shown the utmost personal valour; he had always led from the front, and now this old man prepared to do battle at the head of his troops.

Ascanio de la Corna had made contact with the Mdina garrison soon after landing, and he now took up a position on some high ground near the village of Naxxar. Here he wished to await Mustapha's attack, but his second-in-command, Alvarez de Sandé, and many of the Knights thought otherwise, and stormed down the hill straight at the Turks. Unable to stop them, de la Corna rode with them, and such was the impact of these fresh and ardent soldiers that Mustapha's men soon broke, and he himself was only saved from capture by a devoted band of Janissaries. But the pursuit became overstretched and, as the retreating force reached St Paul's Bay, where some ships had come round to collect it, Mustapha ordered Hassem's arquebusiers to form a rearguard. These men did their work well until forced to retire when confronted with the full weight of de la Corna's force. The embarkation then became a shambles, with many Turks being cut down or drowned, until de la Corna called his men off as the Turkish ships brought their guns into action. As usual, numbers have become exaggerated, but the Turks certainly lost over 1,000 men killed or drowned in this last action. The stench was so appalling round St Paul's Bay that men avoided it for three days.

As the last rays of the sun cast purple shadows across the land on that memorable 8 September, what was left of the Turkish army sailed for Constantinople and an uncertain reception. The siege was over and Malta was, for the time at least, safe, but the cost had been appalling. The Grand Master had no more than 600 men still capable of bearing arms out of an original 9,000; close on 250 Knights and 7,000 Maltese, Spaniards and other nationals had been killed. But the losses they had inflicted on the proud and predatory Turkish army were incalculable. It is thought that no more than

10,000 out of a total strength of nearly 40,000 reached Constantinople, and many of those were wounded or sick. In the story of siege warfare the defence of Malta in 1565, and again in 1942, has become a heroic apologue of spirited defiance in the face of great odds.

It can be no reflection on the courage and steadfastness of the entire Malta garrison, and the superb leadership of Jean Parisot de la Valette, which alone saved the island, to say that the Turks threw away what should have been a comparatively easy victory. They made five colossal blunders. The command should never have been split; Mustapha's strategy of taking the island and safeguarding his rear should have been adopted; immediate steps should have been taken to prevent reinforcements reaching St Elmo; Birgu and Senglea should have been completely sealed off, for which there were sufficient men; and much more use should have been made of the fleet.

The defeated generals had taken the precaution of informing Suleiman of the disaster in advance of their sorrowful landing, which on his orders took place under cover of darkness. He was very ill by now, and was to die the following year while on campaign in Hungary. The victory of the Hospitallers was significant in that it marked the end of any serious Turkish penetration into the western Mediterranean. Their fleet had proved disappointing, and was to suffer a crippling blow six years later at Lepanto. Turkish power, however, remained unbroken for many years to come.

By their fortitude and constancy in war, the Hospitallers had won the respect and gratitude of Europe, now in peace they began to enrich their island which they had finally decided should be their permanent home. On 28 March 1566, La Valette laid the foundation stone of what was to be their new capital on Mount Sciberras, and which was to be called Valletta after the most renowned Grand Master of the Order. He died on 21 August 1568, and was buried in the Chapel of Our Lady of Victory in his burgeoning city. The Order of St John continued in Malta as guardians of the Faith until Napoleon expelled them from the island in June 1798.

CHAPTER 5

Basing House 1643–45

THE story of the Siege of Basing House during the First Civil War between King Charles I and Parliament, is an unusual one, illustrating how political and religious obsession can lead to the employment of forces and loss of life which are quite disproportionate to the military significance of the task. This great fortified house was the seat of John Paulet, the Roman Catholic fifth Marquess of Winchester. In its defence, he was supported by a garrison which was primarily Catholic in character – a fact that was anathema to Cromwell and his Roundheads. On the face of it, the task was not a formidable one yet a blend of gallant fighting by the garrison and a fair measure of military incompetence by the Parliamentary troops, produced a siege lasting two years and drove Cromwell himself to take command in the closing stages.

* * *

When Basing House first came under serious threat, in July 1643, the Civil War had lasted just under a year. Honours were about even, but if anything the King held a slight advantage. In broad terms, the countries west of a line Cheshire-Worcester-Oxford-Hampshire, and north of a line Lancaster-York up to the Scottish border, and including Derbyshire, were predominantly royalist. In particular, matters had recently gone well for the King in the south-west, which was largely due to his distinguished general, Sir Ralph (later Lord) Hopton, who commanded a fine body of Cornish infantry.

In January 1643 Hopton, together with Sir Bevil Grenvile – another good soldier – soundly defeated General Ruthin's troops at Braddock Down. After a minor setback at Scurton Down, in Devon, he and Grenvile again defeated Stamford's numerically superior army at Stratton. This enabled Hopton to leave Cornwall and join Lord Hertford and Prince Maurice at Chard. The juncture of these armies necessitated Sir William Waller, arguably the greatest Parliamentary general, withdrawing his troops from a successful campaign in the Lower Severn Valley. On 5 July, he met Hopton (his friend and comrade in arms in happier times) on Lansdowne Hill. As at Stratton, Grenvile led the Cornishmen in a headlong charge, which gained the royalists an indecisive victory at heavy cost. Grenvile, himself, fell in the last stages of the battle, and Hopton was seriously wounded in an accidental explosion just afterwards. Eight days later, at Roundway Down near Devizes, he was still unfit to command in a battle in which Waller was decisively defeated by Prince Maurice and Lord Wilmot.

Waller returned to London at the end of July to a rapturous welcome. His reputation was too big for it to be damaged by Roundway Down, and soon he was to receive a new commission and make the first major attempt to reduce Basing House. But there were difficulties to be overcome, principally at the hands of the Earl of Essex, the Lord General, who was jealous of Waller's reputation, and determined he should not have an independent command. Parliament was anxious to raise what was called the 'New Army' with Waller in command, and Essex reluctantly signed the commission, but saw to it that recruiting was difficult. On his return to London, after a highly successful march across England to relieve Gloucester, and a strategic success at the First Battle of Newbury (20 September) on the way back. Essex felt strong enough to revoke the commission. It was not until 4 November that Waller's 'New Army', rapidly dying from a lack of men and resources, was reborn under a new name.

He was now to command the Southern Association, whose troops would be found from the counties of Surrey, Sussex, Kent and Hampshire. But the counties were slow and niggardly in their response, and for his attack on Basing House only Colonel Norton's horse and Colonel Jones's Greencoats had joined. But the good performance of the London Trained Bands* at Newbury led to a brigade of these troops being dispatched to Farnham Castle, where Waller had his headquarters. The brigade comprised the Westminster Liberty Regiment, known as the Red Regiment from the colour of its flag, the Green Auxiliaries of London, and the Yellow Auxiliaries of the Tower Hamlets. These men were a numerical reinforcement to Waller's original 3,000 foot and 2,000 horse, but they were an unknown quantity being without any battle experience.

In the Civil War there was not a great deal of difference in the arms and equipment of both sides. The royalist cavalry from the beginning, and the Parliamentarian soon afterwards, was organised in regiments of six or more troops, the troops being commanded by a captain with a lieutenant and cornet under him. Basically, the cavalryman carried a pair of pistols and a sword, but there were variations and some carried carbines, while Cromwell had a troop of arquebusiers. The usual defensive armour was

---

*Trained Bands were mostly infantrymen directly under the Lieutenant of the county and officered by the local gentry. The name Trained Bands indicated that the men were available for training rather that that they had been trained. Those from London and Cornwall were the best organised and equipped, and they alone could be persuaded to fight outside their own counties.

a light headpiece known as a pot, and back and breastplates worn over a buff leather coat – an exception was Sir Arthur Haselrige's more heavily armoured cuirassiers. Dragoons were mounted infantry riding an inferior type of horse. They were armed with sword and carbine.

On paper, an infantry regiment was 1,200 men organised into ten companies but regiments seldom exceeded 800 men, and were often as little as 300. In 1643, there were usually two musketeers to every pikeman. The latter carried a weapon 18 feet long in theory, but usually shortened to 16 feet. Musketeers (except the small artillery guard which carried early flintlocks) were armed with the matchlock, a cumbersome, inaccurate weapon that fired (from a rest) a heavy bullet for a distance of up to 400 yards, although there was no hope of accuracy above 100 yards. The rate of fire was slow, even if the matchlock did not misfire, and the burning match completely eliminated surprise in a night attack. Originally, pikemen wore iron helmets, and back and breastplates but, by 1643, both sides seem to have stopped issuing armour. Musketeers were felt-hatted, and never armoured.

The artillery train contained a wide variety of cannon, ranging from the heavy siege guns, firing a 63 lb shot to the smallest drake (a collective name for the lighter calibre sakers, falcons, falconets and robinets), firing a three-quarter pound one. The culverin, a five inch calibre gun, firing an 18 lb shot and the demi-culverin (nine-pounder) were dual purpose cannon of the type used against Basing House in Waller's attack*. The rate of fire, even with light cannon, was slow, as was the rate of march over the bad roads, for many horses and wagons were needed to move the guns, powder and shot.

In December 1642, Waller had taken Winchester, but Sir William Agle retook it in October 1643 and, at the end of that month, Waller's army left Windsor for Farnham en route for another attempt against Winchester. On 3 November, the troops left Farnham. Lieutenant Archer, who marched with the Yellow Auxiliaries, says there were '16 Troops of horse, eight companies of Dragoons, and 36 foot companies (as appeared by their Colours) our Trains of Artillery consisting of ten peaces of Ordnance, and six cases of small Drakes'. Waller probably commanded a little under 8,000 men. The weather was appalling, and the London Trained Bands were already finding conditions not at all to their liking. On 5 November, the army was near Alton where Waller learnt that Hopton, with a large army, was in his rear, poised to cut off his retreat. He therefore decided it would be safer to fall back and, while awaiting clarification of Hopton's intentions, to take Basing House, 'which by all men was represented to me to be but a small peece'.

*For full range of Civil War Cannon, see Firth pp168, 169, 402, and Adair 'Cheriton', p17.

Basing House was owned by John Paulet, fifth Marquess of Winchester, who came from a family renowned for their service to the sovereign (the first marquess served four Tudor monarchs in high office, and survived). Their motto is '*Aymes Loyaulté*', and Paulet constantly referred to Basing as 'Loyalty House'. He was 45 years old, a patriot and possessed of hard, indomitable grit. Until 1642, when he declared for the King, he had lived a comparatively quiet life as a conscientious landowner.

The house was, in fact, two separate buildings connected by a bridge. The Old House, or keep, was on the site of the Norman ring work and bailey castle, and the New House to its east had been built by the first marquess on a grand scale around a pentagonal courtyard. A wall encompassed the houses, and at the north extremity, there was another wall with towers that enclosed a garden. The park stretched for some considerable distance to the south-west. Here the approach was open and flat, but substantial earthworks with bastions had been erected. Deep, dry moats round the perimeter of the houses completed the formidable fortifications. The house and outworks stood in 14.5 acres, and just to the north was the river Lodden and marshland, which provided a further obstacle to aggressors.

Just as Donnington Castle commanded the main road to the West through Newbury, so Basing House blocked the way through Salisbury. It was of considerable strategic importance, and Parliament was determined to take it, but consistently misjudged its strength, and the courage and stubbornness of its defenders. An earlier attempt, which had been made by Colonels Norton's and Harvey's dragoons at the end of July 1643, might have succeeded, for there were only six men in the garrison capable of bearing arms. But the Marquess had just been to Oxford to plead for reinforcements, and the King had agreed to send Sir Marmaduke Rawdon's regiment. Lieutenant Colonel Peake, making a forced march with 100 of Rawdon's men, reached Basing in time to scatter the Roundheads. Rawdon followed soon afterwards with the remainder of his regiment, and Paulet raised one of his own from local volunteers. In a letter written just before Waller's first assault, Paulet says he has a garrison of 400 men*, and supplies sufficient for three weeks. These latter must have been considerable, for many refugees had come to the house, 'Wee not having lesse than seavenscore useless mouthes'.

The dawn sky was slowly flooding the land on 6 November as Waller's army broke camp at Chilton Candover, and marched for Basing. The troops were before the house shortly after midday, and Waller summoned the garrison to surrender. This formality over, Captain William Archer of the Yellow Auxiliaries was sent forward with a forlorn hope of 500 men. It is not clear whether these were to engage the garrison, or those

*If the strength of Rawdon's regiment is correctly reported at 50 cavalry and 400 foot, this figure must be low.

MAP 5.1

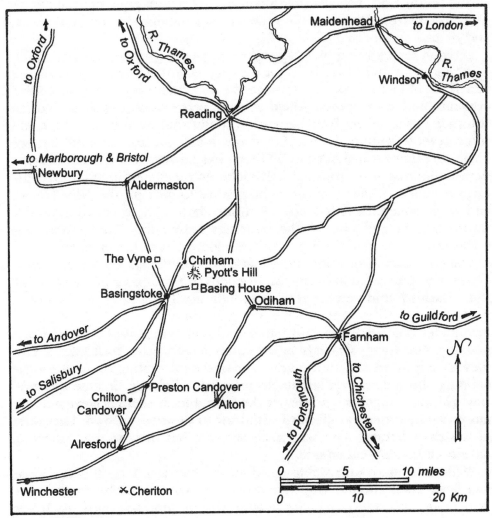

Basing House 1643

troops that held the outbuildings of Grange Farm which Waller, from his
encampment on Cowdrey's Down, rightly appreciated must be cleared as a
preliminary to taking the house. In any event, it was a fairly useless gesture,
for all the forlorn hope achieved was the expenditure of much ammunition
from the lane below the outer wall before being relieved by a regiment of
dragoons, which in their turn accomplished nothing and withdrew with the
darkness.

The garrison then sought a parley, for what reason is not clear. Nothing
came of it save an accusation of Roundhead treachery when two of their
drakes were accidently discharged during the confabulation. Meanwhile,

Waller had established his artillery train on high ground to the north-west of the house, and, between midnight and 4 am, his guns fired about 80 shots to no effect. Waller's cannon was mostly too light to be of much use, and he had no mortars.

Early on the morning of 7 November, he opened a more serious assault with another cannonade. It is not easy to reconstruct the mosaic of this attack, or indeed of the whole siege, because there are many first-hand accounts and recollections which seldom agree as to detail, and often contradict each other. But there is no doubt that on this day there was some severe fighting, lasting for many hours, in and around Grange Farm. Another forlorn hope of 500 men was thrown in and received some devastating case shot from the half-moon entrenchment that covered the farm complex. Waller then brought gunfire to bear on the New House, and at the same time reinforced the forlorn hope. There was considerable skirmishing in and around the buildings before the Cavalier outposts withdrew, to continue the fire fight from loopholes in the outer wall.

The great barn (which still stands), and other buildings, contained a large quantity of provisions and household goods, the sampling of which many Roundheads found more agreeable to fighting. The assault therefore lost momentum and, at the same time, the garrison mounted a sally of picked men under Colonels Peake and Johnson with the purpose of burning those buildings not already set alight by the garrison before the attack began. This they accomplished very thoroughly, and in the suffocating smoke – for the buildings bulged with inflammable material – fighting became difficult. Daylight was fast going, and clearly the Roundheads could achieve nothing more. So the order was given to withdraw to Cowdrey's Down. Casualties in this day's fighting vary with each account, but they do not appear to have been high on either side.

Waller was in an unenviable position. His first attack on Basing House had been thwarted, and Hopton's army was hovering on his flank in the Winchester area. Moreover, the weather that autumn was particularly vile with rain, sleet and snow falling intermittently from a lowering sky and this, together with the recent action, had an adverse effect on his Londoners, who were neither properly trained nor accustomed to harsh conditions. They had been spectators of the Grange battle, and had watched Waller's own regiment, which had borne the brunt of the fight, carry out a fairly orderly withdrawal. However, to their untrained eye, this had the trappings of defeat, and partly accounted for their froward behaviour. This, and the inclemency of the weather, persuaded Waller that it would be best to retire to more wholesome quarters in Basingstoke and The Vyne House. Here he rested his infantry in preparation for a renewed assault on Basing House; meanwhile his horse, active on patrol, somewhat revived his flagging fortunes by capturing Lord Saltoun who was just back from France and carrying large sums of money and important despatches.

For his attack on Sunday 12 November, Waller proposed a more ambitious plan. At some time within the last two days, two men (captured Roundheads) had escaped from the garrison, and given information on the weakness of the eastern wall of the New House. Waller, therefore decided to mount his main attack with 2,000 men from the north-east, while a diversion would go in across the park from the south-west. Waller, himself, would lead the main attack, which he had hoped to begin in the early morning, but such was the disorganisation and slothfulness of some regiments that it was 11 am before the guns could open up.

After an hour's fairly fruitless bombardment, the troops stormed forward. The various first-hand accounts of the next few days are confusing as to the exact direction from which each regiment attacked. Waller had with him his own regiment of dragoons, commanded by Major Strahan, and his infantry regiment, with four companies of the Greencoats. He also had the Yellow Auxiliaries, but the Westminster (Red) Regiment, which behaved badly in an attack on a projecting bastion, and ended up by accidently shooting a number of its own men, was probably in the park, although one account puts it attacking from the south-west.

In the sternly contested main battle, nothing went quite right for the Roundheads. They made short work of the outer defences but, on reaching the walls of the New House, there were no scaling ladders. These had been indented for, but had not arrived. This might not have mattered had the expected breach been made in the wall, but in the heat of battle the petardier (see Figure 5.1) fixed his bomb to a stout gate reinforced by earth, and it made no impression. Meanwhile, the ladies of the garrison were enjoying themselves hurling bricks and stones on the attackers from the roof and, more seriously, a German engineer, with considerable perspicacity, had bored a hole in the house wall from which he and others poured a destructive enfilade fire upon the baffled and exasperated Roundheads.

The attack from the park made even less progress. Indeed, it was virtually pre-empted by the tactical skill of Colonel Johnson, who before the attackers (probably the Green Auxiliaries) could reach the defences, led out, on three separate occasions, a party of 30 musketeers. These lured the Londoners into a lane commanded by the drakes of a half-moon, which showered them with case shot. It would seem that it was on this front too that the sorry spectacle of the Red Regiment's performance at the bastion occurred.

Undoubtedly, the garrison had performed with valour and vigour, but except in the early stages of the main attack from the north-east, there was little collective enthusiasm amongst the Parliamentary troops, although much individual bravery. Even the inspired leadership of Waller himself, who was always in the forefront of the battle, failed to keep the men at their task, and no headway could be made. Darkness came early that afternoon, with rain clouds massing in great banks across the sky, and Waller withdrew

FIG 5.1

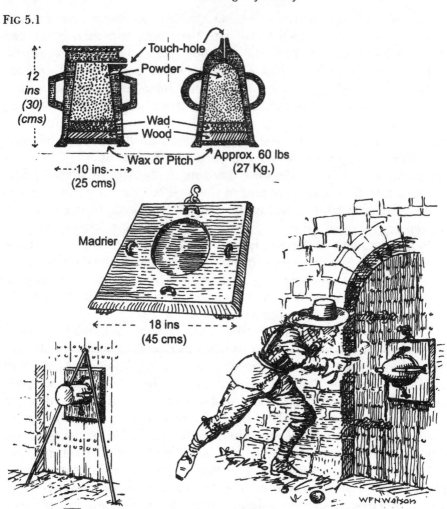

PETARD

The PETARD, a device for bursting gates open, consisted of a truncated cone-shaped metal case with a touch-hole at the breech and four handles for fastening it to the MADRIER, a heavy wooden base. Petards averaged about 8–10 inches (20–25 cms) diameter at the mouth. The Petard was filled almost completely with gunpowder, which was covered with a wad, and then by a wooden cover driven tightly in. The remaining space was filled with wax or pitch and the whole was then covered with a waxed cloth.

The mouth was fitted into a hollow in the madrier and fastened with cords from the handles to staples in the madrier, which was strengthened with iron bands at the back. It was then hung by a hook at the top, either to a spike driven into the gate, or to bipod or tripod legs planted against it, and the fuse was lit.

If the petard was strong enough, the gate was blown in, but frequently, and hardly surprisingly, it was as Hamlet said, "the sport to have the enginer Hoist with his own petar."

his troops to spend a miserable night soaked by the punishing rain in fields around Basing. In his report, he estimated that he had lost 30 men killed and 100 wounded, other accounts give his casualties as high as 300. Lord Winchester reported the loss of only two men in the course of both sieges, 'and some little injury to the house by battery'. He does not mention the wounded, but there must have been quite a few, for the fighting round the Grange had been fairly severe.

Early on the 13th, Waller received information from scouts that Hopton was within six miles of him, and apparently marching to join Sir Jacob Astley's army that had left Reading. He therefore assembled his troops preparatory to marching against Hopton when that general's movements had been clarified. But the Londoners were now on the verge of mutiny, shouting 'Home Home' at him, so that he was forced to threaten them with his pistol. Matters got no better after he had summoned the field officers to see what could be done. Although Archer informs us that his regiment, at least, was longing to meet Hopton, infinitely preferring 'to fight men rather than walls', this sentiment does not seem to have been shared by the others who 'would not march one foot further', and threatened to return to London. Waller therefore had no choice but to fall back on Farnham, where, eventually, pleasanter quarters and the promise of pay and provisions persuaded his fractious warriors to remain in the field.

Meanwhile, during a lapse of five months which followed Waller's withdrawal, a significant incident occurred at Basing House in February 1644. Some of the garrison were becoming wearied and disillusioned by continued confinement. Parliament's new plan for Waller was for him to march to Winchester with his army, which had now been reinforced by 2,000 horses from Essex's army, taking Basing House on his way. The Marquess's brother, Lord Edward Paulet, had been in correspondence with Waller over a plot to surrender the house when attacked. However, the plot was betrayed by that unreliable turncoat Sir Bevil Grenvile, who, on being captured, had offered his sword to Parliament and then absconded to Oxford with much valuable information, including the existence of the Waller-Paulet plot. The Marquess arrested his brother and, by the way of punishment, made him hang his co-conspirators. The plot exposed, Waller decided to bypass Basing House and make for Winchester.

On 29 March 1644, Waller achieved a decisive victory over Hopton at Cheriton Down – the first substantive victory that the Parliamentary army had achieved. This fight was to have several important consequences, one of these being that, with Hopton's subsequent withdrawal to Oxford, Basing House (at which Hopton's beaten army had staged for one night) became much more vulnerable. Waller had troops in the immediate neighbourhood, and a desire to assault the house again, but up to the time of his departure to join Essex at the end of May, he contented himself with attacking the garrison's foraging parties, and indicating that something

MAP 5.2

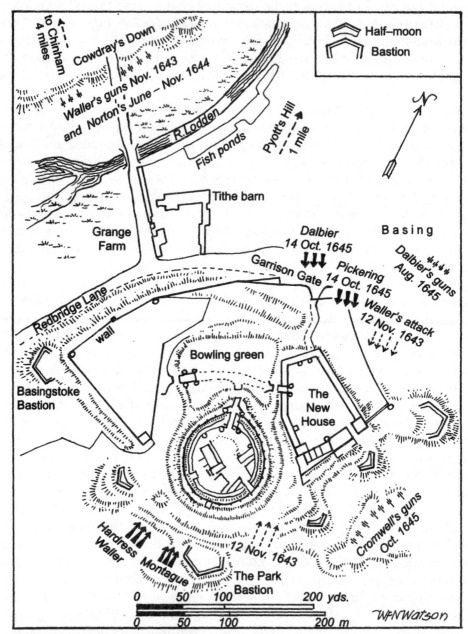

Basing House: the siege 1643–45

bigger was afoot. These overt preparations persuaded the garrison to destroy some houses (including two mills, whose loss they would later regret) that might afford cover in an attack – which, in fact, never came.

At the beginning of June, Colonel Norton, who appears to have enjoyed a roving, independent command in Hampshire, flitting from one trouble spot to another with his cavalry and dragoons, returned to his former stamping ground – this time to besiege. Rawdon, who was still at Basing with his troops, learning of this intention, decided to mount an attack on Norton's headquarters at Odiham. But the plan was betrayed and the attacking party expected. After a brief fight, the garrison's horse were beaten back to the house, and many of their infantry were captured.

Norton's siege of Basing House began on 4 June 1644, and was not raised until November. However, even after he had received substantial reinforcements, bringing his total to around 3,000, the garrison was never so closely confined as to prevent parties, some of them quite large, from sallying out on punitive or foraging raids. Through casualties and other causes, the effective strength of the Cavaliers had been reduced to around 250 men, and there were still many useless mouths to be fed. However, with the exception of a few items (notably beer) there was no shortage of food and powder, at any rate in the first two months. But the pressure on the garrison was intense, for when his numbers increased, Norton was able to bring his trenches in some places within a musket shot of the walls, although during the first siege the lines of countervallation – which eventually stretched to 1.5 miles – had never been completed. The garrison also had to withstand the effects of some heavy shelling, especially in the later stages, when the Roundheads employed two mortars. Considerable damage was done to the buildings (on 2 September one of the Great Towers was destroyed) from gun platforms erected on substantial earthworks in the park and on Cowdrey's Down.

To conserve his limited manpower, Colonel Rawdon laid down that two-thirds of the garrison would be on duty while one-third rested, and sectors of responsibility were allotted to the field officers. Major Cusaude had the works facing the park, Colonel Johnson the Grange, Major Langley the garden, and Rawdon himself took the sector facing Basing. The pattern throughout the siege was fairly similar, with the garrison always striving to hit out with small parties at the Roundhead earthworks, and fortifications in the village (which included the church). On these occasions there was considerable skirmishing, for some of the sorties (notably those of 4 and 14 August) were quite large.

As time went on, the garrison's situation became more serious. The Roundhead cannon began to bite, and Paulet was conscious that although starvation was still not an immediate problem, his stores were getting low, he had destroyed the mills where his corn was ground and by now much of the surrounding land had been eaten out. Foraging parties, when they could get through, found little reward for their efforts. He sent urgently to Oxford for relief, and this was promised for 4 September. It did not arrive on that date – indeed it had not started – but the garrison was sufficiently animated by the expectation to launch one of their more successful sallies against Sir Richard Onslow's works in which, with the help of their artillery, they killed at least 64 Roundheads. One casualty was the captain of a troop escorting Waller, who, being in Basingstoke, 'came forth to see the sport'. His chosen vantage point on Cowdrey's Down proved to be too close, and the captain stopped a cannonball.

The relief force was commanded by Colonel Henry Gage who, like most of the garrison, was a Roman Catholic. He was also a very experienced and distinguished soldier. He left Oxford at 10 pm on Monday 9 September. The delay was fortunate, for Waller had had an army of 3,000 in the area until the 7th. The troops that marched from Oxford were 400 musketeers of Colonel Hawkin's White Coats, and 250 horse – described by Clarendon as 'Horse Gentlemen Volunteers' – nominally commanded by Colonel William Webb, but often by Lieutenant Colonel Buncle, for Webb was Gage's second-in-command. On the march they were joined by men under Sir William Campion and Captain Walters. By then, Gage probably commanded about 1,000 soldiers.

For this tough march, carried out at speed through enemy held country, Gage made his troops wear Parliamentarian colours. But at Aldermaston the disguise was blown, and surprise lost, when Walters attacked a Roundhead patrol that unfortunately got away. From here, Gage sent a message to Sir William Ogle at Winchester bidding him bring 300 foot and 100 horse to take Norton's men in rear from the direction of the park at 5 am on Wednesday, while he attacked from the other side. On his arrival at Chinham Down (just north of Basingstoke), Gage learnt that Ogle was unable to get through, and so he sensibly decided not to divide his army, but to concentrate on one thrust against those troops that were awaiting him there.

The dawn sky was hidden by a dense autumn mist, which made the action confused. Despite all his personal efforts to ease their lot, Gage's infantry, which had covered the distance from Oxford in under 36 hours, were excessively weary. Fortunately, they had little part to play, for although Norton's musketeers showed spirit, they were not supported by their cavalry, which soon left the field when the two wings of Gage's horse came through the fog at the charge. This feeble resistance on Chinham Down was matched by the Roundheads at the Grange, who had been attacked at the same time by Colonel Johnson at the head of some musketeers, and driven from their works all the way to Cowdrey's Down.

The besiegers seem to have been quite demoralised by the arrival of the relief force, for no further opposition was offered to Gage, who now brought his men through the imposing gateway that led to the New House, which still preserved its spaciousness and grandeur, despite the recent battering. Here Gage deposited the ammunition he had brought, together with 100 men of Hawkin's White Coats, before marching back to Basingstoke, which he took quite easily. In the next 24 hours he managed to find sufficient provender, and carts to carry it, to keep the garrison supplied for at least another month.

On Thursday the 12th, while his troops continued their foraging, Gage planned his withdrawal. He was surrounded by the enemy, and clearly his best chance was to steal away that night. This he did, and with the help of two guides from the garrison, and a little deception practised on Norton, made a safe journey to Oxford. It had been a most successful, and well executed operation. For the next two days, Norton was strangely inactive, confining his troops to the fort in the park, but on 14 September he carried out a surprise attack on a party of Cavaliers carousing in Basing. In a sharp fight, the garrison suffered many casualties, including Colonel Johnson, who had come to the rescue. He was a man who could ill be spared.

During the next two months, there was much activity in the Basingstoke area with the King making his way back from a recent success at Lostwithiel, Hopton being around Winchester, and the Earl of Manchester and Waller, having Roundhead armies in Berkshire and Hampshire respectively. There was a minor action at Andover, and on 27 October the Second (indecisive) Battle of Newbury was fought. The King gave much thought to raising the siege of Basing House with a strong army, either commanded by himself or Prince Rupert, but there were very many difficulties and nothing come of these good intentions.

Meanwhile, the position at Basing House remained much as before. The bombardment eased somewhat, and the siege became more of a blockade, but this did not prevent foraging forays, notably to the relatively untapped area of Pyott's Hill, where the provender was more plentiful. Periodically, prisoners were exchanged but, despite the fact there were large Parliamentarian forces in the neighbourhood, the besiegers received few reinforcements and were becoming disillusioned in the face of a still remarkably stubborn garrison.

In November, Colonel Gage (now Sir Henry) was again selected to march to the relief of Basing House with 1,000 men. He set off from Hungerford, probably in the second week of November (accounts differ as to the exact date), but Norton and his men – now reduced from 7,000 to about 2,000 – not relishing the rigours of winter in the field, had raised the siege the day before Gage arrived. It had lasted 24 weeks. In that time, the besiegers are said to have lost not less than 1,000 men. In his saddlebag, each of Gage's troopers carried double rations, which were badly needed, for the garrison was in very poor condition, with provisions for no more than three weeks on short commons.

In the interval between the raising of the first siege in November 1644 and the beginning of the second in August 1645, the most important occurrence at Basing House was the departure of Rawdon's Protestant troops from the garrison. Winchester had petitioned the King for the garrison to be wholly Roman Catholic, and his petition had been granted. Such sectarianism would seem to have been narrow-minded, and was certainly harmful to the garrison, but there had been some dissension, and there might have been a security risk.

At the beginning of August, Parliament approved Colonel Dalbier's suggestion to lay siege to Basing House with the Sussex and Surrey troops. Dalbier was of Dutch extraction, and a veteran soldier of considerable fighting experience. He is credited with having taught Oliver Cromwell the rudiments of soldiering. He had recently commanded a regiment at Cheriton, and among his many skills was field engineering. Dalbier arrived before Basing House on 20 August with only 800 horse and foot, for he had received less than half the promised Sussex and Surrey contingents. This meant that there were insufficient men to complete the investment until the coming of Cromwell's troops on 8 October. However, Dalbier had some powerful cannon, firing from the direction of Basing, with which he destroyed the Great Tower of the Old House besides doing much other damage to both houses. The recent wet weather had made digging easier, and the lines of countervallation were now completed.

Elsewhere, things had been moving apace. The battle of Naseby (14 June 1645) was soon followed by other Parliamentarian successes. Fairfax and Cromwell with the New Model Army swept through the South and West. Sherborne Castle fell in August, Bristol on 11 September, and then it was the turn of Berkeley Castle and Devizes. At the end of the month, Fairfax dispatched Cromwell to take Winchester, and in early October that harsh, puritanical, lightning-charged man made for Basing House to winkle out the 'nest of Romanists'.

Cromwell reached Basing House on 8 October, and he estimated that the total force then present was over 6,000 men. He brought with him five large guns of which one was a cannon firing a 63 lb shot, two were demi-cannon (27 pounders), and the calibre of the other two is not known. After a reconnaissance with Dalbier, it was agreed that the latter's batteries should remain in the area of the Grange, and that Cromwell's guns would be positioned to the south-east. Colonel Pickering's troops would be on Dalbier's left and would therefore assault the New House. Farther to the left would be Sir Hardress Waller's (cousin of Sir William) and Colonel Montague's men. The exact position of their troops is uncertain. Cromwell says they attacked in the area of the guardroom, which may have put them to the south, or just west of south, of the Old House.

On the night of 11 October, Cromwell summoned the garrison (which now numbered around 300 men) to surrender. They must have known they were doomed, for the big guns were tearing the entrails out of the houses, and they also knew that as idolators (in their enemy's eyes) they could expect no mercy. But they fought on. By chance, on a dark, misty morning (the 13th) a party – possibly trying to make good their escape – captured two senior officers of Cromwell's, Colonel Hammond and Major King, while they were riding to inspect a cavalry vedette. Winchester refused to exchange these important prisoners, but it may have been that his courtesy towards them helped his own position when the house was taken.

The breaches made were judged to be sufficiently large for the assault to begin at 6 am on Tuesday 14 October. The signal for the storming parties to go forward was to be four cannon shots. Pickering's men seem to have been the first to enter the New House, while the attack on the Old House from the south had first to drive the Cavaliers from their outworks before Waller's and Montague's troops could bring their scaling ladders into the deep moat. But in every quarter the fight was a hard one. Resolute men clustering on the ramparts gave thrust for thrust, and grenade for grenade. Once inside the New House and on into the courtyards, there was desperate resistance to be overcome from those holding the Old House, and on the connecting bridge it was hack and cut, turn and trample as Pickering's and Dalbier's men stormed forward. Meanwhile, Cromwell's batteries spurted orange tongues of flame as heavy shot pounded against the Old House. In the midst of all this bombardment, and hand-to-hand grapple, the defenders accidentally fired a barrel of gunpowder, and soon a roaring fire was spreading.

The storming was brief, but very furious. One account says it was all over in three-quarters of an hour, others give two hours. But by somewhere around 8 am, the small garrison had lost hope and cohesion, and active resistance ceased. Casualty figures vary, but probably around 100 Cavaliers fell in the fighting, and some 200 were made prisoner. Among the latter were the Marquess of Winchester (the Marchioness is said to have escaped before the house was tightly trammelled), Sir Robert Peake and the 72-year-old Inigo Jones. 'Four Popish clergy priests' were also taken, and numerous women, some of whom were wounded. One woman had been killed in the fighting. Cromwell's report to the Speaker dismisses casualties with the sentence, 'We took the two houses without any considerable loss to ourselves.'

In spite of the great damage done by fire and bombardment, there was still an enormous amount of plunder for the soldiers, besides an unexpected quantity of food and wine. The New House was richly furnished, and there was much gold plate, silver and jewels. It is said that what was taken by the victors exceeded £200,000 in value – a colossal figure for those days. In the midst of all this looting, lechery and breaking of wine casks, some drunken satyrs started another fire, which seems to have suffocated or burnt prisoners herded together in the vaults, and virtually destroyed everything save the walls and chimneys. Thus did this aristocrat among houses perish, to be left a ruin. A senseless symbol of the cruelty and turbulence of war.

* * *

Basing House fell at the very end of the First Civil War. Undoubtedly it had some strategic importance, but it had become an obsession with Parliament. In consequence more men were tied down (and lost) in the two years needed to take it than its value warranted. Access to the west depended much more upon the success or failure of the armies fighting in those regions than in the presence of a small garrison however well sited. After its fall, Cromwell recommended that Basing House should be razed to the ground, for it would need a garrison of 800 men and, in his opinion, it would be strategically wiser to advance the southern frontier, and strengthen Newbury from where Donnington Castle could be held in check.

CHAPTER 6
Vienna 1683

JUST as the Siege of Constantinople had effectively marked the birth of the Ottoman Empire, so would the Siege of Vienna, 230 years later, mark the beginning of the end of the threat which that Empire represented to the Christian world. The techniques of siege warfare had been well developed by the Turks. Their formidable Janissaries, the cream of their army and boasting a great fighting tradition, were still very much a force to be reckoned with. Involving as it did, a very mixed collection of European troops, the defence of the city must have produced many problems of command and control. And yet we find that not only was the defence of the city itself well conducted but that much of its ultimate success was due to the ability of the Allies to engage the Turks in pitched battle outside the actual limits of the siege and to administer some resounding defeats. It was inevitable that there would be internecine squabbles and petty huffs, some of which indeed led to elements of the Allied force returning to their homelands, but fortunately none proved disastrous. As in all campaigns and sieges, there were command faults on both sides but, as is usually the case, victory went to the side whose blunders were of the least significance. In terms of courage and resolution, it might be said that honours were shared in what has been described as some of the fiercest fighting in the history of war in Europe.

* * *

Long before the siege of Malta the citizens of Vienna had experienced the heavy hand of the Osmanlis. In 1529, that same Sultan who had expelled the Knights of St John from Rhodes, and who was to be rebuffed by them at Malta, appeared before the gates of Vienna at the head of a vast army. The siege was raised after three weeks, but there had been a warning; and although with the exception of 1663 and 1664 there had been comparative peace between the Empire and the Sublime Porte in the 17th century, there was an ever present threat, with the Turkish frontier well advanced into Hungary.

There were a number of interlocking factors leading up to the crisis year of 1683, which reached back a long way and which recent European treaties had done nothing to resolve. The Bourbon-Habsburg rivalry; the wooing of Poland by the three great powers; the Hungarian revolt; the desire for expansion by the Turkish sultans, and the need to keep the Janissaries continually on the march, formed the crucible from which emerged one of the great sieges of history.

The Habsburg Emperor, Leopold I, had good reason for disliking the French King, Louis XIV. The latter, not content with his gains from the Nymegen treaty was constantly seeking new opportunities at the expense of the Empire; both monarchs had designs on the Spanish empire in the probable event of Carlos II dying childless and Louis, in his moments of greater grandeur, even appeared to covet the Imperial crown. To this end he made agreements with some of the German Electors to support his nomination. Meanwhile, he was prepared to aid the Hungarian rebels, make welcoming overtures to the King of Poland, and encourage the Turks by letting it be known he would lend no assistance to Leopold. No wonder the marplot peregrination of his agents, and the constant threat of his armies, split the court at Vienna into westward and eastward facing factions.

John III Sobieski had been elected King of Poland in 1674. He was possessed of a commanding presence (although by 1683 inclined to corpulence), a high degree of courage, a certain amount of cunning and plenty of panache and patriotism. He was well aware of the Ottoman danger, but his personal position was as difficult as his country's position was important. Leopold needed the Polish army, for his own was insufficient to protect the frontiers of Empire, let alone to fight on two fronts, and Louis found Sobieski a useful pawn in his constant roiling of the European pot. Sobieski needed money and Louis provided it, but the Polish king steered a canny course, never permitting favours accepted from one of the contending parties to cause a breach with the others. In short he appreciated his country's importance to Bourbons, Habsburgs, Hohenzollerns, Osmanlis and Hungarian rebels; he held good cards, and he knew how to play them.

The situation was somewhat similar in Hungary where, since the early days of Suleiman the Magnificent, much of the country had been occupied by the Turks. The Imperial handling of royal Hungary had, for some years past, been insensitive to say the least, and matters came to a head when in 1664 Leopold, having concluded a successful war against the Turks, made (in Hungarian eyes) a bad peace. Soon afterwards a revolt broke out, and when in 1679 Count Imre Thököly, an ambitious, avaricious and slippery Hungarian nobleman, became leader of the Malcontents (as the rebels were called) raids into royal Hungary became serious. Like Sobieski, Thököly was open to advances from the three major powers, and played his hand so skilfully that before long, styling himself 'King of Hungary', he commanded a strong Magyar patriotic force with which he occupied a fair slice of royal territory. But in 1682, when he took the town of Kosice, he overshot himself,

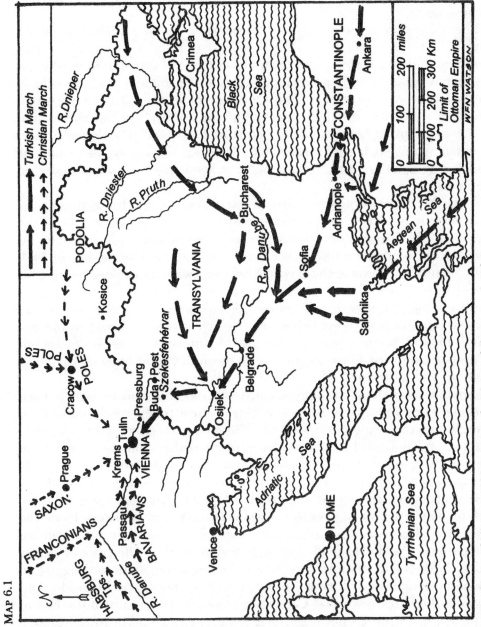

MAP 6.1

The Siege of Vienna 1683: approach routes of the opposing forces

because that greatly alarmed Sobieski who not only withdrew his sympathy from the rebels but also their money supply, for that came from France through his country. To do this he broke with Paris: it was an important turning point.

The Turkish war potential was considerably greater than that of the Empire, for the German states had to be carefully coerced before they would fight for the Habsburgs even in the defence of Christendom, whereas the Sultan could bring an enormous number of soldiers into the field in a comparatively short time. The Ottoman frontiers with the Christian countries stretched for 1,200 miles, and the control and administration of the large provinces was in the hands of *Beylerbeyi*, or with the princes of vassal states, such as Transylvania. War was expensive, but could be paid for by taxation, and Sultans liked to keep their standing armies on the move.

Sultan Mehmet IV was perhaps an exception to this, for although not unintelligent he was a lotus-eater content to leave affairs largely in the hands of his Grand Vezir, while he went his wanton way. Left to his own devices, Mehmet would never have ventured on Vienna, but in 1676 Kara Mustapha, whose ambitions and horizons were boundless, became his Grand Vezir. He was an unpleasant man, whose nature was as black as his name and, although personally brave, his incompetent strategy and tactics were to deprive his troops of victory. He felt certain Sobieski would not march to save Vienna, and he thought his interests would be furthered by cooperation with Thököly. In this he misunderstood Sobieski's political position, and misjudged Thököly's reliability.

Leopold I was deeply religious, courteous, bookish and extremely hard working. Endowed with considerable sagacity he was nevertheless unsure of himself, indecisive and easily swayed. These characteristics led to excessive caution, and not until it was too late did he realise that the threat from the east was more imminent and serious than that from the west. In February 1682, he sent Count Caprara on a peace mission to the Porte, with instructions to extend the treaty of peace due to expire in 1684, and to halt Turkish aggression. Caprara's task was hopeless from the start; he had been authorised to offer extensive bribes, but not territorial concessions. The Turks made outrageous demands for the price of peace, which Caprara had no power to pursue. Pointless negotiations dragged on in Constantinople and, during the march, in Adrianople and Belgrade. And it was in the latter town that Caprara was instructed to inform the Grand Vezir that as all the Emperor's efforts towards peace had been rebuffed, a state of war now existed between the two empires.

Thus, in brief outline, are the events that set the huge Turkish army on its way to Vienna. The number of fighting men summoned from various parts of the Ottoman empire to assembly points along the line of march cannot be accurately assessed, but the army that the Sultan handed over to Kara Mustapha at Osijek probably contained about 180,000 soldiers. They came from places as far apart as Baghdad and the Urals, which caused considerable administrative and supply problems. There were at least 20,000 Janissaries, and although the sharp edge of these élite troops had been slightly blunted in the course of the last hundred years, they were still a very formidable fighting force. Between 15,000 and 20,000 Tartars rode with the army. These wild men were there for the plunder, and the Turks used clouds of them as forward skirmishers. They disliked a sustained campaign, and were ineffective in a set piece battle. The Sultan's professional light and heavy cavalry were excellent, the feudal horsemen were less reliable. The artillery arm no longer enjoyed the superiority over the West that it had had at Constantinople and Malta, and insufficient heavy pieces were brought to Vienna. On the other hand, although the infantry carried a varied assortment of arms, they had many more flintlocks than the Imperialists had, with longer and more accurate range.

The Imperial standing army was no match for this vast array. Until 1680–81, when Leopold decided to increase it by 20,000 men, it had been ludicrously small. Later, as the crisis developed, certain magnates were commissioned to raise regiments. Even so, at Kittsee, where the Emperor reviewed those troops soon to march eastwards, there were no more than 14 regiments of foot, 12 of cavalry and three of dragoons, totalling 35,000 men, with a further 8,000 Hungarians. The Austrians had 72 cannon and the Hungarians 14.

MAP 6.2

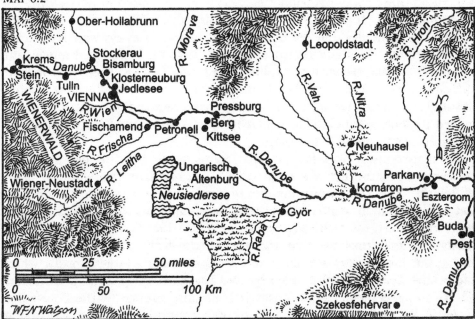

Vienna 1683: the campaign area

Field Marshal Duke Charles V of Lorraine had been given command of the Imperial army. He was a brave and capable soldier, who had seen much fighting. His predecessor in command had also presided over the War Council, but this important post now went to Hermann of Baden. Hermann was to fight well before the walls of Vienna, which earlier he had done much to strengthen, but unfortunately he was on the worst possible terms with Lorraine.

The Austrian infantry regiment had ten companies, and the establishment was for 2,040 men. By 1683 there were almost twice as many musketeers (mostly carrying matchlocks) as pikemen in each company. The heavy cavalry wore the cuirass, and a regiment of five squadrons usually numbered a little under 1,000 horsemen. By 1683, dragoons had replaced arquebusiers. There was a wide range of artillery pieces firing ball, grape and canister, and wagon-borne mortars for siege purposes. Mining and counter-mining were important operations in the siege, and in this the Turks proved more proficient.

The Imperial army alone could never have saved Vienna, and for many months past there had been intense diplomatic activity in Warsaw, Berlin, Dresden, Munich and the Franconian principalities, where Leopold's envoys bargained, bribed and flattered. Some degree of success was eventually achieved, but at a high cost, with Max Emmanuel, Elector of Bavaria, who promised 5,000 infantrymen and 3,000 cavalry from his well trained army; with John George, Elector of Saxony, who agreed to send 7,000 foot, and 3,250 horse and 16 guns; and with Count Waldeck, who ruled three small principalities, and who succeeded in persuading the Franconian and Upper Rhine Circles to dispatch 6,500 infantry and 1,500 horse. The difficulty that confronted the Imperial envoys was that, to the German states, the main threat appeared to come from the French, and some of them had treaties with Louis. The Great Elector, Frederick William of Brandenburg, and the Duke of Hanover resisted the most ardent wooing, although the latter (who had originally promised 10,000 men) eventually agreed to send a battalion in which his son, the future King George I of England, commanded a company.

These promises of some 30,000 troops were helpful, but the most satisfactory – although the most costly – agreement was with the King of Poland. The Poles were anxious to recover previous losses in Podolia, and Sobieski much wanted a successful campaign, in which he might play the leading part, for political purposes. He was therefore prepared to offer substantial assistance once he appreciated the full extent of the Turkish threat, but his country was poor and he demanded a huge subsidy, which might have been difficult to meet but for assistance given by Pope Innocent XI. By an agreement made in March 1683, and ratified by the Polish Diet in April, he undertook to provide 40,000 troops (a figure he was unable to achieve) if Vienna was threatened. These troops were to be mobilised by

July, and he agreed to send 4,000 cavalry to northern Hungary in advance of that date.

Polish-Lithuanian mobilisation was more ponderous than that of the German states for ethnic and territorial reasons. The standing army was very small, and only the cavalry – some of the finest in Europe – was well equipped. The infantry were a motley mélange, and short of discipline, but not of courage. The heavy cavalry and the hussars were superbly mounted. The latter were renowned for their élan, and the demoralising effect of the eerie noise made by the eagles' wings attached to the shoulders of each trooper.

While Leopold's allies were taking time to get their contingents on the march, Kara Mustapha was hastening his huge army across Hungary. There were inevitable delays with so large a host, and the weather in May was very wet. It was 15 June before the army left Osijek. Ten days later, it camped at Székesfehérvár, where the Grand Vezir held a council of war. At this council Kara Mustapha announced that the objective was Vienna. This came as a shock to those present, but of the pashas only Ibrahim, *Beylerbeyi* of Buda (supported by the Tartar Khan), was bold enough to demur. He knew the terrain, and felt sure the army would overreach itself in attempting so distant a target. He was given short shrift for daring to impugn the Grand Vezir's strategy. The army would march, and would march with speed so that the city could be taken before relief arrived. It was too ambitious a project. Ibrahim was right, it would have been better first to capture the border towns and consolidate the position in royal Hungary.

On 1 July, the army was before Györ, where Lorraine had a force of 12,500 infantry and 9,500 cavalry awaiting him. The Imperial Commander-in-Chief had an unenviable task. He was subject to a great deal of interference, and even hostility, from Baden and the War Council, his force was totally inadequate, and he was not conversant with the country he had to fight over. However, it had been his idea to take offensive action in order to divert the enemy from Vienna. His first thoughts had been to take Esztergom before the Turks could reach that place, but his officers raised objections, and only grudgingly gave their assent to besieging the lightly garrisoned Neuhausel (Nové Zamky) a town on the river Nitra north of Komáron. The town was invested in early June, and the outworks were soon taken. But thereafter Lorraine had no success. His orders were not properly carried out, his guns became bedded down in the mud, and he was well aware that his contumacious officers had little liking for the action. On 8 June he raised the siege, and fell back on Komáron.

Here he rested his army for ten days before crossing the Danube and making for Györ. The town's defences were in poor shape, but by hard work, under the expert guidance of the distinguished engineer George Rimpler, who had accompanied the army, some progress was made before the Turks approached. Lorraine supplemented the garrison but decided to meet the enemy on the left bank of the Raba. It was a trappy position flanked by a marsh, and backed by another river.

Early on the morning of 2 July, the Imperial batteries opened up on the Turkish lines to hold the enemy from the right bank of the river. But Kara Mustapha sent a strong detachment of cavalry upstream to cross the river and outflank Lorraine's right, which was seriously weakened by the defection of Count Batthyany's Hungarians, who thought Thököly's prospects were better. Tartars were already over the river and heading for Lake Neusiedl, burning everything they found. Lorraine decided to withdraw, and sent Generals Starhemberg and Leslie, with most of the infantry and guns, across the Danube to the Schutt while he took the cavalry up river to Ungarisch-Altenburg, and then along the river Leitha. Lorraine's rearguard was constantly harassed, but the withdrawal was carried out efficiently and quickly. He still expected the Grand Vezir to besiege Györ, and had hopes of regaining control of the Lake Neusiedl area (the lands of the loyal Count Esterházy). But Turkish intentions soon became clear when the bulk of the army crossed the Raba, and followed Lorraine up the Danube.

The easily traversed plain ends in the Berg-Petronell area, and the ground becomes more defensible for a numerically inferior army. Lorraine planned to concentrate his troops in the area between the rivers Leitha and Danube, and there to block the way to Vienna. But the Turks moved too quickly. Kara Mustapha showed greater powers of generalship on the line of march than ever he was to do before Vienna. He was hard on Lorraine's heels up the Danube, and sent a swift outflanking force sweeping wide to his left and heading for Fischamend. Lorraine's position had become untenable before he had even concentrated his army. Messengers were sent to the War Council saying there was no alternative but to withdraw on Vienna. Leslie and Starhemberg were to march quickly to the capital by way of Pressburg, and Starhemberg soon received orders to hurry ahead to take command in Vienna.

The withdrawal now became rather more ragged and spread out. The wagon-train for some reason was in advance even of the vanguard, which proved too good an opportunity for the Tartars who fell upon it, while at the same time the rearguard under Count Taaffe (Lorraine's friend and counsellor who later became Earl of Carlingford) became heavily engaged near Petronell. This was the first serious fight of the campaign. The rearguard cavalry, which included Prince Louis of Savoy's dragoons, were routed, and Prince Louis mortally injured when his horse fell on him*. Lorraine led a strong force of cavalry to Taaffe's aid, and after a fierce fight,

---

*A casualty that had far reaching consequences, because but for his elder brother's death, Prince Eugene of Savoy might never have left the French service.

in which the Austrians lost more than a hundred men, the rearguard was successfully extricated.

The cavalry, having safely emerged from this potentially dangerous situation, were taken to Leopoldstadt and the Danube islands before crossing the river on 14 July to take position on the north bank at Jedlesee. The infantry, marching fast from Pressburg, crossed the river on the night of the 13th, and entered the city by the Rothenthurm Gate. They were only just in time. Earlier, the precaution had been taken of removing the Hungarian Crown of St Stephen from Pressburg (threatened by Thököly), and the escort of 200 horse sent for this purpose were now ordered to accompany the Emperor, the royal family and the Imperial regalia, on the road to Passau during the night of 7 July. Large numbers of citizens followed the royal example in leaving the city, and many perished at the hands of the Tartars.

Meanwhile, Kara Mustapha had by-passed Györ, leaving a containing force. When the Sultan received information that the army was marching on Vienna, he is said to have been very angry, for the Grand Vezir had exceeded his orders. But there was no stopping Kara Mustapha now. Indeed, as he looked down upon the city on Tuesday 13 July, he could congratulate himself on the rapidity and success of a well executed march. The opposition had, of course, been negligible for which Lorraine has sometimes been blamed, but this is unfair, for his task was impossible. Now he had joined Starhemberg in consultation on the proper defence of the city.

Vienna was partly protected to the north by the Danube and its tributary known as the Canal (which could be waded at the time of the siege), and in the east by the river Wien, but its principal defence was its walls with their twelve bastions, and a number of ravelins. Over the years these had been allowed to deteriorate, and were partly obsolete. Moreover, the suburbs had encroached in places up to the walls, and the moat had gardens in it. Some work had been done in the past 18 months, but not nearly enough, and although Rimpler and other senior engineers had surveyed the defences and made a number of recommendations, work had been so slow that only a few of these had been implemented.

Starhemberg had less than a week in which to galvanise a labour force into doing the minimum essential requirements. He was a well tried and valiant soldier whose appearance was dignified and manner unruffled. He had complete confidence in his own judgement, and a capacity to inspire trust in others, qualities so vital in the difficult weeks ahead. By cajolery, and occasional threatening, much was accomplished. The moat was cleared and deepened, the bastions, ravelins and curtain-wall were buttressed, the counterscarp strengthened and the covered way made useable. All this was important, but even more so was the widening of the glacis. Householders were ordered to remove themselves and their baggage into the city, and set fire to their dwellings. Soon the city was ringed with flames (except to the north where Leopoldstadt on the Prater island was not destroyed), and a disaster was narrowly avoided when sparks went dangerously near the city's nerve centre, the well-stocked Arsenal.

The city's defence force was something of a gallimaufry. The eight companies (totalling under 2,000 men) of the Burgher Militia were not trained, and their arms were obsolete, but the City Guard was more professional, and the municipal artillery had some howitzers among its fifty pieces. At the time of the siege, a number of volunteer companies, organised by professions and including a useful contingent of gamekeepers, were recruited. These meagre defence forces were totally inadequate, but the situation was completely changed with the arrival of Lorraine's infantry and a regiment of heavy cavalry. By 14 July Starhemberg had 72 companies of infantry with a nominal strength of 11,000, the cuirassiers, nearly 5,000 civilian fighters and 317 cannon. The Arsenal held a good supply of weapons and ammunition, and stocks of food were ample, but money was a different proposition. Starhemberg insisted on payment for the troops and labour force throughout the siege, and city funds were insufficient. But thanks to the generosity of certain noblemen, confiscation of assets left behind by those who had fled, and the melting of some treasures, sufficient florins became available.

Kara Mustapha decided (largely on information received from a renegade friar) to launch his main attack at the southern end of the city between the Burg (Palace) and Löbel bastions, where work on the defences was still being carried out. Here the land sloped gently to the glacis, which had not been completely cleared allowing the troops a partly covered approach to the moat. The rising ground was suitable for his guns and, more importantly, the watertable in that area was low enough to permit digging and mining. The number of men positioned here for the main assault is not known, but it is difficult to believe there were more than 20,000, for with men left in the Györ and Pressburg areas, the number of fighting soldiers before Vienna was probably a little less than 100,000, and there was a formidable area to cover. Before the Prater was occupied the troops stretched in a large semicircle from the Canal just south of the island, passing between Simmering and the river Wien, crossing the Wien north of Gumpendorf and present-day Schönbrunn, through Hernals and Währing and on to Dobling, a village north-west of the suburb of Rossau.

Overnight a circle of tents sprang up as though a new suburb surrounded the city. The hub of this juggernaut wheel was the Grand Vezir's luxurious tent of golden brocade encrusted with gems, and its garniture of gardens and fountains, for he was campaigning in style with his seraglio, eunuchs and slaves. The tent was pitched approximately between the villages of Penzing and St Ulrich, and here was the treasury and court of justice; here also was George Kunitz, Leopold's envoy, who had been compulsorily

MAP 6.3

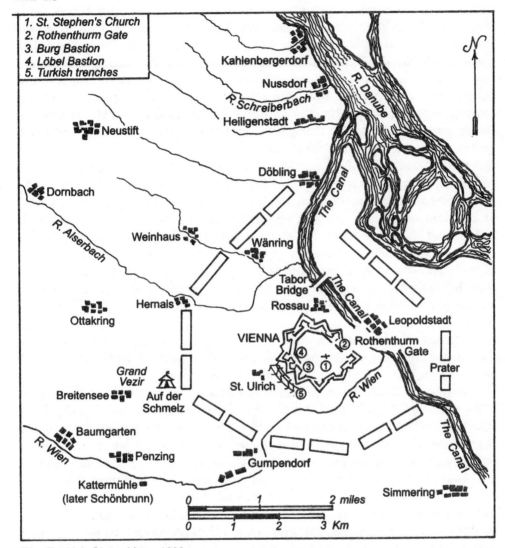

1. St. Stephen's Church
2. Rothenthurm Gate
3. Burg Bastion
4. Löbel Bastion
5. Turkish trenches

The Turkish Siege Lines 1683

detained. In the afternoon of 14 July, Kara Mustapha rode into St Ulrich to arrange the assault dispositions with the Aga of the Janissaries and the *Beylerbeyis*. He would take personal command of the centre sector with the Janissaries, and troops of the *Beylerbeyi* of Rumelia. His advanced headquarters were to be in a house on the road that led from St Ulrich to the Burg gate, and the troops of the other pashas were allotted sectors to his right and left.

An offer to surrender on the usual Turkish terms was made to Starhemberg, who predictably rejected it, and that night (the 14th)

entrenching began. There were, of course, many men available, but even
so the work was carried out with commendable speed. Digging began some
300 yards from the palisades, the trenches were deep enough to give a
standing man protection, and they stretched between the Burg and Löbel
bastions (about 400 yards), with dugouts for command posts, and battery
positions. By the evening of the 15th only a farther 70 yards remained to
be dug. But this feat had not been achieved without casualties for, despite
a strong supporting bombardment, many Turks, unable to keep their heads
down, had succumbed to the gamekeepers' fine marksmanship, and the
garrison gunners had also taken toll.

As the Turkish parallels, and the elaborately constructed zigzag trenches
edged ever nearer, Starhemberg ordered sorties to interrupt the work. The
trenches were deep and trappy, and although results were fairly satisfactory
in the first attack, in the second the casualties were disproportionately
heavy, and it was decided that sorties should cease for a while. Once the
trenches had reached almost to the palisades the fighting became some
of the fiercest and most sustained of any siege in history. For almost two
months, with hardly a pause, the two sides were locked in hand-to-hand
combat. From 23 July, when the Turks exploded their first mines, the boom
of cannon, the roar of explosions and the sharp crack of musket fire was
never absent by day, nor for much of the night. It is impossible to portray
the savage intensity of the passions which this bitter struggle aroused. It
became a fight to the death in a symmetry of blood.

Fortunately, apart from a severe bombardment of the northern walls
from guns in Leopoldstadt (which the Turks occupied on 16 July) little
offensive action was attempted other then the main assault. And so
Starhemberg could concentrate a large proportion of his men to fight
on the parapets, along the covered ways, in the moat and on the ravelins
and bastions of the threatened sector. To break the defences the Turks
relied largely on mines, for they lacked heavy cannon and mortars.
The defence found hand grenades did considerable execution, and their
artillery was well handled. In particular, although having to give ground
inch by inch with great stubbornness as the Turks descended into the
moat and surrounded the ravelins, the Austrians never lost the offensive
spirit. Counterattacks were mounted, retrenchment carried out with speed
and efficiency, covered ways were sealed off against enfilade fire, and
chevaux-de-frise blocked the breaches. This and Starhemberg's splendid
leadership sustained them through days of butchery in a ditch strewn
with the stinking bodies of many men.

The succession of events in the evolving destiny of Vienna at this time
stand out clearly. The first major Turkish achievement came with the
successful explosion of two mines on 29 July. These caused considerable
casualties, and destroyed a section of the palisade and parapet leaving
a large hole that opened up the moat. This was the time for a major

assault, but Kara Mustapha – who throughout fought the battle from a forward command post – for some reason failed to order it, and a great opportunity was missed. Perhaps it was because at this stage he was still confident of an eventual surrender from which he, and not his troops, would be the principal beneficiary. The besieged, despite being exposed to very heavy small arms fire, made good the damage within two hours, and not until 3 August did Turkish soldiers first descend into the moat.

In the course of the following three days the fighting was particularly fierce. Starhemberg personally led a counterattack which failed with the loss of Rimpler and two other senior officers. By 6 August the Turks had a firm lodgement in the moat, and had entrenched themselves beneath the ravelin. Throughout the next week mines were constantly exploded, but despite much damage and heavy casualties the ravelin held. And then on the 12th an even greater explosion occurred which threw up sufficient earth to form a causeway from the moat to the ravelin over which fifty men abreast could storm. A furious struggle, in which the losses to both sides were cruel, left the ravelin partly in Turkish hands. Now the scene shifts to the bastions, and on 16 August the Austrians at last had a notable success. After days of mining and countermining two sorties were launched against the Turkish galleries, which did such damage that the sector in front of the Löbel bastion was quiet for the next ten days.

The siege had now lasted a month. The Austrians had suffered some 1,500 casualties, and the Turks many more. Both sides were feeling the effects. The Turkish troops, particularly the Janissaries, were grumbling at the amount of time taken to achieve little, and the situation in Vienna was beginning to get very serious. The worst problem for both armies was disease. Turkish hygiene was non-existent, and their entrenchments were a foul mess spreading every kind of complaint. In Vienna, great efforts were made towards cleanliness, but disease was rife, particularly dysentery from which Starhemberg suffered. Inevitably, there were too few hospital beds and medical supplies. There was no serious threat of starvation, but fresh meat was dwindling. Horses were eaten, and the citizens organised cat hunts over the rooftops. Foraging was forbidden, and offences against security were punished by execution. It had been a month of great danger, stress and ceaseless toil, but cool heads without cold feet kept despair, and disaster, at bay.

News from outside was slender. Kunitz contrived to send reports on the bad state of the Turkish lines, which boosted Austrian morale, but his messenger was eventually caught. However, some communication was maintained with Passau, and occasionally with Lorraine, through brave men getting through the lines in disguise.

Inevitably, the continuing struggles and torments of the second month were harder to bear than the first. Kara Mustapha, realising at last that 'A Captain, in the time of war, hath not the ordering of his hours', urged his men to greater efforts. Senior commanders were replaced, reinforcements were hurried into the lines, and mining was stepped up. Once the last defenders had been thrown off the Burg ravelin, guns could be mounted to fire at close range into the fortress, while the engineers continued their remorseless task underneath the bastion. By the end of August, the Austrian soldiers were totally exhausted with continual fighting, and through having insufficient men to man the walls; the Turkish troops were also weary, disillusioned and, in some cases, mutinous. But both armies fought on, dulled into a delirium of death and killing, not only in the breaches but in the prison cages, where both sides committed appalling atrocities.

Despite undoubted weariness, the fighting reached the height of its ferocity in the first week of September. The 4th was nearly a disastrous day for the Austrians when a well-placed mine blew a huge hole in the Burg bastion, and several thousand Turks surged forward and upward. As so often, Starhemberg was at the place of peril, personally conducting the valiant efforts of his men to throw out the Turks, which they did with enormous slaughter. Then, bringing up a mobile *cheval-de-frise*, they blocked the gap. They had suffered more than 200 casualties, but it was only a temporary respite. Two days later, as more mines caused havoc to the bastion and to the antiquated fortification in its immediate rear, the Janissaries again stormed forward to be met by a solid phalanx of Austrians, and a withering enfilade fire from the Löbel bastion. So packed were the ranks that men died on their feet. But once again, the Turks were hurled back.

For some days past, rockets had been fired from the top of St Stephen's Cathedral to add urgency to messages previously sent for help. Until 6 September, these distress signals had not been answered and merely gave encouragement to the Turks. But on that night, answering rockets went up from the high ground of the Wienerwald. The relieving armies were almost at hand. Kara Mustapha also saw the rockets, and as he had dug no lines of circumvallation, he had to pull out troops and make hasty arrangements to meet this threat to his rear. But the besieged, although exhilarated, were not left unmolested. The mining continued with even greater intensity under both bastions, and there were still Janissaries and others to storm the breaches. Starhemberg was making preparations for barricading the streets in anticipation of a Turkish breakthrough. It is probably true to say that had the relief been delayed only a day or two, the Turks would have been into Vienna.

While the fate of Vienna still hung in the balance, what was happening in the surrounding countryside? Here Charles of Lorraine, and his army of (mostly) cavalry and field artillery were very active. Lorraine had important and difficult tasks to perform, which included trying to discover what was happening in Vienna, keeping in touch with the Imperial court at Passau,

Map 6.4

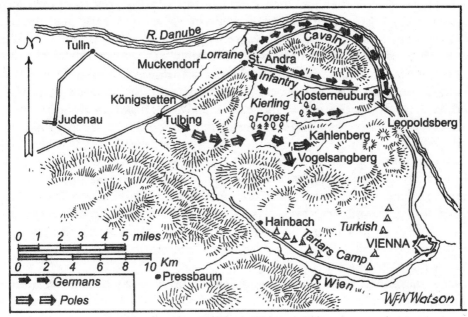

The Christian advance across the Northern Wienerwald

sending hasteners to the relieving armies – particularly to Sobieski through the commander of his advance cavalry, Prince Lubomirski – keeping a watchful eye on Thököly and his Turkish allies along the lines of communication to Györ, and clearing the countryside of large roving bands of Tartars. In this latter duty he was only partially successful, for there were too many Tartars indulging in arson, rape and plunder over a large tract of country ranging from Klosterneuburg to Lake Neusiedl. But the dragoons of his lieutenant, Count Dunewald, operating from Krems, had one very successful encounter against a band of eight hundred.

Towards the end of July, a report reached Lorraine's headquarters at Jedlesee that Thököly, and a force of probably around 25,000 Turks and Magyars under Kör Huseyin Pasha, *Beylerbeyi* of Eger, were marching on Pressburg, where it was intended to bridge the river, march westwards and – among other things – threaten Sobieski's march in the Sisamberg-Tulin area. Lorraine acted with speed, sending an advance party of 500 to reinforce the garrison, and following himself with 1,000 horse. Unfortunately, the advance party got cut up, and Thököly's followers were permitted to enter Pressburg. Lorraine was undecided. Dare he risk his small, and very important, army against so large a force? Greatly encouraged by the young and adventurous Margrave of Baden, whose troops had been with the Imperial army for some time, and by Prince Lubomirski, he offered battle. In the event there was not much of a fight, for the bulk of his enemy were Magyars, and they had little stomach for the affair, but the Turks gave Lubomirski's Poles plenty to do before being driven from the field, leaving 600 dead and a large number of wagons containing useful booty. Lorraine, having admonished the burghers of Pressburg, retired across the Morava.

As Commander-in-Chief, Lorraine had an important voice in the War Council's deliberations on the best line of approach for the relieving armies, and he strongly advocated the more direct, although steeply wooded, route over the top rather than round the southern edge of the Wienerwald. He had recently obtained information from Starhemberg which made him uneasy about the situation in Vienna, and he was therefore anxious to move his army to Tulln to safeguard the bridges on the Tulln-Krems stretch of water. He also wished to begin the march before the full relief force had assembled. Leopold and his advisers eventually agreed to his suggested route, but were adamant that Lorraine should remain north of the river until the arrival of Sobieski. By 19 August, the latter was four days out of Cracow, and so well on the way.

As it happened, any premature advance on Vienna became academic when Lorraine learnt that his Pressburg opponent, Kör Huseyin Pasha, having obtained several thousand Tartar reinforcements from Kara Mustapha, was marching to join the Turkish camp. By 24 August, he was across the Morava. Lorraine was at Stockerau on his way to Tulln, but sending General Leslie forward to guard the bridges, he and Lubomirski, with about 15,000 horse, turned back to meet the Pasha at Bisamberg. The ensuing battle was to end disastrously for the Turks. Almost half of their 12,000 men were Tartars, who were no match in organised battle for the Imperial and Polish squadrons. Again, the Turks fought valiantly and with initial success, but with their right in disarray they lost heart and broke. Their retreat became a shambles. Over a thousand men, including Kör Huseyin, were slaughtered or drowned, and many standards were captured.

This decisive victory, and Thököly's disappearance from the scene (he was meant to have joined the Turks before Bisamberg), made it possible for most of Lorraine's troops to take part in the relief of Vienna. This began to take definite shape with the meeting of Lorraine, Count Waldeck and the King of Poland at Ober-Hollabrunn on 31 August. Sobieski had finally mustered only about 18,000 of his promised 40,000 men, but these included 13,000 of his splendid cavalry. This meant there were rather over 60,000 soldiers, and large wagon-trains, assembled on the Danube at the beginning of September. There had been a lot of rain which made crossing to the south bank very difficult, because the water had risen and the ground was boggy. Bridges at Stein and Tulln were used, and some sort of movement order was worked out by the Bridge Captain. The passage at Stein was accomplished without too much difficulty, but the Poles experienced considerable trouble at Tulln, and their wagon-train was delayed. This was serious because the

Tartars had scorched the surrounding land. However, concentration on the south bank was completed by 8 September.

There had been considerable concern as to who would command the allied army. The obvious choice was Sobieski, and he himself was most anxious for this prestigious post, but if the Emperor took the field he, as the most illustrious Christian sovereign, should properly head the crusade against the infidel. Pressure was brought upon Leopold to sacrifice his dignity in the interests of success. Sobieski, even before he had been confirmed in command, had set out the Order of Battle which, with only one alteration, was agreed. On the left was Lorraine with the Imperial cavalry and infantry, with John George's Saxons on their immediate right; the Bavarians and Franconians were to march in the centre, and the right wing was found by the Polish army. The artillery was to be distributed between the various contingents, and the infantry (with the guns) would precede the cavalry across the Wienerwald, giving place to the horse when the open ground was reached. Individual Imperial and German forces would be commanded by their rulers under the general direction of Lorraine, while the King of Poland exercised supreme command.

Meanwhile, Kara Mustapha was hastening to make belated amends. In the course of operations before Vienna, he had committed three grave errors. He had hopelessly underestimated the time it would take him to reduce the city; he had persisted in believing that Sobieski would not march; and he had taken virtually no precautions to safeguard his rear. There had been no line of circumvallation, his observation posts were weak and he had left it to the Tartar Khan to prevent any new bridging at Tulln, which the latter had signally failed to do. Too late, he learnt that Sobieski's Poles were upon him, and not until the beginning of September did he send to Györ for Ibrahim and some 13,000 men.

On 8 September, at a council of war with all the Pashas, Ibrahim advocated raising the siege (he had never favoured it), taking up a defensive position with the whole army and, once the Christian attack had been blunted, using the cavalry to envelope their army. Some of the pashas agreed, but the Grand Vezir would have none of it, and refused to let go his grip on the city which he estimated (rightly) was at its last gasp. He withdrew the troops from Leopoldstadt, and with 22,000 horse, 6,000 infantry and 60 guns* he took up a position in the defiles beneath the Kahlenberg height, in the area Nussdorf, Heiligenstadt, Grinzing, Währing. Ibrahim had overall command of the right wing, with Kara Mehmet Pasha in the van beneath the Kahlenberg. On receiving more detailed information of the Imperial line of march, Kara Mustapha strengthened the right wing with some Janissaries under their Aga. There was little time to make a strong defensive position, and with only 28,000 men in the line, plus a

*Stoye p257.

few thousand rather unreliable Tartars and Wallachians the Turks were hopelessly outnumbered. Moreover, weariness, shortage of food and the Bisamberg disaster had greatly damaged their morale.

On the same day as Kara Mustapha was holding his conference, Lorraine had sent out an advance party of 600 dragoons, and it was decided to begin the march across the Wienerwald in the early hours of 9 September. The line St Andra-Konigstetten was reached that night, and the objective for the 10th was the Weidling valley. At St Andra, Lorraine split his force, the cavalry going round the northern slopes, while the infantry took the steeper route. It rained hard, sheets of water created rivers of mud, and the high ground was shrouded under a thick haze. The Poles, who had lost time awaiting their wagon-train, found the going particularly heavy on the right, and everywhere some gun carriages had to be abandoned. Not all the troops made the valley that night, indeed the Poles were no farther than Kierling Forest, but contact was maintained.

By about midday on the 11th, the great ridge had been climbed by all the troops save the Poles, and they were not far behind. From the Leopoldsberg-Kahlenberg-Vogelsangberg line, the soldiers got a pano-

MAP 6.5

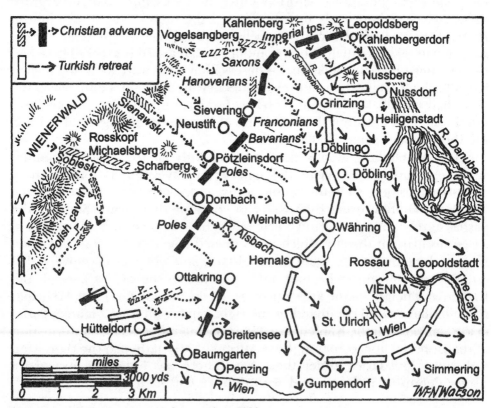

The Battle of Kahlenberg 12 September 1683

ramic view of the city, and for some who imagined it would now be an easy decline there was considerable chagrin at the sight of more hills and ravines before the plain. But to go round to the south was ruled impracticable, and the attack was to be launched from the ridge on the 12th. One small alteration in the order of battle was made when Sobieski asked Lorraine to send some Habsburg infantry to support his cavalry.

The Battle of Kahlenberg began at 5 am on the 12th, when Kara Mehmet's advanced troops made an attack from the direction of Nussdorf on a battery position General Leslie was constructing on the forward edge of the ridge in front of Leopoldsberg. The rain and mist had gone, and the day was to be blisteringly hot with the sun beating down on troops clambering over rough and rugged ground. Indeed this thick country was to mean that much of the action was fought by isolated groups under junior leadership, although the two principal commanders retained a fair grip throughout. Visibility was splendid for those watching anxiously from St Stephen's tower.

It was not long before Lorraine committed the whole of his left in a drive towards the Nussberg feature, and the village of Nussdorf which lay to its south-east. Once the hill had been taken, Leslie could mount his cannon and pulverise the village, but the left had got too far ahead of the Bavarians and Franconians advancing down the centre. The result was a dangerous gap which was filled just in time by a battalion of Hanoverians acting on their own initiative. Sobieski had now joined Lorraine, and measures were taken to stabilise the line and make certain that the Duke of Sachsen-Lauenburg's Bavarians could link with the Polish left under General Sienawski, when the latter debouched from the defile below Neustift.

The left was to bear the brunt of the morning's fighting, and so far Lorraine could be well pleased. But Kara Mustapha was alarmed by the loss of the Nussberg and launched a strong counterattack. At first, the Turks were held and driven back to the river Schreiberbach, but the charge of their second wave shook the Saxon-Habsburg line, and the situation was only restored when the dragoons and heavy cavalry were sent in. The Elector of Saxony was unhorsed and nearly killed in this engagement. The fighting for Nussdorf was particularly fierce, and the village was not taken until Colonel Heisler's dragoons, riding up from Kahlenbergerdorf, gave added momentum to Hermann's Habsburg infantry. The advance then continued to Heiligenstadt, and when that was taken – soon after 11 am – Lorraine held a line from there through Grinzing to Sievering.

In the midday heat there was a short involuntary pause by both sides on Lorraine's front. But the Poles, with their centre axis down the Alsbach river towards Dornbach, had ground to make up, and although honours were to be shared by every unit that fought on this glorious day, a lot depended on the Poles, for the battle could scarce be won without them. They had had a very difficult march, and much of their heavy cannon had to be abandoned, but Martin Katski, their General of Artillery, had 28 light guns firing case shot. Sobieski had spent much of the morning hastening the march and by 2 pm, although still only between Michaelsberg and Schafberg, the Poles came in sight of the allied left whose troops raised a mighty cheer. As they came down the Alsbach valley the Bavarians were fighting hard on their left, and they themselves were engaged, but after the Schafberg was reached, at about 4 pm, the ground became more open and the columns could deploy.

In the afternoon, Kara Mustapha had grown anxious for his line of withdrawal across the river Wien. To safeguard this, he brought Ibrahim's troops to his left flank. The Poles were therefore faced by a mass of infantry and horse in depth. The time was about 5 pm, and a decision had to be taken as to whether to stake all and go forward, or to consolidate after many hours of bitter fighting and await the morrow. The commanders decided to go forward to Vienna. Some of the hardest fighting of the day now took place, with the outcome often in the balance. More than once the Polish cavalry broke through, only to be flung back by the Turkish horse. It was hack and thrust, charge and countercharge. Sobieski called for assistance, and Generals Schultz and Sachsen-Lauenburg sent German troops. Gradually the Christian avalanche gained momentum, and victory became assured.

Lorraine changed direction from the shortest route to Vienna, and swung his men in a left wheel to hit the Turkish right, while the showmanship of Sobieski was to bring the battle to a spectacular close. The action took place on the plain in the Weinhaus-Ottakring-Baumgarten area, and the King rode in the forefront of his army dressed in oriental splendour, with his young son at his side. His magnificent hussars with their leopard skins, and outspread eagles' wings making their weird and hideous whirring, rode at the Turks knee to knee, their sabres flashed and fell and so did men and horses in the fearful mêlée. The Turkish right and centre was already bending, and now the reinforced left become badly shaken under this impressive display of flailing steel, but it did not immediately break. It was left to Count Jablonowski to administer the *coup de grâce*. In the advance he had commanded the Polish right with a cavalry flank guard to brush Tartars out of the way. Now he delivered a powerful punch that put the whole Turkish army into rapid retreat across the river, and on their way to Hungary. Almost the last to go was the Grand Vezir, and his bodyguard with the great banner of the Prophet. Kara Mustapha may have conducted the battle unwisely, but he did not lack courage.

As is often the case, with the victory gained, the allies began to fall apart. Predictably, and principally for home consumption, Sobieski arrogated to himself and his Poles the greater share of the triumph. This did not please Lorraine, or the German rulers, whose troops had fought just as bravely and skilfully, and it was partly the reason for John George taking his

Saxons home three days after the battle in something of a huff. Count Waldeck was not prepared to join any pursuit with his Franconians, and the Duke of Sachsen-Lauenburg, whose troops had plainly had enough, also withdrew. This unfortunate disharmony, together with the looting – mainly by the Poles who reached the Grand Vezir's marvellous tent and treasure first – and, sadly, the ghastly atrocities perpetrated by the victors on their prisoners, delayed what must have been a successful pursuit of a broken army.

Meanwhile, Kara Mustapha and the remnants of his army reached the outskirts of Györ on the 14th September. Here he attempted to revitalise his dispirited and disorganised troops. He also sought scapegoats for the recent disaster. In his deep-seated bitterness he killed greedily. Ibrahim and the Tartar Khan were obvious candidates for the cord, and several other pashas joined them. Thököly had wisely ignored the summons to the camp. His blood-lust satiated, the Grand Vezir retired to Buda, leaving others to handle the army in the event of more fighting.

Leopold re-entered his capital on the 14th, and the next day met Sobieski outside the city* for formal and slightly frigid pleasantries. There followed consultations among the commanders before a decision was taken to march into Hungary and take Esztergom. On the 17th the army left Vienna. The Poles, with their flamboyant king, were in the van; Lorraine who appears to have received no outward recognition for his leadership at Kahlenberg, and Starhemberg, who had been made a field marshal for his valiant defence of Vienna, headed the Imperial troops; the ebullient Margrave of Baden was present, and the Elector Max Emmanuel joined in time for the battle, even some Brandenburgers making their first appearance.

Difficulties in crossing the Danube delayed the march, and it was the beginning of October before the Turks were engaged at Parkany. There were two battles fought there before Esztergom was captured. In the first, the Poles attacked prematurely, and were only rescued from disaster by Imperial and German troops. But in the second battle, the Turks suffered a crushing defeat, their heavy losses being compounded when a bridge across the river was destroyed by gunfire while crowded with troops. It is estimated that some 9,000 men died in the fighting or in the river, bringing the total Turkish losses in the campaign to around 60,000, of which 10,000 soldiers fell in the Kahlenberg battle. Allied losses in that battle were only about 1,800, but more than 5,000 lives were lost in Vienna.

The defeat at Parkany sealed the Grand Vezir's fate. The Sultan had been prepared to forgive his failure before Vienna (after all he was in distinguished company), but pressure was now too strong, and reluctantly Mehmet gave way. On the day the victorious Christians celebrated the birth

---

*The Polish king had entered the city in state before the 14th!

of their Founder, Kara Mustapha met his Destiny at the hands of the official strangler.

It would be fair to say that after 1683 Ottoman power ceased to be a danger to the Christian world. When the War of the Holy League, a natural successor to the events of 1683, ended in 1698, almost all Hungary had been recovered, and the great Habsburg empire was rising on firm foundations.

CHAPTER 7

Londonderry 1689

THERE have been many important, and often bloody, landmarks in Ireland's turbulent history, and the Siege of Londonderry is amongst the foremost. The bitterness created between Catholic and Protestant, Irishmen and Ulstermen, which persists to this day, may have had its origin in James I's Protestant Plantation but it was exacerbated by later events, not the least of which in importance was the Siege of Londonderry, which dragged on for 105 days and saved Scotland from an earlier, and possibly successful, Jacobite invasion.

Most people are familiar with pictures of the Apprentice Boys' Marches, held annually through modern Derry and probably know that they commemorate the siege – but how many know the story of that siege, which the determined action by the Apprentice Boys sparked off?

* * *

Two eminent historians (Sir Charles Petrie and Hilaire Belloc) have written that there never was a siege of Londonderry, or even a blockade. They base these conclusions principally on the strengths and armaments of the rival forces. It is true that, at the beginning of the siege, numbers were mainly equal, and the besieged had superiority in fire power, whereas Napoleon laid it down that for success the besiegers should have four times the strength of the besieged. Therefore, in theory, the Protestant garrison should have engaged the Jacobite Irish in open fight, and never allowed themselves to be closely confined for 105 days. But this simple solution is not in accordance with the facts, and the reader can judge for himself when the story has unfolded, whether those two distinguished men were right.

The present outrages perpetrated by the Irish Republican Army are largely the work of terrorist thugs determined to cause the maximum mayhem at minimum risk. They are not in the main motivated by religious or patriotic considerations, although there is undoubtedly a deep divide between the Protestant and Catholic communities. A study of Irish history from the time of Elizabeth I does much to explain the bitterness that still exists between the two faiths, born of the appalling atrocities committed first by one sect and then by the other in the 16th and 17th centuries and, to a much less degree, thereafter. Such a study also shows the very real part that patriotism has played in the continuing troubles. The Irish Jacobites of 1688–89 cared nothing for the Stuarts, but regarded James II as a useful stepping stone to the suppression of the Protestant Plantation imposed upon them since the beginning of the century, and to liberation from the conqueror's yoke. Conversely, in the struggle between James and his son-in-law, William of Orange, nearly all the Protestants saw the triumph of William as their only means of salvation.

James II succeeded his brother in February 1685. He was a declared Roman Catholic and so his accession was greeted with cautious optimism by the predominantly Catholic population of Ireland, and with some anxiety by the Protestants. However, the former's optimism was somewhat dampened when James did not at once repeal the Acts of Settlement which, in 1652, had legalised gifts of land to all who had supported the Parliamentary cause, and resulted in two-thirds of the land being in Protestant possession. The King had need to proceed with care over this, for the colonists were successfully established, and had many supporters in England. But his removal of the Lord-Lieutenant, the Duke of Ormonde, was unwise, for although not a great proconsul, he had striven to keep a fair balance between Protestant and Roman Catholic, and he was intensely loyal to the Crown.

In Ormonde's place, James sent his brother-in-law, the Earl of Clarendon, to be viceroy. This might have been all right had he not at the same time disregarded the Test Acts (which forbade anyone from holding the King's commission or posts of authority who did not first declare his disbelief in the Roman Catholic dogma), by giving important positions to his Catholic friends. Among those so favoured was Richard Talbot, whom he made Earl of Tyrconnel, and gave him command of the army in Ireland.

Tyrconnel was descended from those Talbots to whom Henry II gave the lordship of Malahide. He was an ardent Catholic and, in the fulfilment of his overriding ambition to promote the welfare of his co-religionists, he was vindictive and devoid of scruple. He arrived in Ireland in June 1686, and very quickly took the measure of Clarendon for whom he had scant respect, frequently going over the Lord-Lieutenant's head in matters of policy, particularly those affecting Catholic appointments to senior military and civil posts. It was not long before he persuaded James to recall Clarendon and appoint him (Tyrconnel) as viceroy, although James downgraded the title to Lord-Deputy.

Such demotion was meaningless, for Tyrconnel now had virtually unfettered control of Irish affairs, and he at once stepped up his work of increasing the army's strength, and replacing Protestant officers with Roman Catholics, many of whom had little or no military knowledge. He then turned his attention to civilian affairs introducing Catholics into positions of importance inside and outside Parliament. Catholic administrators were to be the axle on which the wheel of state turned. Inevitably, many Protestants – soldiers, administrators, dispossessed landowners – made their way to England, or in some cases to Holland, for no one would trust Tyrconnel's assurances of protection, more especially as all Protestants were being disarmed.

Towards the end of 1688, Roman Catholics held almost all posts of importance in Ireland. Protestants in the south had suffered more severely from Tyrconnel's scourge, for they were a very small ruling caste, isolated among a large majority of unprivileged and uncultured peasants. In the north, however, Protestants were on almost equal numerical terms with Catholics, and had many leaders of distinction. Tyrconnel had garrisons in a few towns in the north and throughout Ulster Protestants were in a state of considerable fear. But the Catholic grip was not absolute. Londonderry, where the new predominantly Catholic Corporation had been rejected by the staunchly Protestant citizens, was garrisoned by Lord Mountjoy's regiment. Mountjoy and his second-in-command Colonel Lundy, happened to be Protestants, and so were the majority of his men.

Londonderry had been razed to the ground during the Protestant Plantation troubles at the beginning of the 17th century, and rebuilt with the help of the City of London Guilds. In recognition of this, its ancient name of Derry was changed*. At the time of the siege it was very small, with a single wall of which the circumference was less than a mile. The wall, which had seven bastions and two demi-bastions, was neither particularly high nor strong, and had fallen into a sad state of disrepair. To defend it there were eight sakers and twelve demi-culverins† given by the City Guilds. At the end of the four principal streets that divided the oblong-shaped city were large gates with either a drawbridge or portcullis, these were in bad condition with rusted chains. There were some outworks, and about 450 yards beyond the southern, or Bishop's Gate, there was the important Windmill Hill feature. To the east the River Foyle gave some protection, and on the west side of the city there was a bog, passable over a built-up causeway leading to Butcher's Gate. But Londonderry was not built to withstand a siege, and in the opinion of Count d'Avaux (Louis XIV's personal representative with King James in Ireland) it could be easily taken by one battalion.

Towards the end of November, Tyrconnel withdrew Mountjoy's troops from Londonderry, and ordered the Earl of Antrim to raise a regiment to replace them. This caused great concern to the citizens when, very shortly

---

*It is now again called Derry, but I shall continue to use the name as it was at the time of the siege.
†The saker was a light cannon of varying sizes. The demi-culverin had a 4½ inch bore, and could fire a 10 to 12 lb shot upwards of 2,000 yards.

MAP 7.1

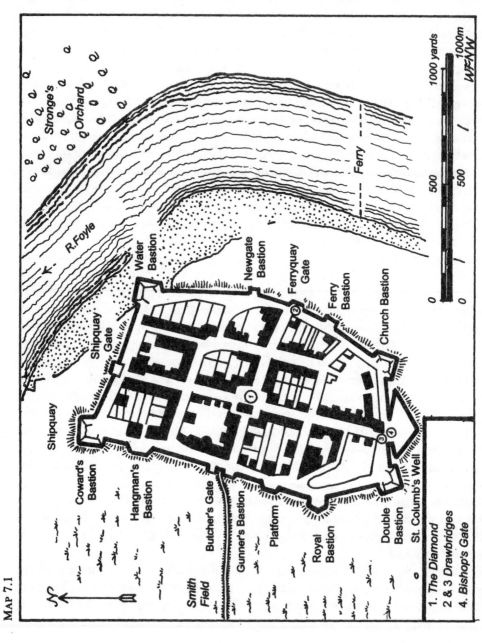

Stronge's Orchard

R. Foyle

Ferry

Water Bastion

Shipquay Gate

Newgate Bastion

Ferryquay Gate

Ferry Bastion

Church Bastion

1000 yards

1000 m

WNW

500

500

0

0

Shipquay

Coward's Bastion

Hangman's Bastion

Butcher's Gate

Gunner's Bastion

Platform

Royal Bastion

Double Bastion

St. Columb's Well

Smith Field

1. The Diamond
2 & 3 Drawbridges
4. Bishop's Gate

Londonderry in 1689

afterwards, an anonymous letter was circulated naming 9 December to be the day for a general massacre of Protestants throughout Ireland. Fortunately for Londonderry – and perhaps for England – Antrim took his time. Had he relieved Mountjoy at once, as ordered, resistance would have been impossible, but in the fortnight's interval the citizens had time to think. Suspicion grew that the replacement of Mountjoy's mainly Protestant regiment (almost the only one to escape Tyrconnel's purge) by a Catholic one might be part of an overall plan to exterminate them on 9 December.

Antrim's motley collection of men eventually reached the waterside on 7 December, and began to cross the river. There were still two days to go, and the city dignitaries were undecided as to what to do. The burden of decision was taken from them by the prompt and resolute action of a handful of apprentice boys, who ran to the guardroom, collected the Ferry Gate keys, raised the drawbridge (one marvels that it worked) and locked the gate when Antrim's men were less than 100 yards off. The boys then took similar action with the other three gates. December the 9th passed off peacefully, but a brotherhood known as the Apprentice Boys of Derry commemorates the courage of these City Guild apprentices.

Antrim's men may have been little more than a poorly armed rabble, but they represented the King's authority which the city had defied, and there were some, including the Bishop of Derry, who felt the action was unjustified. Most of these men left the city, but at the same time a number of armed retainers, who had been marshalled independently and privately as protection against Tyrconnel's troops and prowling rapparees (secret bands of Catholic raiders), rode into the city. On learning of Londonderry's insolence, the Lord-Deputy flew into one of his fearful rages – which frequently took the form of throwing his hat and wig on the fire – but he refrained from taking punitive action, for he had just heard of William of Orange's arrival in England. He therefore decided that until matters were more certain, he would try persuasion, and Mountjoy was ordered to return with his troops to Londonderry bearing a slightly withered olive branch.

However, having come to terms with their act of defiance, and sent a messenger to England explaining their position, the citizens of Londonderry were for the most part in no mood to compromise. Moreover, arms and stores had been reaching the city in fair quantities, and the former had been distributed among volunteers who were being organised into companies and allotted military duties. Therefore, when Mountjoy reached Londonderry – having sent an officer forward from Omagh with his terms for surrender – they were prepared to listen and to argue, but not to admit any Catholics. The upshot of these protracted negotiations through late December was that Mountjoy's men retired to Strabane where two companies were reorganised on a purely Protestant basis, and these were admitted into the city. Colonel Lundy came with them, and he immediately took over the governorship from Colonel George Phillips.

Tyrconnel recalled Mountjoy, and at the same time alerted Antrim to be ready to reduce Londonderry. But nothing came of this threat, for the Lord-Deputy had more important matters on his mind, one of which was an attempt from London to convert him to the Williamite cause. Whether Tyrconnel ever seriously considered changing sides is extremely doubtful, for he had too much at stake in Ireland, but William was persuaded to send Richard Hamilton to make generous offers to the Lord-Deputy and his followers if they would own allegiance to the new King. Hamilton was a member of the Catholic branch of that great family, many of whom played important parts in Irish affairs of this time. He had been a brigadier in the Irish army, and had accompanied those regiments sent to England by order of King James. Here again it is impossible to know if Hamilton had any intention of trying to convert Tyrconnel, with whom he was on excellent terms. Most probably not, for in the event he changed sides and was soon firmly attached to the Irish cause, being sent with an army to subdue the north.

This army, which started for the north at the beginning of March 1689, numbered rather more than 5,000 of which one-third were regular soldiers. They had five pieces of artillery, but represented only a fraction of the vast cohorts Tyrconnel was raising throughout Ireland. There was no shortage of recruits, but there was a considerable shortage of good officers, arms, training facilities and money. Macaulay estimated that at this time there were 100,000 men under arms of which perhaps 50,000 had some military pretensions, while the other 50,000 were armed marauders, capable of doing a tremendous amount of damage to life and property, whom the government (as represented by Tyrconnel) was unable or unwilling to suppress.

Throughout the country, there was little to stop the enormity of sorrow that unfurled its way across the land, although the Protestant gentlemen of Ulster did what they could to form companies or regiments with what weapons were available. There may have been as many as 4,000 of these yeomen turned soldiers, and they had some gallant and determined leaders. However, in a miniature campaign, fought in atrocious weather through the counties of Tyrone and Antrim, the Protestants, although registering some successes, eventually found themselves outmanoeuvred by superior numbers. By the end of March, they had fallen back to Londonderry and Enniskillen which, apart from some outlying garrisons, became the only strongpoints left them in all Ireland – and they were not very strong*.

---

*The gallant defenders of Enniskillen gave indirect, but very considerable, support to their Protestant colleagues in Londonderry throughout the siege.

MAP 7.2

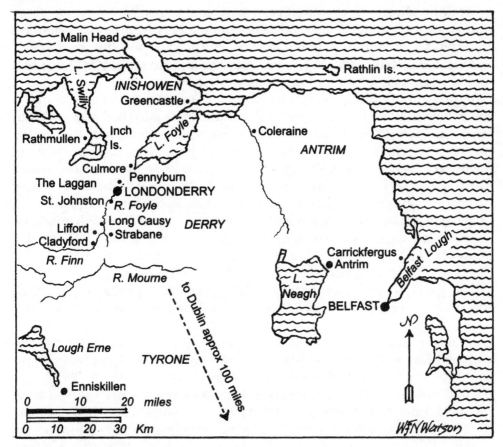

North-Western Ulster

On 21 March, Captain James Hamilton (later 6th Earl of Abercorn and not to be confused with Richard Hamilton) arrived at Londonderry from England in the *Deliverance*, bringing with him arms, ammunition and military stores. He had been instructed to withhold this consignment until Lundy and the garrison had sworn an oath of allegiance to King William. Lundy's loyalty had always been somewhat suspect, and there was now considerable controversy as to whether he had in fact taken the oath, but, eventually, Hamilton was satisfied that he had and handed over the arms. By the beginning of April, the garrison's prospects were looking much better. There were now 341 officers and 7,020 combatants, who were divided into eight regiments (seven of foot and one of horse), and there were muskets, long-barrelled duck guns (a lethal weapon), pikes and swords for everyone, and a good stock of ammunition and powder. The artillery arm, however, was very weak, for there were no mortars and the

20 pieces of cannon were old and none too reliable. Perhaps the garrison's greatest handicap was the number of non-combatants. Many thousands of oppressed Protestants had poured into Londonderry from the surrounding countryside. At one time there were 30,000 packed into the confines of this small city, although later – and surprisingly – some 10,000, classified as deserters, were permitted by the Jacobite Irish to leave.

Shortly after Captain Hamilton had landed his much needed supplies for the garrison, King James arrived in Dublin. Louis XIV had received him kindly in France, and while he was not prepared to lend him troops, for his own commitments were considerable and James was not a particularly good risk, he saw that it was greatly to his advantage to back the Stuart cause. He therefore sent him about 400 officers and technicians under such top ranking soldiers as Generals Conrad de Rosen (an unpleasant man of Latvian extraction), Maumont, and Pusignan, together with muskets, powder and ball, and a very considerable sum of money. Besides this imposing military mission, James brought with him his illegitimate son, the Duke of Berwick, and a number of his own subjects.

The party landed at Kinsale on 12 March, and proceeded to Cork where they were met by Tyrconnel whom James at once made a duke. The Lord-Deputy was full of optimism, telling James that the south was quite subdued, and that Hamilton had the north pretty well under control, although Enniskillen and Londonderry still held out, but they presented no problem. James then made his way to Dublin where he arrived on 24 March. He had already sent Pusignan to assist Hamilton, and shortly afterwards he dispatched Berwick. There followed arguments as to whether James should stay in Dublin or join the army. His Irish, French and English counsellors advanced forceful and differing persuasions, and it was a little time before James decided to go north.

Meanwhile, in Londonderry, Governor Lundy's behaviour was causing grave concern. Save for the building of a ravelin in front of the Bishop's Gate, he had done little to improve the defences; he had called in the garrisons of outlying towns against their wishes, and with the loss to the enemy of valuable stores; and now, in early April, he had refused to heed the warning brought by the Reverend George Walker, the militant parson of Donaghmore, that the enemy, in considerable strength, were almost at the gates. His only positive reaction to this was to send a cavalry vedette to watch the river crossings.

These fords were important, for Richard Hamilton was rapidly approaching from the direction of Antrim to join the main Irish army at Strabane – indeed his vanguard had made a detour to fire a monitory round at Londonderry's wall from across the Foyle – with the obvious intention of attacking the city from the west, and occupying the rich pasture lands of the Laggan. It was David Cairns, an officer who had just returned from a mission to London, where he had been received by William, who persuaded the Governor to hold a council of war. At this council, Lundy was urged from all sides to take positive action. Good men, deeply depressed by the Governor's lack of enthusiasm and lethargy, were leaving the city, a state of affairs that had to be halted. After some debate Lundy agreed to lead a force to contest the river crossings.

The rivers Finn and Mourne join the Foyle at Lifford. A crossing could be made in three places, at Lifford itself, at Cladyford three miles upstream from Lifford and at Long Causy, three miles downstream from Lifford. The many accounts of this affair are confusing and contradictory, but none of them is to the credit of Lundy. He posted orders for the assembly of the troops that merely said 'On Monday next, by Ten o'clock, all officers and soldiers . . . and all other armed men whatsoever of our forces and friends, enlisted or not enlisted . . . shall appear on the fittest ground near Cladyford, Lifford and Long Causy . . . and to bring a week's provision at least with them.' Not surprisingly this rambling, imprecise operation order resulted in thousands of men wandering about on the river banks with no sort of cohesion, discipline or leadership. The Duke of Berwick, who was present, said the Irish had no more than 600 horse and 350 foot, and that the Protestants numbered around 10,000. Captain Ash, who marched with the Protestants, gives the numbers – perhaps more realistically – as five to one in their favour.

The main crossing was made at Cladyford, where the river was swollen and the bridges down. The Irish horse plunged boldly into the water and swam across; some of the infantry hitched a lift from the horses' tails while others patched up a bridge and crossed that way. No arrangements had been made to bring up ammunition for the Protestant army, but in the circumstances this may not have mattered. It seems that the sight of a thousand Irishmen thrashing through the water so unnerved the milling mass that they managed to kill only one officer and two private soldiers (and they may have been drowned) before bolting for home led by Lundy. The Jacobites pursued and claim to have killed some 400 men in this fiasco. Lundy then compounded his poltroonery by closing the city gates in the face of George Walker and the regiment he had led at the Finn. These men had to spend the night outside the wall, at considerable risk, before being admitted. Lundy's feeble and unacceptable excuse for this was that he had insufficient rations to feed more troops.

This fight took place on 15 April, and events of much importance came crowding in during the next few days. Eleven ships from England, carrying 1,600 troops, arms and ammunition had anchored off Greencastle, at the entrance to Lough Foyle, on that very day. When Lundy had returned from the shambles of the Finn he received a communication from Colonel Cunningham (the senior officer of the relieving face) asking for orders, because his instructions were to comply with Lundy's wishes. The Governor replied that the troops were to remain on board, but that he (Cunningham), and his second-in-command, Colonel Richards, should come to Londonderry.

They arrived the next day, and Lundy immediately convened a council of war comprised only of the few men he could rely on. At this council he gave detailed reasons as to why the city was untenable – the poor state of the defences, the lack of reliable artillery, the grave shortage of food, and the strength of the opposition, which he exaggerated to being 25,000. There was much truth in what he said, the city was in very poor shape to withstand a siege or major assault, but he was not aware that the Irish army was also short of artillery, small arms and much else besides. Moreover, and more importantly, he was also not aware of – or if he was he was not prepared to disclose it – the strong determination of the garrison to stand firm.

The two colonels were not inclined to call in question the Governor's survey of the situation, and the council resolved that no troops or supplies would be landed, and that the fleet would withdraw. Lundy also obtained agreement that no mention of this resolution should be communicated to the garrison. But in this he reckoned without the clerk, John Mogridge.

It so happened that at this time Richard Hamilton, commanding the Jacobite army, had offered the garrison generous surrender terms, to discuss which Lundy ordered another council, and at this it was decided to send a delegation on 17 April to negotiate. By the time the delegation returned that night, the people had learnt from Mogridge the truth about the relief force. Such was their anger that, for some time, the delegation was denied re-entrance to the city. The answer to Hamilton's terms was to be given by midday on the 18th, the very day on which King James arrived before the city.

James had left Dublin on 8 April and had had a miserable journey. Neither the weather nor the accommodation on the way was fitting for a king. He had brought with him General de Rosen, and a most unwilling Count d'Avaux. As each bulletin arrived from the front, James became more undecided. At one stage, he turned back for Dublin, but then better news was received, coupled with a message from Berwick saying that all that was needed was for the King to appear before the city and it would surrender. Buoyed up by such misplaced optimism, James duly arrived before the wall, with an impressive escort and standard bearers, to be met with a volley of shots and cries of 'No surrender'. Whereupon the royal party wisely withdrew out of range, and sat bewildered and disconsolate while straight spears of rain streaked down on them.

Lundy attempted to make amends by sending an apology to James for such churlish behaviour, which he assured the King was against his orders, and James replied by sending the Earl of Abercorn with his personal offer of a free pardon for everyone on their surrendering the city. But by now Lundy had lost control, and the people would hear nothing of it.

James returned to Dublin with de Rosen, leaving Maumont, Hamilton and Pusignan to complete the investment and conduct the siege.

It was now that the garrison found a true fugleman, a man of action and audacity, who was ready and willing to come to grips with events. Colonel Adam Murray was a young man of Scottish extraction who farmed in the area and had command of a recently raised regiment of horse. He may have been present with his regiment at the Finn encounter, but he had certainly heard while at Culmore how his fellow Protestants in Londonderry were feeling under Lundy. He decided to bring his troops to the city. As he approached, he was met by a relative, sent by Lundy, ordering him to turn back. Disregarding this, he rode on, and the captain of the city guard ordered the gates to be opened for him.

Murray soon found that *au fond* there was no lack of loyalty and determination among most of the people. All they needed was positive leadership, and this he was willing to supply. Lundy had to admit him to his council, which was then drawing up surrender terms that Murray was asked to sign. Indignantly refusing, he at once attacked the irresolution, if not treachery, shown by Lundy during his governorship. So forceful was his condemnation that Lundy was overthrown, and placed under house arrest. Many of his cronies left the city, and in due course he himself was allowed to escape in disguise*. Murray refused the post of governor, believing he would be of more value in command of troops, and a Major Henry Baker was then unanimously chosen. He asked that the Reverend George Walker should assist him in the role of co-governor, with responsibility for administration.

During April, the Irish army remained at some distance from the city, and Avaux censured Maumont and Hamilton for allowing so many Protestant mouths to depart, but from the beginning of May troops moved from St Johnston to form a much closer investment. There was a strong contingent posted at Pennybrook Mills to the north of the city, and some 3,000 men were in Stronge's Orchard east of the river, almost opposite Shipquay Gate. These men had at least one mortar and, Walker says, four demi-culverins. The mortar (lobbing bombs of 272 lbs) did much damage inside the densely packed city, but the Protestant gunners scored a direct hit on the battery killing several men including Lieutenant Colonel O'Neil.

The size of the Irish army before Londonderry is not accurately known, for they had outlying garrisons (such as Culmore Fort, which had recently surrendered to them), and their open communication with Dublin allowed them to be frequently reinforced. The army's total strength would seem to have fluctuated between 10,000 and 12,000. The fighting unit was the company of which there were 13 to a battalion each of 62 men, and

*On 18 December every year the Apprentice Boys of Derry burn a huge effigy of Lundy.

approximately three-quarters of these were musketeers, the remainder carrying pikes. At least that is what they should have been carrying, but there was a lamentable shortage of weapons, both for horse and foot, and there was no siege artillery train. At the end of May, James sent some 'battering guns', but these made little impression on the wall, although, in contrast, their shelling was most troublesome. The Irish placed their main hope for reducing the city on starvation.

Within the city, the Governors had available, as already mentioned, 7,020 fighting men, of whom only about four companies were regular troops, the remainder were all volunteers with plenty of courage, but no experience. The eight regiments were commanded by senior officers such as Colonels Mitchelburne, Whitney and Murray, and in those companies whose commanders had deserted, the men were allowed to choose their captains. The city was divided into eight sections, one for each regiment, and each company knew its own bastion, or place of defence. Two regiments stood-to each night, and there was 'no Drinking after Eight of the clock at night or candles lighted'.

Of the twenty pieces of artillery, two were placed on the cathedral tower, four at each gate, four (presumably sakers) at the Diamond, or centre of the city, to command the four principal streets, and the remainder on the bastions. A small detachment occupied Windmill Hill, and they probably had two or three cannon in the enclosure, although this is not specifically mentioned in any account. To begin with, the soldiers' weekly ration was quite generous. Each man had a salmon and a half, two pounds of salt beef and four quarts of oatmeal, but food was to become very scarce, and there were 20,000 non-combatants to feed.

The garrison made their first sortie on 21 April. General Maumont, who had his headquarters at Culmore, had ordered Colonel John Hamilton (yet another officer of the same name) to occupy the village of Pennyburn, which lay a mile north of the city on the west bank of the river. Murray, observing this movement decided to intercept the Irish. He rode out with 200 horse, half commanded by himself and the other half by Major Bull. Along the hedges that lined the lane leading from the city he placed 500 musketeers, and a further party of 500 occupied high ground covering his left.

Hamilton's small infantry force was no match for the Protestant strength, and so he sent urgently to Maumont for reinforcements. The general, hastily summoning a troop of horse and another of dragoons, led them at the gallop to reach the field in time to engage Murray's cavalry in a very hot skirmish, and drive them back to the city along the lane. In the fight Maumont was killed and Murray unhorsed, but he gained the city unscathed. However, the Protestants had the victory, for the musketeers lining the hedges did terrible execution to the pursuing Irish, killing at least 80, which would have accounted for most of their horse. Protestant losses were said to be three officers and less than a dozen men. Six days later, the Irish were back in Pennyburn, and Murray again sallied forth. In an all-day battle, the Irish, reinforced by Brigadier Ramsey when severely pressed, just managed to hold the village. In this fight another Frenchman, General Pusignan, whom they could ill afford to lose, was critically wounded. He died a few days later, entirely due to lack of proper medical attention, for the Irish were virtually without a field hospital service.

There were to be other sorties by the garrison, for they were great morale boosters, and a welcome interlude from the heavy bombardment General Hamilton (now in sole command) ordered his gunners to deal out by day and night. But the next engagement was on a larger scale than Pennyburn.

Hamilton had decided that Windmill Hill would make a good gun position for the heavy cannon he was expecting and, on the night of 5/6 May, Ramsey's brigade had no difficulty in driving in the Protestant detachment. But Governor Baker could not allow the position to be occupied by the enemy, who were already entrenching themselves, and so, on 6 May, an assault force of over 1,000 men was detailed by taking ten men from every company. Simple, and in this case effective, but one wonders how such a mixed force fighting without cohesion, and under no chain of command, managed to dislodge Ramsey's brigade of 3,000 men. However, in fierce hand-to-hand combat, they did so, leaving (according to Walker and Mackenzie) 200 dead Irishmen on the field and taking many wounded prisoners. Among the latter was Brigadier Ramsey, perhaps the best of their officers, who died of his wounds and was buried with full military honours in the Long Tower, just outside the city walls, where a church still stands. After this, Baker extended the fortifications to the south of the city with a line of redoubts from the bog on the western side across the windmill to the river, which gave the garrison more room to manoeuvre.

The month of May was comparatively quiet, and this was not good for the besieged. The tension of waiting, trapped as it were in time and tightly trammelled, is always demoralising. Raiding parties were dispatched, but they achieved little, and on at least one occasion ended in disaster. Water became a problem. The city wells had become muddy and this water almost undrinkable, the river was tidal and drawing from St Columb's Wells outside the wall was extremely hazardous. The constant bombardment claimed many lives each day and food was beginning to get short. As the month wore on tempers became high and vitality low. Moreover, there was disagreement and disloyalty in high places. Colonel Whitney, in command of a regiment, had been found guilty of corruption and imprisoned; a major row broke out between Governor Baker and Colonel Mitchelburne; and serious charges were proffered, although never substantiated, against Governor Walker. Such troubles were bound to occur when there were still men in the city who, if not Jacobites, were certainly defeatists. Baker rose to the occasion, and through his institution of a representative Council of Fourteen to organise city affairs, loyalty and a sense of purpose were gradually restored.

At the beginning of June, the Irish, who also had their troubles, for the conditions under which they lived were appalling*, were able to step up the bombardment with the arrival of bigger calibre guns. They now had enough cannon for Hamilton to complete the blockade by sealing off the river. The idea of sinking ships to establish the blockade was abandoned, for it would be too permanent, but under the guidance of the French artillery expert, the Marquis de Pointis, a boom was made of stout timbers, yet light enough to float with the tides, joined by cables and chains, and firmly fixed to the shore on each bank†. This barrier was protected by gun emplacements in Fort Charles on the left bank and Grange Fort on the right. Other forts were constructed above and below the boom.

On 4 June, Hamilton mounted a strong attack on the Windmill Hill defences with 15 squadrons of horse, and 12 battalions of infantry, probably totalling between five and six thousand men. The cavalry were to attack on the river side in three successive waves, the infantry were allotted the centre between the river and the Windmill, with the massed grenade companies of each battalion on their left. Baker, who was to show considerable military competence in his control of the battle, had ordered a full muster of the garrison as soon as he saw the Irish at their assembly points. In contrast to the first Windmill Hill battle, the Protestants must have been well trained and competently led, for we are told that they fought in three ranks in order to obtain successive volleys, which is a difficult operation requiring skill and precision.

On the Protestant left, it was not until the defenders lowered their fire to bring down the horses that the first wave of cavalry was checked, for Irish cuirasses proved bulletproof. But the tangled heaps of writhing animals broke up the following waves, and those that got through found the entrenchment impossibly high. Only Captain Butler, Lord Mountgarrett's son, was sufficiently well mounted to leap the bank, and he was made prisoner. The infantry in the centre, bravely led by their commanders, fared no better than their cavalry colleagues. The leading ranks carried bundles of faggots to deflect the bullets, but unlike the cuirasses these were easily penetrated and must have inhibited their freedom of action. On the

---

*According to an intercepted letter they had 3,000 men out of action.
†It seems fairly certain that a boom was in position before the relieving fleet (see page 116) arrived, although some authorities say it was constructed about 13 June, and condemn General Kirke for losing his best opportunity of relieving Londonderry. Walker's diary makes no mention of it before 15 June, but there were two booms, and very likely the second was made after the fleet's arrival on 11 June.

MAP 7.3

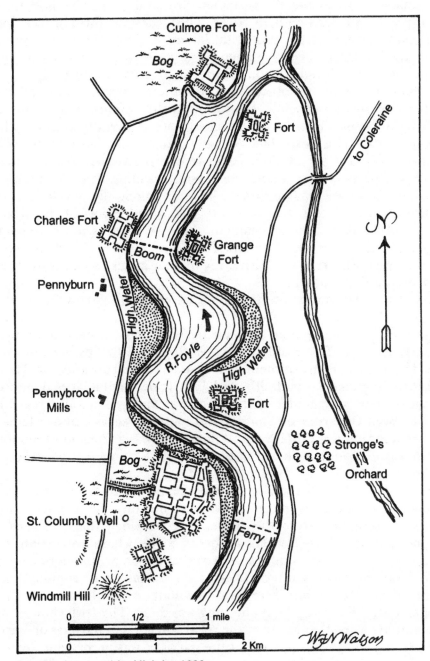

Londonderry and its Vicinity 1689

left of the line, however, the Irish grenadiers broke the defence, but Baker had reserves in hand for a successful counterattack.

So stubborn was the defence, and so well organised was the ammunition supply by the women of the garrison, that within a few hours the Irish were unable to withstand the sustained fire, and broke. In their retreat, they carried their dead on their backs. This gruesome form of pick-a-back saved many a soldier from Protestant bullets, but had there been any sort of pursuit it must surely have been an uneven race. Accounts of losses, in this the biggest single action of the siege, vary considerably. On the Protestant side only one officer and six other ranks are reported dead, which seems suspiciously low, even though the defence had far the best of the fight. Nicolas Plunket, a Catholic supporter, writing in 1711, admits to at least 200 Irish dead, but Walker's estimate of 400 may be nearer the mark. Perhaps the greatest harm to the Irish cause was the loss of morale and despondency among the troops resulting from the numerous desertions, and the damaging recriminations among the senior officers in the aftermath of defeat. Avaux was to give a bad report of the affair to James, and Plunket's acerbic comment, 'You see here, as you have seen all along, that the tradesmen of Londonderry have more skill in their defence than the great officers in the Irish army in their attack', could scarcely help to smooth ruffled feathers.

Only a few days after the defenders encouraging performance at the Windmill, the masts of a relieving fleet from England became visible in Lough Foyle. These were an advance party of three ships headed by the frigate *Greyhound*. The main fleet consisting of 30 ships arrived on 11 June. These ships, many of them men-of-war, carried around 2,000 troops from three regiments – 2nd, 9th, and 11th Foot – and a large quantity of provisions. The commander of the force was Major General Percy Kirke, who had been Governor of Tangier and had seen service under James II at Sedgemoor but was now loyal to William. He was a cruel, loud-mouthed, brutish sort of man, but he had proved himself a competent governor and soldier.

Captain Richards, an engineer and senior officer of the advance party, had spotted the boom from the *Greyhound*'s maintop; he had also had an unpleasant reception from the shore batteries when the *Greyhound* ran aground and was nearly lost. His report to Kirke, whose instructions were not to hazard the fleet unduly until the situation in Londonderry was known, was therefore sombre. There were no means of communication between fleet and city, and Kirke was unwilling to run the gauntlet of the shore batteries. For several days nothing was done. The Irish showed signs of decamping when they learnt of the relief force, yet as the days of inaction went by, they took fresh heart. But the garrison was in torment, for their great elation on sighting the vessels was turning sour.

Frantic attempts to communicate were made by both sides. Colonel Adam Murray took a boat party which was intercepted, and they were lucky to get back with only one casualty – a graze wound to Murray's head. Two messengers from the fleet were caught, one of whom was hanged, but a man called James Roche, whose adventures would fill a book, got to Londonderry. On the return journey, however, he was severely wounded and had to swim back to the city. The last of these messengers, called McGimpsey, said he would swim to the fleet, and was dispatched with a message in a bladder attached to his neck. He was drowned, and his body recovered by the Irish with the useful information that the garrison's food supplies were so drastic that, unless relieved, they must surrender in six or seven days.

The situation had been painted blacker than it was, in order to stir Kirke into immediate activity. Nevertheless, the Protestants' plight was becoming extremely serious. The horsemeat from the slaughter at Windmill Hill was nearly finished, and the diet was now mainly dogs, cats, rats, mice and melted tallow. The familiar irritations and backbiting were soon to be exacerbated when Hamilton felt the time was ripe for another offer of generous terms. But before these had been lobbed into the city in an empty shell, the garrison was faced with the return of de Rosen with orders from James to prosecute the siege more vigorously. His means of doing this will be seen later, and were not in keeping with a strange attempt at this time by the men of Lord Clancarty's regiment to force Butcher's Gate. This vainglorious young nobleman set out to fulfil some ancient and obscure prophecy that a Clancarty would 'one day knock at the gates of Derry'. He almost bettered the prophecy by overrunning the outworks, and getting some miners into a cellar under the Gunners' Bastion. But Captain Noble, leading a party out of Bishop's Gate took Clancarty's men in the flank and drove them back across the bog, leaving behind the miners and some 40 casualties.

Two days later, to add to the garrison's woes, Governor Baker died – probably from pneumonia. He had been a stalwart of the defence, and almost the only man respected by everybody. His one quarrel with Mitchelburne had soon been mended, and on his deathbed Baker had recommended that Mitchelburne should take his place, with Walker continuing as Co-Governor in charge of administration.

When the garrison refused to agree to Hamilton's latest peace offer in the 24 hours de Rosen allowed, he resorted to an act of terrorism. He had thousands of Protestants, from the surrounding countryside, irrespective of age or sex, herded beneath the city wall. Those who had survived the rigours of the march were to be left to starve unless admitted to the city, which de Rosen knew meant its surrender. Mitchelburne ordered a gallows to be erected on the Double Bastion from which all the Irish prisoners would be hanged unless de Rosen gave the Protestants safe passage home. This threat, and the pleas of the Irish prisoners, persuaded him to do so. King James was furious with de Rosen when informed of his maleficent action.

Meanwhile, at the end of June, when the Protestants were contending with the loss of their Governor, the braggadocio of Clancarty and the devilry of de Rosen, Kirke called his senior officers to a council of war. At this he argued that as there had been no message from the garrison their plight could not be desperate, and the relief's purpose would best be served by sailing round Malin Head, entering Lough Swilly and anchoring off Rathmullen. This would enable the troops to get some much needed exercise ashore, allow the fertile land which had been provisioning the Irish army to be occupied, and form a base from which Londonderry might be relieved and Enniskillen protected. On 18 July, soon after their arrival, Berwick attempted to dislodge the troops, but with the help of the naval guns he was beaten off. Kirke then fortified the island of Inch.

It was while he was at Inch that, at long last, communications were established with the garrison. Through the ingenuity and courage of a small boy, messages got through the Irish lines, and Kirke was fully appraised of the garrison's desperate situation. Indeed both sides were now nearly at the end of their tether. So anxious was James to have Londonderry that he allowed Hamilton to offer such advantageous terms as it was almost impossible to refuse. The garrison sent commissioners to treat, but – probably deliberately in order to gain time while the relief was being planned – they grossly overplayed their hand. Even so, negotiations foundered on only three points with which the Irish felt it impossible to agree.

Walker's facts and figures make it easy to see why the garrison was willing to accept good terms. On 17 July the effective strength was down to 5,114 very weak men, and the weekly wastage was over 100. John Hunter, as good a man as any, reports that he was so weak he fell under the weight of his musket, his face blackened with hunger. But there was still some food to be bought for those able to pay half a crown for a dog's head, 5/6d a pound the haunch, one shilling a rat and sixpence a mouse. Dogs had scavenged well on the killing grounds. A raid on 26 July by 500 sadly emaciated men failed to achieve its object of securing Irish cattle from the Pennyburn fields, and it was probably then that Murray was severely wounded. By now the Irish were in scarcely better shape, for despite their having slightly more generous rations, they were dying fast from fevers, smallpox and other complaints.

About the middle of July, Kirke received a positive order from General Schomberg, William's commander-in-chief of the army destined for Ireland, that he was to break the boom at all hazards and waste no more time in relieving Londonderry. This objurgation, coming from so distinguished a source, had immediate effect. Leaving troops to safeguard the Protestants of Inshowen, Kirke returned to Lough Foyle.

One of the merchant ships was the *Mountjoy* commanded by Micaiah Browning, who had been foremost among those condemning inaction. He now volunteered his ship for the honour of breaking the boom. Accompanied by the *Phoenix*, carrying a precious cargo of food, and escorted by the *Dartmouth* (Captain John Leake) a frigate mounting 36 guns, Browning set sail on the evening of Sunday 30 July. There was much danger, for the tide was out and the only navigable channel was close to the left bank where Irish defences were prominent. But Leake handled his ship with extreme skill, and his guns played upon the shore batteries, and protected the merchantmen.

When the boom was reached Browning sailed straight at it. The great timber baulks, groaned, creaked and splintered, but such was the impact that the *Mountjoy* ricochetted backwards, and was stuck in the mud. A huge shout of joy rose from many Irish throats, but it was premature, for *Dartmouth*'s cannon were still active, and the shudder of *Mountjoy*'s own guns dislodged her from the mudbank. Meanwhile the *Phoenix* had passed through on a rising tide, and forging through the broken boom reached the quay at about 10 pm. It had been a successful operation in the highest tradition of the British navy, but sadly Micaiah Browning, in his hour of triumph, received a musket ball in the head.

The garrison had passed through moments of elation and apprehension as first the advancing sails were seen, then the Irish cheers seemed to announce disaster, and finally came the marvellous sight of the *Phoenix* coming alongside. The whole city was there to greet her, and barricades were quickly thrown up to protect the unloading of great casks of meal, bacon, cheeses, butter, brandy and many other delights that were almost dangerous to shrivelled stomachs. The siege of Londonderry was over.

The Irish gunners kept up a sporadic bombardment throughout that night, and much of the next day, but on 1 August fires were seen from their camp as the army prepared to withdraw towards Strabane, destroying everything in their path with iconoclastic fury. They had lost about 8,000 men (Walker's estimate), and for many of the survivors there was to be another and more final fight at the River Boyne in the following year. The effective strength of the garrison had been reduced from 7,000 to about 3,000, and one of the citizens who endured the 105 days of the siege* put the losses among the non-combatants as 15,000 men, women and children, 'many of which dyed for meat'. But 10,000 would be a more realistic figure, and concurs with a later report to the House of Commons.

It is always fascinating to examine the 'ifs' of history, but it is not usually a fruitful exercise. Had Londonderry not stood firm, James would have taken an army to Scotland to join the Earl of Dundee, who was fighting so strenuously on his behalf. Could he then have marched south to topple William from a throne not yet consolidated? Probably not, but at least his prospects would have been better than those of his grandson 50 years later. Slightly more possible, and certainly more importantly, would Louis XIV

---

*The siege is reckoned to have begun on 18 April and ended on 1 August.

have been able to make Ireland a springboard against England? These
are imponderables, but there is one undoubted reason for our gratitude
to the loyal Protestants of Ulster. In the words of G. M. Trevelyan, 'before
Britain could send her armies to fight France on the Continent she had
first to secure her own shores . . . .' We owe, in some part, to the men and
women of Londonderry the glories of Blenheim, Ramillies, Oudenarde and
Malplaquet.

CHAPTER 8

The Third Siege of Badajoz
March–April 1812

THE Peninsular War of 1812–14, in which the British fought the French in Spain and Portugal, is regarded by many as one of the truly great campaigns in the history of the British Army. Under Wellington's guiding hand, the Army grew into a most formidable fighting machine and in the story of its achievements lie many of its finest traditions. The Third Siege of Badajoz is not only the story of an epic battle in which unparalleled courage and superb and fearless leadership brought a resounding success – albeit at terrible cost and despite what may, with the benefit of hindsight, be seen as some imperfections in its actual conduct – but it is one that marks a very significant milestone in the history of the Army in that, as a result of Wellington's recommendations after the siege, the first professional corps of military engineers, the Corps of Royal Sappers and Miners, was born. What British commander today would dream of undertaking an operation of almost any sort without the support of the Royal Engineers, the direct descendants of those gallant men who masterminded much of the siegework at Badajoz.

* * *

In the early years of the 19th century, Spain was an uneasy ally of France and in November 1807, following a Franco-Spanish treaty partitioning Portugal, General Junot invaded that country. The Portuguese sought help from Britain, which in July 1808 sent an expeditionary force under Sir Arthur Wellesley. Wellesley, the youngest Lieutenant General in the British Army, was put in an awkward position when joined by three other generals – Sir Hew Dalrymple, Sir John Moore and Sir Harry Burrard – all senior to himself. Meanwhile, Napoleon on the pretext of not wanting a Bourbon king on a neighbouring throne, but chiefly because he wanted Spain as a bridge to North Africa with control of the Mediterranean, deposed the Spanish king and, backed by a large army, imposed his brother, Joseph, on the Spaniards. These fierce, passionately proud people immediately rose in revolt at this heavy-handed blunder.

A month after he had landed in Mondego Bay, Wellesley decisively defeated Junot at Vimiero, but unfortunately Burrard, who had arrived just too late to take command, was in time to refuse Wellesley's wish to exploit the victory and destroy Junot. Worse followed when, shortly afterwards, the even more cautious Dalrymple arrived, and Junot was permitted to evacuate his entire army, together with its loot, under the advantageous terms of the Convention of Cintra. Dalrymple, Burrard and Wellesley returned to England, leaving Sir John Moore in command of a reinforced army with which to aid the Portuguese, and Britain's new ally Spain.

Later in the Peninsular campaign, Spanish armies were to give Wellington (as Wellesley had become) a great deal of trouble. They were badly organised, ill-disciplined, and not particularly well led, but individually Spaniards were bold fighters and their guerrilla bands were to prove invaluable. Sir John Moore had early experience of this unreliability when, with Spanish aid, he rashly attempted to march against the French lines of communication when Napoleon, albeit briefly, happened to be in Spain himself. His army only just avoided annihilation and became involved in a long, hard withdrawal, in the depths of a bitter winter, to Corunna and embarkation. Although's Moore's leadership at this time undoubtedly saved his army, the final battle with the French cost him his life.

The British Government was determined that Portugal should be held and, in April 1809, Wellesley returned to take command. Ten thousand soldiers had been left there after Corunna, and this number was now more than doubled. Wellesley's brief was primarily to defend Portugal. To help in this, he was to train, and to a certain extent officer, the Portuguese army. His task was hazardous, for by now Marshal Soult was in Oporto with a large army and threatening Lisbon from the north, while Marshal Victor, with an even larger one, seemed to be poised to attack from the east. Leaving 11,000 British and Portuguese troops to watch Victor, Wellesley struck north at great speed, and with some of his finest strategem and manoeuvre he routed Soult on the Douro, and by mid-May had driven his much damaged army into Galicia.

Meanwhile, Victor had crossed to the north bank of the Tagus and advanced to Talavera. Wellesley felt that with the full cooperation of the large Spanish army encamped at Almaraz, he might get between Victor (who had with him King Joseph) and Madrid. But he reckoned without the old, obdurate and incompetent General Cuesta in command of the Spanish Army. In the closing days of July 1809, the great battle of Talavera was fought. The British bore the brunt of the battle against an army twice their size and, although the victors in the end, their casualties were grievous. The French withdrew, but pursuit was out of the question and, with the Spaniards unable to protect his flank, Wellesley fell back.

On 3 August (six days after Talavera) Wellesley learnt that Soult with 50,000 men was marching south from Salamanca to cut off his withdrawal, and had pushed aside an inadequate Spanish force guarding the Baños

Pass. The withdrawal became a hasty retreat under conditions of great hardship, for transport and supplies promised by Cuesta had not arrived, and the countryside had been denuded by Victor's troops. By 3 September, the army was on the Portuguese frontier, half-starved, riddled with fever and now shorn of a third of its strength.

A period of comparative quiet enabled Wellesley, now Viscount Wellington of Talavera, to put new strength into his own and the Portuguese Army. With Soult now operating in Andalusia, Napoleon sent Masséna to command the 70,000 strong Army of Portugal. He took the fortresses of Ciudad Rodrigo and Almeida, and advanced south on Lisbon. Wellington fell back before him, but on 26 September 1810, the British and Portuguese troops gave Masséna a bloody nose at Busaco, before retiring farther. Masséna thought he could drive Wellington into the sea when, quite unexpectedly, he found the British and Portuguese firmly entrenched behind the famous lines of Torres Vedras, with its 152 redoubts, which thousands of Portuguese labourers had been constructing in great depth across the mountains since October 1809. Quite unable to make any progress, and eventually short of all stores, Masséna withdrew, closely followed by Wellington.

At the end of January 1811 Soult, who had belatedly responded to Napoleon's orders to support Masséna, laid siege to Badajoz, a strongly fortified town on the south bank of the Guadiana, which commanded the principal southern route into Portugal. So long as Masséna held on in Portugal (which he did until towards the end of March) Wellington could spare few troops for the relief of Badajoz, and the Spanish commander surrendered in early March before the place had even been assaulted. This was a serious business, for Wellington needed Badajoz – and Ciudad Rodrigo – as secure bases while he advanced into Spain. General Beresford was therefore sent to retake it. Wellington rode south to oversee arrangements and outline the plan, but his presence was required with the main army to fight the battle of Fuentes de Onoro.

Badajoz town is situated on high ground above the river Guadiana, and is dominated by the castle at the north-east end which stands, behind a high turreted wall, some 130 feet above the river, near its confluence with the much smaller Rivillas. Except on the north, where the river did duty, the town wall was strengthened by eight bastions and a deep ditch. In the ditch were ravelins, although these were mostly incomplete. There were four outlying defences. San Cristobal, 150 yards north of the river, was a strong enclosed fort which commanded the castle from a rocky eminence. East of the Rivillas stream, and about 400 yards from the south-east angle of the wall, was the lunette Picurina, and to its north, but nearer the walls was the small lunette, or ravelin, San Roque. Almost in the centre of the southern wall, and some 300 yards from it, stood the crownwork Pardeleras. There

MAP 8.1

Portugal and Western Spain 1812

was a road bridge across the Guadiana from a north-west gate, leading to a bridgehead fort.

The plan for the first siege of Badajoz was to make the main effort against San Cristobal, for once this strongpoint had been taken it should be comparatively easy to breach the castle walls. There were to be subsidiary attacks on Picurina and Pardeleras. But nothing went quite right. It has to be remembered that the British Army at this time had virtually no experience in siege warfare, and the engineers were neither trained nor equipped for such operations. There probably was a siege train in Portugal, but it was still in store ships on the Tagus. Cannon of sufficiently heavy calibre, and siege stores of every kind, were lacking, and Beresford had to rely on local Portuguese resources. The siege lasted from 4 to 13 May, and it is hardly surprising that, with their lack of experience and equipment, Beresford's men found San Cristobal too tough a proposition.

Casualties were mounting and progress was almost at a standstill when it was learnt that Soult was coming up from the Sierra Morena, and was within 80 miles. Beresford therefore raised the siege, and marched south to meet him. The action took place 14 miles south-east of Badajoz at Albuera. The battle was a seven-hour shambles of bloodshed and butchery. Beresford's inept leadership was only rescued by the courage and stubbornness of the British infantry which lost two thirds of its number.

The second siege of Badajoz was no more successful than the first. Wellington hoped to take the place before the French recovered from Fuentes and Albuera, and hurried south at the head of two divisions to conduct operations personally. His plan did not differ greatly from the earlier one, but this time Major Dickson, the artillery officer charged with finding siege guns, had managed to collect a number of larger calibre cannon, albeit fairly ancient. The trenches were opened on 29 May, and the whole operation was on a larger scale than the previous attempt with all the actions carried out simultaneously. But the French garrison fought with great skill and valour. Again, San Cristobal proved too strong. On 10 June, Wellington realised that he had miscalculated, and raised the siege.

As it happened, the Badajoz garrison was down to almost its last biscuit, but Wellington was fearful lest his army be crushed between the upper and nether millstones. He had some 45,000 men sandwiched between Marmont (who had succeeded Masséna) and Soult, whose combined strength was very considerably greater than his. He therefore left the marshals to meet in Badajoz and, glad to be clear of the unhealthy Guadiana valley, headed north with thoughts on the reduction of Ciudad Rodrigo.

This time Wellington would make sure he had a proper siege train, and the indefatigable Dickson was given most detailed orders for the assembly and conveyance of 68 heavy pieces, and large quantities of ordnance and stores, from Lisbon to Almeida via Oporto by sea, river and road. This great battering-train began its tortuous journey at the end of July, and it was not until 22 November that it entered Almeida. There had been inevitable hold-ups, the longest of these being due to the fighting round El Bodon (six miles south of Rodrigo) at the end of September.

Wellington waited patiently for the overall French position to favour him. He knew that Marmont was under pressure to succour Suchet in Valencia, and although he had to withdraw his investing troops when Marmont closed in on Rodrigo, he thought, correctly, that this was only a relief operation. His chance came when, at the end of December, Marmont moved 16,000 men eastward, and had the rest of his army strung out in cantonments round Salamanca. The first parallel was dug on the night of 8 January 1812, and by the night of the 19th, with Marmont's relieving army still 20 miles away, Ciudad Rodrigo had fallen. This time everything had gone well, and what Wellington feared might be a 30-day siege had lasted only eleven. But the army had suffered 1,121 casualties, half of which – including 59 officers – occurred during the storming, and of these the greatest loss was the brilliant commander of the Light Division, General Crauford. The survivors of the garrison were made prisoner, and the entire siege train, including 153 heavy guns and much ammunition, fell to the besiegers.

Wellington now only needed Badajoz, as a safeguard against any invasion of southern Portugal by Soult from Andalusia, to enable him to take the offensive farther into Spain. Therefore as soon as work to repair the Ciudad Rodrigo breaches could be completed, and a strong Spanish garrison for that fortress brought in, the troops could begin their march south to Elvas, where Wellington would establish his headquarters.

Arrangements for assembling the 52 heavy siege guns had been put in train even before Rodrigo fell. Major Dickson had been sent to Lisbon to organise their collection and transport by sea to Setubal, and from there by river and road to Elvas. Sixteen 24-pounders had recently arrived from England, and a further 16 24-pounder howitzers were in store ships on the Tagus, but more were required and Admiral Berkeley, commanding the fleet, was asked to supply naval guns. His ships did not carry 24-pounders, but he promised 20 18-pounders; these were accepted although firing, say, at 400 yards, the battering power of an 18-pounder made it a poor substitute for the bigger gun. Moreover, when Dickson arrived to take possession these naval pieces turned out to be old Russian guns in poor condition from a Lisbon store.

Great care was taken by Wellington that the French should not realise that his entire army was moving south from Rodrigo. Divisions were dispatched at intervals from 19 February, and not all by the same route. Wellington himself delayed his departure until 5 March, and by then all but 5 Division and the 1st Hussars of the King's German Legion had left. The latter were to act as an outpost line along the Agueda as the last piece of deception. The Spanish armies of Galicia and Estramadura, with some Portuguese units, were now left to garrison Ciudad Rodrigo and hold Marmont's formidable army. The latter could easily have dealt with them, and spared troops to relieve Badajoz, but fortunately Napoleon had ordered Marmont to concentrate his army for an invasion of Northern

Beira. But the threat, and that from Soult in the south, was ever foremost in Wellington's calculations.

By the second week in March, the army, with the siege train, was concentrated around Elvas, and a pontoon bridge had been thrown across the Guadiana four miles west of Badajoz. On the 16th the town was invested. On the same day a covering force in two sections of 19,000 and 16,000, under Generals Graham and Hill respectively, was pushed out towards Llerena and Merida with orders to drive the divisions of Drouet (Graham) and Daricau (Hill) out of the Estramadura plain. At Badajoz, on the evening of 17 March, a working party of 1,800 men, covered by a further 2,000, began, in foul weather conditions, to dig the first parallel 160 yards from Fort Picurina.

After the second siege, the French had greatly strengthened the fortifications. The damage to San Cristobal had been repaired, and a redoubt built upon the site of Wellington's breaching battery; the Rivillas had been dammed near San Roque causing an inundation opposite La Trinidad bastion, and in the ditch there a deep *cunette* had been dug below the counterscarp, which held several feet of water; much work had been done at Pardeleras and to the whole southern *enceinte*; and the south-west face of the fortress had been elaborately mined. Wellington, who at the time of the investment had carried out a careful inspection, could not, of course, see much of these improvements, but fortunately, a French sergeant major of sappers had deserted with a map of the defences.

In view of what he had seen and heard, Wellington decided that this attack would differ substantially from the previous two. The counterguard of Trinidad's right flank was unfinished, and the base of the wall could be breached by a battery firing from Picurina; moreover the curtain wall between Trinidad and Santa Maria was said to be comparatively weak. The basic plan therefore was first to take Picurina, and from the area of that fort, breach the two bastions Trinidad and Santa Maria. San Cristobal would not be attacked this time, and the castle does not appear to have been a target at this juncture. A simple plan to crack a hard nut, for within this fortress there were almost 5,000 tough, resolute Frenchmen commanded by a fighting general in Armon Phillipon. The place was well supplied, and could mount 140 cannon, although ammunition was thought to be short, for several convoys had been intercepted.

As mentioned above, the first parallel and approaches to it were begun on the night of 17 March. By daylight on the 18th, some 600 yards three feet deep and three feet six inches wide had been opened. For the next eight days and nights, work parties, almost always in excess of a thousand men, laboured to perfect and extend the parallel, trace the various battery sites, and bring up the guns. The conditions under which they had to work were appalling. The rain fell in punishing quantities almost the entire time, the trenches became flooded and the soil a soggy, unworkable mess; the

Guadiana flooded the fixed bridge and swept away the pontoons, cutting communication with Elvas. So bad was the weather that, on the 22nd, raising the siege was seriously considered.

Nor was the weather the only impediment the work force had to face. As soon as the Picurina garrison realised what was afoot, they poured a destructive fire on the trenches. Then at 1 pm on the 19th, a strong sortie of 1,500 foot and 40 horse left the main fortress by the Talavera gate. Making use of cover provided by the communication trench from San Roque to Picurina the infantry were able to enter the parallel. The work force were taken by surprise, and suffered casualties before they could pick up their arms; meanwhile the cavalry rode round the right flank to the engineer park behind the Cerro de San Miguel from where, after a sharp action, they were driven off. Little damage was done to the trench, but there were 150 casualties including the Chief Engineer, Colonel Fletcher, who was wounded. The French lost double that number, but collected a few entrenching tools for which General Phillipon had offered a reward.

There were no further destructive raids of this kind but, owing to a shortage of men, the investment had not been complete. As soon as Phillipon discovered this, he placed a battery on the right bank of the Guadiana which could enfilade the right end of the parallel. Similarly, guns from the Pardaleras area caused trouble on the left. Counter-battery work was mainly successful, and the 5th Division was ordered to move from Campo Mayor to clear the right bank of the river, and to invest San Cristobal. This had been done by 24 March.

Despite interruptions from the weather, and interference from the garrison artillery, by the 25th, the parallel had been completed to a point opposite the castle on the right, and to the Seville road on the left. Ten 24-pounders, eleven 18-pounders and seven 5½ inch howitzers had been brought into action in six battery sites. This was a great achievement in the prevailing conditions, with Colonel Fletcher a casualty and no properly trained sappers available. On this day, the batteries opened a furious bombardment on Picurina and San Roque and the latter was put out of action. Although the Picurina gunners retaliated with some success, Wellington considered the garrison sufficiently subdued to warrant an assault. Accordingly, Major General Kempt was ordered to attempt the task that night with 500 men from 3 Division.

Fort Picurina, which resembled a detached bastion, was a great deal stronger than it looked. The wall rose sheer for nine feet from the bottom of the ditch where the revetment gave place to earth, and the angle was such that men could scramble up it, but it was protected by horizontal rows of poles (Fraises). The parapet had been repaired with sandbags, and the deep ditch was flanked by four splinter proof casemates. At the gorge in rear, which was the fort's most vulnerable side, there were three rows of palisades which could be covered by enfilade fire. A loopholed gallery, with mines beneath the counterscarp, had not been completed, but the fort carried seven light cannon, and was held by upwards of 200 men (each with two muskets) under Colonel Gaspard-Thierry.

For the assault, Kempt divided his force into three parts. Two hundred men were to take the fort from the left, a further 200 were to attack on the right (or north) side, and 100 men were to remain as a reserve at No 2 Battery. Major Shaw, who commanded on the right, was to detach half his force to guard the communication trench with the main fortress. One hundred men of the 52nd from the Light Division, armed with axes, ladders and crowbars, were to precede the assault parties. Owing to the short time available for preparation the attack did not go in until at least 9 pm, and some contemporary accounts mention 10 pm. The night was still, and the weather perfect, for there had been no rain for two days.

A gun fired from No 4 Battery was the signal, and Major Rudd's column on the left made the gorge unhindered but, on the right, Shaw was soon discovered, and his force had many casualties. Both in the gorge and on the north flank, the fire was so furious that neither party made progress. Shaw drew in towards Rudd, but those in the ditch found the ladders too short, and a dangerous impasse had been reached until one of Shaw's officers had the idea of throwing three ladders across the ditch, thus forming a bridge over which his men scrambled. After some fierce fighting, a few of these men gained an entrance. By now, Kempt had launched the reserve straight at the salient angle, where the defences had been badly mauled by the bombardment. After an initial failure, and great difficulty in surmounting the fraises, the issue was decided when a party gained the top in sufficient strength to drive the French from the parapet. Meanwhile, Shaw's detachment guarding the communication trench had successfully dealt with a relieving force, and the 52nd's axemen had broken down a gate at the rear, which was no longer covered by fire.

Only one officer and about 40 men of the garrison escaped to the town. The commandant, two other officers and some 80 men were captured, the rest either died in the fighting or were drowned in the inundation. Phillipon had expected, and wanted, the fort to be held for several days, and was displeased at its early collapse. Certainly the defence had failed to make use of the many shells and combustibles assembled on the parapet, but undoubtedly they had fought gallantly, as the British losses showed. Out of an assault force of 500 there had been 319 casualties, of which four officers and 50 men had been killed.

Phillipon now realised that the main assault would not be made against the castle as he had anticipated, and he hastened with many working parties to strengthen the defences of the two threatened bastions. He also directed a heavy bombardment on the Picurina area, making it difficult for the British to consolidate their gain, and two attempts at a lodgement were necessary. Meanwhile, work on the communication trenches, the second parallel and new battery sites, was a perilous business involving many casualties. It was not until 30 March that the first of the new batteries could begin firing. Number 7, of twelve 24-pounders, was to breach the right face of Trinidad bastion, Numbers 8 and 9 batteries, of six and eight guns respectively (mixed 18 and 24-pounders), firing from just outside the Picurina gorge, were aimed at the left flank of Santa Maria, and Number 10, of three 24-pounder howitzers, was sited in the first parallel to enfilade the ditch and prevent the erection of obstacles.

It took four or five days for the breaching batteries to make any real impression on the solid masonry of the bastions, and San Roque also stood defiant. The inundation caused by the dam there meant that the assault could not go in from the trenches, and it was therefore decided to take San Roque and destroy the dam. The second parallel was extended across the Talavera road, and the engineers did their best to sap forward to the ravelin. But time was too short for these partly trained men, and it was decided to make a direct attack on the dam. This was bravely attempted by Lieutenant Stanway and twenty sappers, but there was too much water running for the explosion to be carried out satisfactorily. The breaches would have to be assaulted from the west bank of the Rivillas.

On 30 March, news that Soult was across the Sierra Morena caused Wellington to bring back Graham and Hill to Zafra and Merida respectively, and to send 5 Division in support. A contingency plan was made to leave two divisions in the trenches, and march the rest of the army to meet Soult at Albuera. Happily this proved unnecessary, for by the morning of 5 April the remorseless pounding of 38 guns against the two bastions had enabled the engineers to inform Wellington that the breaches would be sufficiently large by sunset to justify an assault. This was therefore ordered to take place that night.

A memorandum of instructions, containing 27 paragraphs, had been prepared by Wellington for a three-pronged attack against the castle and the two bastions. The main points of this memorandum were that one brigade of 3 Division would cross the Rivillas and assault the castle by escalade; 4 Division was to storm the breaches of La Trinidad, and the Light Division those of Santa Maria; these two divisions would advance west of the Rivillas with the 4th nearest the stream. The Light Division was to put 100 men into the quarries near the Santa Maria covered way to keep down enemy fire from that bastion, and both divisions were to leave 1,000 men in reserve in these quarries. Each was to have advance storming parties of 500 men with a forlorn hope furnished with 12 ladders, axes, and bags of hay for entering the ditches; an element of these 500 advance troops was to act as a firing party spread along the crest of the glacis for the same purpose as the 100 men in the quarries. Major Wilson of the 48th, with the trench guards, was to storm San Roque and General Power's Portuguese brigade was to make a feint at the bridgehead. 5 Division (which had been recalled that day) was to send two brigades to occupy ground vacated by pickets of the Light Division and 48th Regiment, and leave one brigade at the Cerro del Viento.

Wellington's memorandum is reproduced in full in Colonel (as he then was) Jones's journals, and it raises some interesting points. It was written for the attack on 5 April which did not take place, and that accounts for the reserve role of 5 Division and the minor attack on the castle, for the commanders of 3 and 5 Divisions had not yet sought permission for their divisions to play a more active part. But it seems to show quite clearly that at this time (and therefore presumably earlier when the plan was first formed) there was no intention of making a third breach.

However, when Colonel Fletcher (just recovered from his wounds) made a closer inspection of the two breaches, he became convinced that the French had made such strong retrenchments behind them that a third was necessary. This, he reckoned, could be made quickly in the weaker curtain wall between the bastions. Wellington therefore agreed to postpone the assault by 24 hours, and eight 24-pounders and six 18-pounders got to work with such effect that (according to Jones, although some accounts say earlier) a third breach had been opened by 4 pm on 6 April.

In the memorandum, the attack was timed to begin at 10 pm, but there is some evidence that 7.30 pm was the intention for 6 April, which, for some reason, was later found to be too early. Be that as it may, the final orders were for 10 pm, but the guns remained silent, certainly after 7.30 pm, some say earlier. Why this was so is not known, but it allowed Phillipon some precious hours for improving his defences, and he made good use of them. The ruined parapets were hastily rebuilt, much of the debris that had fallen into the ditch from the day's bombardment was cleared, and the mines and shells buried in the ditch could be safely fused. The ditch had now become extremely deep and hazardous, for Wellington had chosen to ignore one of the principal rules of siegecraft, that before an assault, the counterscarp should be blown into the ditch.

Apart from the possible time change for the assault, the only alteration to the original instructions concerned 3 and 5 Divisions. At General Picton's request, and after being given more information about the castle, Wellington allowed the whole of 3 Division to take part in the escalade. Similarly, at General Leith's importuning, one brigade of 5 Division was to assault the San Vicente bastion, and the Portuguese brigade of that Division was to demonstrate against Pardeleras.

Around 8 pm the battalions were mostly in their assembly areas. No guns fired, and a mist had risen from the Rivillas which muffled sounds, save the constant croaking of frogs, until (according to Grattan) some regimental bands played selections of music. If this was so, it would undoubtedly have eased the tension, for the men were well aware that for many this would

MAP 8.2

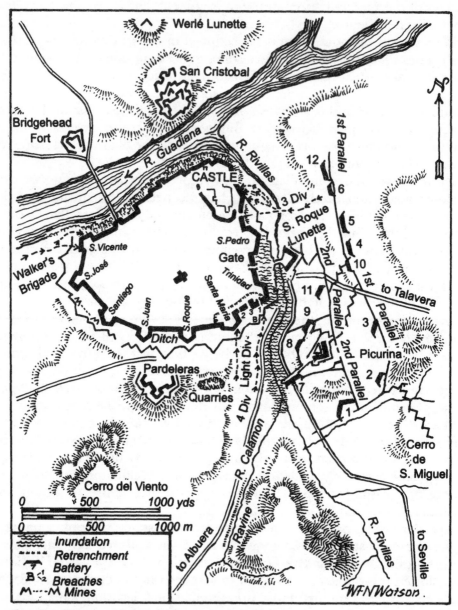

The Third Siege of Badajoz March–April 1812

be their last night on earth. At about 9.30 pm, arms were unpiled and formations prepared to move off.

In the event, the attacks were not simultaneous. The troops destined to assault San Roque opened fire 15 minutes in advance of time, and this caused a fireball to be blazed from the castle which illuminated the men from 3 Division as they were crossing the Rivillas by the broken bridge, and they had no alternative but to go forward at once. On the other hand, the officer in charge of the ladder party for 5 Division's assault lost his way from San Miguel, and that attack was more than an hour late in starting. Only the main assault went in more or less on time.

San Roque lunette was easily disposed of. The defenders were engaged frontally by intensive fire, while the escalading party attacked from the rear. Lieutenant Knowles of the 7th Fusiliers, who, at the head of a small band of men from his regiment, formed the forlorn hope, describes the short sharp action in a letter to his father. The surrounding wall was 24 feet high, but his party got a ladder up despite 'being exposed to the hottest fire I was ever under.' Knowles was the third man up the ladder, but on reaching the top was 'knocked over by a shower of grape', however the only casualty was his sword. The garrison of 150 put up little fight; 60 were soon captured, and the rest bolted for the town.

The main assault was a truly terrible business. The 4th and Light Divisions, under General Colville and Colonel Barnard respectively, advanced in parallel columns. Their uniforms were ragged, their appearances unkempt, but their muskets and rifles were bright, and high and proud was their bearing. Disaster struck early, and was never far removed. The leading files of 4 Division met the ditch where the French had dug the *cunette*; not waiting for the ladders, nor realising the depth of water, many men leapt down, and 100 Fusiliers and Portuguese were drowned. The men behind instinctively swung to their left, and this brought the storming parties of both divisions into close confusion. Somewhere around 1,000 men were now in the ditch when the French fired their fougasses, explosive shells and powder barrels. The spectacle was tragic. Hundreds of men lay dead (including all the engineers who were guides to the breaches), others staggered about mutilated and bleeding from ghastly wounds. The whole scene was lit by lurid bursts of flame from burning debris in the ditch, leaving those who still stood illuminated targets for French muskets.

But nothing daunted, the main bodies of the two divisions were soon jumping on to what hay bags there were, or descending by the few ladders left, to forge their way through the inferno and reach the foot of the breaches. In the general chaos, some men mistook an unfinished ravelin for the foot of the breach, and this caused further confusion. The covering party on the glacis had been shot away from their exposed position, leaving French soldiers free to hurl everything they had against men striving to storm the breaches. Those few that overcame every form of obstacle – crowsfeet, nailed planks, fascines – and reached the top, were confronted with a quite impenetrable *chevaux-de-frise* of sword blades firmly set in thick beams, and here swift destruction engulfed them.

For two hours this dreadful bloodletting went on, for the troops refused to give up, and perhaps as many as 40 assaults were made. It so happened that in the general mêlée most attempts were made against La Trinidad breach, only a few by the Light Division against Santa Maria, and almost none on the curtain wall, where the breach was less strongly defended, and there was no retrenchment.

Around midnight Wellington, who had positioned himself near the quarries and had been receiving reports, each more distressing than the one before, called the attack off. The casualties had been crippling. But Wellington would not be denied. A message was sent to Picton to redouble his efforts against the castle, and the weary, bloodstained and battered men of the 4th and Light Divisions were ordered to reform preparatory to storming the breaches again. At which news even the bravest were seen to blanch.

However, by the time Picton received Wellington's message his 3 Division had just completed the capture of the castle, although Picton himself may not have entered it until the morning for, as the columns splashed their way across the Rivillas to the roar of cannon, mingled with the sharp crack of musketry, he received a spent bullet in the groin which put him temporarily out of action. Command devolved on Brigadier Kempt until he was wounded, by which time Picton had partly recovered, although probably not sufficiently to climb a ladder.

Many fell crossing the stream, but once over that obstacle, the palisade was soon broken, and the storming party quickly reached the walls. The garrison was no more than 300 men (mostly Hessians), but they were well provided with every sort of weapon. Pikes, rocks. logs, shells and fireballs were thrown down at the climbers, while a destructive enfilading fire from the flanking bastions cut them and their ladders to pieces. The first escalade was attempted between the bastions of San Antonio and San Pedro, where the cross-fire was far too punishing for any success to be achieved. Both Kempt's brigade and Champlemond's Portuguese had fallen back baffled after trying for three quarters of an hour to scale the walls. But better fortune attended the efforts of Campbell's brigade, for his attack was made farther to the right where the wall had been breached in the earlier siege. The breach had, of course, been repaired, but the wall here was slightly lower, and not so well covered. Moreover the long, heavy ladders were eventually erected in several places, and the small garrison could not be everywhere at once.

Colonel Ridge of the 5th Fusiliers, and Ensign Canch, commanding the battalion's grenadiers, were among the very first to gain a footing. They had found an empty embrasure below the top of the wall and, once in it, they gallantly held the place with a few men while the ladders were brought up. As soon as the Colonel had collected about 20 men, he made for the ramparts and encountered small resistance, for the French appeared surprised that the castle had been entered so quickly. Only in the keep was there a spirited defence. Soon after 11 pm, most of 3 Division were over the walls.

Grattan says there was much butchery and that only a few prisoners were taken. Some men may have got away, but this would not have been easy because the French had barred up all the gates except one small postern. For this reason, the division found it difficult to leave the castle to join the main battle. However, at one gate – or possibly at the postern – a brief engagement took place when Phillipon, anxious for his stores and ammunition, sent a reserve battalion to regain the castle. These men had to advance on a very narrow front, and were quickly driven off by Ridge at the head of his Fusiliers, but sadly, the Colonel was killed in the fight. Of him Napier was to write, '. . . . no man died that night with more glory – yet many died, and there was much glory'. But the carnage at the castle was considerably less than it was at the breaches. Out of 4,000 men who assaulted, there were 500 British and 200 Portuguese casualties.

While Picton's men were vainly trying to leave the castle around midnight, in order to help the main attack, the closing phase of this memorable siege was being fiercely fought at the far end of the town's defences. Owing to the delay with the ladders, it was after 11 pm before the Portuguese brigade of 5 Division could begin their feint against Pardeleras, and General Walker's brigade the assault of San Vicente bastion.

As Walker's men reached the glacis, they were seen by the garrison and subjected to heavy artillery fire. However, they rushed the palisade and reached the ditch without much damage, but the drop was 12 feet and the French had dug a *cunette* that was five feet six inches deep, and six feet six inches broad. This obstacle, although obviously formidable, does not appear to have taken the same disastrous toll as the one encountered by men of 4 Division, but the wall immediately ahead was sheer for 31 feet. The bastion was not strongly held, for men had been withdrawn from the riverside defences to aid those at the breaches, but there were quite enough defenders left to cause serious trouble to the besiegers as they floundered about in the ditch, trying to raise ladders that were anyway too short.

The escalade seemed doomed, until some soldiers discovered that on the north side of the bastion the ascent appeared perfectly possible. Here the perpendicular face stretched only for 20 feet, and above it was an easier gradient left in a rough state where it had once been intended to build a tower. And so, while a strong party was left to engage the attention of the besieged from the front, ladders were placed round the north end and men of the three regiments (4th, 30th and 44th Foot) stormed up them and over the wall.

Taken in flank, the small garrison broke, hotly pursued by Walker at the head of the first 200 troops he could collect. The men in San José were quickly swept away, but sterner resistance was met from two battalions at Santiago. Here an unlucky incident started a quite unnecessary panic. A lighted port-fire, dropped by some gunner, was mistaken for a mine fuse, and with men whose every nerve is stretched by the confusion and inevitable chaos of close-quarter night action doubts and fears come speedily to the brain. The cry of 'Mine' was sufficient to send these hitherto undaunted soldiers back the way they had come in an undignified scramble, closely pursued by cheering Frenchmen. This unfortunate affair was made worse by the fact that Walker had fallen gravely injured in the action.

Fortunately General Leith had sent a reserve battalion, the 2/38th, into San Vicente. Although no more than 230 strong, these men very quickly restored the situation, and two brigades of the division then advanced along the ramparts. At some point, a detachment broke off and entered the town. Proceeding through the silent streets – for every house was barred and shuttered, the inhabitants awaiting, as they hoped, a peaceful relief from the French – they came upon the rear of those men still holding the breaches. With the bugles sounding the advance from the ramparts, the town and the castle, the garrison lost hope. Although there was desultory fighting in pockets throughout the town, organized resistance was over. The Light and 4th Divisions, on being ordered to advance once more, were relieved to find the breaches almost deserted, although even then the obstacles placed in them were overcome only with the greatest difficulty.

Most of the garrison were made prisoner but General Phillipon, who had led a most skilful and resolute defence, and was himself wounded, crossed the bridge and entered San Cristobal with a handful of officers and about 100 men. Napier gave the time as 1 am (Grattan says 2.30, but he had been wounded and evacuated early on), and with the departure of the Governor the town could be officially considered captured. Early the next morning, after a feeble attempt to gain terms, Phillipon surrendered unconditionally to Lord Fitzroy Somerset, but he had previously sent some cavalry, that had crossed the bridge with him, to tell Soult that Badajoz had fallen.

The taking of the town had cost the British and Portuguese soldiers very dear. In the 21 days of the siege, there were 4,824 casualties, three quarters of them British. Of these, 72 officers and 963 men were killed. The losses in the actual assault were 59 officers and 744 men killed, and 258 officers and 2,600 men wounded. The 43rd and 52nd suffered the worst with 347 and 323 casualties respectively, but the 95th Rifles was not far behind with 258 (Harry Smith of that regiment wrote later, 'There is no battle, day or night I would not willingly react except this'). But in percentages, the 4th Foot of 5 Division were hardest hit losing 230 men out of 530 all ranks. Included in this mournful roll call were six general officers wounded, and four battalion commanders killed. To be put against these appallingly high figures is a loss to the garrison in the assault of only a little over 100 and, in the sortie of 19 March, of 317 all ranks.

Could Badajoz have been taken earlier, and at far less expense? Certainly, in the first two sieges, Wellington's usual meticulous forethought and breadth of view seemed to be lacking, and in the third it is possible to point the finger at one or two apparent errors. Would the attack have been more successful against some other part of the defences? Major Burgoyne had always maintained (and as acting Chief Engineer had presumably communicated his thoughts to Wellington) that the castle was the weakest point, and that by opening a parallel opposite that place, the town could be taken in less than ten days – a point of view shared by the French, who regarded the castle as the key to the town.

In any case, having committed himself to assaulting the two bastions, and with the certain knowledge that the breaches had been retrenched, could not Wellington have blasted these retrenchments prior to the attack? Why did the guns remain silent that evening, allowing the French to work in the ditch? And why was the counterscarp not blown in? These are all questions it may seem impertinent to address to the shade of the Great Duke, and there are some answers. There were no mortars for counter-retrenchment (but there were howitzers); there were no trained sappers; and time was vital. These answer some of the questions, but the fact remains the town was taken in the end not by the planned assault (although that played a very major part in drawing men off), but by two diversionary attacks that were somewhat reluctantly wrung from Wellington by two importunate generals.

One must draw a curtain across the horrors of the sack of Badajoz. It was one of the most disgraceful in the history of the British Army, if for no other reason than that it was perpetrated against a town owned and occupied by an ally. But there were other reasons for shame, even allowing for the licence normally granted the conquerors when a garrison has not surrendered. However, at least some good came out of these two days of hell and horror for one British officer and, vicariously, for Britain.

Through the shambles of broken wine casks, and lecherous louts with liquor dribbling from mud-caked mouths, two terrified Spanish girls of high birth threaded their way. With ears bleeding from having the rings brutally torn from them, they sought protection of the first two officers they found. One of those officers was Captain Harry Smith of the 95th, who two days later married the younger of the girls, the beautiful Juana Maria de los Dolores de Leon, who accompanied him throughout the Peninsular campaign, sharing and enduring all the hardships of war. Harry Smith was to achieve greatness, and in the accomplishment of this greatness the talented and devoted Juana played an important part. Many years later, when her husband was Governor of the Cape, she herself achieved eponymous fame in giving her name – Ladysmith – to a South African town, the siege of which is later described in this book.

The taking of Badajoz opened the way into Spain but, perhaps more importantly, it was as a result of this siege, and that of Ciudad Rodrigo, that a properly trained corps of sappers and miners became a part of the military establishment. Wellington had always recognised the courage and energy of the volunteer engineers from the Line, but was equally aware that they lacked the necessary skill and training. In a letter to Lord Liverpool (then Secretary for War) he says, 'These great losses [at Badajoz] could be avoided, and, in my opinion, time gained in every siege, if we had properly trained people to carry it on'. He further declared that at Badajoz, 'the fortress must have surrendered, if I had been able to "approach" the place'. In other words had had men skilled at sapping forward to the counterscarp. Wellington ended this letter, 'I earnestly request your lordship to have a corps of sappers and miners formed without loss of time'. This request was complied with and, by 1813, trained companies of the new Corps of Royal Sappers and Miners had joined the Peninsular Army.*

*This was not, however, the origins of the Corps of Royal Engineers, which was formed in the 18th Century.

CHAPTER 9

Lucknow
May–November 1857

LUCKNOW, probably the greatest siege of the Indian Mutiny, will always hold a special place in the annals of the British in India. The name conjures up a popular conception of a glamorous relief with Sir Colin Campbell at the head of his Highlanders, the pipes skirling 'The Campbells are Coming' and the mutineers being driven from the field at the point of the bayonet. In truth, the story was very different, as this chapter will show. It is a story to which the courage and endurance of almost every man, woman and child in the hard-pressed garrison contributed in no small measure. When relief came, after some intense and very bloody close-quarter fighting, Campbell had no option but to impose upon the shattered garrison a brilliantly planned and executed withdrawal and a long march, for the mutineers were by no means dispersed but remained in the ruined city in their thousands. The whole story of the Mutiny is a tragedy which should never have occurred. It says much for the Indian Army, which would replace the Army of the East India Company once the Mutiny was over, that the fearful suffering and bloodshed and the bonds of comradeship in battle which the Mutiny produced, should have become woven into the high tradition of service to the British Crown which would be so glorious a feature of that army through countless minor campaigns and the carnage of two world wars.

* * *

The Indian Mutiny, which erupted at Meerut on 10 May 1857, and which was not officially declared over until 8 July 1858, was notorious for the appalling cruelty practised by both sides. Virtually no prisoners were taken by the mutineers; wounded troops, women and children who fell into their hands were butchered, and British soldiers were determined that sepoy blood should flow in expiation of their crimes. Prisoners were usually summarily executed by bullet, rope or at the muzzle of a gun. But the savagery of a barbarous war was relieved by numerous acts of heroism, self-sacrifice, devotion to duty and, among many of the sepoys and native

139

servants, heart-warming instances of loyalty to the Company*, and to their masters.

This is not the place to detail the causes of the Mutiny. History moves upon the pivot of intrigues and passions, and at this time India had its full share of these. But the spark which put flame to smouldering embers was the introduction of the new Enfield rifle with its grease-topped cartridge that had to be torn open by the teeth. Agitators were not slow to assert that the grease was cow and pig fat, and that the British were attempting to break the caste system, and convert Hindu and Moslem to Christianity. This was untrue, and belatedly the cartridges were ordered to be issued ungreased, but the damage had been done. Another cause for unrest was the policy of annexing some Indian states carried out by the last Governor General, Lord Dalhousie. Particularly was this so in the kingdom of Oudh, of which Lucknow was the capital, and which had been annexed as recently as February 1856. The Bengal Army, which was the army most affected by the Mutiny, drew two-thirds of its recruits from Oudh.

The Mutiny flared first in Meerut, from where, having killed their British officers and massacred most of the women and children, the mutineers made their way to Delhi which they soon took. There they proclaimed the restitution of the Mughal dynasty in the person of Bahadur Shah II, a direct descendant of the great Mughal emperors, but now a pensioner of the British. Soon Cawnpore, weakly garrisoned, came under attack, and the treacherous Dandu Pant (better known as Nana Sahib) having wiped out the garrison, perpetrated an horrendous massacre of the women and children. Oudh lies immediately east of Cawnpore across the Ganges, and ever since annexation there had been considerable unrest in the province.

In March 1857 Sir Henry Lawrence was appointed Chief Commissioner of Oudh. He was a brilliant administrator, and a great servant of the Company and of India. Although only 51, Lawrence was not robust, but much knowledge, deep thought, courage and a will to work were embedded in his nature.

A contributory factor to the initial horrors of the Mutiny was that many senior British officers and Civil Servants were unwilling to believe that their native regiments or subjects would rebel. Therefore regiments whose loyalty was clearly doubtful were not always disarmed, nor towns put into a proper state of defence. Lawrence was not totally innocent of this misplaced confidence, but for some time he had had misgivings about the state of the native army, and while he would not immediately disarm regiments whose loyalty was doubtful, he took a number of safety measures. He moved the

---

*At the time of the Mutiny the East India Company ruled India as agent of the British Government, who through the President of the Board of Control held a watching brief on the Company's Board of Directors. On 1 November 1858 the East India Company was abolished, and India was ruled directly by the British Government.

European families into the Residency buildings in Lucknow, he collected large stocks of food and ammunition, and, in the time available, he did what he could to fortify the Residency area. But he took care to emphasise that these were only precautionary measures.

There was much for Lawrence to do, and little time in which to do it. His predecessor, Coverly Jackson, had been a thoroughly tactless man, who had upset not only the natives, but also his own staff. Lawrence did what he could to mend fences, but both the Revenue Commissioner, Mr Gubbins, and the Judicial Commissioner Mr Ommanney (especially the former), were very difficult. The discontent in Oudh, fermented by Jackson, was exacerbated when at the first signs of mutiny men of disbanded regiments came into the province. As early as April, the 48th Native Infantry in the Mariaon cantonments had shown incipient signs of mutiny, and this was followed by trouble over the cartridges with the 7th Oudh Irregular Infantry. Lawrence became increasingly concerned with the distances that separated his slender forces.

Apart from a detachment of 50 men of the 84th Regiment, which General Wheeler had generously sent him a few days before he himself was attacked in Cawnpore, Lawrence's only European regiment was the 32nd, of some 700 men. Their barracks were a mile and a half to the east of the Residency. The main garrison in the Mariaon cantonments was four miles north of the river, and comprised three Native Infantry (NI) regiments, the 13th, 48th and 71st, together with a European Light Horse Battery, and two Oudh Irregular Horse Batteries. The 7th Native Light Cavalry was even farther away towards Mudkipur, and although the Military Police and two regiments (4th and 7th) of the Oudh Irregular Infantry were stationed south of the river they were two miles upstream of the Residency compound.

As soon as Lawrence received news of the mutiny at Meerut, he hastened his defence measures. His plan was to hold the Residency position, the cantonments and the Machchi Bhawan. The latter was an old fort that stood on an eminence about half a mile to the north-west of the Residency. It had fallen into disrepair, but its commanding position made it the key to any defence plan. Between 17 and 23 May a large labour force was employed to bring this fort to a high standard of readiness and in it, protected by a strong garrison, were some European families. Nothing much was done to strengthen the cantonments, but centring on the Residency a defensive area was traced, roughly in the shape of a diamond, and with a perimeter of one and a quarter miles covering about 35 acres. The boundary of this trace was put into a state of defence, as labour became available, by blocking the streets, barricading and loopholing the buildings, and erecting earthworks where gaps occurred. Fortunately Oudh remained calm during the period of this work, but even so there was not time to prepare properly the various selected strongpoints, nor to clear all the houses necessary to give the defending troops a reasonable field of fire. In consequence, when the fighting began, the opposing forces were often within only a few feet of each other.

Lawrence took other wise precautions, such as separating the Sikhs* from the sepoys, calling up pensioners of whose loyalty he felt assured, and sending out cavalry patrols to show the flag in outlying districts. But he continued to remain optimistic (in spite of warnings) that the prevailing calm conditions would continue. It came, therefore, as a considerable shock to him when at 9 pm on the evening of 30 May, while he was dining in his house at Mariaon, the native cantonments erupted. The officers' mess and bungalows were set afire, and one or two officers were killed, including Brigadier Handscombe, commanding the Oudh Brigade, but the rest of the night passed quietly. The 13th NI and most of the 71st remained loyal and joined the 32nd in the British camp. The next morning those troops, with artillery, attacked the mutineers who quickly broke, but as the 7th Native Cavalry had mutineers in their ranks, no pursuit was possible. Native troops in the city and its immediate environs remained calm, but for Lucknow 30 May was the beginning of the Mutiny.

There was to be a further month before the city was invested, which gave Lawrence much needed time to improve the defences. Individual owners fortified their houses, some of which (Gubbins's for one) achieved almost fortress standard. Voltunteers were called for, and came from many nationalities and every walk of life, but for most the musket was a mystery. Lawrence, with the help of Major Anderson his Chief Engineer, spent long hours in the saddle touring the defences, advising and encouraging the labour force. But his health was in decline, and he took the precaution in a letter to Lord Canning, the Governor-General, to recommend, in the event of anything happening to him, that Major Banks should be in charge of civil affairs, while Colonel Inglis should command the troops.

The news was usually depressing. Mutineers were reported from outlying Oudh stations and Lawrence, whose optimism was waning, wrote 'Every outpost (I fear) has fallen, and we daily expect to be besieged . . .'. The weather was sizzling hot, with a dangerous sun and men, seen through wavering heat bars, toiled at the defences, hauled cannon and dug trenches. Soon the rains would come, but the heat would continue. In the Residency the atmosphere remained tense, but confidence abounded in Lawrence. It was a time of divided loyalties when none could be certain between friend and foe. On 12 June, the military police, at least, declared their true colours when almost 1,000 of them departed from the city with their arms. Mutineers were drifting into Oudh to swell the indigenous bands, and some *talukdars* (the landowning class), hitherto moderately content, were now said to be siding with the mutineers. At the end of the month,

*The Sikhs formed part of the Oudh irregular forces.

came reports of trouble nearer home. A formidable force of mutineers were concentrating at Nawabganj 25 miles north-east of Lucknow.

The mutiny of 30 May, and the subsequent flight of other mutineers, had very considerably diminished Lawrence's native troops. Of the three regiments in the cantonments, there were left 200 men of the 13th NI, 57 of the 48th and 120 of the 71st. Sixty of the 7th Light Cavalry remained loyal. Many of the Oudh irregulars had gone, and in all there were about 700 loyal native troops. These, together with the Queen's 32nd Foot, a number of artillery details, the volunteers, and British officers from the mutinied regiments, had to protect the Residency compound with its huge number of non-combatants, and almost 600 women and children.

On 28 June, after information had been received of the enemy concentration at Nawabganj, Lawrence brought the troops from the cantonments into Lucknow, and on the 30th he decided to march against the mutineers. He had previously applied for, and been granted, command of all the troops in Oudh with the rank of Brigadier General. His previous military experience was confined to a brief spell in the artillery in early years, and it was a pity he did not leave the leadership of this ill-fated expedition to Colonel Inglis, his second-in-command, for besides his lack of experience, Lawrence was a very tired man.

However, he now placed himself at the head of 520 foot (of whom 300 were from the 32nd), 116 horse (36 European volunteers and 80 Sikhs), and 11 guns, and marched up the Chinhat road as far as the bridge over the Kukrail. The intended dawn start had been delayed until the sun was well up, for some of the troops had been drinking the previous night and were late on parade, and there was an administrative muddle resulting in no breakfast, which meant that the troops marched on empty stomachs. On reaching the bridge, no enemy was sighted, and Lawrence gave the order to withdraw. However, at this juncture a patrol reported a small force at Chinhat, and after some hesitation, and a little pressure from the senior officers, Lawrence countermanded the withdrawal. Rations had been brought, but the opportunity to distribute them was not taken, and by now most of the water-carriers had deserted. The troops therefore were in bad shape, and the native artillerymen were showing distinct signs of unrest.

The advance was resumed, and round a bend in the road a force – not small as reported, but later estimated as being about 5,000 foot and 800 horse – was drawn up in a strong position. It must be remembered that in many instances whole regiments mutinied *en masse*, taking with them their arms, equipment, ammunition and even the colours. The mutineers were brave and well trained, but very seldom well led, and for this reason throughout the Mutiny the British had the edge. As it happened, this force had two competent leaders in Burket Ahmed and Khan Ali Khan, but with such preponderance of numbers leadership was of no great account.

Lawrence's force was soon in danger of being encompassed, and his only hope was in a speedy but orderly withdrawal. His behaviour throughout was magnificent, and the stand made at the bridge – thus enabling the troops to cross the river – was largely due to his inspiring and fearless leadership, supplemented by a gallant cavalry charge against the enemy guns. But after the bridge the orderly withdrawal became a retreat, and the retreat a rout, although the native infantry fought a most courageous rearguard action, thereby stopping the enemy horse doing more damage. As the stragglers gained the safety of Lucknow, the price of this expedition was seen to have been a heavy one. Nearly 300 men had fallen, with a further 78 wounded, and six guns (including a much valued 8-inch howitzer) had been captured. The 32nd alone lost their commanding officer, Lieutenant Colonel Case*, three other officers and 111 men.

These severe battle casualties were not the only serious consequences of Chinhat. Lawrence's principal object in advancing to engage the mutineers was to drive them back from Lucknow, so as to give more time for work on the incomplete defences before the city was invested. In the event, Chinhat precipitated investment, which by sunset on 30 June was almost total. Moreover, once the mutineers reached the city, the two regiments of Oudh local forces quartered in the vicinity, as might be expected, deserted. The squalor in the old city was hardly affected by the influx of many thousands of sepoys, but in the beautiful north-eastern quarter, with its hitherto pleasant and comparatively uncluttered atmosphere, all was chaos. Trees were being felled, gardens wrecked, houses cleared, and among the majestic palaces and stately mosques, with their delicate minarets, loose horses careered, bullocks trampled and soldiers looted. Fortunately, the mutineers contented themselves with heavy, but random, firing, for had they made a determined attack it would have been difficult to prevent a breakthrough.

But some semblance of order was soon restored within the defended area, which Lawrence now saw had to be restricted. There were insufficient troops to hold that dominating, but comparatively isolated, fortress the Machchi Bhawan. Accordingly on 1 July Colonel Palmer, who had recently commanded the mutinous 48th NI, was ordered to evacuate the building, and convey the women and children, the sick and political prisoners to the Residency. He was to take what guns he could and the remainder, together with the magazine, were to be blown up. Palmer began his withdrawal at midnight on 1/2 July. The fact that most of the mutineers were busily engaged looting enabled a very well planned operation to be executed without what might have been a disaster. As the last man reached the Residency, the Machchi Bhawan went up with a thunderous roar throwing

*At the bridge, before deciding to continue the advance, Lawrence is said to have asked Case whether his men were fit to go on, and Case replied 'no'. But Inglis, who had previously commanded the 32nd, overruled him.

valuable stores, and a drunken Irish soldier, high into the air. The stores perished, but the Irishman continued his disturbed sleep where he fell, and the next day arrived at the Residency with two bullocks he had found on the way.

The first siege of Lucknow, which was to last until 25 September (88 days), had now begun. A brief description of the area Lawrence decided to defend makes the subsequent fighting clearer. The only piece of open ground on which the enemy could form up for a major attack lay to the north of the perimeter, where the ground sloped down to the river from the plateau on which the Residency stood. Here the natural bank had been scarped, and a ditch dug in which obstacles were strewn. A parapet topped with sandbags crowned the bank. The commanding feature was the so-called Redan battery, which projected from the curtain wall enabling its three guns to bring enfilade fire. Immediately in front of the defended area ran the Cawnpore road through a built-up street known as the Captan Bazar which it was planned to hold, but after Chinat there were insufficient troops, and there had been no time to demolish it.

Moving to the east, the main defence was the strong Residency wall, and its principal entrance the substantial Baillie Guard Gate, but along the Cawnpore road were houses which the mutineers loopholed, although any attack from this area had to be made in column through narrow alleys. At the south-eastern corner was Anderson's well defended house, and the important Cawnpore battery. On the south front the Martinière (a school), the Brigade Mess and Sikh Square had been made strongpoints, but just outside the perimeter stood the dominant Johannes House. Like the Captan Bazar there had not been time to fortify or destroy this building, an omission which was to prove costly. On the western flank, the ground was open for 150 yards and, being in musket shot, was not used by the sepoy artillery. Two strongly fortified posts on this side were Gubbins's house and the Slaughter-house. Beyond the church, to the north-west was Innes's post and battery, which projected from the line of entrenchment.

To man these defences, Lawrence had 1,720 combatants, 712 of whom were native troops. English soldiers manned the Redan and Cawnpore batteries, and the 50 men of the 84th were a reserve in the Residency. The loyal sepoys of the 48th and 71st NI held the Hospital post, which was the banqueting hall of the Residency; men of the 13th NI were posted at the Baillie Guard Gate, and Sikh cavalry were in Sikh Square, all the other posts were held by mixed European and native troops. The principal weakness of the defence was that although there were more guns than could be manned (many of the ex-King's having been found) except on the northern front, and before the Baillie Guard Gate, there was no opportunity for flanking fire.

Of the individual posts undoubtedly the most vulnerable were at the angle of the eastern and southern fronts (by the Cawnpore battery), and at the

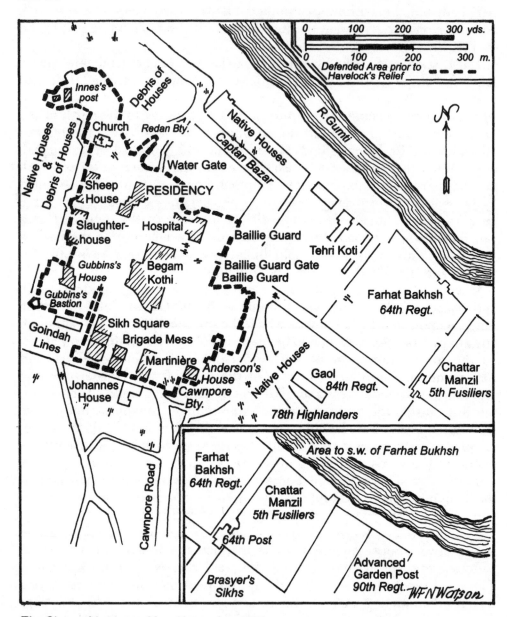

The Siege of Lucknow May–November 1857

south and west angle between Gubbins's bastion and Sikh Square. Each of
the posts had a commandant, who had virtually an independent command,
for central control was impossible. The 133 British officers were mostly
armed with rifles, which proved invaluable, for the inaccuracy of Brown

Bess* made the penetration of enemy loopholes a very chancy affair. Thanks to Lawrence's foresight there was, in the early days, no shortage of fresh meat and most other supplies. Water was plentiful from wells, but hospital facilities were to prove inadequate.

At the beginning, the number of hostile mutineers was probably about 6,000 but they soon increased to over 10,000. They had a number of useful guns, but eventually became short of shot and shell. They then had to hope that unexploded British shells would prove more obliging on the return journey, and those cannonballs that could be retrieved were returned to their owners. The *Talukdars* retained low caste tribesmen who fought mainly with bow and arrow, but they were skilled miners, and were constantly employed in this work. But the principal reason why this vast mass of manpower failed in their objective was through lack of leadership and discipline. Among the leaders there was complete disagreement as to who should be chief, and even when a new Nawab had been elected leadership was divided, and the sepoys continued in disobedience.

The city of Lucknow in 1857 covered twelve square miles, and was bounded on the north by the river Gumti, and on the east and south by a canal which the Cawnpore road, approaching from the south-west past the Alam Bagh, crossed at the Char Bagh. The mutineers occupied all of the city outside the entrenchments, as well as the many beautiful palaces and gardens in the north-east residential quarter. Chief among these were the Kaiserbagh, the older Chattar Manzil palace, the Sikandarbagh, the small Moti Mahal – or pearl palace – and across the canal the Dilkusha Park.

On 2 July, the garrison suffered a tragic loss. Enemy guns commanded the upper storey of the Residency, and Colonel Palmer's daughter, heedless of warnings, had already had her leg taken off by a cannonball in one of the upper rooms. On the same day (1 July), a shell from the captured 8-inch howitzer exploded in the room where Lawrence and his secretary were working. On that occasion, miraculously, neither occupant was hurt, but although Lawrence had reluctantly agreed to change his quarters, he had not done so when at 8 am the next day a second shell found its way to the same room. This time Lawrence was mortally wounded, and two days later was dead. In accordance with his instructions, Major Banks and Colonel Inglis took over the civilian and military duties respectively, until less than three weeks later Banks was killed by a sniper's bullet, and the whole command devolved on Inglis – now an acting Brigadier-General.

The horrors and hardships of this siege have been well documented. From the families' viewpoint the wife of the officer commanding, and the widow of the commander of the 32nd Foot, among others, kept daily diaries, and Captain Wilson, chief of staff to Inglis, recorded the military

*Brown Bess. The standard musket in use by the British Army for much of the 18th and 19th centuries.

events of the first siege. By the end of June, the rains had started, but the heat was still intense, humid and oppressive. It is not difficult to imagine the sufferings of the families in conditions that were totally unfamiliar.

The women and children were distributed throughout the various posts, so far as possible in the interior ones, and only in the more fully protected out-posts. The post commander kept them strictly to the ground floors and *taikhanas* (basements), where they were comparatively safe from gunfire. Practically every servant had left, and native labour was needed on the defences and with the commissariat. The women, therefore, found themselves in the novel position of having no cooks, *dhobis*, nor *ayahs*.* Most of them quickly learnt to compete with conditions, but at no time was it easy, and for all of the time extremely unpleasant and dangerous.

As the siege progressed everything became short. Inevitably food had to be strictly rationed with the fighting men getting the greater share; firewood was important, but very scarce, and the commodity most seriously missed was milk for the children. Throughout the siege babies were born, and many died because their mothers' milk dried up through strain, illness, malnutrition or fear. Those families quartered in houses whose owners had made careful provision were lucky. The occupants of Gubbins's house, for instance, dined and wined in considerable luxury for much of the time – to the envy of many, for Gubbins was not popular.

The squalor became appalling. Great care was taken to drive out wounded animals before they died, but even so there were horses and bullocks killed whose carcasses quickly became putrid. Whenever possible these were taken outside the perimeter for burial, but the risk was great. Everywhere there were clouds of flies, the windows had to be barricaded, there was no one to work the *punkas*,* and in the fetid air, and stench from no drainage, disease became rampant. Cholera was the greatest killer, but smallpox and dysentery also took their toll. Many of the women, who had no children to care for, worked in the hospital. During the first week of the siege, before people learnt to keep their heads down, there were between 15 and 20 deaths a day, mostly from bullets, and many more were wounded. Thereafter, throughout the first siege, no day passed without at least one death – save one day in August. In the hospital, conditions were dreadful despite all that was done by the devoted doctors, women, and boys from the school.

For the soldiers, the greatest deprivation was lack of tobacco. Tea-leaves did duty instead, and when tea ran out green leaves were used. Huge prices were paid for every type of luxury, and for essential items such as clothing. With sentry and other duties so heavy, there was often little sleep for officers

---

Dhobi = Laundryman or woman. *Ayah* = Children's nurse.
†*punka* = fan.

or men, and even many women lay down at night fully dressed. When the soldiers could lay their hands on any alcohol, there was some drunkenness, and a constant worry to everyone was an almost total lack of communication with the outside world. The Sikh cavalry, whose loyalty was under grave suspicion, had some contact with the city, but information received through that channel was unreliable.

Under terrible heat, short rations, constant vigil and heavy pounding, men and women could be smitten by a catalepsy which required great strength to overcome. As the besieged gradually became accustomed to the appalling conditions, the daily presence of death, the suffering and loss of loved ones, they became transmogrified. Close-knit by constant danger undreamt of, bonds were formed that sustained them through days of doubt and despair. Lucknow was a siege rich in anonymous heroes.

From 1 July until the arrival of General Havelock's force in September, which marked the end of the first siege, the fighting went on continuously. It was the high period of the monsoon, temperatures were over one hundred degrees fahrenheit day and night, and conditions for living and dying were as nasty as could be. The mutineers kept up a fairly constant gun and musket fire from various gun emplacements around the perimeter. To begin with, the gunfire was not particularly damaging, although the incendiary shells supplemented by flaming arrows caused considerable trouble. The small arms fire was more dangerous, and men, women and children learnt to live with the whistle of bullets, all too many of which found their mark. The garrison would make the occasional sortie for a specific purpose, such as the one to silence an enemy battery opposite Innes's post, which was successful, and another on 7 July to destroy Johannes House, which although occupied after some hard fighting, had to be abandoned before the mission was accomplished.

Enemy buglers could be frequently heard sounding the advance, but mostly the attacks were poorly supported, and easily repulsed. But there were to be three major assaults. Throughout the siege, the garrison kept look-out posts on prominent buildings from which early warning could be given of enemy concentrations. The first such warning came from the Residency post on 20 July, when the enemy were preparing to launch a serious offensive against the Redan battery and Innes's post. The explosion of a mine at 10 am was the signal for the attacks to begin, but the mine, exploding at the end of a 160-foot gallery, was well short of target and out of line, so that when the debris cleared the assault party found themselves confronted by the full battery, and were soon dispersed. At Innes's post, however, the attack was more sustained, and for a time the post was in danger of being cut off, but eventually well-directed grapeshot broke it up.

The explosion of the Redan mine was the first of its kind, but from then onwards mining was to play a leading part in enemy operations.

The garrison, under the skilful and daring leadership of Major Anderson and Captain Fulton, became expert at detecting the enemy tunnels, and countermining. Nevertheless, there were a number of explosions that did severe damage, and on at least one occasion a potentially dangerous breach was made in the defences. However, in general, the post-explosion assaults lacked élan and leadership.

Two days after the first major attack, Brigadier Inglis led a sortie through a hole in the wall of Gubbins's compound to drive out the enemy from the Goindah Lines immediately in front of the vulnerable south-west angle. Throughout the siege, Inglis was everywhere, encouraging, advising and occasionally reprimanding. He had a most difficult task, for so much depended on him morally and technically. He impressed himself upon all ranks by the quality of his performance.

The second and third major attacks took place on 10 August and 5 September respectively. As before, the onslaughts were timed to begin with the explosion of mines. On 10 August, there were two, directed at the Martinière and another post on the east side, but the subsequent attacks were not restricted to these posts, and went in at points along the whole line of the perimeter, except the north and north-east. Because there had been many sepoys dispatched to observe the movements of General Havelock's relieving force the assault forces were comparatively weak, and easily held. The third, and last, general attack on 5 September followed much the same pattern. The mines directed against Gubbins's house and the Brigade Mess exploded short, and a third one near the Baillie Guard Gate failed to explode. But the storming parties were much more resolute than usual, and had taken severe punishment before being forced to retire. In all these major attacks the garrison casualties were small, but the mutineers lost heavily.

Lesser attacks against various points of the perimeter were almost continuous, and carried out with great courage, but nearly always without success. The garrison, hard pressed for manpower, had to restrict their sorties, but on 21 August there was a most successful one against the troublesome Johannes House. Only five days before, the enemy had silenced the Cawnpore battery from this post, and it was time to make a determined effort. This was to be the garrison's sole mining offensive, and it was meticulously planned by Lieutenant Innes, and executed by men of the 32nd. The shaft was sunk close to the Martinière wall on 17 August, and the gallery ran for 50 feet with two branches at its end. Complete secrecy was achieved, and all was ready by dawn on the 21st, when musket fire alerted the enemy who piled into the house just seconds before the two mines were fired. The destruction was complete, and the subsequent two-pronged sortie totally successful. The Cawnpore battery could resume its defensive task.

One other important feature of the fighting, which ran parallel to mining and countermining, was battery and counterbattery manoeuvre. The enemy would shift their guns from one commanding site to another from which heavy fire would be opened in support of an assault, or in general bombardment. The garrison would bring guns to bear in an attempt – usually successful – to silence the enemy's fire. On one occasion an enemy battery opposite Gubbins's house was put out of action by the ingenuity of Lieutenant Bonham, a gunner officer, who mounted an 8-inch mortar as a howitzer. This strange weapon became known as 'the ship', and was thereafter manoeuvred to many parts of the perimeter, always proving most effective.

Nevertheless, despite excellent counterbattery work, by mid-September enemy guns and mines, helped by the effect of continuous hard rain, had made a shambles of many buildings. Much of the Residency, Anderson's house and the Brigade Mess had collapsed, and even Gubbins's stronghold began to look battered. The hospital was always full, medical supplies were short, chloroform was finished, flies were plentiful, and everywhere the stench was appalling. Diseases proliferated, accounting for many women and children. But for the garrison, the most grievous losses were their skilled engineers, Major Anderson and Captain Fulton. Anderson died of dysentery in August, and a month later Fulton was felled by a cannonball. By September, one of the Army chaplains was dead, but church services continued to be held regularly. By now there was no more room in the small graveyard.

It may seem from the above that the garrison's casualties were crippling, but, in fact, considering the amount of lead that was flung at them they were surprisingly light, and the greater number were from disease. The children suffered most with 54 of the 270 dying, mainly from lack of proper nourishment; eleven women died and three were killed. Eighty-one soldiers and four officers of the 32nd were killed during the defence, and a further 52 other ranks died from disease. Artillery officers were hard hit, losing five out of nine with three others wounded. Losses among the native troops, who had fought splendidly (although 25 Sikhs had deserted), were never known exactly, but were not heavy, although the 13th NI had quite a few men wounded more than once.

It is time to leave Brigadier Inglis and his troops, still locked in deadly combat with a force whose strength was inexhaustible, and turn to Major General Havelock's relieving army, which is a story in itself that can be told only in brief outline here. He had fought his way into Cawnpore on 17 July, and there found himself with an army reduced by battle casualties, cholera and sunstroke to 1,200 British troops, 300 native soldiers and ten guns – a force that was quite inadequate for the relief of Lucknow, although Havelock made the attempt more than once, only to be forced back to deal with threats to his rear.

It was not until 19 September, after he had won several victories with

MAP 9.2

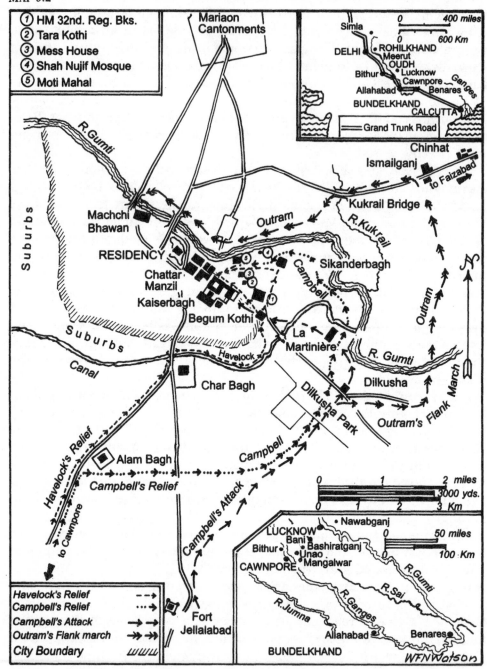

1 HM 32nd. Reg. Bks.
2 Tara Kothi
3 Mess House
4 Shah Nujif Mosque
5 Moti Mahal

Mariaon Cantonments

0   400 miles
0   600 Km

Simla

DELHI   ● ROHILKHAND
          Meerut
          OUDH
Bithur ● Lucknow
          Cawnpore
Allahabad Benares
BUNDELKHAND
          CALCUTTA
━━━ Grand Trunk Road

Chinhat
Ismailganj
Kukrail Bridge
to Faizabad

R.Gumti

Machchi Bhawan

Outram

R. Kukrail

RESIDENCY

Sikanderbagh

Chattar Manzil

Campbell

Kaiserbagh

Suburbs

Begum Kothi

La Martinière

R. Gumti

Havelock

Suburbs

Canal

Char Bagh

Dilkusha

Dilkusha Park

Outram's Flank March

Outram's Flank March

Havelock's Relief

Alam Bagh

Campbell

Campbell's Relief

Campbell's Attack

to Cawnpore

0   1   2 miles
0   3000 yds.
0   1   2   3 Km

LUCKNOW ● Nawabganj
Bani
Bithur ● Bashiratganj
          Unao
CAWNPORE Mangalwar

0   50 miles
0   100 Km

R. Gumti
R. Sai
R. Ganges
R.Jumna

Havelock's Relief   - - →
Campbell's Relief   ··· →
Campbell's Attack   ━→
Outram's Flank march   ⇉→
City Boundary   ⊔⊔⊔⊔

Fort Jellalabad

Allahabad   Benares

BUNDELKHAND

WFNWatson

Lucknow 1857: routes of the relieving and attacking forces

this small force, that Havelock received sufficient reinforcements to bring his army up to 3,179 men. Included in this number were five British regiments, the 5th Fusiliers, the 64th, 84th, 78th Highlanders and 90th

Light Infantry. But by now, Havelock had been superseded in command by General Sir James Outram. Both men were excellent soldiers. Havelock, at 62, had had the greater experience in battle, Outram, eight years younger, the greater in administration, having been Resident of Oudh at the time of annexation. Havelock had devoted himself to the deep study of his profession, for comfort he turned to religion; Outram, no less professional, was more of an extrovert and heroic figure – the author's fourth uncle (Sir Charles Napier), himself a distinguished general, dubbed Outram 'the Bayard of India'. He at once created a favourable impression with the soldiers by allowing Havelock to continue in command, and finish what he had begun. A noble gesture indeed, but sadly marred by his frequent interference which resulted in divided command.

The rains cascaded down as Havelock's men sloshed their way past the sites (Unao and Bashiratganj) of recent victories. There had been one short, sharp action at Mangalwar, but no serious opposition was met before the Alam Bagh. Here Havelock carried out a neat flanking and storming operation (Outram in the van wielding his Malacca cane) to overrun this potentially strong position. The next day (24 September) was spent at the Alam Bagh depositing stores, surplus supplies, the wounded and sick. On the 25th the advance was resumed, a garrison of 300 being left at the Alam Bagh. There was a choice of four routes to the Residency, and here was an instance when Outram overruled Havelock. He insisted that on account of the wet ground south of the canal, Havelock should take the army by the shorter route, crossing the canal at the Char Bagh, even though this would involve dangerous and difficult street fighting.

Opposition at the canal bridge, and from the Char Bagh, was strong. A battery was positioned on the far side of the bridge, supported by musketeers in loopholed buildings. Havelock's men suffered heavy casualties in assaulting the bridge, and from enemy guns firing from a covered position on his flank. But the Madras Fusiliers, charging in the second wave before the enemy gunners could reload, carried the bridge and the buildings. Five guns were captured, and the advance was continued. It is impossible to tell whether Havelock's favoured route via the Dilkusha would have been better, but certainly the fighting and confusion that took place around the strongly held Kaiserbagh, and among the maze of narrow streets with their trenches and loopholed houses, proved extremely costly. Before the badly scarred Baillie Guard Gate was reached, Brigadier-General Neill, a forceful, fine fighting soldier had been killed, and Colonel Tytler and Havelock's son wounded.

On 26 September, Outram abandoned his assumed civilian status, and took full command of the defence. His first task was to extricate the rearguard, which had not reached the perimeter the previous night, and was now holed up in an area between the Kaiserbagh and Moti Mahal fighting desperately. This was eventually achieved, but not without loss. In the fighting between crossing the Ganges on 21 September, and bringing in the rearguard on the 26th, Havelock lost 535 men, but he still brought into the Residency nearly 3,000 additional mouths to help consume what was understood to be a rapidly diminishing food supply.

However, a few days later a large store of grain was located in the swimming bath. The reason for its late discovery could be explained, and Inglis had genuinely believed his urgent messages* to be correct, but understandably Outram felt he had been hastened unnecessarily. This was not the opinion of Lieutenant Innes, who was certain that with the vast increase of mutineers following the recapture of Delhi, Havelock's men had arrived just in time to prevent another Cawnpore-type disaster. The original garrison had now shrunk to 979, but there were still over 500 women and children.

Outram quickly realised he was not strong enough, nor had he sufficient bullock carts, to withdraw the garrison and families. At first he contemplated leaving the 90th with the old garrison, and fighting his way out with his other troops, but when the new supply of grain was discovered it seemed that with care there was food for everyone for at least a further month. He therefore determined to await relief. Meanwhile he extended the existing perimeter to take in the Tehri Koti, Farhat Bakhsh, Chattar Manzil and the gaol, so as to accommodate the new arrivals, and on the north side push the defences down to the river. Once the buildings had been secured, the 64th occupied the Farhat Bakhsh, the 5th Fusiliers the Chattar Manzil, the 90th a forward garden post, the 84th the gaol, and the Highlanders a post immediately south of the gaol. New defences were hastily erected – there was now no manpower shortage – and the old ones repaired. Havelock commanded the new position, while Inglis remained in charge of the old perimeter.

The enemy directed most of their energy to extensive mining operations, and to bombarding the palaces, but the original position received some attention from cannon, which, because it was now shooting from a greater distance, could better lift shot and shell into the middle of the compound. Even so, only nine people were killed there from gunfire during the second siege. The garrison at the Alam Bagh had been strengthened by 750 men and two guns from Cawnpore together with ample supplies. Attempts by the mutineers to break the position by bombardment was foiled by the skill of the garrison's gunners.

The second siege was a much less fraught affair than the first. To begin with, the position was now sufficiently strong as to be virtually secure from being overrun, despite the continuing increase in numbers of

---

*During the siege, native messengers occasionally performed the difficult and dangerous task of getting important letters from Inglis through the enemy lines for a high reward. The letters were usually written upon a very small piece of paper in Greek characters and concealed in a sealed piece of quill.

mutineers. And in addition to this, means of communication had become more efficient, so that news of large-scale operations for a proper relief, as opposed to Havelock's reinforcement operation, kept spirits constantly buoyant. Nevertheless, the enemy kept up the pressure, especially with mining, and military casualties from sorties against gun positions, and civilian ones from disease, continued to fill the hospital where conditions got steadily worse.

The wounded and the dying lay tightly packed side by side. The surgeons and the ladies performed their errands of mercy efficiently and unflinchingly, but the groans from amputations unalleviated by anaesthetic, and from which little hope of survival could be expected, made their work the more pitiable. Moreover, by November food had again become a problem, but Outram, in his report to the Commander-in-Chief, Sir Colin Campbell, forecast that with careful rationing it should hold out to the end of the month. Meat was very short, although in the event it held out, the last issue being made on the very last day of the siege.

It was therefore in a state of considerable anxiety that the garrison received periodic information concerning the long awaited relief, which was to be commanded by Sir Colin himself. Campbell had arrived in Calcutta in August to succeed General Anson, who had died of cholera. He had considerable battle experience at brigade level, and was a brave and thrusting commander, but he had never exercised high command.

By the time he joined the army, just short of the Alam Bagh, on 9 November, there were about 5,000 troops, of whom 400 were to be left there, This army had converged on Cawnpore in two columns. Some 2,400 men under Colonel Hope Grant had fought their way south from Delhi, and in this column there were 1,800 infantry, 600 cavalry and 16 guns. The other column comprised troops from Benares, and regiments that had been diverted at the Cape while on their way to China. An unusual component of Campbell's army was the Naval Brigade under Captain William Peel RN, of 300 Marines from HMS *Shannon*, fresh from their exploits in the Crimea, and having with them a valuable heavy artillery train of two 8-inch howitzers, six 24-pounders and some rocket launchers.

While at the Alam Bagh, Sir Colin received a letter from Inglis brought through the enemy lines, and the city, at very considerable risk by a civilian called Thomas Kavanagh, a wild Irishman who would dare all things. Dressed as a native, and with a genuine native to help him, he overcame incredible perils, and for his valour was awarded the Victoria Cross. In his letter, Inglis advised the Commander-in-Chief not to cross the canal at the Char Bagh, but to march south of the canal to the Dilkusha, from there northward to the Martinière (parent of the small city building), cross the canal at the bridge close to the Gumti, and thence to the Sikandarbagh. From here onwards he would be following Havelock's route, and was certain to meet stiff opposition in the streets, for the sepoys would be expecting him to come that way. This in fact happened, but Corporal Mitchell of the 93rd Highlanders tells how Kavanagh's knowledge of the alleyways saved many lives.

November 13th was spent capturing a small mud fort between the Alam Bagh and the Dilkusha, and securing the army's rear, before the troops advanced on the Dilkusha the following day. This palace, with its beautiful deer park full of blackbuck, was relatively untouched and here, on the 15th, the Arcadian and the heroic merged, for there was tough fighting – particularly by the 93rd, supported by Peel's guns – before the compound, and the entrenchments in front of the Martinière, were cleared of the enemy. From the Martinière that afternoon communication by semaphors was established with the Residency, using a code brought out by Kavanagh.

The 8th Foot, some cavalry and five guns were left to secure the Dilkusha while the rest of the army, now 4,200 strong, crossed the canal unopposed on the 16th, and advanced through an enemy held village to the large, and strongly fortified, Sikandarbagh palace – and to some of the fiercest fighting of the whole siege. As soon as the outbuildings had been cleared, the heavy cannon were brought up to pound the palace at short range. This was dangerous work, for the place was resolutely defended from well sited loopholes, but after half an hour a breach was made just sufficient for men of the 4th Punjab Infantry to lead an assault, followed very closely by the 53rd and 93rd. The latter cheered on by that soldier of the regiment, the Commander-in-Chief with the words 'Colonel Ewart, bring on the tartan – let my own lads at them'. Once inside the palace, the slaughter was appalling, both sides fighting in a white heat of undisciplined passion. The place was held by a brigade of three full regiments, and a large number of unattached sepoys; by the end of the morning nearly 3,000 of them lay dead, for quarter was neither asked nor given.

Campbell hurried the men forward, anxious to capture another strong-point, the Shah Nujif mosque, before nightfall. Peel's heavy guns could make no impression on the impregnable walls, and his gunners suffered severely. The Commander-in-Chief was about to call the attack off when a small opening was found at the rear, and in went the 93rd again. However, there was little fighting, for the Highlanders found the sepoys desperately trying to dodge Peel's picaresque rockets which were chasing them round the forecourt. That completed operations for the 16th.

Early on the 17th, Sir Colin took steps to secure his left flank, which meant occupying the two-storey Mess of the 32nd (the former Khoorsheyd Munzil) and the small observatory (Tara Kothi) close-by. Both places were strongly held – particularly the Mess – and it was not until 3 pm that they were captured. There then remained only the Moti Mahal before the relief force joined hands with the besieged. Captain Garnet Wolseley (who would later become Commander-in-Chief of the British Army) had led three companies of the 90th in their successful assault on the 32nd Mess, and driving the enemy helter-skelter towards the Moti Mahal he determined to exceed his orders and press on. He was soon joined by men of the 53rd, and he and his troops were determined to have the Moti Mahal before Sir Colin ordered in his precious 93rd. But it was no easy task, and several men were lost by flanking fire from the Kaiserbagh, and in eyeball to eyeball firing through the loopholes, before breaching tools arrived and access was gained.

Just as this was accomplished, a loud explosion occurred in the west wall, and through the debris came men of the garrison. Soon the commanders of the old and new forces, mercifully escaping showers of lead directed at them by a still active enemy, were greeting each other. Lucknow had been relieved. In achieving this, the first part of his task, Sir Colin had lost 45 officers and 496 other ranks. His own regiment alone had lost nine officers and 99 men.

Campbell soon decided he must evacuate Lucknow. He had good reasons for this decision, but for those who had for almost five months walked daily with death, and existed in appalling conditions to keep the flag flying above the Residency, it was a bitter pill to swallow. Inglis told Outram, who passed it on to the Commander-in-Chief, that with 600 men and without the families, the sick and the wounded, he could hold the position. This figure was unrealistic, and Campbell was adamant on withdrawal. And Campbell was right. The evacuation would give a temporary boost to enemy morale, but mindful of the pressing danger of Cawnpore from the large Gwalior contingent, he needed the men, and once clear of the city he would garrison the more easily defended Alam Bagh against his return next year.

There was no time to lose, and 1,500 women, children, sick and wounded, together with all the troops had to be got out of the city which was still held by many thousands of well-armed mutineers. The withdrawal was to be along the same route as the advance, and the recently captured posts were to be held until the operation was concluded. Canvas screens were erected to give cover from view in the open places, and the artillery played endlessly on all enemy strong-points, particularly the Kaiserbagh, and battery positions beyond the Gumti. During 19 November, the families were filtered in small batches as far as the Sikandarbagh, and that night they went, as a body, to the Dilkusha. The garrison was leap-frogged along the same route in the course of the next two days. By the 22nd, everything including food, treasure, and guns not destroyed, was clear, and the last units of the rearguard reached the Dilkusha in the early hours of the 23rd. Throughout, the enemy remained in total ignorance. It had been a brilliantly planned and executed manoeuvre. Sadly, at the Dilkusha, Havelock, worn out by his exertions succumbed to dysentery. He died secure in the knowledge that those he had striven so successfully to succour were on their way to safety.

The army spent the next few days at the Alam Bagh, putting the gardens and buildings into a strong state of defence. General Outram, with a mixed force of 4,000 men, was to hold this position to cover the withdrawal to Cawnpore, and as a base for the reconquest of Lucknow. A further force of 500 was to be positioned lower down the road at Bani on the river Sai. On 27 November, the army left the Alam Bagh for Cawnpore. The march for the families was a nightmare, food was short, alarms were plentiful, the dust was appalling and the procession – because that is what it was – stretched over nearly nine miles. General Windham, whom Campbell had left at Cawnpore with a force of 500 Europeans and some Sikhs, was soon faced by a vastly superior army of mutineers under their ablest general Tantia Topi. Windham was forced to give battle and was overwhelmed, but before the sepoys' guns could destroy the vital bridge over the Ganges, they were silenced by the British siege batteries, and Sir Colin's leading troops, who had covered 47 miles in under 30 hours, crossed over in safety. On the next day, (29th), the enemy was cleared from the river bank and by the evening of the 30th, the whole column was across the river. Four days later, the long-suffering families, the wounded and the sick, piled into creaking bullock carts and left for Allahabad. The Commander-in-Chief watched their departure thankfully and turned towards Tantia Topi and more accustomed tasks.

In March 1858 Sir Colin once more marched on Lucknow, this time with the largest army so far assembled in India. Since the evacuation the mutineers had considerably strengthened the defences, but Campbell gained an initial advantage by a powerful pincer movement, with a strong flanking force coming in from north of the Gumti. This had been Havelock's preferred route, but never having been used, was unconsidered by the sepoys. Nevertheless, there were to be more than ten days' fighting, followed by some unpleasant butchery, and a good deal of looting before Lucknow was cleared of rebels.

But the fruits of victory eluded Sir Colin, partly through the incompetence of some subordinates, but mainly through his own handling of the action in its final stages. Thousands, perhaps tens of thousands, of mutineers got away to fight another day in another place. The victors were left with a city in complete ruin, the symbol of the cruelty and turbulence of this unhappy period of Indian history.

CHAPTER 10

Vicksburg
May–July 1863

THE American War between the States was not only a milestone in the story of the development of warfare but, like the Indian Mutiny, a vast human tragedy. It says much for the United States Army that, despite the bitterness of that war, the traditions of courage, service and fine leadership which it generated live on today. It is not always easy to realise how close it was to our own time. One of the great generals of American history, Douglas McArthur, was the son of a man who won the Congressional Medal of Honor at Chattanooga less than six months after the end of the siege with which this chapter is concerned.

Both sides in the Civil War produced great commanders, of whom Ulysses S Grant must rank as the foremost on the Federal side. The Siege of Vicksburg will not be seen as his greatest battle, for historians may fairly allege that the extent of the Federal losses was due, in part at least, to his failure of judgement. But, as the story shows, Grant had achieved a tactical and strategic triumph in his famous approach to the city, during which he won no less than five resounding minor victories, inflicting grievous losses upon the Confederates.

The significance of the siege lay in the fact that Vicksburg was the key to the control of the Mississippi, one of the principal logistic highways of the war. Grant's success was to prove the lynchpin upon which the remainder of the war would turn and so contributed in no small measure to the final collapse of the Confederate cause.

* * *

The American Civil War, or the War Between the States, as it is more usually called by the American people, started in the early hours of 12 April 1861 when Confederate batteries opened fire on Fort Sumter – a fortress built to guard the entrance to Charleston harbour. The next day, the Federal commander surrendered, and what was to be a long and bitter struggle, with all the tragic consequences of a civil war, became inevitable.

The Confederate States of America elected Jefferson Davis, a soldier turned politician, to be their President, and the seat of their government was to be in Richmond, Virginia. In Washington President Lincoln had taken office at the head of a Republican administration just a month before Fort Sumter, and he went to war primarily to preserve the Union. Eleven slave-holding states of the South had seceded, ostensibly because they considered their sovereign rights under the constitution had been violated, but *au fond* it was fear of the abolition of slavery that drove them to this step.

Both sides entered the war entirely unprepared, and both armies had to resort to a *levée en masse*, obtained first from volunteers and later by conscription. The difficulty was not in procuring recruits, but in arming and equipping them. This was especially so for the South whose industrial capacity could not match that of the North.

When war broke out, the overall commander of the United States forces was General Winfield Scott, who was an old and virtually immobile seventy-five year old. He had been a good general, and he was sufficiently perspicacious to see that although the war could be lost (as it nearly was) in the east, it would be won eventually (as indeed it was) in the west. However, Lincoln was right to remove him after the Federal defeat in the first major engagement of the war. Until March 1864, when General Ulysses S Grant was given command of all the Federal armies, the North suffered from dissension among its senior generals, which inevitably led to frequent changes in the higher echelons.

The Confederate field armies had independent commanders until February 1865 when Robert E Lee was appointed to supreme command. Lee, one of those regular soldiers who had resigned their commission to fight for their native state (in his case Virginia), was the most outstanding general of the south, and arguably the most outstanding of either army.

The first major battle of the war was fought on 21 July 1861, when General Irvin McDowell was sent by Scott to seize the important Manassas Junction just south of Washington. General Beauregard commanded the Confederates, and Scott hoped that McDowell would defeat him before General Joseph E Johnston's troops could come up from the Shenandoah Valley. But Johnston arrived in time and, after some initial success, the Federal troops were severely defeated.

In November, Scott was replaced in overall command by General George B McClellan, who is best remembered for the excellent work he did in training and organising that fine fighting force the Army of the Potomac, rather than for his prowess in the field. Urged by Lincoln to show some results, in April 1862 he landed his army at Fortress Monroe and began an advance on the Confederate capital between the York and James rivers. There followed the Peninsular campaign which lasted until August. After the first large-scale engagement at Seven Pines (31 May–1 June), in which General Johnston was severely wounded, President Davis gave Lee the command of what now became the Army of Northern Viriginia.

Between 26 June and 2 July, four battles and one or two minor engagements were fought, which collectively became known as the Seven Days Battle. McClellan's objective was to take Richmond, Lee's was to destroy McClellan's army, but neither general succeeded in obtaining his objective. The campaign cost McClellan 16,000 casualties and 6,000 men taken prisoner. The Confederates had preserved Richmond at a staggering cost of 20,000 casualties.

In the course of the 12 months that separated the Seven Days Battle and Gettysburg, there was to be some severe fighting and, on the Union side, constant changes in the army command. In January 1863, General Hooker was given command of the Army of the Potomac and engaged Lee at Chancellorsville. The battle which lasted from 1–4 May resulted in a Confederate victory, but it decided nothing, and Lee suffered the grievous loss of one of his most brilliant commanders General 'Stonewall' Jackson.

The famous battle of Gettysburg between 1 and 3 July, is well known to every student of military history. It was a battle of majestic splendour, but terrible slaughter, in which were displayed the hideous cruelties as well as the nobilities and sacrifices of war. Approximately 160,000 men were engaged, and by the end of the third day, rather more than one in four lay dead or grievously wounded. Although Lee lost the battle, he carried out a perfectly orderly retreat to the south, but the crippling casualties he had suffered ensured that there could be no other invasions of the north.

The war in the east, threatening as it did the two capitals, has always commanded the limelight, but until the Gettysburg campaign, the most important fighting had been done in the west. There battles had been fought which were to have a definite influence on the outcome of the war.

The Federals had troops at Cairo, an Illinois town on the Mississippi, commanded by Brigadier General Ulysses S Grant, who was under Major General Halleck*, and another force east of the Cumberland river under Major General Buell. The Confederates held a line in southern Kentucky from Columbus, a strong-point on the Mississippi, east through Bowling Green. They were commanded by the very able General A S Johnston. He made the first move in 1862 by sending a force from the right of his line across the Cumberland in January, but Buell had little difficulty in crushing this thrust and thereby unhinging Johnston's right. Halleck then ordered Grant, in co-operation with Commodore Foote's gunboats, to take Fort Henry on the Tennessee. The fort submitted fairly quickly to the pounding from the ironclads, and Grant marched east against Fort Donelson, which proved a much tougher proposition, but after three days it too surrendered.

These reverses forced Johnston to relinquish Columbus and to pull back

---

*In July 1862 Lincoln summoned Halleck to Washington to become Commander-in-Chief.

as far as Corinth. Near there, he decided to offer battle to Grant before the latter could be joined by Buell, who was marching towards him from Nashville. The two armies were more or less matched with between 45,000 and 50,000 men apiece, and on the first day (6 April) of the battle of Shiloh the Federals were worsted, but Johnston was killed. On the second day of this particularly bloody battle (23,000 casualties for the two sides), Grant's men rallied, and the Confederates left the field, but the Union men were too bruised to pursue.

Within two months of Shiloh, the Federals looked poised to sweep their enemy clean out of the Mississippi Valley. That battle had denied the Confederates west Tennessee, the fleet and other Federal troops had cleared the river as far as Memphis, and Admiral Farragut had taken New Orleans from the sea. But fortune does not favour the big battalions if they are ineptly handled. Halleck had enough troops at Corinth to defeat anything put against him, but he failed to press his advantage, and instead split his force. By July (when Halleck had departed for Washington), the Confederates had recovered sufficiently to be preparing a brilliant, if short-lived, counterstroke.

Their army of Tennessee was now commanded by General Braxton Bragg, and in August he swept through and past Buell at Cumberland Gap. Grant (now a major general commanding the Federal Army of *The Tennessee*) had to send men to Buell's assistance, and at the same time deal with other Confederate troops from across the Mississippi. Leaving Buell to catch him if he could, Bragg pressed on towards the Ohio. But then suddenly and unaccountably his attack lost momentum, and he withdrew to eastern Tennessee. Meanwhile, Grant had defeated Major General Van Dorn at Iuka on 20 September, and again at the much bigger battle of Corinth on 3/4 October. As a result of this battle, Major General Rosecrans, who had led Grant's troops in it, replaced Buell as commander of the Army of the Cumberland.

After a period of reorganisation, Rosecrans moved his army south from Nashville to meet Bragg, who was waiting for him at Murfreesboro. The major engagement of this savage and very costly fight took place on 31 December, but the armies maintained contact until 3 January 1863 when Bragg withdrew. Both sides claimed the victory, but in fact little was decided, except that such was the punishment given and received that neither army was fit to fight again for many months.

In October 1862, the Federals had regained the initiative, but now their prospects in the west had again become clouded. All depended on Grant, who was preparing to capture Vicksburg and clear the Confederates from the Mississippi Valley. He was a first class fighting general who showed energy and enterprise, moreover he was prepared to take calculated risks in the face of odds, and in defiance of his superiors' expressed caution.

Vicksburg is situated on the east, or left bank of the Mississippi. That

MAP 10.1

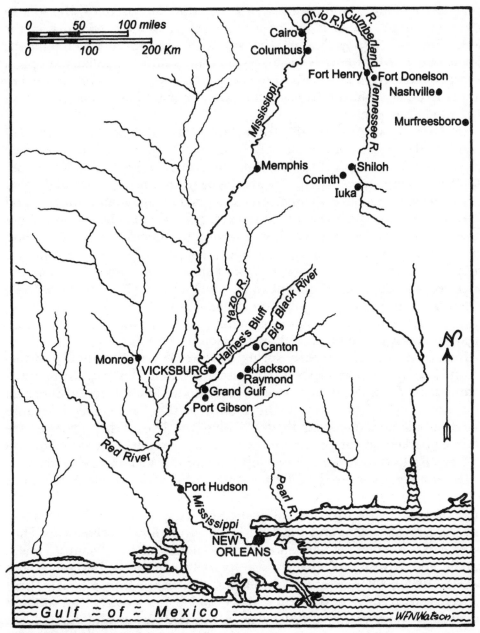

The Mississippi Valley

great waterway was of enormous importance to both the Union and the Confederacy. For the Union, it formed the main artery in a part of the country that was short of roads, for the transportation of industrial products from the north to much-needed markets, and for transportation of troops which, using the various navigable tributaries, could campaign into the very heart of the Confederate south. For the Confederates, the loss of the river meant the isolation of a large chunk of their territory in the west, from which they obtained (by way of the Red River, which joins the Mississippi north of Port Hudson) big quantities of food, military supplies, and personnel from Louisiana, Texas and Arkansas. Vicksburg was the key to the river, and Lincoln had said that the war could not be won 'until that key was in our pocket.'

In the Vicksburg campaign, Grant's two principal opponents were General Joseph E Johnston who, having recovered from his wounds, had been given overall command of the Confederate armies in the West in November 1862; and, more immediately, General Pemberton, whose army had the task of defending Vicksburg. Pemberton was a good administrator, diligent and hard working, but he had a task that better generals than he was would not have found easy. He was faced with having to defend a very wide front, virtually without the aid of cavalry, and throughout the campaign he was subjected to contradictory orders from Johnston, his immediate military superior, and Davis, his President and Commander-in-Chief. In April 1863, when Grant began his campaign on the east bank of the river, Pemberton had around 50,000 troops under command, but they were dispersed from near Memphis in the north to Port Hudson in the south.

During the winter and early spring of 1862–63 Grant made five unsuccessful attempts to take Vicksburg by land and water. The first, an approach march from Memphis to tie up with a force under Major General Sherman that sailed down the river to the mouth of the Yazoo, failed because the Confederates managed to get behind the line of his advance. He then embarked on four separate operations, in conjunction with Admiral Porter's fleet, to turn the right or left flank of the Vicksburg defences.

Grant's army consisted of four corps one of which – the 16th under General Hurlbut – was left at Memphis to protect communications. Of the other three, the 13th was commanded by Major General McClernand, the 15th by Sherman, and the 17th by Major General McPherson. They were camped wherever there was dry ground amid the swamps, creeks, canals and bayous* of the Mississippi delta. Between December and March, in appalling weather conditions, the troops dug a canal, spent weeks clearing trees and stumps above and below water in an attempt to open a route of some 400 miles to the Red River, and carried out two abortive amphibious operations aimed at turning the right flank of the Vicksburg defences. Although nothing was achieved, Grant felt that these canal-bayou expeditions had not been wasted, for they served to keep the troops occupied, alert and in good condition until the coming

*Intersecting streams or channels amid the large alluvial deposits.

of the dry weather when he would be able to begin operations on a plan he had envisaged for some time.

This plan was for the navy and transports to run the gauntlet past the Vicksburg batteries at night, and to be at hand to ferry the troops (which could now march down the dried-out west bank) across the river at Grand Gulf, or some point below. On the night of 16/17 April 1863, Porter's fleet passed the batteries with the loss of only one vessel, although a few nights later, when the barges carrying supplies made the run, seven out of eighteen were lost. Meanwhile, the troops had completed the tough march to aptly named Hard Times. However, as the naval bombardment failed to neutralise the Grand Gulf batteries, the troops were marched a few miles farther down the river to be landed safely from the barges at Bruinsberg on 29 April. Grand Gulf was held by General Bowen with 8,000 men who fought stubbornly, but were far too few for McClernand's whole corps, and two divisions of McPherson's. Port Gibson was taken on 2 May, and Grand Gulf soon afterwards.

Grant's strength for the campaign was much the same as Pemberton's, but he had to detach troops for various duties. Nevertheless, by the time Sherman's corps (which had initially remained in the Vicksburg area to create a diversion) had joined him, his numbers actually engaged in rear of Vicksburg would have been between 40,000 and 45,000. He was well aware that speed was vital, for Johnston was heading for Jackson (the state capital) with an army that was being reinforced from various Confederate strongholds. He therefore decided on the bold concept of cutting himself off from his base, and advancing to Jackson across enemy territory, relying on the country to supplement what few rations he had.

Pemberton, meanwhile, was in the most unenviable position. Through his lack of cavalry, he was uncertain of what Grant was doing, and he was at the receiving end of two plans differing from his own, which was to hold Vicksburg and to protect his important railway communication with Jackson. To do this, he favoured holding a line on the Big Black river, resisting Grant's certain attack, and then getting behind the Federal line of withdrawal. President Davis urged him to hold Vicksburg at all costs, and to stay close to it, while Johnston wished to cut loose from Vicksburg completely and avoid a major engagement until Confederate forces could be concentrated. Pemberton tried to reach some sort of compromise, which resulted in his brigades becoming scattered thereby making it much easier for Grant to defeat him in detail, as well as to cope with any threat from Johnston.

Grant left Grand Gulf on 7 May, and moved towards Jackson. On the 12th, his path was barred by one brigade at a stream two miles from Raymond. By this time Sherman's corps had rejoined, and after about two hours of stiff fighting weight of numbers prevailed, and the Confederates fell back to Jackson. As soon as Johnston arrived in the capital, he ordered Pemberton, whose main force was at Edward's Station, to attack McPherson's rear. Pemberton disregarded this order, and instead planned a south-easterly stroke against Grant's supply line, which did not exist. Johnston was later to aver that had Pemberton obeyed him, Vicksburg might have been saved.

Meanwhile, on 14 May, Grant's leading corps closed in on Jackson, and by 4 pm both McPherson's and Sherman's corps were in the city, having suffered a little above 300 casualties between them. The Confederates lost 845 men and 17 guns. Johnston, who had taken steps to evacuate valuable material by rail to Canton, marched his troops north towards that town. Thus there was the ludicrous situation of some 45,000 Confederate soldiers, well separated in three different areas – Vicksburg, south of Edward's Station, and north of Jackson – faced with about an equal number of Union troops all within close support of each other.

From six miles north of Jackson, Johnston sent another despatch to Pemberton urging him to make all speed to unite with his force. Grant anticipated this move, and took immediate steps to hasten an engagement with Pemberton before he could join Johnston. Unlike his enemy, he was working on interior lines, and the concentration of his army, given the nature of the country, was a comparatively simple matter. The result was the battle of Champion's Hill which began at 11 am on 16 May. There was a lot of very hard fighting for about four hours on the left of their strong position before the Confederates broke. This meant General Bowen's division in the centre had no alternative but to fall back. General Loring's division on the Confederate right had not been heavily engaged, and was ordered to cover the withdrawal. Unfortunately, the retreating troops failed to hold the ford at Baker's Creek for Loring, whose division was consequently cut off, and forced to break away south to join Johnston. In this battle, Pemberton lost 3,839 men (380 killed), 24 guns and the future use of Loring's division. Grant suffered 2,408 casualties, which included 397 men killed.

The Confederates fell back to the Big Black river. Grant ordered Sherman's corps to make all speed for Bridgeport, a few miles up river, from where he would be in a position to outflank the Confederates holding the line of the river. But in the event, this was not necessary, for a frontal attack, which began at about 8 am on 17 May, routed them after one and a half hours. There was some bloody fighting at the only bridge, where 5,000 men tried to cross. Some got away – often without arms – some were drowned, and 1,751 were captured along with 18 guns. But the bridge was destroyed, and the Federals spent the rest of the day, and well into the night, building three new ones. This delay enabled the Confederates to call in the bridgehead at Haines's Bluff, which place Sherman had rendered untenable, and to withdraw their troops in moderately good order to the prepared defences at Vicksburg.

Grant had every reason to be satisfied. With virtually no supply train,

MAP 10.2

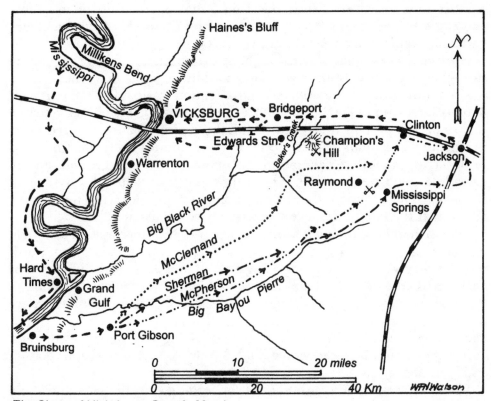

The Siege of Vicksburg: Grant's March

the Union troops had marched an average of 180 miles, fought and won five battles, and accounted for some 12,000 Confederate soldiers captured, wounded or killed, for a total loss to themselves of 4,379. It was a tactical and strategical triumph. He now hoped that his enemy were sufficiently demoralised to allow him to take the city by storm. In this he was soon to be disappointed.

The Vicksburg terrain is admirably suited for defence. The city is situated on the river slope of a range of bluffs that are about 250 feet high. The strong loess, semi-indurated clay soil, is of such a tenacious quality that when cut vertically, for roads or fortifications, it will retain its sides against all weather for many years. But the constant erosive action of running water over the centuries had resulted in the whole plateau being broken up into deep ravines with very steep sides, gullies, and narrow twisting ridges which have complete command of the ravines. The city is encompassed by a prominent ridge, which begins some two miles to its north-east, and curves in an arc following an irregular course, but retaining an unbroken fairly level crest for some nine miles, until it meets Stout's Bayou which empties into the river. Along this ridge, making full use of its salient and commanding points, Major Lockett, Chief Engineer of the Vicksburg garrison, prepared a strong defensive position.

Work had been going on throughout the summer of 1862, mainly in strengthening the existing river batteries and making new ones, and it was not until 1 September that serious attention was paid to the rearward defences. As soon as Pemberton took over command in October, the tempo was stepped up. The first priority for the negro labourers, hired from neighbouring plantations, was to clear large chunks of virgin woodland in order to establish a general line on the commanding ground, and to provide a good field of fire. Then came the laying-out of a system of redoubts, redans, lunettes and smaller field-works, all connected by rifle pits so that the line of defence was virtually continuous.

The earth walls of the nine forts were up to 20 feet thick and 10 feet high, and in front of them (with the exception of the 3rd Louisiana redan, which was atop a very narrow ridge) was dug a seven foot deep ditch. The line was anchored on the left at Fort Hill, and on the right at South Fort, but Haines's Bluff on the Yazoo river and Warrenton, six miles below Vicksburg, were fortified as flank positions. To attack this formidable line Federal troops had to cross broken, difficult ground, and having negotiated ravines and gullies they would be faced with a ditch 8 ft deep, 14 ft across at its bottom and 18 ft at the top.

There were six roads and one railway leading into the city, and these now form useful guides to the disposition of the two armies. On the right of Pemberton's line was General Stevenson's division, which stretched from the Warrenton road to the railway line, then came General Forney's division in the centre, with its left on the Graveyard Road, and the left was held by General M L Smith's division. Forney's and Smith's divisions had not been engaged in the recent fighting, and were comparatively fresh; Bowen's, which had borne the brunt of the last battle, was placed in reserve on the left centre. To defend the perimeter Pemberton had around 20,000 troops fit for duty out of an army now reduced to 31,000 men, and 172 pieces of artillery of which 36 were siege guns*; the river batteries mounting 31 heavy calibre siege guns and 13 pieces of field artillery, were still intact.

There was another ridge a few hundred yards east of the Confederate line, and running roughly parallel to it on which Grant positioned his army after crossing the Big Black. Sherman's corps held the right of Grant's line from the high ground, from where it overlooked the Yazoo, to the Graveyard Road, then came McPherson's from the Graveyard Road to near Baldwin's Ferry Road, and the left was held by McClernand's corps.

*The Chief Engineer reports only 102 guns ready for service on 18 May.

His troops had a large area to cover, and initially the investment was by no means complete, for there was a gap of some four miles on McClernand's left. By 15 June, this had been filled by Generals Herron's and Lauman's divisions from Missouri and Memphis respectively. There was no chance that Pemberton could break out of this gap, but small parties could use it for communication purposes. On 22 May Grant gave his strength as 40,000 men available for the siege, but his numbers fluctuated as reinforcements arrived, and divisions were detached to guard against a relieving force. He had no siege guns, and had to borrow some large calibre pieces from Admiral Porter.

There had been some early skirmishing, especially on the right of the Federal line, where Sherman's corps was close to the Confederate defences. At 2 pm on the 19th, Grant ordered an assault, hoping by a swift *coup-de-main* to make a rapid breakthrough. He was quickly disillusioned when Sherman's men tried to storm one of the nine forts (the Stockade Redan near the Graveyard Road) that was resolutely defended by Brigadier General Shoupe's troops of Smith's division. The Confederates, secure behind their defences, were very different troops from the men who had been driven from Champion's Hill and across the Big Black. Two determined assaults were repulsed with heavy loss. The second reached the ditch but, getting no support from McPherson's and McClernand's men, who were too far back, they withdrew.

It had cost Grant a thousand men, and nothing to show for it save the bringing of two corps closer to the enemy, and to learn that he almost certainly had a siege on his hands. But he was not a man to have his confidence shaken so easily. He spent the 20th and 21st consolidating his line to, on average, 800 yards from the Confederate works, and improving his communications with the Yazoo, before attempting a more serious attack on the 22nd. Grant's decision to launch this second attack so soon against almost impregnable defences was not a piece of pig-headedness, but taken partly because he knew the mood of his troops. They shared his confidence, and were loath to resort to the drudgery of digging. But more important was the position of Johnston, who was known to be assembling a large army with which to relieve Vicksburg.

The Confederate troops had not been idle in their two days' respite. They had spent the time in improving their defences by the erection of traverses as protection from enfilade fire, and in digging covered approaches between camp and forward areas as protection against Federal sharpshooters. They were absolutely ready when the assault went in at 10 am on 22 May.

The Federal attack was planned on a three corps front, extending to some three miles, and covering the right of M L Smith's Confederate division, the whole of Forney's, and the left brigade of Stevenson's division, which in terms of Confederate forts was from Stockade Redan to Fort Garrott.

The attack had been carefully prepared: the field batteries had carried out an intensive bombardment on the rearward defences at the same time as Admiral Porter shelled the river batteries. The assaulting troops had been brought through the thick cover to within 200 yards of the defences, in some places. This was necessary, for the divisions had to attack on a narrow and vulnerable front, mainly using the roads that ran along the ridge tops, the surrounding country being both dense and very trappy. Sherman, having had such trouble with the ditch on the 19th, had the idea of bridging it. The only timber suitable for this purpose had to come from the General's headquarters. Grant obligingly allowed his shack to be dismantled.

The Federal guns were silent at 10 am, and the attack went in simultaneously along the whole line. On the right, a forlorn hope of 150 men from General Blair's division of Sherman's corps, carrying the wooden planks, bravely headed the charge against the Stockade Redan. The Confederates lay low until the leading Federal troops were almost in the ditch, when up they sprang to deliver an intensive and destructive fire that flared and crackled along the whole line.

The forlorn hope was swept away, but not before a few men had climbed the parapet and planted a colour which waved triumphant until nightfall. Blair committed all three of his brigades (Ewing's, Giles Smith's and Kilby Smith's) in successive attacks, and when the Graveyard Road became impassable through mangled bodies heaped upon it, the two rear brigades deployed, finding some cover on the ravine slopes, and forging their way through the thick growth to the ditch. It was here that the fighting was fiercest. The fort walls had not been breached and, as men struggled to climb them, the Confederates lining the parapets used shells as hand grenades to blast them to pieces. It was an uneven contest which continued without a break for over two hours, but the Confederates had not fought off Blair's men unscathed, for many of their number had been killed as they hurled destruction into the ditch from the parapets.

McPherson attacked with two divisions (Logan's and Quinby's) and Ransom's brigade of McArthur's division. But the fighting on his front was done mainly by Logan's division using the Jackson Road, for Ransom, on the right, and Quinby, on the left, were opposite a re-entrant. To have entered it, would have entailed heavy casualties from murderous cross-fire. The defences were held by General Forney's troops in three principal forts – 3rd Louisiana Redan, the Great Redoubt, and the 2nd Texas Lunette – and the story was much the same as on Sherman's front. Time and again, men fought their way into the ditches but, once there, suffered severely without making any headway. Some men of the 7th Missouri from J D Stevenson's brigade of Logan's division did manage to place their flags on the wall of the Great Redoubt, but lost six standard bearers in the process.

McClernand also had two divisions up and a brigade of a third, with one division in reserve. Carr was on the right with Baldwin's Ferry road as his axis, Osterhaus advanced between the railway line and Fort Garrott, Hovey's only brigade was on Osterhaus's left, and A J Smith's division was in rear, supporting Carr. The only entry in the whole Federal attack was made by men of two regiments (21st and 22nd Iowa) of Lawler's brigade of Carr's division, who stormed the Railroad Redoubt, and briefly entered the fort before all of them, save one sergeant, were killed or captured in some exceedingly fierce hand-to-hand fighting with Colonel Waul's Volunteer Texas Legion. The sergeant, by name Joseph Griffith, somehow managed to escape with a party of prisoners. An attempt to regain the fort by a brigade of the reserve division was beaten off with severe loss, but the colours of the 22nd Iowa, and the 77th Illinois, remained firmly on the parapet for nine hours.* Carr's other brigade (Benton's) on the Baldwin's Ferry road gained the ditch in front of the 2nd Texas Lunette, where they suffered heavy casualties in trying to enter the work, but they managed to place some colours on the parapet before being driven off. On the extreme left, Osterhaus's and Hovey's men fared no better.

All along the Federal line, the pattern was the same, with every fort attacked. The troops suffered casualties in reaching the ditches, many more during their attempts to scale the walls, and only in one instance was a fort entered. As it happened, this led to an even bigger disaster. Grant had taken up a position on the high ground by the Jackson road from which he had a fairly good view of the principal forts under attack, but communication in this type of country was difficult, and inevitably the elliptical notes scribbled by the commanders took time to arrive. By 11.30 am it looked to Grant as though the assault would never succeed, and he was on the point of riding over to confer with Sherman when he received a despatch from McClernand saying he was hard pressed and could McPherson create a diversion to relieve the pressure on him? Grant ordered him to look to his own reserves, and went on his way to Sherman, where he received a second note from McClernand saying he had used his reserves, but he had now achieved such success in entering one of the forts that he felt a vigorous effort on all fronts must succeed. A third, equally optimistic, communication arrived shortly after 1 pm.

Grant regarded these reported successes with some scepticism, for they did not tally with his own observations, but the hour was getting late and there was not time for him to ride over to McClernand. He felt he could scarcely ignore the persistent importunities of an allegedly successful corps commander, and so he ordered McPherson to create the diversion. Sherman immediately renewed his attack with a fresh division (Tuttle's),

*This regiment, a part of A J Smith's division, had gained the parapet of the fort when in support of Carr's 14th Division.

Quinby, whose division had hardly got into the fight, was ordered to move in support of McClernand, and the latter was given permission to make use of McArthur's two brigades thought to be coming up from Warrenton – in fact they did not arrive in time.

The fight was thus continued until almost dark, and the slaughter of the morning was repeated in the afternoon with precisely the same results. Grant had committed 35,000 men in the attack, and lost 3,199 of whom 502 had been killed. The Confederates, who manned the defences with 13,000 men, lost a little over 500. Grant blamed McClernand (whose corps, incidentally, suffered the worst with 1,543 casualties) for the Federal heavy losses, and this was reflected a little later when he lost his command. But Grant was ultimately responsible. He had mistrusted McClernand's reports, he had seen for himself that the forts were virtually impregnable, and yet he allowed the attack to be repeated – almost certainly against his better judgement.

Grant now reluctantly realised that he had a siege on his hands, and that his men would have to dig lines of countervallation, and quite possibly of circumvallation as well, for there was every indication that Johnston would attack. More troops were necessary to complete the investment and to guard against relief. These were to come from Grant's 16th Corps at Memphis, and from appeals to Halleck in Washington.

There was no shortage of labour to dig the parallels and saps, but there was a shortage of skilled engineers. This meant that progress was a little slow in constructing the ten approaches, of which the four most important were the Graveyard, Jackson, Baldwin's Ferry and Warrenton Roads. There was ample material for gabions, fascines and sap-rollers to protect and assist the pioneer companies. The latter did well to have advanced their saps and parallels to within 150 yards of the defences by 4 June, and as close as 90 feet in two places by the 8th. This close proximity of the lines led to some fraternisation, for both sides put out pickets at night, and these would exchange greetings and persiflage. It was a feature of this civil war that while the actual fighting was some of the fiercest on record, whenever an opportunity occurred during a lull, the soldiers of both armies often conversed happily together.

It was not easy for the Confederates to block the slowly winding saps. Unlike their opponents, they were becoming dangerously short of ammunition and had little answer, other than to resort to hasty retrenchments, to the hard pounding they received from Federal guns and improvised wooden mortars. They do not appear to have ventured any sorties in the early stages, although later, as the trenches got closer, there was some hand-to-hand grapple in them. A slight check in the sapping occurred when a Confederate soldier discovered a clever way of setting the sap-rollers alight, but this was soon countered by the Federals keeping them wet. Countermining was begun in the ditches with limited success, but when the trenches came

MAP 10.3

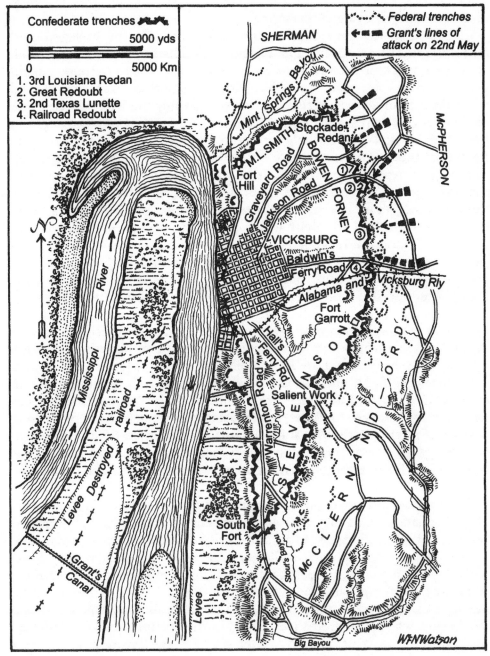

Vicksburg: The Siege Lines

close enough barrels of powder and shells were ignited and rolled over the parapet which caused a temporary withdrawal of the besiegers. By the end of June no less than twelve miles of parallels had been dug, and 233 guns were in position, which included a battery of 13 heavy guns manned, and commanded, by naval personnel.

Life for the besiegers is invariably easier than for the besieged, and Vicksburg was no exception. The Federal troops had never lacked for food, with the important exception of bread, but water was to become a slight problem. They were well provided with every sort of ammunition, and when the reinforcements arrived, those men holding the front line trenches could be regularly relieved. This was not the case for the Confederates, who needed to be vigilant the whole time, and had not sufficient men to rotate front line duties. They suffered continual bombardment, and bringing up rations from rear to the forward areas was extremely hazardous, nor was the food particularly palatable when it did arrive, although Pemberton thought mule most nutritious. Coffee was soon finished, and a nasty substitute was found for flour which produced a nauseous composition. However, Pemberton reckoned (as he told Johnston in a letter of 15 June) that on reduced rations they could last a further 20 days.

Civilians fared no better. Bombardment to them was nothing new, for they had endured it from the river for over a year, but during the siege it became almost hourly. The nightly pyrotechnics of the giant 13-inch mortar were most spectacular for those watching at a distance. Lives were saved through a troglodyte existence in the many caves dug into the ridges on which the city is built. Damage to buildings was considerable, but civilian casualties were light, and the ladies of Vicksburg did excellent work in tending the evacuated wounded, for hospital facilities and medical supplies were tightly stretched. In sieges, as in most forms of warfare, there are long periods of intense boredom, and for none more so than for the besieged. Vicksburg was one of those places where an attempt to boost morale was made through the publication (latterly on wallpaper) of a daily paper, or news-sheet.

Grant was always looking over his shoulder for the approach of Johnston. His information as to that general's apparent preparations was doubtless correct, but it is permissible to ask how seriously did Johnston contemplate relief? When Pemberton first withdrew into Vicksburg, and Haines's Bluff had become untenable, Johnston informed him that without Haines's Bluff 'Vicksburg is of no value and cannot be held ... if it is not too late, evacuate Vicksburg and march to the north-east'. This note, which horrified Pemberton, who considered Vicksburg to be the linchpin of all Confederate operations in the West, was dispatched on 17 May. Throughout the next six weeks, the official records show correspondence in much the same pessimistic vein. All that Johnston ever contemplated was an attempt to extricate the garrison, and he was not overzealous in that. On 15 June, he even went so far as to inform his government 'I consider saving Vicksburg hopeless'.

He had his problems. Assembling a large enough army to defeat Grant, even with the aid of Pemberton's men, was not easy. Loring had arrived at Canton with virtually no equipment, and other troops had to come long distances over a railway largely destroyed by Colonel Grierson's splendid cavalry raid at the end of April. The whole time Johnston was under constant, and often contradictory, pressure from Richmond to save Vicksburg and the Mississippi Valley. To attempt the relief of Port Hudson (one piece of advice from Davis) would expose Jackson, and to take a substantial force from General Bragg in Tennessee would endanger that state. Probably the task of saving Vicksburg, or even the army, was impossible, but because Johnston lacked the will to win he never put it to the test.

By the end of June, he had managed to assemble an army of some 31,000 men comprising four infantry divisions and 3,000 cavalry, which he marched cautiously down the Big Black, not, as he said, 'in the wild spirit that dictated the despatches from the War Department', but as a reconnaissance in force to see if there was any chance of saving the Vicksburg garrison. The city he knew to be doomed. He was still reconnoitring when he ultimately learnt of the garrison's surrender.

Nevertheless, Grant had to assume that Johnston would make a determined effort to break through his lines, or at least draw him off to accept battle. He therefore needed substantial reinforcements to guard against this threat. The obvious first call was on his own 16th Corps at Memphis. Hurlbut had already sent him one division (Lauman's) which eventually took post on McClernand's left, and when the siege began, he sent two more which Grant positioned at Haines's Bluff under the command of Major General Washburne. As already mentioned, Grant had asked Halleck for more troops and General Burnside, commanding the Department of Ohio, sent two divisions from his 9th Corps commanded by General Parke, which had arrived by 15 June. Grant also received General Herron's division from Missouri, and when that had been ferried across the river on 14 June, and come into position on Lauman's left, the investment of Vicksburg was complete.

By the time all the reinforcements had arrived, Grant had an army of 71,000 of which (he reported to Halleck on 8 June) 30,000 were available to repel anything from the rear. Most of these 'spare' troops were in the Yazoo river – Haines's Bluff area, and were periodically dispatched (particularly the cavalry) to guard or watch the various crossings of the Big Black. The only action fought outside the lines of countervallation was at Millikens Bend, when one brigade of Sherman's corps and the Marine brigade, which Grant had been lent, crossed the Mississippi to help two gunboats drive off a Confederate division from the Trans-Mississippi Department, which had responded to Johnston's call to bring relief to Pemberton. This short action principally concerned a mixed black and white Federal outpost, had no hope of success, nor bearing on the siege, and need not be described in detail.

Throughout the month of June, the siege proceeded along very much the usual lines for such operations. Conditions within the Confederate camp became daily more difficult, depressing and dangerous; duties increased, food decreased, and ammunition had to be very carefully husbanded. Johnston was still able to communicate with Pemberton, and asked him to formulate a breakout in support of an attack. Pemberton replied (21 June) suggesting Johnston should attack north of the railway while his troops tried to cut their way out by the Warrenton road. It was a plan that both generals must have known had little hope of success, and was never implemented. In the face of great hardship, and daily loss of life, the garrison had passed from the stimulation of hope to the deadness of despair, and even their courage began to grow dim.

Two events stood out at this time to enliven the monotonous routine of the besieging army, which was becoming accustomed to the constant false alarms of Johnston's imminent approach. On 18 June, Grant dismissed McClernand, and replaced him by General Ord, who had been severely wounded fighting under Grant at Corinth in the previous October. McClernand had not been an easy subordinate, and had particularly annoyed Grant when he persisted (in Grant's view quite wrongly) for the attack to be renewed on the forts, but the actual cause of his dismissal was quite different. He had published a congratulatory Address, without consulting or informing Grant, in which he greatly praised the performance of his own men, and used the opportunity to vilify the other corps, and even his commanding general. The Address appeared in a Memphis newspaper, and much annoyed Sherman and McPherson. Writing to Halleck, Grant said, 'I should have relieved him long since, for general unfitness for his position'.

The other notable event of the month was the attempt to break the defence by mining. Shortly after the disastrous attack of 22 May, Sherman, holding the right opposite Fort Hill, had decided to reduce that fort with naval aid. This had ended in complete failure when the US gunboat *Cincinnati* had the worst of an artillery duel with the shore batteries and was sunk. The method of destruction was then switched to mining, and the target was to be the 3rd Louisiana Redan which, it will be remembered, had no ditch. Tunnelling started some distance from the salient, and was deep by the time the parapet was reached. McPherson, in whose sector the fort lay, gave 3 pm on 25 June as the time for the mine to be exploded, and Grant had ordered an artillery bombardment all along the line to coincide with the explosion. The top of the redan was blown off, but the breach was too small for a full-scale assault. Those men who made the attempt were soon repelled with losses when they met the retrenchments.

The depth of the tunnel had prevented successful countermining in time to save the explosion, and Federal miners were again under the 3rd Louisiana parapet by 29 June. At 1.30 pm on 1 July, one and a quarter tons of explosive virtually destroyed the redan. The Confederates were hard pressed to shore up their retrenchments, and a quick, resolute attack through the large breach must have captured the position, but the failure of the last assault deterred them from making another.

Grant now decided to withhold any further explosions until three or more mines could be set off simultaneously, combined with a general assault. His men had got their trenches to within a few feet of the parapets at three different points, one in front of each enemy corps. He knew from fraternisation that the Confederates were nearing the end of their tether, and he also knew (and this time it was correct) that Johnston had an army quite close. The time was ripe for a final push, and preparations went forward in compliance with orders for a full-scale assault on 6 July. Men were immediately put to widening the approach trenches so that troops could pass four abreast, while others were cutting timber from the scrub woodland suitable for bridging the ditches. But all to no purpose, because three days before the attack was to go in, Pemberton sought terms.

He had done what he could to save Vicksburg, for he was convinced of its importance, but now, with relief a long-vanished dream, and the temper of his men uncertain, he considered the only two courses left open – to cut his way out, or to ask for terms. On 28 June, he had received an anonymous letter signed 'from many soldiers' couched in respectful, and indeed laudatory, terms; but at the same time making it quite clear that the men could no longer continue to fight in the prevailing conditions of hardship and malnutrition. The latter, Pemberton knew, was partly responsible for his having between seven and ten thousand men unfit for duty. These near-mutinous sentiments were only kept in check by the absurd promise that, within a week, sufficient boats would be built for evacuation. And indeed this dissembling was carried to the extent of actually constructing a large number of very crude boats.

Nevertheless, before taking any irrevocable step, Pemberton – as was his wont – discussed the choice with his divisional commanders. All but Stevenson were in favour of immediate capitulation, and this course was almost unanimous among the regimental commanders. And so, at 10 am on 3 July, white flags appeared on the Confederate defences. Soon afterwards, a preliminary meeting took place between the Confederate General Bowen, and Grant's divisional commander A J Smith. At this meeting it was agreed that Grant and Pemberton should meet at 3 pm in front of McPherson's corps.

Grant sent a note to Pemberton confirming this and intimating that his terms were unconditional surrender. At their meeting, Pemberton demurred at such terms, but Grant was not prepared to palter, and the meeting ended inconclusively. Grant made some minor concessions in a letter to Pemberton that evening and, subject to one amendment, these were agreed. Officers were to be allowed their side-arms and clothing, mounted officers one horse each, the rank and file to be allowed only their clothing. Pemberton's amendment was that the Confederates should be allowed to march out with their colours and arms, and then to stack them in front of their lines before returning to their camp as prisoners. This little ceremony took place at 10 am on 4 July. Later, Grant entered the city that had defied his troops for 47 days, and went aboard Admiral Porter's flagship to thank the navy for their very considerable assistance.

The campaign for the Mississippi was now virtually over. Johnston, on hearing of the surrender, had withdrawn to Jackson, and Grant ordered Sherman with a mixed force of 48,000 men to pursue. Sherman wisely refrained from attacking the strongly held defences and Johnston, who was not equipped to withstand a siege, made a clever withdrawal under cover of darkness across the Pearl river, and was not pursued. Grant had lost 545 men killed during the siege, 3,688 wounded (many only lightly) and 303 missing. Since landing at Bruinsberg his total losses for the campaign were 10,142, but his troops had accounted for at least 45,000 of Pemberton's Mississippi army. In the actual siege Pemberton lost some 3,500 men killed or wounded, and Grant writing to General Banks on 4 July gave the number that surrendered as 27,000, with 128 pieces of field artillery and a large number of siege guns*.

The twin defeats of Vicksburg and Gettysburg, and the loss in less than six months of Chatanooga, sounded the death-knell of the Confederacy. There was to be much hard fighting still to come, but there were few, if any, in the South who now thought in terms of victory.

On 9 July, the commander of Port Hudson, who had been under siege since 23 May, on hearing of the loss of Vicksburg, surrendered with 6,000 men. The last of the Confederates had been cleared from the banks of the Mississippi and now, in Lincoln's memorable words, 'The father of waters rolls unvexed to the sea'.

---

*All 172 guns were surrendered.

CHAPTER 11

Ladysmith 1899–1900

THE British Army which found itself in South Africa at the outbreak of the Second Boer War in October 1899 was both ill-equipped and ill-prepared for its task of fighting a highly mobile enemy that had mastered the arts of guerrilla warfare. Furthermore, that army was led by a general, Sir Redvers Buller, who would readily confess that he felt himself lacking in the experience of high command which his new appointment demanded.

The little town of Ladysmith and its garrison of some 14,000 men held out against General Joubert's encircling forces, who held all the high ground overlooking the town, for three months whilst Buller made no less than four attempts to relieve it, the last one being successful. General Sir George White VC, the commander of the garrison, has been criticised by historians for his ineptitude but, as this chapter shows, he was not lacking in courage or resolution and the survival of the garrison owed much to his leadership and determination not to surrender. Despite the failings of the British Army in that war, a number of officers who were to gain fame only 14 or 15 years later, learned much from the experience. Two of White's most valuable officers in the siege were Colonels Hamilton and Rawlinson, both of whom would later command armies and become household names.

* * *

In 1652, the Dutch East India Company took possession of that part of Southern Africa that became known as Cape Colony. During the Napoleonic wars, the British seized the Cape of Good Hope and surrounding land, and in 1814 they purchased the colony from the Dutch. There thus began an uneasy, indeed for much of the time turbulent, relationship between the British and their Afrikaner* subjects. For much of the early years, the British administration was inept, although there were difficult problems to be solved, chief among them the handling of the black majority and its relationship with the colonists. It was this, and particularly the abolition of slavery, that finally decided a large number of disgruntled

---

*Afrikaners. People born in South Africa of Dutch descent. Known also at the time as Boers.

Boer farmers to begin the Great Trek in 1834, and to establish the South African Republic (the Transvaal), and the Orange Free State.

It was not long before the Voortrekkers, as those who took part were known, were in confrontation with their Zulu neighbours in Natal, and Sir Harry Smith (who it will be remembered married Juana after Badajoz), the Governor of Cape Colony, annexed Natal. He also expanded Cape Colony, and seized Boer land across the Orange and Vaal rivers. But these latter conquests were repudiated, and by the Sand River Convention of 1852 the independence of the two Boer republics was guaranteed. Twenty-seven years later, British troops, under Sir Garnet Wolseley, broke Zulu military power and the British were peacefully established in Pretoria where they sought to rescue the republic's bankruptcy and to promote federation of the four colonies – the Cape, Natal, Orange Free State and Transvaal.

The intention was admirable, but the whole business was thoroughly mishandled both in Westminster and in Africa. Nothing was done to alleviate the Transvaal's economic chaos, nor towards federation, and the Transvaalers were angered by what had become a simple case of annexation. In 1880 they rose in revolt. The First Boer War brought little credit to British arms, and shortly after General Sir George Colley had suffered an ignominious defeat at Majuba Hill, on 27 February 1881, Gladstone's government opted for a peaceful solution. By the Pretoria Convention, the Boers, very reluctantly, accepted self-government for the Transvaal subject to British suzerainty.

For the years between the two Boer wars the South African scene was dominated by two men. Paul Kruger was elected President of the Transvaal in 1883 by which time Cecil Rhodes had begun his Parliamentary career in Cape Colony, where, in 1890, he became Prime Minister. Kruger's ambitions centred on an independent South African Confederation under Boer hegemony, while Rhodes strove to promote an Anglo-Saxon domination. Had the two men been able to co-operate, the story might have been a much happier one. As it was, they were poles apart.

The South African problem was greatly complicated by the discovery of gold in the Transvaal hills in 1886. Thousands of British immigrants, and a strong minority from other countries, swarmed into Johannesburg to make their fortunes in the Rand goldfields. These Uitlanders, as they were called, created difficulties in the Boer republic when Kruger consistently refused them the vote. It was largely to obtain a redress of the wrongs which were alleged to have been done to them, that the Uitlanders were encouraged by Rhodes to stage a revolt, which he would support with a force of 500 armed mounted men under Doctor Starr Jameson. When the Uitlanders discovered that Jameson's aim was British annexation of the Transvaal, instead of a reformed Transvaal government, the revolt was called off. However, undaunted Jameson entered the Transvaal unsupported, and his men were ingloriously defeated in short engagement at Doornkop. It had greatly damaged the Imperial position in South Africa, and brought the Second Boer War a long step nearer.

In 1897, Sir Alfred Milner was appointed High Commissioner at the Cape. His immediate authority was in Cape Colony, but his principal problem concerned the Transvaal, where Kruger had offered the Uitlanders limited franchise in return for the withdrawal of suzerainty, a condition Kruger knew would be unacceptable. Milner was soon telling Joseph Chamberlain, the Colonial Secretary, that the solution to the Transvaal was drastic reform or war, and reform seemed unlikely. He urged the sending of 10,000 troops, for a show of force, he felt, might persuade Kruger to co-operate.

In due course troops were on their way to Natal from India, Malta and Crete, but the bluff did not work, and long negotiations achieved very little. By the summer of 1899, both sides realised that war was inevitable, it was merely a case as to who would act first. The Uitlanders, who had closed the mines and left Johannesburg, guessed rightly that it would be Kruger. On 9 October, an ultimatum was handed to the British agent in Pretoria. Its demands were unacceptable and, by 5 pm on 11 October, Britain was at war with the South African Republic.

Not for the first time, nor the last, Britain entered upon a war quite unprepared. There were insufficient troops available, even for a small war, and the Secretary of State for War, Lord Lansdowne, had delayed mobilisation until almost the day of the ultimatum. There was a shortage of certain ordnance stores, most importantly maps, which were not only insufficient, but incomplete and unreliable; and General Sir Redvers Buller, chosen to command the troops, was reluctant to accept the responsibility, having had no experience of senior command in war.

However, almost all the reinforcements from India (British troops) had arrived in Natal by the outbreak of war, and although Buller was still in England awaiting the completion of mobilisation of the Army Corps of 47,000 men, Britain had in Natal just over 13,000 regular troops and 2,781 local forces. The initial Boer invasion of the colony was estimated at 17,000 men (another 20,000 were on the Cape Colony border), and they were soon reinforced. Their mobilisation figure was given as 48,216 troops from both republics. General Joubert had succeeded Kruger as Commandant General of the Boer forces. He w,s old and cautious, but in Louis Botha he had a highly skilled lieutenant in Natal. Command at lower levels occasionally suffered from the Boer preference for individual rather than collective fighting.

Another British failing, that of underestimating the skill of the enemy was soon, and painfully, corrected. The Boers were unparalleled in fieldcraft, and their marksmanship was excellent. In this they were aided by the .276 millimetre German Mauser (which was a better weapon than the British Lee-Metford). They had over 50,000 of these, and almost as

MAP 11.1

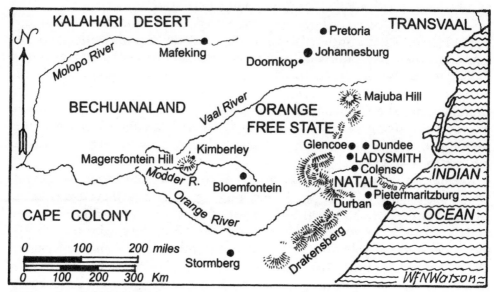

Eastern South Africa in 1899

many Martini-Henry. Their commando system* was geared to instant mobilisation; organised by the field cornet, and led by the commandant, the size of a commando varied from 300 to 3,000 depending upon the district. Natural horsemen, Boer mobility was a feature of the fighting, and brought out the need for more British mounted infantry. In defence, the Boers were stubborn and dangerous, but they had a very healthy respect for the bayonet, and tended to avoid close-quarter fighting. The artillery arm was a part of the regular forces, and excellent. The Boers possessed French Creusot guns (6-inch and 3-inch), Krupp howitzers, Vickers-Maxim quick-firing guns and Vickers mountain guns, and these they fired and manoeuvred with great skill. But they never learnt the value of concentrated fire, which, on occasions, proved fortunate for the British.

Lieutenant General Sir George White was appointed to command the troops in Natal, where he arrived a day or two after the war began, and took over from Major General Penn Symons. The latter had decided on a forward defence, and had troops at Glencoe near Dundee. White, quite rightly, favoured a more southerly line, perhaps along the Tugela river, but the governor of the colony, Sir Walter Hely-Hutchinson, supported Symons' plan on political grounds, and White allowed himself to be overruled, establishing his headquarters at Ladysmith.

*The commandos were a citizen fighting force based chiefly upon the Boer farmers. Their mastery of guerrilla warfare led to the adoption of the term 'commando' for specialised raiding forces in the Second World War.

The first engagement of the war took place on 20 October at Talana Hill – a few miles north of Dundee. The hill was taken from the Boers by a frontal attack at the heavy cost of ten officers (one of whom was Symons) and 31 other ranks killed, and nearly 200 wounded. A further 245 cavalry and mounted infantrymen were made prisoner when cut off during the pursuit. The lesson was obvious (but sadly not learnt) that to attack the Boers frontally was a very dangerous practice.

Brigadier General Yule, now in command, requested reinforcements, but these were refused, for another battle was in progress at Elandslaagte, a railway town north of Ladysmith, where a large force of Boers had cut White's forward communications. This was a more satisfactory victory, for although British casualties at 250 all ranks were again quite heavy, once the infantry had cleared the Boers from the ridge they were holding, the cavalry, which included the Imperial Light Horse (ILH) (a fine body of men raised by the Uitlanders) took heavy toll in the pursuit. On 22 October, Yule was ordered to withdraw to Ladysmith, where his weary men arrived four days later, having been constantly under attack and in danger of being cut off. On the 29th, a reconnaissance patrol reported a strong concentration of Boers with heavy guns on Pepworth and Long Hills. White made plans to break up this threat of investment the next day.

To accomplish this, he used almost his entire force. The main attack was to be made by 7 and 8 Brigades and preceded by a heavy artillery concentration on the Boer positions. 8 Brigade was to advance along the Modder Spruit and take Long Hill in flank, while 7 Brigade would be in reserve until that feature was carried and would then assault Pepworth Hill to complete the operation. The right flank of the attack was to be protected by a cavalry brigade, and on the left two battalions and a mountain battery under Lieutenant Colonel Carleton were to hold Nicholson's Nek (three miles north-west of Pepworth Hill) to guard that flank, and open the way for a cavalry pursuit.

The plan was sound, except for the grave error of sending infantry out on a limb with only light mountain guns; but the intelligence was faulty, for the Boer line extended much farther than was thought. In consequence 8 Brigade, while still in the Modder Spruit, found itself heavily engaged, and partially outflanked. 7 Brigade, having taken Limit Hill, was constantly called upon to send troops to stabilise the front. Neither brigade, despite considerable help from the cavalry on the right, could make progress and, at 11 am, White ordered them to withdraw. A difficult operation was carried out under severe artillery fire, which was largely neutralised by the fortuitous arrival from Durban, at about 10 am, of Captain Hedworth Lambton RN with four 12-pounders and two 4.7-inch naval guns on improvised carriages. The troops were back in camp by 2.30 pm having suffered 318 casualties.

The disappointment of the main attack was overshadowed by the disaster on the left. Colonel Carleton's force had a long and difficult night march at the end of which they ascended the wrong hill by an almost precipitous track. The mules panicked, and went crashing to the bottom with the guns. When dawn came, the force found itself exposed to heavy Boer fire with virtually no protection. After raising what cover they could from boulders, and suffering many casualties in the extremely confused fighting, one company commander, thinking his troops were cut off, surrendered. With the Boers advancing over open ground to take the surrender, Carleton found himself compromised and felt his position so weak that he decided to surrender the whole force of 37 officers and 917 men. It is easy to understand why this black day became known thereafter as 'Mournful Monday'.

Sir Redvers Buller arrived in Durban a day later, and it was quickly apparent to him that White would not be able to hold Natal. Indeed, White informed him at once that he was now besieged, although he did not regard this as a calamity, for he had supplies for three months, and so long as Ladysmith held, Maritzberg and Durban were safe. Nevertheless, after a few days' consideration in Cape Town, Buller decided that his place was in Natal to direct the relief of Ladysmith with some of the reinforcements now on the way.

Ladysmith in 1899 was a small town with about 5,000 inhabitants. It stood on the left bank of the river Klip at the western edge of a flat plain some three miles wide. There were two main streets of galvanized iron-roofed houses and shops. The town was sheltered to the west by a ridge of boulder-strewn *kopjes* (or small hills), and a little over a mile from its southern edge was an elevated ridge running east-west, and there was a similar ridge, but closer, to the north. It was a very difficult place to defend if there were not sufficient troops to hold the outer hills that overlooked the town. To the north these were Thornhill's Kop, Surprise Hill and Pepworth Hill; to the east was Umbulwana, Lombard's Kop and Gun Hill; to the south, Middle Hill; and on the west, Lancer's Hill, Rifleman's Ridge and Telegraph Ridge. These outer features were mostly about four-and-a-half miles from the town centre, with Lancer's Hill six miles. None of them could be held by the garrison, and in due course most were held by the Boers. A Royal Engineers balloon section, under Captain Heath, was used to spot Boer battery positions in these hills.

At the beginning of the siege, White had 13,496 officers and men and 51 guns. The perimeter of some 14 miles was divided into four sections. Section A to the north and north-east was commanded by Colonel Knox and held by the 1st Devons, 1st Liverpools, two companies of the 1st Gloucesters, and half a company of the 2nd Royal Dublin Fusiliers. Section B to the north and north-west was commanded by Colonel Howard, with the Leicesters, King's Royal Rifles and Rifle Brigade. Section C on the south and south-west was under Colonel Hamilton (later to gain fame as General

Sir Ian Hamilton) who had the Gordon Highlanders, four companies of the Manchester Regiment and two of the Royal Irish Fusiliers, and Section D which reached from Hamilton's left to Section A was commanded by Colonel Royston, who had various regiments and detachments from the Natal volunteers. Troops not allotted to sections were initially held in reserve. The naval guns were positioned on features in the two northern sectors, and the six field batteries were treated as a mobile reserve. White's headquarters were on Convent Hill, which stood 500 yards north-west of the town.

Joubert was convinced that the capture of Ladysmith would add enormously to his chances of success, because it would bring large numbers of waverers both in Natal and Cape Colony to his side. He therefore postponed any action farther south, and concentrated on the investment of the town. For this purpose he employed twelve commandos of varying sizes, a so-called Irish Brigade of 200 men, and some German detachments, in all 17,000 men, to form the inner circle. In outline, his plan was for the Free State forces to occupy the western side of the town and the Transvaalers the eastern, the dividing line in the north to be the Klip, and in the south, Nelthorpe.

The strong Pretoria Commando (2,300) and the Johannesburg police were given the northern sector east of the Klip, and the Irish Brigade was on the Elandslaagte railway. From Long Hill through Lombard's Kop to Umbulwana were the Lydenberg, Heidelberg and Wakkerstroom Commandos. South of Bester's Valley was held by the Utrecht, Vryheid and Harrismith men, and the troops occupying the south and western heights from Lancer's Hill through Rifleman's Ridge to Telegraph Ridge were the Heilbron, Kroonstad and part of the Winburg Commandos. Each commando had its own artillery detachment, and the heavy 6-inch Creusot guns were in position on Pepworth Hill and Umbulwana. These were the guns that caused most trouble, and it was fortunate that in the soft ground many of the percussion shells failed to detonate. Joubert had his headquarters a mile and a half north-east of Long Hill on the Modder Spruit.

The encirclement was complete by the early days of November, and there were other commandos brought up during that month to make the total of investing troops to around 23,000. In this, as in all wars, there were unpleasant incidents such as the abuse of the white flag, but generally speaking the Boer War was carried out in a comparatively humane manner. Joubert permitted some of the women and children to leave Ladysmith and, on representations from White, he sanctioned the setting up of a large neutral hospital on the Intombi Spruit three miles south-east of the town.

After a few days of consolidation and entrenching by both sides, the Boers moved on Limit Hill and took it from a small cavalry picquet, and on 3 November, Major General Brocklehurst, in command of the cavalry, carried out a reconnaissance in force towards Lancer's Hill. Nothing was achieved, and in a smart skirmish the ILH lost two officers and four troopers killed, and 14 wounded. The Boers retaliated three days later with a limited offensive against the southern defences which came to nothing, but a larger operation was mounted on 9 November. After an intensive preliminary bombardment from an estimated 25 guns, an attack developed on Observation Hill at about 6 am. This was successfully held after the post had been reinforced by two companies of the 2nd Rifle Brigade, and other commandos forming up in front of Lombard's Kop were dispersed by gun fire. But the main purpose of the operation had been to seize the prominent southern ridge in Colonel Hamilton's sector, and this was repulsed by his brigade, supported by 42 Royal Field Artillery.

The failure of this attack strengthened Joubert's long-held opinion that Ladysmith would be a hard nut to crack. He now determined on a diversion in the form of a strong raid to the south and, accompanied by Botha, he set out on 13 November at the head of 2,000 troops, two guns and two maxims. This raid was a tactical gem, for although the British had been recently reinforced, the Boer mobility enabled Joubert to get in between the British brigades and gain a number of minor successes. Much booty was collected, and the armoured train that brought Winston Churchill to prominence was captured. But it proved far too ambitious a project, and ended in a hasty withdrawal to the Tugela, with Botha in command, for Joubert had been seriously injured when his horse fell.

Meanwhile, at Ladysmith, the Boers settled down to a close investment, heavy bombardment, occasional raids on outposts, and hopes of success through starvation. To further the latter, the garrison was forced to accept large numbers of kaffirs and Indian labourers from Dundee. But the Commissariat Department, under the excellent handling of Colonels Ward and Stoneman, had few feeding problems initially, although on 25 November White thought it necessary to reduce the ration, and refused absolutely to accept another batch of 250 natives.

The garrison and civilians very quickly settled down to siege routine of discomfort and long periods of boredom, punctuated by those moments of chill horror that seize upon the viscera as the shells come crashing down. But it was remarkable how little damage was done to personnel by the bombardment, which was very heavy and persistent at times. There were a number of amazing escapes. A 96-lb shell from one of the Creusot 'Long Toms' landed within a few feet of where White and his staff were sitting their horses, and failed to explode; and on another occasion, a shell ploughed through the wall of Hamilton's brigade headquarters and exploded under the dining-room table, laid for breakfast, just as the commander, his brigade major and Colonel Rhodes (Cecil's brother) were about to enter the room.

MAP 11.2

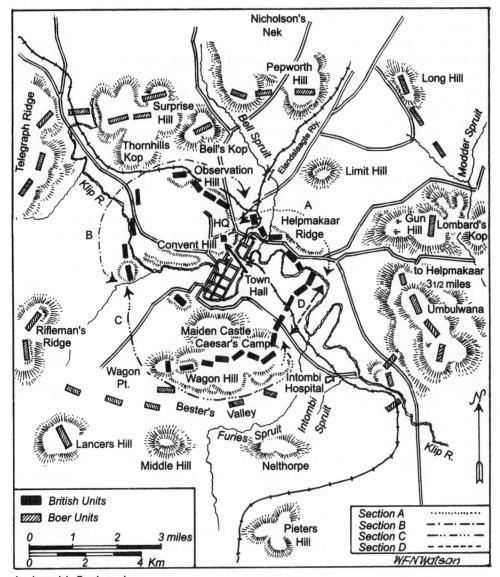

Ladysmith Besieged

Nevertheless, there were a few casualties every day when places like the Royal Hotel, Town Hall and shops (before they closed) were hit, and the occasional tragedy when a direct hit was scored on troops at duty. The Natal Carbineers and the 5th Lancers lost men and horses when shells struck them at morning stables, and the Gloucesters had five men killed and nine wounded by one shell. The Boers laid their guns on the batteries by day, and the streets by night. There were spies among the native drivers who undoubtedly gave the Boers useful military information, but most of the civilians escaped the nightly cannonade through seeking the protection of caves in the riverside bluffs.

No one could impugn White's courage, for he had been in the forefront of many fights and had won the Victoria Cross, but now, at 64 he was faced with a kind of fighting new to him. In General Hunter and Colonel Rawlinson (who would command the 4th Army on the Western Front in the First World War) he had on his staff two first rate soldiers to whose counsel he should have paid greater attention. There were more opportunities for offensive action than he was willing to take, and although always accessible he was seldom seen. He spent most of his time closeted in his quarters, seemingly smitten by a damaging catalepsy. This was unfortunate, for of all the operations of war, the siege offers the best opportunity for the general to impress his personality upon the troops, and to influence morale.

On 7 December, White was able to establish heliographic communication with Generals Buller and Clery, who were preparing to advance to his relief. Back in England, the siege of Ladysmith had an emotional connotation well in excess of the town's strategic value, and Buller, now with 21,000 men under command, was determined on its relief. The timing had yet to be fixed, but White organised a mixed mobile force to be specially trained to help at the appointed hour. Meanwhile, the garrison had become greatly troubled by an increase in Boer fire power, whilst its own artillery, especially the naval heavy guns, was short of ammunition, which had to be carefully husbanded. White was therefore prevailed upon to carry out raids on enemy gun positions.

The first of these, against Gun Hill on the night of 7/8 December, was under the personal command of General Hunter. He took with him 500 men of the Natal Carbineers, 120 ILH, a detachment of Engineers, and a detachment of No 10 Mountain Battery. A cavalry force was to guard his left flank, and the 1st Devons were sent to hold a covering position on the Helpmakaar Ridge. The approach march through Stygian darkness was skilfully accomplished, and the base of the steeply faced hill was reached at 2 am. Some of the Carbineers were detailed to guard the immediate flanks of the attacking force. The picquet at the foot of the hill was taken by surprise – a most unusual occurrence – and the ILH and remaining Carbineers stormed up the hill and overran the gun positions. The 96-pounder and 4.7-inch howitzer were then blown up. That same night two companies of the 1st Liverpools and a squadron of 19th Hussars captured Limit Hill.

Encouraged by these successes, a further raid was made on gun positions on Surprise Hill on the night of 10/11 December by 450 men of the 2nd Rifle Brigade under their commanding officer, Lieutenant Colonel Metcalfe, with a detachment from the Engineers and the 69th Battery RFA. The party started from Observation Hill and covered the 6,000 yards uneventfully. The assault up the steep, rocky hill was successful, but the first charges placed under the guns failed to ignite, and the delay in setting new ones meant that the drop-off troops at the bottom of the hill were hotly engaged, and the whole party had to fight its way out losing 19 men killed and 44 wounded.

This last raid coincided with the beginning of what became known as 'Black Week'. The British Army had not fought opponents with modern weapons since the Crimean War, more than 40 years before (and its generals there were no Napoleons), and now in South Africa from Buller right through the divisional and brigade commanders experience was limited to small native wars. Inevitably, mistakes were made in handling large formations against a cunning and skilful enemy armed with excellent weapons. Almost certainly, the job was too big for Buller. He handicapped himself from the start by dividing the newly arrived Army Corps to fight on three fronts, and not remaining centrally placed to take command himself. Between 10 and 16 December, his army suffered serious setbacks on the western, central and eastern fronts.

Lord Methuen, commanding the division on the left, attempted a difficult night march against some 5,000 Boers entrenched on Magersfontein Hill, and fell into a trap, losing nearly 1,000 men killed and wounded. Meanwhile General Gatacre, in the centre, suffered almost as many casualties through a series of muddles in his attack on Stormberg. But the worse reverse of 'Black Week' befell Buller himself in the fierce Colenso battle, fought on 15 December.

The Boers held a very strong position on the left bank of the Tugela, and in their recent southern raid they had destroyed the principal bridge. Buller planned to send a brigade up river to cross at some fords and attempt to outflank the right of the Boer line, but the main punch was to be a frontal attack – so beloved by the school of native warfare – across the river by two brigades. The key to the battle was Hlangwane Hill, a feature on Buller's right south of the river. It was strongly held by 800 Boers who, unless driven off it before the main attack went in, could cause considerable trouble with enfilade fire. Lord Dundonald's mounted brigade and the South African Light Horse were given the task of taking it, but it proved beyond them, and when they called for reinforcements, Buller was unwilling to take men from the centre.

The operation went wrong from the start. The flanking brigade never found the fords, and were badly mauled before being extricated by the neighbouring brigade. In the centre, repeated efforts to achieve a crossing were foiled by Botha's resolute defence and, by the middle of the morning, it was painfully clear that the battle was running the enemy's way, and that Buller had lost control of it. Soon after 11 am, realising nothing was being achieved, he gave the order to withdraw to camp. His casualties were 74 officers, 1,064 men, and 10 guns in this his first attempt to relieve Ladysmith.

Colours were no longer taken into battle, but the guns had the same connotation of sanctity. Colonel Long may have misunderstood his orders when he brought twelve 15-pounders into action ahead of the leading troops, and well within range of everything the Boers had. It was almost the only time the Boers concentrated their fire, and after the gunners had expended most of their ammunition they could stand the punishment no longer, and retired to the shelter of a *donga*.* Numerous exceedingly gallant attempts were made to retrieve the guns, and two were brought in. But the effort was far too costly, and Buller eventually stopped it. Five Victoria Crosses were awarded to those who had tried and failed. Among them (posthumously awarded) was Lieutenant Frederick Roberts, the only son of the man who was shortly to relieve Buller in overall command.

'Black Week' confirmed that Buller was not up to the task, and the government had already decided to send out Field Marshal Lord Roberts with Major General Kitchener as his chief-of-staff. The reverse Buller suffered in Natal was compounded by his defeatist telegram to Lansdowne, and helio message to White, saying he was doubtful of being able to relieve Ladysmith and suggesting an attempted break-out or surrender. But White was made of sterner stuff. He replied at length to Buller saying he had rations to last well above a month; it would be wrong to sacrifice 12,000 men; he had no intention of surrendering; and he urged Buller to keep in touch with the Boers until strong enough to renew the attack.

Buller's helio message, which coincided with a bout of very heavy shelling (on 18 December there were 18 casualties) had a depressing effect on the troops who were now suffering badly from typhoid and dysentery. By the end of the year, there were 1,650 officers and men in hospital, and the death rate had risen to 23 weekly. Christmas came with some early morning shelling. One of the unexploded 15-pounder shells was stamped 'with the compliments of the season', and contained a synthetic plum pudding! Food was now becoming short and monotonous. Fresh vegetables from the local gardens were virtually finished, and what there were sold at fantastic prices; there was still a small daily ration of meat, but milk was in very short supply. Eggs could be bought occasionally, as much as 23 shillings a dozen being paid. It was a shut-in world, fed upon rumour, but there were concerts to be enjoyed and even polo for some; above all, there was no thought by anyone of surrender.

The new century opened quietly, but within six days the garrison was called upon to withstand a major offensive which rolled against the southern defences for fifteen hours and bade fair to determine the fate of Ladysmith. Joubert, somewhat unwillingly, for he was mindful of 9 November, and under pressure from the two state presidents, agreed to an attack with between five and six thousand men from both armies

Donga. A ravine or gully.

under the general direction of Botha and Commandant De Villiers of the Orange Free State. With their natural eye for country the Boers had always realised the importance of the southern ridge, known as Wagon Hill and Caesar's Camp, and their principal attack was to be against the troops on this feature.

This east-west ridge extends for two-and-a-quarter miles. It includes two separate heights joined by a neck, of which the eastern one (Caesar's Camp) is much the larger in area. At the western end of the ridge are two knolls, Wagon Hill and, at its western extremity, Wagon Point. Typically, the ridge was barren but covered with huge boulders, and at its eastern edge, mimosa bush in the valley offered an excellent covered approach. The ridge was exposed to Boer batteries on Umbulwana, Middle Hill and Rifleman's Ridge. On the night of 5 January, Caesar's Camp was held by the 1st Manchesters, the Natal Volunteers, and a naval detachment, Wagon Hill by six companies of the 2nd/60th and a squadron of the ILH, and Wagon Point by another squadron of the ILH. A detachment of sappers under Lieutenant Digby Jones arrived that evening to erect a platform for a 4.7-inch naval gun. Colonel Ian Hamilton was in overall command.

The attack began at 2.45 am on 6 January when some deception was practised on the ILH sentries which gained the Boers a small advantage, and they were soon storming their way up Wagon Hill and Point where there was considerable confusion. The sappers were still working on the gun emplacement when the Boers arrived, but young Jones led them and some Gordon Highlanders in a bayonet charge which cleared the crest of the hill. Both squadrons of the ILH then joined in the fray, and Major Gore Browne answered an appeal for help with a company of the 60th. A close-quarter fight continued hotly and confusedly on this part of the ridge until dawn.

Orange Free State Commandos had assaulted Wagon Hill and 20 minutes later, it was the turn of the Transvaalers to storm Caesar's Camp. Partly owing to shortage of manpower, but also to inefficiency, this feature had not been properly fortified nor had the mimosa scrub been cleared. In consequence some men of the 2,000-strong Heidelberg Commando were able to infiltrate between the left picquet of the Manchesters and the Natal troops. Soon the Commando had overrun two lines of weak *sangars,** and had established a foothold on the crest. Here, as on Wagon Hill, the fighting was fierce and confused, but the Boers were firmly held to the eastern edge of the ridge.

The battle had hardly started before the headquarters staff were rudely awakened by the thunder of guns echoing round the hills, for the Boers had launched a number of feints, the most persistent being that against

---

*Sangar. A fire position protected by a parapet of large stones and rocks which, on occasions, might serve a whole platoon but more usually a section or less.

MAP 11.3

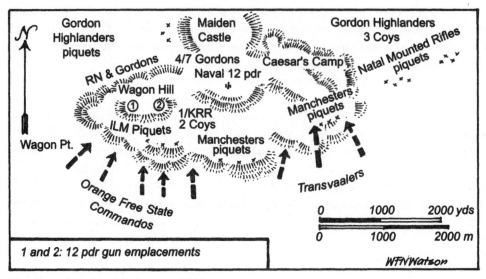

The Boer Attacks of 6 January 1900

Observation Hill. At the same time, requests for reinforcements reached White from Hamilton. White rose from a sickbed and, with Hunter and Rawlinson, was quick to respond. More ILH were sent to Wagon Hill, and the 2nd Gordon Highlanders to Caesar's Camp. Here Captain Carnegie's company of Gordons cleared the Boers from a dangerous enveloping position which they had established after outflanking the left hand picquet of the Manchesters in their initial assault. At about the same time, Major Abdy's 53rd Battery, which was part of White's reinforcements, came into action east of Maiden Castle. Despite being pounded by the Umbulwana gun, the battery got off 138 rounds of shrapnel, which cleared the enemy from the south-east slopes of Caesar's Camp. But the crest still swarmed with Boers and six companies of the Rifle Brigade were brought forward to deal with these. On arrival, they found no one in charge, received no orders and, joining the general mélange, suffered heavy casualties.

This hiatus in local command was due to Hamilton having galloped off to Wagon Hill on hearing the opening shots, and remaining there when it became obvious that that feature, unable to receive artillery support, presented the more dangerous situation. Repeated, and most gallant, attempts to drive the Boers from the summit all failed, but by 11 am both sides had temporarily fought themselves to a standstill, and the firing almost ceased. On Caesar's Camp the crisis had passed by this time, for there were now quite sufficient troops there (White, having no further infantry to spare, had recently sent six squadrons of cavalry to the ridge). Indeed, the Boers, probably realised that, having failed to capture the two positions in the early hours before reinforcements arrived, their chances of success were now very slender. Nevertheless, there were men among them not prepared to give up, and at about 1 pm a fresh assault, led by Commandant De Villiers and Field-Cornet De Jagers, suddenly erupted upon Wagon Hill.

The appearance of the leading Boers, after two hours of inaction, took the forward troops completely by surprise. They were swept back, and once again it was the action of the intrepid Digby Jones, assisted this time by Major Miller-Wallnutt of the ILH, and indeed by Ian Hamilton himself, that retrieved a very nasty situation. These three men were at a gun emplacement, and their first intimation of the attack came when a sapper was shot dead in front of them. Jones immediately seized a rifle and made for the open. His first shot killed De Villiers, and someone felled De Jagers at the same time. Hamilton stood rock steady, revolver in hand, endeavouring to halt the backward movement, for the Boers were pouring lead into the retreating troops mowing them down, spinning them round. Jones and Miller-Wallnutt went back to bring up the reserves, and rally those men that had broken. In this they were successful, but both lost their lives in the doing. The dismounted cavalry did fine work, and by 2 pm this attack, which had not been well supported, was beaten off. However, for the next two hours there was a fierce mingle-mangle on Wagon Hill.

By 4 pm, the Boers appeared to have had enough, but they stubbornly hung on to the crests from which the exhausted defenders were unable to shift them. They were probably waiting for darkness to cover their retreat, but White wanted the ridge cleared before then, and decided to withdraw the 1st Devons from their key position on the perimeter. All day a blazing sun had burnt down upon the troops from a clear sky, but now one of those extremely violent South African thunderstorms burst upon them, and the hills and sky merged together in massive black clouds. As the weary defenders, led by the fresh Devons with bayonets fixed, chased the Boers off the ridge, the storm that had lasted nearly two hours flooded the *dongas*, and drowned many of the Boer wounded lying in them. The remainder disappeared into the darkness accompanied by claps of thunder and a vicious crackle of musketry. It had been a hard day's fighting, and until the coming of dawn and reinforcements it was a close run affair. Great courage, determination and, at times, tactical skill had been displayed by both sides. Five Victoria Crosses (including Jones and Miller-Wallnutt) were awarded. 175 officers and men died in holding back this dangerous Boer inroad and more than 200 were wounded. Boer casualties were thought to have been slightly heavier.

There were to be no more assaults upon Ladysmith. But the garrison was so weak now that White's mobile force could no longer support a breakthrough by Buller. The 5th Division, under Sir Charles Warren, had recently arrived in Natal and Buller decided to carry out the plan he had previously abandoned in favour of Colenso. This was a flank march westwards to cross the Tugela at Trikhardt's Drift and attack the right of the Boer line. Lord Roberts arrived in Cape Town on 10 January and was informed by Buller of this plan. He did not favour it, but felt it unwise to overrule the man on the spot. Buller gave command of the main operation to Warren merely acting himself as adviser. It was not a good idea, for Warren lacked experience of handling large numbers (he had some 15,000 men under command), and Buller breathing down his neck probably did not help.

The Tugela was crossed on 17 January, and the main force was to attack two features on the Rangeworthy Heights (Tabanyama), while General Lyttelton's force of 9,000 men remained north of the river at Potgeiter's Drift. The Tabanyama attack was only partially successful, for the Boers had brought troops from Ladysmith and extended their right. Warren and Buller then decided to switch the attack to Spion Kop on the night of 23 January (there had been spasmodic, indecisive actions north of the river between 19–22 January). A battle raged on that height throughout the 24th. Lyttelton sent reinforcements, and also created a useful diversion by attacking and taking Twin Peaks to the east. On Spion Kop there was a certain amount of muddle over the command of the operation, and by 7 pm, with no progress made and the situation looking dark and uncertain, Brigadier General Thorneycroft, who had recently been put in command, decided to retire. The skilful withdrawal was perhaps the only real success of a day on which Buller had over 1,000 casualties, and achieved nothing.

The relieving army was now back behind the Tugela, but despite two serious reverses, Buller's habitually cheerful disposition did not desert him. To what extent his men remained cheerful is a different matter, but there was only a little grumbling, and much enthusiasm for the next round. After a few days for reorganisation and rest, this was to be aimed at the ridge to the east of Spion Kop called Vaal Krantz. It was thought to be the left of the Boer line on that range of hills, and when taken should open the way across nine miles of flat country to Ladysmith. But in fact it was not the Boers' extreme left and, in the absence of good maps, important details of the feature were unknown at the time of the attack.

The river was to be crossed by three pontoon bridges, and while the main attack was to be made on Vaal Krantz by Lyttelton's 4 Brigade supported by 2 and 5 Brigades, 11 Brigade was to make a feint against Brackfontein, a hill some three miles to the north-west. That brigade moved off at 6 am on 5 February and the Boers, in position on the reverse slope, allowed it to come within a thousand yards before opening heavy fire which effectively held up the advance.

Meanwhile, for various reasons, 4 Brigade did not cross the river until

2 pm, but by 4 pm it had taken Vaal Krantz. It then became clear that the feature had little value so long as Hill 360 to the left and Green Hill on the right remained in enemy hands. But Buller had now become nervous of once again suffering heavy casualties with no positive results, and held 2 Brigade back until receiving assent from Roberts that heavy casualties could be accepted. He then sent that brigade, on the evening of 6 February, to relieve Lyttelton's embattled men on Vaal Krantz. Throughout the 7th, the troops there were scorched by the sun and blasted by shell fire from which the flimsy sangars gave only limited protection. The brigade commander reported that prospects of taking Hill 360 seemed remote, and after Buller had gone forward to see for himself, he realised that this third attempt to relieve Ladysmith must be abandoned. By the evening of the 8th, the army was once again south of the Tugela. Vaal Krantz had cost Buller 370 casualties against a mere 30 or so lost by the Boers.

While Buller was making these attempts to relieve them, the troops and civilians in Ladysmith were facing diminishing food stocks with fortitude and firmness. When the last trek-ox had been eaten, White gave permission for the more robust horses to be killed. Forage had become very short, necessitating the retention of a bare minimum of horses for the artillery and cavalry. The remainder, and the mules, all skin and bones, were either turned out or converted into a ingenious form of Bovril called 'chevril'. The daily ration in February was 1 lb of horsemeat, ½ lb of biscuit, ⅙th oz of tea or coffee, ½ oz of sugar, and ¼ oz of salt. Vegetables, milk, and the mealie meal for porridge had disappeared from the menu.

The scanty rations were no doubt partly the cause of the enormous number of sick by the first week in February, when as many as 110 men a day were being sent to the hospital. In the Intombi hospital, designed for 300 beds, there were over 2,000 sick and wounded, more than half of them suffering from typhoid, and the death rate was eight per day. A contributory cause to illness, especially mental illness, was the extreme nervous tension caused by the remorseless pounding of the Boer heavy guns, the scarcity of news of Buller's progress, and the agony of hopes deferred as the rumble of his artillery sounded close and then receded.

A little over a week after the failure at Vaal Krantz, Buller made his fourth, and as it turned out final, attempt to relieve Ladysmith. Much had been learnt from Colenso, Spion Kop and Vaal Krantz and this time he got it right, for he saw that no progress could be made unless he cleared the Boers from Hlangwane and their other positions south of the river. It was to be a very tough battle lasting many days, for the Boer position was a strong one, running from Cingolo and Monte Cristo to their left through Hlangwane and across the river almost to Grobelaar Kloof. This was rough, rugged country made for defence, where 8,000 good men might have defied Buller's two divisions (about 25,000 in all) had they not been hopelessly outgunned.

MAP 11.4

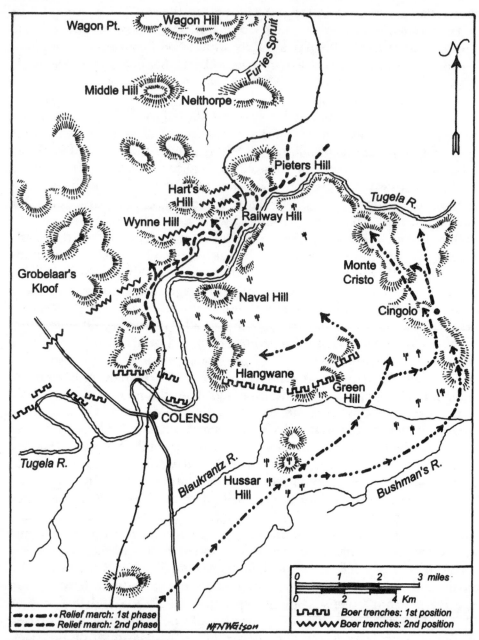

Buller's Relief of Ladysmith

General Lyttelton's 2 Division (he had succeeded General Clery who was sick) advanced on the right, and General Warren's 5 Division on the left. On 14 February, Hussar Hill was quickly taken, and Lyttelton's 2 and 4

Brigades made for Cingolo and Monte Cristo, and these two features fell on the 17th and 18th respectively. On the 19th, Warren's 6 Brigade had captured Hlangwane. There was now a partial panic in the Boer line, and large numbers were seen retreating. Had they been resolutely pursued, much subsequent hard fighting might have been avoided, but they were given time to recover on the 20th and 21st. Nevertheless, by the morning of the 20th, there were no Boers south of the Tugela.

5 Division now took the lead, and crossing the river by a pontoon bridge near Hlangwane on the afternoon of the 21st had a very tough time fighting its way down the left bank. On the 22nd, 11 Brigade captured Wynne's Hill, but on the 23rd there was some exceptionally heavy fighting for Hart's Hill and Railway Hill. Very little progress was made, and there were many casualties. Buller now made a major reappraisal. After a truce had been agreed for succouring the wounded and burying the dead, he left two brigades and a battalion on the captured ground, and withdrew all the other troops back across the river.

The final phase of this drawn out battle began on the morning of 27 February. Basically, the plan now was for 6 Brigade (Barton's) to cross the river by the new pontoon bridge and work its way round to storm Pieter's Hill, known to be the left of the Boer position, from a flank. As soon as this attack developed, a frontal assault was to be launched on Railway Hill and Hart's Hill by 11 and 4 Brigades respectively. A very heavy and concentrated artillery bombardment preceded and accompanied these attacks, all of which were entirely successful. By the end of the day, the Boers were seen to be riding away all along the line, and there was much cheering in the British ranks – probably an expression of triumph and relief, but a few may have recalled it was Majuba Day. British casualties in the 14 days were just over 2,000 all ranks of which 307 had been killed. The Boers reported a loss of only 420 killed and wounded.

On 28 February, dawn broke through dark, heavily laden clouds that promised rain. There was nothing to indicate to the Ladysmith garrison that this the 118th day of the siege was to be the last. Periodic messages had been received from Buller, but his forecasts had not always proved accurate. However, at about midday, large numbers of Boers with their wagons were seen trekking north, east of Umbulwana. Clearly this was a major retreat, and relief was at hand. There was little the greatly weakened garrison could do, but a mounted column of Natal Carbineers was sent out on horses that could hardly canter. The Boers conducted a masterly retreat saving all their guns, but the Carbineers inflicted a few casualties on the rearguard without loss to themselves.

It was about 6 pm when Lieutenant Colonel Gough with two squadrons of Mounted Infantry rode into the town to be greeted by a greatly rejoicing, but sadly emaciated garrison, and an immaculately turned out General White, who was said to have aged more than ten years from his ordeal.

Inevitably, his performance was to be subjected to a critical, and none too friendly, scrutiny. Through many very trying days he may not have shown the fire and spirit of a great commander, but he had never given way to despair, or ever contemplated surrender.

In the course of the siege the garrison had lost 270 men killed, 629 wounded, and 541 had died from disease.

CHAPTER 12

Port Arthur 1904–05

THE story of the Russo-Japanese War of 1904–05 is not well known yet, like the American Civil War, it was to have much influence on the techniques of warfare in the years ahead.

The siege of Port Arthur, one of the two principal engagements in that war, was remarkable in two respects – the sheer heroism shown by the junior officers and their soldiers and the failure of command, both Russian and Japanese, which were to be paid for at a terrible price in human lives. The Russian commander was little better than an incompetent poltroon. In consequence, he was in constant conflict with his subordinates and command became split. The Japanese General Nogi, on the other hand, lacked any sort of finesse and drove his troops like a bull at a gate. In five months, over 120,000 men lost their lives in battle or through disease.

Port Arthur fell on New Year's Day 1905. Five months later, the great Russian fleet which had been sailed half way round the world to bring relief to their forces in the Far East, was decisively defeated in the battle of Tsushima and the power of Russia in that theatre was extinguished.

* * *

The siege of Port Arthur was one of the epics of the Russo-Japanese war, which had its origins mainly in the Russian occupation and control of Manchuria and Korea. Russia had had expansionist ambitions in Manchuria since at least 1860 when she persuaded the Chinese to cede her a maritime strip from the river Amur to the Korean border. Other concessions (such as the Siberian-Vladivostok railway) and encroachments followed, but her greatest coup was a 25-year lease from 1897 of the Liao-tung Peninsula with its valuable ice-free Port Arthur. Shortly after that she got a foothold in Korea where she obtained concessions to establish a timber company with rights to exploit forests on both banks of the Yalu river.

Japan, recently emerged from a long medieval sleep, and working hard to become a modern nation, had viewed these Russian moves with deepest suspicion and a growing resentment. She too looked towards Manchuria and Korea partly as a solution to a fast expanding population, although mainly as a security buffer. Indeed, it was largely because she thought

China incapable of upholding her suzerainty in Korea that she went to war with her in 1894. As the fruits of victory, she obtained from the Chinese the Liao-tung Peninsula. But, at the time, was not strong enough to withstand European pressure on her to return the Peninsula to the Chinese, who two years later leased it to the Russians.

The two immediate causes of the outbreak of war were Russia's failure to withdraw her troops from Manchuria, and the strengthening of her presence in Korea, where Japan also had commercial interests. Russia had used the Boxer Rebellion as a pretext for pouring troops into Manchuria to protect her railway, and in 1902 had agreed with China to evacuate them in stages. But after the first stage had been completed that October, it became clear that nothing more would be done. Moreover, towards the end of 1903, the large number of troops on the Yalu, ostensibly there to guard the timber company's position at Yonggampo, were put on a war footing.

Throughout 1903 and January 1904 there were endless negotiations and conferences in St Petersburg and Tokyo, and much diplomatic activity, all of which amounted to little more than shadow boxing, for while both sides thought war inevitable, and were making preparations for it, neither wanted to enter into it before they were ready. In the end, it was the Russians, having misjudged Japanese strength and been unwisely provocative, who found themselves faced with a war for which they were not properly prepared.

At an Imperial conference in Tokyo on 4 February 1904, it was decided to go to war with three clear objectives – to regain Port Arthur, to prevent a Russian lodgement in southern Manchuria, and to secure the Japanese position in Korea. Negotiations would cease and Admiral Togo was ordered to send a squadron to deal with the Russian fleet at Port Arthur, and cruisers to cover the landing at Chemulpo. The troops were safely disembarked there on 8–9 February and, at about the same time, the Russian fleet, anchored in the roadstead at Port Arthur, was taken completely by surprise, suffering very considerable damage from the Japanese squadron. War was declared 36 hours later. By this pre-emptive strike, the Japanese had gained command of the sea. They had done the same in 1894, and were to do it again at Pearl Harbour in 1941. The lessons of history are not easily learnt.

The Japanese Army was a formidable fighting force. Germany, the leading military power of the time, had been asked to shape it, and the raw material at their disposal was excellent. There was a great military tradition to build upon, and a keen desire to master modern technology. Their armament was modern, their tactical training had been thorough with much attention paid to night operations, and their Intelligence Service was excellent. The rapidly changing Manchurian climate, from heavy rains to sizzling heat, to bitter cold, did not seem to worry these peasant-soldiers, every one of whom was a warrior utterly contemptuous of death.

The Russians possessed a very much greater reserve of manpower than their enemy, but most of their troops were far distant from the scene of action, and for much of that distance the rail track was single line. They had only 95,000 men in Manchuria at the outbreak of war and so, provided that the Japanese could retain command of the sea, Russian troops were likely to be outnumbered for a considerable time. The Russian soldier was a more stolid individual than his Japanese counterpart, but every bit as brave and efficient when well led. Russian tactics were more ponderous, and the Crimean practice of volley firing and fighting in column still prevailed. In light weapons there was little to choose between the two armies, but in the latter part of the siege the Japanese outgunned the Russians.

Naval action played a comparatively small part in the siege, although had the Russian Pacific Ocean Squadron been more enterprisingly handled, it could have had a greater bearing on the campaign. With one exception (Admiral Makaroff, who was killed soon after taking command), it was badly led, and many of the ships were substandard. It was Admiral Togo's aim to destroy or neutralise the Russian fleet as quickly as possible, and certainly before it could be reinforced by the Baltic fleet. In this he was to be largely successful, although his three attempts to block the harbour were not a total success, for a passage always remained open.

There had been a difference of opinion in Russian war councils, where only General Kuropatkin, the Minister for War, appeared to realise the full extent of the Japanese threat. Admiral Alexeiev, recently appointed Viceroy in the Far East, belittled the Japanese armed forces and argued strongly for holding the Yalu, and defeating any Japanese invasion on that river. Kuropatkin saw clearly that if command of the sea was lost, and the Russian forces were divided, they would be defeated in detail. Even though it meant the temporary loss of Port Arthur (the fleet would sail for Vladivostok) it would be better, he stressed, to pull back the Yalu force to the Mukden-Harbin area until sufficient reinforcements had arrived to sweep the Japanese off the Peninsula. Events proved his counsel to be the wisest, but it was not accepted, and when, shortly after war broke out, he was appointed commander of the armies in Manchuria, he reluctantly had to give battle on the Yalu.

The Japanese troops that landed at Chemulpo on 8–9 February marched north up Korea to cover the landing of the rest of the 1st Army at Chinampo as soon as that port was ice-free. The Japanese plan, in outline, was to isolate Port Arthur and drive a wedge between the troops there and Kuropatkin's main army at Liao-yang. Having gained command of the sea, the intention was to land the 2nd Army on the Liao-tung Peninsula, and in due course to make a converging movement to the north with three armies, leaving one army to capture Port Arthur. It was a bold plan which was to be executed in masterly fashion by Field Marshal Oyama.

The Japanese 1st Army fought its way across the Yalu between 25 and

MAP 12.1

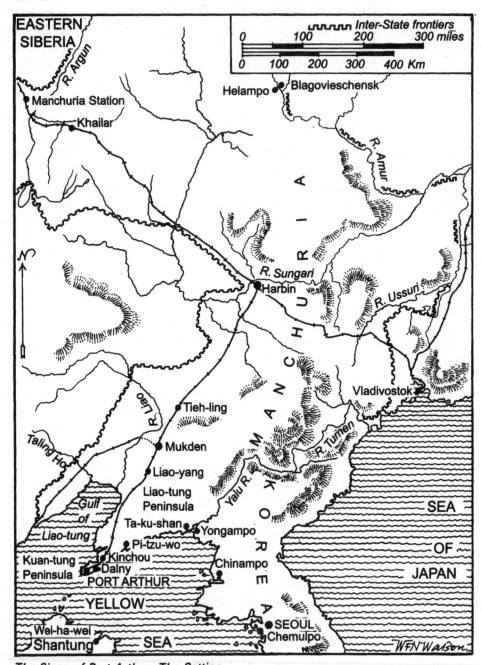

The Siege of Port Arthur: The Setting

30 April, and engaged General Zasulich's force of 20,000 men with double his numbers on 1 May. The Russians put up a magnificent defence in this as in subsequent actions, but they were too thin on the ground. By the end of

the day, they had been thrown back with a loss of 2,200 men, 600 prisoners and 21 guns. The Japanese had a little under a thousand casualties. The consequences of this the first battle of the war far exceeded its immediate result, for it was the first time a European army had been defeated by an oriental one in modern warfare, and what the Japanese gained in morale (and it was a lot) the Russians lost in proportion. Moreover, the Japanese also gained considerable international respect.

By 20 May, the Japanese 2nd Army had completed its landing at Pi-tzu-wo, and the next objectives were Kinchou and Namsan at the neck of the Kuan-tung Peninsula. During 25–26 May, the Japanese took these two places after some extremely fierce fighting. The victory not only gave them the valuable port of Dalny, but it effectively cut off the 45,000 or so troops in Kuan-tung from Kuropatkin's northern army.

After this battle, the double movement north and south of the Japanese armies, in accordance with their master plan, was carried out successfully. This fine strategic manoeuvre resulted in the 1st, 2nd, and the recently arrived 4th, armies moving north towards the Russian forces south of Liao-yang, and taking no further part against the troops in the Kuan-tung Peninsula.

However, the 2nd Army's 1st Division now reverted to the 3rd Army, which at first had only one other division, the recently landed 11th. This army, which was commanded by General Nogi, a veteran soldier who had taken Port Arthur in a day in the 1894 war, marched south from Dalny with the task of repeating Nogi's feat albeit with a greater time allowance. The Russian troops opposing it had fought at the Yalu, Kin-chou and Namsan, and were under the overall command of General Stoessel, with Lieutenant General Smirnoff acting as Fortress Commandant. They comprised the 4th East Siberian Rifle Division (ESRD) under Major General Fock, the 7th ESRD commanded by Major General Kondratenko, and detachments from the 5th ESRD. There were two artillery brigades, three battalions of Fortress Artillery, a squadron of Cossacks and various details, making a total of about 47,000 all ranks.

After their defeat at Namsan, the Russian troops moved back to the first of the outer defences known as the Green Hills. The line ran along the contours from the north coast at Shuang-tai-kou to Lao-tso-shan in the south, with two strong outposts some way in advance. Nogi was in no hurry to attack it, for he was expecting the arrival of the 9th Division, and although he took the outposts at the end of June he did not move against the main line until the end of July, by which time he had the 9th Division. The fighting on the 26th and 27th was very bitter, and the Russians put up a tremendous defence, but they could not hold against the weight of numbers and the heavy bombardment. They then fell back to their second outer line, the Wolf Hills. However, because they had put such faith in being able to hold the Green Hills, this position had been sadly neglected. Little resistance was offered there, and the Russians retired behind their permanent defences. In capturing these two positions between 26 and 31 July, the Japanese had lost 139 officers and 3,931 men.

In their withdrawal from the Wolf Hills, the Russians held on to two important features, Ta-ku-shan and Sia-gu-shan, which lay just outside the main fortifications on the south-east of the perimeter. These were attacked on 7 August, and after another stubborn defence in which the Japanese took terrible punishment as they stormed across the steep, open ground, both features were in Japanese hands by the evening of the eighth.

While the Japanese were advancing down the Peninsula, Kuropatkin had been doing his best to remove Stoessel in favour of Smirnoff, for he quite rightly considered Stoessel was not up to the job, whereas Smirnoff possessed that fiery dynamism which could generate success. Accordingly, he sent Stoessel two signals ordering him to hand over to Smirnoff and leave Port Arthur. Stoessel not only refused to leave, but informed Kuropatkin that he, and certainly not Smirnoff, was the only man capable of saving Port Arthur. All this left an unpleasant atmosphere in headquarters, where anyway there were too many chiefs – 45,000 men scarcely justified a General, a Lieutenant General and six Major Generals to look after them. It is hardly surprising that, in due course, there was to be a most damaging obfuscation of command.

The permanent fortifications of Port Arthur stretched across the heights surrounding the harbour in a semi-circle of some eleven miles. They had been started soon after Russia obtained the lease, but with the improvement in modern artillery, they were too close to what they were intended to defend. The line of the hills running from Nytonsu through Ho-shan to Ta-ku-san, behind which the Japanese had their base, would have been better.

Against attacks from the sea there were 21 coastal batteries, and the principal land defences were five forts (a sixth was sited, but had not been begun), and five fortifications. These latter were added after it was found that owing to the hilly ground the forts were not in visual communication, and they were given corresponding numbers to the forts. Starting from the south-east of the line there was Fort 1 (Pai-yin-shan); Fort 2 (Chi-kuan-shan); Fort 3 (Erh-lung-shan); Fort 4 (Yi-tzu-shan) and Fort 5 (Ta-yang-kou North). Hereafter they will be referred to as F 1, 2, 3 ....., and for the fortifications Fn 1, 2, 3 ......

At the beginning of the war F 2, 3 and 4 and Fn 4 were nearing completion, but the others still needed considerable work. Although fairly formidable, none of these works was entirely satisfactory; no proper armour was used in their construction; the concrete – between three and four feet thick only – was not proof against the 458 lb shell of the Japanese 11-inch guns; the parapets were poorly revetted; there were no covered communications and, as there were no traverses, some trenches could be enfiladed. They were held initially by one company of 200 men, but in the later days of the siege this number was increased.

At various intervals in the semi-circular defences there were permanent concrete battery emplacements. These were lettered A to D, A Battery being about 1,500 yards north of F 1, and D Battery the same distance north-east of Fn 5. Close behind the fortifications, from A Battery to Fn 3, was the old Chinese Wall which, built of mud and stones, stood some ten feet high, was twelve feet thick at the base and had a banquette and parapet. This wall had been considerably strengthened and improved by the Russians, and became a very important part of the defence. Along the crest of the heights behind the Chinese Wall was a line of batteries connected by trenches, and behind this second line was a third. It was one of the weaknesses of the defence that many of the heavy guns were placed forward on conspicuous hill sites where they attracted a heavy concentration of fire.

To the north-west of the main perimeter was a north-south line of hills known as the Metre Range. The chief importance of Angle Hill (174 Metre Hill), Long Hill (Namako-yama), and Flat Hill (Akasaka-yama) was that they guarded 203 Metre Hill (Ro-ya-san) which was vital to the defence, for it commanded the harbour. Earthworks connected this feature with F 4. There were a number of other outworks, usually connected by entrenchments, principally the redoubts in the north such as Temple, Water Supply (Fort Kuropatkin) and Rocky, while Signal Hill beyond the extreme south-east of the line, was held throughout the siege.

Early in August, Admiral Witgeft, who had succeeded Makaroff when the latter went down with his flagship, was ordered by the Viceroy in Mukden to sail the patched up fleet to the safety of Vladivostok. There was some opposition to this in Port Arthur, for many of the fleet's heavy guns were operating on shore. These were hastily dismantled. Nevertheless on 10 August the fleet sailed short of six 10-inch guns. Admiral Togo's squadron was ready and waiting, and in the subsequent engagement, although no ship on either side was sunk, the Russian fleet was roughly handled. The *Tsarevich*, wearing the Admiral's flag was severely mauled and Witgeft was among the many killed. A battleship, three cruisers and three destroyers sought refuge in neutral ports, where they were eventually destroyed or dismantled. The rest of the fleet limped back to harbour badly damaged. It was its last sally, but the sailors continued to fight bravely on land.

Nogi had taken his time pushing the Russians back to their permanent defences, but now he was under considerable pressure from Oyama to take Port Arthur, for the Russian Baltic fleet was reported to be sailing for Eastern waters, and anyway the Field Marshal wanted the 3rd Army in the north. Nogi therefore made preparations to attack in the second week of August. The result of a dangerous balloon reconnaissance decided him to aim for the very heart of the defence, the north-east sector and in particular the commanding feature of Wang-tai. It was the strongest part of the perimeter, and as yet Nogi lacked heavy guns, for these had been lost in the sinking of the *Hitachi Maru* by the Vladivostok squadron in June. However, he firmly believed he would succeed, and was perfectly prepared to be prodigal with his troops in doing so. He felt that with the centre broken, the wings would cave in, but he realised that to protect the right flank of his assault he would need to neutralise some of the north-western defences.

This task was given to the 1st and 9th Divisions, and the objectives were Kan-ta-shan, north of Siu-shuing village, Headquarters Hill, and the northern part of the Metre Range for 1 Division, and the Water Supply Redoubt for the right hand brigade (the 18th) of the 9th Division. The 1st Division began operations at 9 pm on 13 August when the 1st *Kobi* (reserve) Brigade advanced on Headquarters Hill. The weather was appalling, hindering the supporting efforts of the divisional artillery and the 2nd Field Artillery Brigade, and there was little fighting on the first four days. On the 18th, Kan-ta-shan was occupied unopposed, but the fighting on the 19th and 20th was very bitter. Headquarters Hill, and Hills 331 and 305 fell to the Japanese, but Division Hill was never taken; on Angle Hill, Colonel Tretyakov, in command, asked urgently for reinforcements which Fock delayed sending until it was too late, and the 5th East Siberians were eventually forced back on to Long Hill on the afternoon of the 20th. This ended the fighting in the north-west, in which the Japanese had lost nearly a thousand men.

While 1 Division was battling for the north-western heights, the 18th Brigade attacked the Water Works Redoubt, which had been heavily shelled by naval guns on the night of 19 August. There was some stiff fighting, but an advanced trench was captured at heavy cost, and on the 20th the 19th Regiment of the brigade secured a lodgement on the prominent salient of the Russian position. However, a strong counter-attack from the direction of Pa-li-chuang drove the Japanese back to the trench. The casualties were heavy – the 19th alone lost two-thirds of its strength – and the attack was called off. This important redoubt was not captured until a month later.

On 16 August, Nogi made a formal representation to Stoessel for surrender, which was politely rejected, and three days later the Japanese began the first of their very costly assaults on the north-east sector of the perimeter. The whole line from Fn 3 to B Battery was subjected to a 'long and heavy pounding, and 9 and 11 Divisions moved forward that night for the assault.

It is difficult to follow the exact details of these operations, for much of the fighting took place at night and was very confused. In general, it can be said of the Russian forward defences that although of necessity improvised, they were innovative with all sorts of cunning devices (planks across the ditches with upturned nails for sandalled feet) hastily laid out to hinder the close assault. Their counterbattery work was not particularly successful, but their artillery gave good close support, and they had a preponderance of machine-guns whose scything fire sheared the Japanese to shreds. For the Japanese, it can only be said that in this assault, as in the later ones, they went forward to the slaughter in their thousands, utterly disdainful of death, mindful only of the soaring glory of the Rising Sun, mad with battle lust and determined to kill before being killed.

There had been much recent rain, and the water courses which served as partially protected approaches were soon a morass of mud and blood in which densely packed troops were periodically illuminated by Russian flares and searchlights. The attack was on a wide front, and the principal fighting was for the two redoubts East and West Pan-lung, and Wang-tai. After a damp and misty night, during which many Japanese had died, with little progress made, 20 August dawned bright and sunny. Again the Russian defence proved too strong and, although Japanese gunners laid down a heavy concentration between Q Work and West Pan-lung, the fortifications and the Russian battery sites were never completely broken. Every attack was pinned down, with enfilade fire from the repaired Water Works Redoubt proving particularly dangerous. On the Japanese left, an attack by the 10th Brigade of 11 Division from the direction of Wang-chia-tun across fairly open ground was easily held by A and B Batteries and Fn 2. The day ended with heavy Japanese losses and no progress made, nor was there any on the 21st.

On 22 August, just as Nogi was considering calling off the attack, he received information that East Pan-lung had been taken. This was an exaggeration, for in fact only a tenuous lodgement had been made in a trench around the battery, and every attempt to enlarge it was being thrown back by the fire from West Pan-lung. Some Japanese got as far as the parapet, but all were killed. Eventually, a junior commander, realising that West Pan-lung held the key, rallied two companies and, with surprisingly few casualties, gained the parapet. By 6 pm the redoubt had been cleared of Russians. With the suppression of supporting fire from West Pan-lung, the eastern redoubt became vulnerable. The 7th and 35th Regiments of the 6th Brigade once again stormed up the hill on which so many of their comrades lay dead, and despite the fact that a *Kobi* regiment ordered to support them failed in its duty, by 8 pm they had captured East Pan-lung. Russian attempts to retake these redoubts on the night of 22–23 August failed.

That same night, the 6th Brigade was to go into action again, this time with the 10th Brigade in an attack on Wang-tai, using the captured redoubts as a jumping off base. Nogi had misjudged this whole assault; he did not realise the strength of the positions he was attacking without heavy artillery, and Wang-tai in particular was an impossibly ambitious target at this stage. The night attacks were a mess, troops lost their way, others were dazzled in the search-lights and mown down. On the 24th, the fighting was a desperate business and the attacks went on piecemeal due to lack of liaison between the two brigades.

After the troops had fought their way across the Chinese Wall, they came under a withering fire from the defenders as they struggled up the steep hill and were assaulted and fired upon from the rear by troops in F 2 and on the Wall, as well as the guns of H Battery. The lucky ones regained the Pan-lung redoubts, but hundreds lay dead on the slopes where they were left to rot, and in the warm, damp weather the sickly smell of death soon poisoned the air. When Nogi eventually called the assault off he had lost between 15,000 and 18,000 men (the 6th Brigade alone lost over 2,000) for the capture of two redoubts that were of little value.

In the midst of the battle there was a cleavage in the Russian command. The defenders of East Pan-lung desperately needed reinforcements and Smirnoff, who had an instinctive affinity for the front line, ordered Fock (who had not) to send up the 14th Regiment. This order Fock virtually refused to comply with (he had been reluctant to reinforce both at Namsan and Angle Hill), and Smirnoff dismissed him, giving command of the land defences to Kondratenko. Fock retired to headquarters unemployed, where he sided with Stoessel in making trouble for Smirnoff and Kondratenko.

While the Japanese spent early September bombarding and nibbling forward, the Russians took stock of their situation. Their biggest handicap was Stoessel, who by now was almost universally discredited and distrusted. Although not so well off for food as the Japanese soldiers, they were certainly not starving, and at present they suffered far less from disease than did their enemy, who had literally thousands afflicted with beri-beri – probably caused by fermented rice and dirty water. However, these, and other losses, could be made good from their base at Dalny. By mid-September, Nogi was ready to begin preliminary operations that would pave the way for his next big attack.

The 1st Division was now given the task of pushing the Russians off the last two prominent features they held on Metre Range. The 3rd Regiment of the 2nd Brigade of that division had the Temple Redoubt as their objective, and the 18th Brigade of the 9th Division was to attack the Water Works Redoubt. Sapping in the hard ground had been very difficult and dangerous. The Japanese took to encasing their sappers in armour, which must have made the work harder, and only marginally safer. The problem was not quite so great in front of the two redoubts as on Metre Range. The former were attacked on 19 September and by 2 am on the 20th, Water Works had been taken and, later that day, Temple Redoubt also. Loss of the Water Works left only the brackish fresh water lake for the garrison.

The defence of the north-west was very stubborn, and the attacking force must have been grateful for the considerable support they received from the naval and field artillery guns, which pounded the Russians in their shallow trenches on Long Hill. The fighting here began on 17 September, but not until the 20th were the Russians driven off that hill. 203 Metre Hill has two peaks 150 yards apart, connected by a ridge on which the Russians had their guns. The Japanese attacked it on 20 September, bypassing Flat Hill. The fighting here was the fiercest of all these preliminary operations and, although the Japanese made a lodgement on the south-west of the feature, they were unable to hold it. Once the Russians had located and got the range of their reserves, their guns did great slaughter. The hill was found to be too strong and, as the dispirited Japanese were driven off it, Russian rifle and machine-gun fire lashed them like wind-driven rain. This abortive attack had cost Nogi 2,500 men.

The capture of the redoubts enabled the Japanese to sap right up to the Russian main defences on their north-east sector during October, and in some places to tunnel mines under the counterscarp. The most sensational of these operations occurred at F 2, where the Japanese had a mine almost ready to explode before the Russian engineers were able to locate the tunnel in the left gallery. Hasty preparations were made for a camouflet, and it became a desperate race as to which explosion would occur first. The Russians won when Smirnoff, personally and at considerable risk, pressed the firing key on 27 October. The defenders' own tunnel and caponier, with all those inside it, were blown to bits, but the damage done by the explosion was so considerable that there was now an entrance into the fort.

At the end of September, while these mole-like activities were in progress, Nogi at last got his long awaited 11-inch guns. Their arrival was a grave down-turn for the Russians, who could never accurately locate them because of their smokeless powder and well concealed positions. Nogi also received 8,000 reinforcements from Dalny. With the help of these, and the new guns, he hoped to present Port Arthur as a birthday present to his Emperor on 3 November.

G Work was taken on 16 October, and for the next ten days the whole Russian front was subjected to heavy shelling by the 11-inch guns and the field batteries, while under cover of this fire sapping went forward to the glacis trenches. The Russian soldiers, well supported by the sailors, made the Japanese fight for every inch of the ground. At least one sortie was successful, but generally these were made with too few men to retain any position retaken. The concrete casing of the fortifications could now be penetrated, and considerable damage was being done by the bombardments, with guns being put out of action in some cases. By 29 October, the advanced trenches were mostly in Japanese hands and Nogi was ready to begin the second major assault. This was to follow very much the same pattern as its predecessor, and indeed as its successor at the end of November, with a demonstration against the north-west defences, and a frontal attack against the north-east sector.

Early on the morning of 30 October, the Japanese artillery began to

MAP 12.2

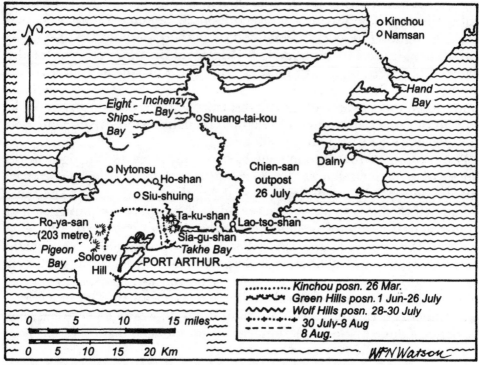

*The Kuan-tung Peninsula, showing the Russians' successive defence lines
from 26 March 1905*

pound the defences from Fn 3 to Q Work with every calibre of gun in their
powerful arsenal. The Russians were not slow to reply, and soon the air was
full of the screech and explosion of shells, for it was the liveliest cannonade
so far. Even the Russian ships joined in, although this was not too popular,
for faulty fuses caused short-falls in the town. At about 1 pm, the Japanese
troops left their trenches, which in places were less than 100 yards from
their objectives. The Russian gunners were ready, and their shrapnel tore
the advancing ranks assunder making the slaughter truly terrible.

The attack had to be delivered simultaneously along the whole line, for
the Russians had so many opportunities for enfilade fire, but it soon became
obvious that the principal targets were Fn 3, F 3, P Work, F 2, Q Work, Kobu
and B Battery. Success or failure depended on how much of a battering
these fortifications had previously received, the extent to which they could
be supported by their neighbours, the condition of the wire entanglements
and the distance of open ground (which nowhere exceeded 165 yards) to
be traversed by the attackers.

Kobu fell quite quickly, for it was not strongly defended and there were good gaps in the entanglements, but P and Q proved much tougher. P was eventually taken by the battle-scarred 6th Brigade whose men, led by their commander, General Ichinohe, stormed up the steep slope, slipping and sliding over their dead comrades. In his honour, P was renamed Fort Ichinohe. Q, a strong lunette built into the Chinese Wall, resisted every attack, nor did the Japanese succeed in taking F 2, where initially they were established on the counterscarp. The attack on F 3 was a disaster, for the scaling ladders were found to be too short, and the attacking force got trapped in the ditch. The 1st Division also failed to take Fn 3, where the storming party of 2 Brigade reached the counterscarp, but the crest of the glacis was all they managed to hold. The fighting lasted six days and was almost continuous, with the Russians making prodigious efforts each night to repair their broken parapets. When Nogi called a halt, he had gained only two provisional fortifications, P and Kobu, and it had cost him 124 officers and 3,600 men.

Nogi was having a bad war. He had sacrificed thousands of his best men, and so far had achieved very little; he had already lost one son in the fighting, and would shortly lose another. He was constantly under pressure from Oyama to take Port Arthur, and bring his army to the north, where Kuropatkin would soon be receiving massive reinforcements, whereas Japanese reserves were almost fully committed. The extraordinary thing is that General Nogi never seems to have appreciated the great value of 203 Metre Hill, for once again he decided to go bull-headed into the strong north-east sector, and made preparations for his third major assault.

Throughout the first three weeks of November, the Russians had to bear an almost ceaseless bombardment, and their manpower situation was now a cause for concern. Sickness, while still not on the same scale as among the Japanese, had become extremely serious. Typhoid, dysentery and scurvy cases were greatly overloading the hospitals, and only a few of the men so affected would return to duty during the siege. This, and battle casualties, caused a problem in manning the defences, and troops could no longer be risked on sorties.

By the middle of the month, Nogi had received various assorted reinforcements, including the whole of the 7th Division which he placed in reserve in the centre of his line. By the 26th, his sappers and miners had gone as far as they could. At about 1 pm on that day, a mine was sprung under the parapet of F 2, which was the signal for a general advance against the same objectives as before.

The story does not require repetition, although this time failure was virtually accepted at the end of the first day. But before admitting defeat, Nogi attempted a last forlorn hope. The risk was so great that volunteers were called for from all four divisions with the 7th Division providing 1,200 out of a total force of about 2,600. It was to be a night attack with the bayonet against Tumulus Battery, for it was thought (almost certainly erroneously) that, with that taken, the line could be rolled up from a flank. It went wrong. Some troops got detached and blundered into a post thereby losing surprise. Searchlights then beamed on to the attackers, who struggled bravely against great odds until 3 am. At least half the force never got back; the wounded had to be left, many to perish from cold, for winter had set in with frozen intensity. Thus ended the third attempt in which Nogi had lost over 4,000 men, and achieved nothing. The Russians lost about 500.

Perhaps stimulated by a visit from General Kodama – Oyama's deputy – who, unbeknown to Nogi, had instructions to take over if he thought it necessary, the next major attack was to be against the Metre Range. Since September, the Russians had strengthened the defences on both peaks of 203, and Flat Hill. The approach to the latter from the north was almost precipitous, and fougasses had been liberally sprinkled in the valley below the hill. Trenches could not be deep, but they were loopholed and there were breastworks. On the highest peak of 203 there was a bombproof fortification. Both features were as near to being inexpugnable as nature and man could make them. The original garrison numbered about 2,200, but during the fighting almost as many men again were sent up.

The attack was to be made by the 1st Division but, later, regiments from 7 Division were to be withdrawn from the eastern investment line. Sapping had been continuous for some time, but was found to be almost impossible on the rocky ground approaching 203. However, effective covering fire from riflemen on Long Hill and Ridge 590 kept Russian heads down as the troops advanced to the attack between the two features.

The attack began at 8.30 am on 28 November* on the twin peaks of 203, and Flat Hill, but all the Japanese could do that day, after some close-quarter fighting, was to carve passages through the entanglements. The Russian battery on Solovev Hill, near Pigeon Bay, had never been eliminated and now did the Japanese much damage. That night, the attacks were resumed and a lodgement was made at the south-west corner of 203 (in much the same place as in September), but at great cost. On the morning of the 29th, the ground right up to the breastworks of both peaks was thick with Japanese dead.

The 30th showed some of the hardest fighting of the siege. Regiments from 7 Division had now been thrown in with the divisional artillery, and these joined in the heavy bombardment, for Nogi realised that if he was to gain the hills he must blast the Russians out of them. There was a fearful drumming in the air as the ground trembled beneath the avalanche of shells that pounded the defences. All the time, the attacking soldiers inched forward, but after the severest fighting, some of it at hand grenade range,

---

*Thus the Official History, but some accounts give 27 November as the start of the battle. All agree it ended on 5 December.

the positions still held throughout that day and night. And so it was on 1 December. On the next three days, there were no assaults. The cannonade went on continuously and the Japanese pushed forward their trenches until Nogi was ready for the final phase of this desperate battle.

On 30 November, at a council of war, Stoessel and Fock had demanded immediate withdrawal. Fock, in particular, was most insistent that no further reserves should be sent forward. Smirnoff, while admitting that the struggle would be desperate, and the losses cruel, urged defiance, for he at least realised the importance of 203. Tretyakov, in direct command, strongly supported him and, to the honour of Russian arms, their counsel prevailed.

At 1.30 pm on 5 December, men from the 13th and 14th Brigades rose from the parallels and, in extended order with bayonets fixed, once more climbed Flat and 203 Hills respectively. The heavy artillery concentration of the past days had thinned the defence, and what reserves that could be brought up were blasted with HE and shrapnel. Moreover, Tretyakov had left the field severely wounded, and the heart had gone out of the devoted troops he left behind. The Japanese took the twin peaks with surprising ease, and by 4.30 pm all was over. Two attempts to retake both hills that night reflected more courage than any hope of success. In the words of the Russian war correspondent, it had been 'the bloodiest scene of carnage of the whole war'. The Russians had lost over 3,000 men, and the Japanese about 12,000.

Nogi had paid a high price, but he had captured a feature that not only overlooked the harbour, but Fn 3 and F 2 as well. Now he had the Russian fleet at his mercy. Remorselessly, the Japanese gunners pulverised the helpless ships, while many of their erstwhile sailors, now fighting on land, looked on in misery. It was like shooting sitting ducks, and Admiral Togo himself climbed 203 to witness the destruction, in the sure knowledge that he was now master of the seas, even if the Baltic fleet did arrive. Only one captain, von Essen, attempted to save his ship by leaving the harbour. He took the battleship *Sevastopol* into the roadstead at the southern end of the Tiger's Tail where, for three weeks, he gallantly held out against all attacks, sinking two Japanese destroyers and damaging several others, finally scuttling his ship.

With the loss of the fleet, much of the importance of Port Arthur had gone, but by no means all. The garrison could still hold the Japanese 3rd Army from reinforcing the northern troops. The situation in the town inevitably became much worse. Some hospitals were hit, and many houses reduced to rubble, their inhabitants left to face the bitter cold and the bullets that buzzed about the street. Food was still sufficient, with plenty of horses to be eaten, and luxury items such as pigs and eggs occasionally available but at colossal prices. In a council of war on 8 December, the egregious Fock showed every sign of defeatism. However, he lacked the

MAP 12.3

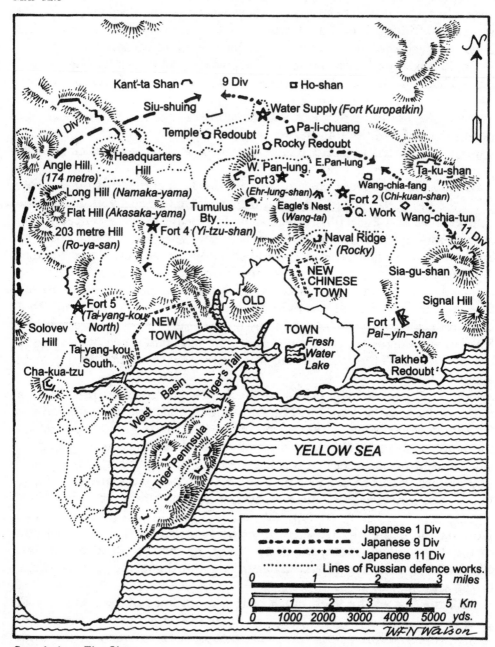

Port Arthur: The Siege

support of Stoessel, who had been slightly wounded, and neither Smirnoff nor Kondratenko would hear of surrender while there were men to fight and food to eat.

As the Japanese closed in for the kill, Fortune, who had shown herself indifferent to sacrifice, now declared for the stronger side. On 15 December, Kondratenko was, as usual, in the forward defences conferring with officers in F 2, when an 11-inch shell scored a direct hit on the casemates killing him and seven other officers. The terrible blow to morale caused by the death of this well loved and efficient officer might have been lessened had Smirnoff's immediate request to assume the duties of field commander as well as Fortress Commandant been granted. But Stoessel, unfortunately recovered from his wound, refused this sensible suggestion and, in a stormy interview with Smirnoff, gave the job to Fock. Incredible as it seems, the first directive this man made was to reduce the strengths of the forts and intermediate works, an order that must have seemed to the troops to have all the odium of military treachery.

The last great battle began on 17 December, when men of the 7th Japanese Division took the heights north of F 5. At 2 pm on the next day two mines exploded beneath F 2, destroying the rampart and wrecking one angle of the fort. Immediately, a battalion charged into the breach, but the interior of the fort was undamaged and the storming party met with fierce opposition. For the rest of that day, and well into the night, there was bitter fighting, until shortly after midnight 25 men, all that was left of a garrison of 300, slunk away ghost-like into the night. The fort was of no great value to the Japanese, for it was overlooked by Wang-tai and other works, but it was the first of the permanent defences to be taken and, as such, was a fillip to morale.

From then on, there was fighting every day, ground was taken and sometimes retaken and the defences were continually subjected to the most punishing bombardment. On 26 December, the 7th Division at last took Solovev Hill where the garrison had resisted attack throughout the siege – only 15 men were left to retire. The exposed western front was now continually bombarded from new battery positions.

Two days later, at 10 am, mines exploded under F 3 with much the same result as at F 2. Savage hand-to-hand fighting followed on the ramparts and the cavalier, and even in the surviving labyrinth of counterscarp galleries, until the fort and ten guns were captured that evening. The capture of Forts 2 and 3 had cost the Japanese well over 1,000 men. On 29 December, the Russian chiefs were again in council. Smirnoff no longer had the support of Kondratenko, nevertheless he persuaded the faint-hearted to fight on. But Stoessel was only awaiting time and opportunity to surrender.

On New Year's Eve, Fn 3 was taken. That left the Chinese Wall as the only serious obstacle, for once that had gone, Wang-tai would be isolated. On that night, General Ichinohe received information that the Wall was only lightly held and, advancing at once at the head of his famous 6th Brigade, he succeeded in taking this the last Russian main defence line by dawn. On New Year's Day 1905, Wang-tai fell. Even before that feature was lost, Stoessel had despatched a letter to Nogi seeking arrangements for surrender.

The constant scene of strife and struggle among the Russian commanders did not end with the fighting, for Stoessel had sent his *parlementaire* without a council of war. It was a decision taken by himself, Fock and Colonel Reuss, his chief-of-staff. Smirnoff knew nothing and was astounded, as also was Nogi who fully expected to have much more fighting. The latter was to become even more amazed when no fewer than 875 officers and 23,491 men marched out later as prisoners, and large quantities of food and ammunition were handed over.

Smirnoff, who refused to have anything to do with the capitulation, sent a cipher telegram on 2 January to Kuropatkin which read, 'General Stoessel has entered into negotiations with the enemy for surrendering the Fortress without informing me, and in spite of my opinion and that of the majority of the commanding officers'. No doubt this helped his acquittal at the eventual court martial of the senior officers, when Stoessel was condemned to death.

From the day on which the Russians fell back to their permanent defences to the day of surrender, the siege had lasted almost exactly five months. It had been an epic of courage and resolution on the part of the junior officers and rank and file of both armies, but Nogi's performance had not been distinguished, and Stoessel's had been both caitiff and catastrophic. The Official History puts the Russian losses at 31,306 of which perhaps 10,000 had been killed or died from disease. The Japanese lost 57,780 all ranks killed and wounded, while a further 33,769 died of illness.

By the middle of January, the 3rd Army was on its way to join the fighting in the north, where the Japanese were inexorably pushing the Russians deeper into Manchuria. The war was to go on until June 1905 when, largely through the skilful diplomacy of President Roosevelt, a peace conference was held at Portsmouth, New Hampshire, and on 5 September, the Treaty of Portsmouth was signed. The Russians, who had had very much the worst of the conflict, were treated remarkably leniently. The Japanese, who had been persuaded to forgo their indemnity demand, felt that the immense sacrifices they had made justified more than a reversion of the lease of the Liao-tung Peninsula, and the islands of Sakhalin. Serious rioting erupted throughout the country, and there was a bitterness towards the United States that lingered on.

CHAPTER 13

Kut-el-Amara 1915–16

THE surrender of Kut-el-Amara in Mesopotamia on 29 April 1916 has long been seen as a dark day in the history of the British Army and the name of its commander, Major General Townshend has been held in contempt by many, perhaps not least because he spent the subsequent years in captivity in considerable luxury whilst his soldiers rotted in Turkish prison camps. However, the siege is of great interest. Even as the troops had been put into the field in South Africa with serious deficiencies of essential equipment, so did Townshend find himself leading a division up the line of the River Tigris woefully short of almost all the essentials for fighting a war in undeveloped country.

The whole of the expedition to Mesopotamia, of which Townshend's division formed only a part, had been the subject of deplorably muddled handling by both the British Government and the Government of India, so that the aim seems to have been far from clear. Launched up river in this highly unsatisfactory situation, Townshend was faced by a strong Turkish force under German command. Once again the British had underestimated the strength and ability of the enemy. Whilst the name of Kut is associated with that of Townshend, we shall see how the whole business of his relief seems to have been doomed from the outset. The lessons of Kut are legion.

* * *

In 1914, the large tract of land watered by the two great rivers Tigris and Euphrates, which now forms the Republic of Iraq was that part of the Ottoman Empire known as Mesopotamia. Kut-el-Amara was a small town with about 6,000 Arab inhabitants, situated in a U-bend of the Tigris some 250 miles up river from Basra. The Arabs had a saying that when Allah made hell, he was not satisfied and threw in Mesopotamia as well. Certainly it has a pretty fiendish climate with the bone-searing heat of the July sun sending the temperature to around 120 degrees fahrenheit. In the searching cold of December, it can fall below freezing. The rainfall is low, but comes in torrential storms and between March and May, the melting snows of the highlands cause vast tracts of land to be flooded. In the campaign, the principal means of transport was by river.

The English presence in countries bordering the Persian Gulf had been active ever since the days of the East India Company, but at the beginning of the 20th century, the Germans had become a dangerous catalyst in the crucible of Turkish politics. Their active interest in the Near East and the railway they had built, and were about to extend, posed a threat not only to India but to the important oil concession obtained from the Shah of Persia. In the event of war with Turkey, the pipeline and refinery of the Anglo-Persian Oil Company at Abadan would be very vulnerable. In October 1914, it was decided to send a composite brigade of the 6th Poona Division to the head of the Persian Gulf.

At this time there was a field army in India of just over seven divisions, and five cavalry brigades; with garrison and other army troops the total was about 150,000 Indian and 80,000 British soldiers. At the outbreak of war, three divisions were earmarked for service in Europe, and some other troops for East Africa which, after internal security, including the important North-West Frontier, did not leave much for Mesopotamia. There was also a chronic shortage of key personnel and equipment such as staff officers, medical officers, hospital equipment, wireless/telegraphy, aeroplanes (there were only four in the sub-continent) and, most necessary for the type of operations likely to be involved in the Gulf area, gunboats and river craft.

These restrictions on manpower and equipment were to be compounded by the unsatisfactory dichotomy in the management of military matters. Until later in the campaign, the Government of India, which was the Viceroy (Lord Hardinge) in Council, had control of operations and administration, but the India Office, under the Secretary of State (first Lord Crewe and then Austen Chamberlain) liked to have the final say in the scope of operations. As neither the powers in Whitehall nor in Simla had a very clear idea of the conditions that prevailed in Mesopotamia, or the strength of the opposition, there was a great deal of cross-telegraphing and very little co-ordination. It was understandable, perhaps, that with strictly limited resources operations should at first be confined to safeguarding the pipeline and refinery through the occupation of the Basra *vilayet**, but as the campaign got under way the indecisiveness of the sachems severely handicapped the commander on the spot, who was to have considerable difficulty in obtaining permission to advance even so far as Amara.

When Turkey entered the war on 5 November 1914 the composite brigade, which had been waiting at Kuwait, advanced up the Shatt-al-Arab demolishing the Turkish mud fort at Fao on its way. This was the beginning

*Vilayet. A Turkish district.

of a series of operations in Lower Mesopotamia that can only be touched
upon in outline.

There was a brief engagement at Sahil, but Basra was occupied unopposed
on 21 November. By this time, General Barrett, commanding 6 Division, and
most of his troops – now to be known as D Force – had arrived, and the next
objective was Qurna, the legendary Garden of Eden, which lay some 30
miles up the Tigris. It was of strategical importance to D Force, and Barrett
pushed his men up the left bank of the river, through mud made deep and
glutinous by recent heavy rain, to take the place on 9 December.

So far everything had gone pretty well, but already the lack of medical
facilities and equipment, and particularly transport both for land and water,
was beginning to be felt. To make matters worse, Lord Crewe was pressing
for a force to go up the river Karun to protect the pipeline. Apart from
shortages, operational planning was inhibited by the unknown factor of
Arab intentions. These riverine tribesmen were thought to be hostile to
their masters, even though co-religionists, but in fact they were merely
out for what they could get, and this pointed to a policy of supporting
the winning side. Nevertheless, the Turco-Arab force near Ahwaz was a
threat to the pipeline and Barrett despatched a battalion there at the end
of January 1915.

On 9 April, General Nixon succeeded Barrett, who was ill, and he arrived
in Basra with a much larger brief which even included a possible advance
to Baghdad. But that step was to be subject to many hesitations before it
was finally sanctioned. Meanwhile, Nixon's primary task was the original
one of safeguarding the pipeline and to gain control of the whole of Lower
Mesopotamia, which clearly indicated taking Nasiriyah, where the Turks
appeared to be building up troops for retaking Basra. Nixon now had
command of a corps, for General Gorringe's 12 Division had arrived in
March with certain other troops, and even two aeroplanes (but without
pilots!). Gorringe would shortly be despatched to Ahwaz to drive the Turks
off the pipeline, for the battalion there had only been saved from disaster
by the resolution and courage of a platoon of the Dorset Regiment.

On 11 April, the first major engagement of the campaign began. The
Turks made a determined effort to regain Basra with a strong attack on
the British entrenched camp at Shaiba. The battle lasted three days, and
there was some very hard fighting on land as well as on water, where British
troops made use of small boats known as *bellums* and *mahailas**. But by 14
April, the Turks were in full retreat, although they escaped unscathed,
because the cavalry were wrongly placed for pursuit, and the mirage –
that constant source of bafflement – obscured the gunners' target.

Mahailas were native craft, 50 or more feet long holding up to 70 men, and carrying
a lateen sail. *Bellums* were smaller, flat-bottomed boats only 20 feet long, and paddled
or poled.

MAP 13.1

Mesopotamia 1915–16

A week after the battle ended, Major General Townshend arrived at
Basra, having been specially asked for by Nixon, who was impressed by
his military record. He took the vacant command of the 6th Division.

Well read, especially in military history, Townshend was an urbane man, equally at ease on the battlefield and in a London drawing-room. He had considerable fighting experience which included being besieged in Chitral's fort, where he had handled a difficult situation skilfully. Although he had served for a time in the Indian Army, he never liked Indian soldiers, nor they him, but he inspired great loyalty and devotion in his British troops. There have been vilipenders ready to traduce his character, and criticise his behaviour in Kut; much of that criticism was unjustified, although it has to be said that his undoubted merits were somewhat tarnished by the alloy of a tiresome urge for military promotion.

At this stage there was another divergence of views between Whitehall and Simla, but the Indian Government was beginning to act independently, and favour the wishes of the local commander. The near disaster at Ahwaz had strengthened Lord Crewe's desire to restrict operations to safeguarding Persian Arabistan, but Sir Beauchamp Duff (Commander-in-Chief India) was prepared to stand by his original orders to Nixon, and allow an advance up river. The next step on that journey was Amara.

Amara was taken at the beginning of June in quite incredible circumstances. Much of the land north of Qurna was flooded, and the Turks held a series of island posts. Both sides took to the water in gunboats, and the British organised 500 *bellums* (some of them with armoured shields) carrying ten men to a boat. Townshend's Regatta, as it was called, steamed and poled its way up river engaging the enemy craft and, under cover of a barrage, landing men on the islands. The operation was entirely successful, and the Turks were in full retreat when the gunboats were halted by mud. But Townshend, the naval commander and about 100 soldiers and sailors, transferred to three armoured launches and a paddle-wheel yacht, and continued the chase. So demoralised were the Turks by the trouncing they had received from this strange armada that Townshend was able to bluff the Amara garrison of at least a battalion into surrender.

Attention now switched to Nasiriyeh, which was an important Turkish base for any further attempt to retake Basra. With it in British hands, Nixon reckoned that the Basra vilayet would be quite secure. Gorringe, back from his task of driving the Turco-Arab force off the pipeline, was given command. In operations that lasted almost a month, he had prised the Turks from their last position by 24 July, and Nasiriyeh was taken.

Shortly after capturing Amara, 6 Division temporarily lost its commander, for Townshend was one of a large number of men in the expeditionary force who succumbed to fever. At first it was thought he would die, but he recovered sufficiently to be sent back to India, where, during convalescence, he had talks with Duff. He was able to acquaint the commander-in-chief at first hand (for Duff had never visited Mesopotamia) how serious was the shortage of everything concerned with the medical and transport departments, and he made it clear that while he could advance to Kut, for any approach to Baghdad he would need to be reinforced. Whitehall was still wavering on how far Nixon should go, but he was determined on Kut at least, and was supported by the Viceroy and Duff. It was certainly a logical step if Baghdad was contemplated, but Nixon's lines of communication would become badly overstretched.

Nevertheless, on 23 August the advance on Kut was authorised, but beyond that place Nixon was not to go. Townshend rejoined his division at Amara on 28 August and, on 1 September, he started to move his troops to their forward concentration area at Ali Gharbi. For the first time in the campaign, the 6th Division now operated with all three brigades (16th, 17th and 18th), and Nixon had allotted 30 Brigade from 12 Division to guard Townshend's line of communications. With divisional troops, he now had about 11,000 men and was accompanied up river by three gunboats.

Turkish troops, thought to number about 6,500 infantry with 23 guns and under the command of Nur-ud-Din Pasha, were entrenched across the river at Es Sinn a few miles east of Kut. Townshend planned to make a feint on the right bank, pass troops across the river on a pontoon bridge, and deliver his main attack on the left bank, where he would attempt to outflank the Turkish left by a fairly long night march. The battle was fought between the 26th and 28th of September, and Nur-ud-Din was completely surprised by Townshend's strategy. Tactically it was successful in so far as the feint worked, and the troops crossed from right to left bank, but General Hoghton's 17th Brigade lost direction on their flank march, leaving Delamain's 16th Brigade to attack the centre unsupported, for the 18th Brigade on his left was also in trouble. However, Delamain's men drove the Turks from their positions at bayonet point and, when the morning of the 28th came, it was seen that the battle was won. The gunboats had been active in the first part of the fight, but the Turks had obstructed the river, and it was some time before they could join in the pursuit which went on through Kut, for Nur-ud-Din was falling back to Ctesiphon.

By 10 October, Townshend had concentrated his troops at Aziziya. Here, in advance of Nixon's directive from India, he awaited the outcome of conferences and cables between Whitehall and Simla. He himself was not anxious to head for Baghdad without being reinforced, but London wanted something to offset Gallipoli, which was not going well. Nixon assured Duff that he could take Baghdad, provided that he obtained reinforcements from France to hold the place if Gallipoli collapsed. Nixon won the argument, and Townshend began his advance on 11 November.

He had 16 battalions (the 30th Brigade had also been allotted him), 11 squadrons of cavalry, 29 guns and, with divisional troops, some 13,700 men. Aerial reconnaissance had shown the Turks to be strongly entrenched on both banks of the river at Ctesiphon, and they numbered about 12,000 men. But changes were coming in the Turkish forces; masses of reinforcements were arriving in Mesopotamia, the much more resolute Khalil Pasha had become number two to Nur-ud-Din, and the German Field Marshal von der Goltz was appointed to command the 6th Turkish Army.

The very hard fought battle of Ctesiphon lasted for three days (22, 23 and 24 November), with the British in many ways having the best of the fighting, but they were overcome by weight of numbers. The fighting took place on the left bank of the river, and Townshend divided his force into three columns – a holding column on the left, a flanking one on the right, supported by a flying column, and a centre column for the main thrust. He had three gunboats in support. The left column opened operations early on the 22nd, and the fighting that morning was entirely favourable to the British. By 1.30 pm the key position (known as VP), and the whole of the Turkish first line was in Townshend's hands. A counterattack by the Turks that afternoon failed. But when evening came, it was clear to Townshend that his troops were in no condition to resume the offensive the next day, for units were disorganised, the men were short of water and exhausted, and arrangements for the wounded were more chaotic than ever.

The 23rd was spent by the British in reorganisation, while Nur-ud-Din launched a series of half-hearted, fruitless counterattacks. But on the 24th, now apparently aware of Townshend's plight, he put in a major attack which almost, but not quite, succeeded in regaining his lost positions. That evening, with casualties for the three days amounting to 4,300, Townshend sought permission from Nixon (who had witnessed the battle) to withdraw to Lajj. This was successfully accomplished, and two days later it was decided to fall back first to Aziziya, and then to Kut. The Turks, with greatly superior numbers, pressed the division hard. At Umm-al-Tubul, some twelve miles below Aziziya, they caught up with the withdrawal. In a stiff fight on 1 December, Townshend lost another 536 men and two of his three gunboats. Kut was reached on the morning of 3 December without further interference. But by 8 December the Turks had invested the town thereby putting an end to the telegraphic consultations between Townshend, Nixon and the Indian Government as to whether Kut should be held or evacuated.

Townshend, as ordered, had sent most of his cavalry and wounded away just in time, and he now had 8,893 combatants of which 7,411 were infantry, 3,560 Indian non-combatants, and all Arab householders had been allowed to stay – a fact Townshend bitterly regretted later on. There were 43 guns, and the gunboat, *Sumana*, was retained. Except for tea and meat, which would last 34 days, Townshend reported 60 days' rations for British and Indian troops, and he considered that his men had been so weakened by the recent fighting that they must start on full rations. There was also meat on the hoof from the large number of horses, mules and 100 bullocks, for all of which there was sufficient fodder.

The principal justification for staying in Kut was that the Turks would have to take it before attempting to push the expeditionary force into the sea; it therefore acted as a good buffer while reinforcements were on their way from France and India. On the other hand, the nature of the surrounding countryside, particularly with the flood season not too far away, made its relief a difficult problem. It was also something of a trap, being enclosed by two arms of the river in an area two miles long, by one mile wide.

The existing defences of Kut were mainly aimed at keeping out Arab marauders, and were totally inadequate for a modern siege. They comprised a mud-walled fort at the north-eastern corner, and four blockhouses connected to the fort by barbed wire entanglements. This, the first line, was too far forward and was overlooked by some prominent sandhills, but obviously, with only five days' grace, it had to be accepted. There was much digging to be done to protect the river flanks and to construct a middle and second line of defence. On the right bank of the river, in Yakasub, the woolpress village, there was a liquorice factory in which was a grain store. For some inexplicable reason, Townshend felt it should be held as an outpost – perhaps the grain could not be shifted in time.

The peninsula upon which Kut stood was divided into three sectors – north-east, north-west and southern. The north-east sector, which included the fort and up to the second blockhouse, was held by the 17th Brigade (Hoghton); 16 Brigade (Delamain) held the north-west sector; the southern sector (which included the liquorice factory and woolpress held by two battalions) was allotted to 18 Brigade (Hamilton); and 30 Brigade (Melliss) was in general reserve.

The Turks lost no time in mounting an assault. On 9 December, the whole position, and particularly the fort, came under heavy shellfire. That afternoon, waves of infantry advanced against the north-west sector in extended order. This attack was easily held but, during the night, the Turks dug in and formed a line just out of rifle shot of the defence. The bombardment continued on the 10th and 11th and there were further attacks in which the Turks suffered heavy casualties for a slight advancement of their line. Townshend had lost 531 men in the three days, and the garrison had expended 61,000 rounds of rifle ammunition on the 10th alone.

For the next ten days the Turks confined their activities to normal siege operations (mainly sapping towards the fort), but their recent attacks had clouded Townshend's optimism. In a telegram to General Aylmer, recently appointed to command all troops on the Tigris, he reported his casualties as running to between 150 and 200 a day (which must have been an exaggeration), his ammunition was becoming dangerously short, and the morale of some of his troops (this implied the Indians whom, as we know, he never liked) as 'not what it was, to say the least of it'.

After the initial assaults had ended, aerial reconnaissance confirmed Townshend's thinking that he was faced by around 12,000 Turks. It was learnt from prisoners that von der Goltz was at Turkish headquarters, and said to be against wasting men in assaults when the garrison could be starved into surrender. If this was true, it may have accounted for the ten-day lull during which the garrison were able to carry out much needed improvements to the defences, and to launch a most successful raid against the Turkish saphead near the fort. Whether von der Goltz had disapproved or not, Nur-ud-Din, whose stock was running low, was determined to take the town by a *coup de main*, and on Christmas Eve (perhaps in Goltz's absence), he launched his most serious attack so far.

Throughout the night of 23 December and the morning of the 24th, Turkish gunners kept up a bombardment against the whole position, including Woolpress village. When this ended at about noon the main thrust of the attack was delivered against the fort. The 103rd Mahrattas, the 119th Native Infantry and a few men of the 43rd Light Infantry held the fort, with two 15-pounders that were soon put out of action. Despite the very destructive fire which the defenders poured into the advancing ranks, a lodgement was made on the north-eastern wall and on the bastion. The next half hour was a very bloody business with the Indians and the few 43rd fighting magnificently in hand-to-hand grapple, and the 4-inch guns of the 104th Heavy Battery pulverising oncoming reinforcements. The Rajput company of the 119th, which held the trench outside the fort with great courage, poured a withering enfilade fire into the attacking ranks and this, perhaps more than anything, determined the Turks to break off the fight.

There was then a lull of several hours that enabled the men to make minor repairs to the battered bastion and fortress walls, and for more of the 43rd to come into the line. But at 8 pm, Turkish infantrymen, headed by lines of bombers, once more threw themselves against the walls and the stockade (part of north-east bastion). Once more, they were met by a punishing fire. Although no high explosive shell was available, the ground over which the attackers struggled was continually sprayed with shrapnel and star shells, but men of the 52nd Turkish Division, bravely buffeting against the storm of lead, closed upon the stockade which for a time was down to a handful of defenders, and the situation became critical.

The 48th Pioneers were working on the second line, and they were rushed forward to fight most gallantly. At about midnight there was a pause while Nur-ud-Din regrouped his men, but at 2.30 am they came forward again. However, by now much of the impetus had gone and they were unable to dislodge the Pioneers who still held the stockade. The whole attack collapsed. The Turks had lost some 2,000 men in this Christmas Eve assault and gained nothing. The garrison casualties were 382, of which 315 were suffered around the fort's walls and stockade. This brought Townshend's losses since 3 December to 1,625.

After this failure, Nur-ud-Din came round to von der Goltz's thinking,

MAP 13.2

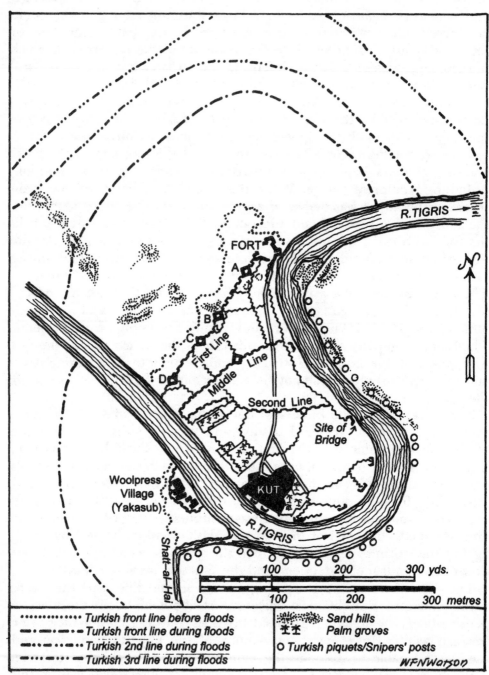

The Siege of Kut-el-Amara

and abandoned any further attacks in favour of a close investment, and a
division of troops so as to take up a strong position against the advance of

a relieving force. On 29 December Aylmer informed Townshend that his relieving force comprised 'roughly two divisions with a brigade of cavalry', so the garrison were in high hopes of his arrival during January, although Townshend must have appreciated the difficulties, and known this to be an unlikely forecast. Nevertheless, he was confident enough to keep the garrison on full rations, and – in accordance with his practice at Chitral – he issued occasional communiqués, which were usually over optimistic.

The major feature now, as in most sieges, was boredom, compounded for those in the trenches by acute discomfort in conditions that were deteriorating quickly as the weather became nastier. Those not on duty and in the town were comparatively well off, the officers had reasonable billets and beds, while the men were at least warm and able to take exercise, and even enjoy a few luxuries. The town was by no means safe, for Arab informers pinpointed targets for Turkish gunners, and divisional headquarters, among other buildings, came in for some accurate shelling. The worst worry was snipers, and those in most danger from them were the *bhistis** who gallantly kept the garrison supplied with water, and often got picked off with dum-dum bullets for their pains. Casualties were now down to about 30 a day, but already there were some cases of dysentery and *beri-beri*. There was hospital accommodation for 1,450 patients, who were at constant risk from shellfire.

The scene now shifts to General Aylmer's relieving force to be known as Tigris Corps. Eventually it was to comprise the 3rd (Lahore) and 7th (Meerut) Divisions with the 6th Cavalry Brigade and corps and divisional troops. However, coming from France and Egypt, formations arrived piecemeal and were hastily dispatched up river to meet Townshend's 60 days deadline. It was all most unsatisfactory, for units that had never trained together became mixed, the troops could be given no time to acclimatise, and in many instances they were short of equipment and important supplies. But the best had to be done under very difficult conditions, for Basra lacked proper facilities for unloading, and for the long river trip there was a lamentable shortage of transport, particularly shallow-draught vessels.

Major General Younghusband was promoted to command the 7th Division, and his 28th Brigade, being the first to arrive, was sent straight up to Ali Gharbi. Other units of the division began to build up in Basra towards the end of December, but brigades of the 3rd Division would not start to arrive much before early January 1916. Aylmer was anxious to concentrate as much of his corps as possible at Shaikh Saad before any major advance, although he told Townshend that he would certainly act in an emergency. The latter, in numerous telegrams, was constantly urging speed. He did not

---

**Bhistis.* A water-carrier.

M<small>AP</small> 13.3

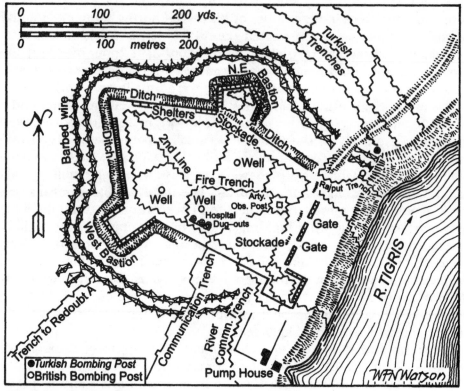

Kut-el-Amara: The Fort

consider suggestions that he should break out in support of the advance as
practicable, although there could be opportunities for sorties.

Aylmer ordered Younghusband to begin his advance on 4 January for
what he thought would be a comparatively easy first step, but which turned
out to be an exceedingly costly battle, lasting three days, in which he had
to employ every available soldier. Younghusband had three brigades (19th,
28th and 35th), three cavalry squadrons and a heavy artillery brigade at Ali
Gharbi. The Turks at this time had about 30,000 men with 70 or more
guns around and down river of Kut of which perhaps 16,000 infantry,
1,600 cavalry and 30 guns now faced Younghusband at Shaikh Saad. He
decided to attack up both sides of the river with the main punch directed
against the Turkish lines on the left bank. Three gunboats accompanied the
advance, and the steamer *Julnar* brought up the rear as a hospital ship.

Aylmer joined Younghusband on 6 January, and learnt that the fighting
that day had made very little progress. The 7th could have been a day of
disaster, for the brigade ordered to carry out a flanking attack against the

Turkish left opened up a big gap, and began its sweep before reaching the extremity of the Turkish line. It might have been demolished had it not been for the effective artillery and gunboat fire which caused the Turks to hole up for the night a short distance from the British line. The British troops had made a succession of gallant attacks all of which were defeated, and the casualties were very heavy. On the right bank of the river, Kemball's 28th Brigade had made some better progress, but here again losses had been high, and they were held by the second line of defence.

After a miserably wet and cold night, the troops, many of whom were out of condition from long journeying, were in great need of a day's rest, and Aylmer decided on a night attack. But again the weather was foul, the mud deep and the darkness intense. The guides lost their way, and the troops became exhausted so that operations were suspended. The next day the Turks, who had defended their lines so stubbornly, began to pull back. It seemed surprising, but in fact their food had run out, for with their line of communication virtually blocked at Kut, and a shortage of transport, their problem was almost as great as that of the British. Their casualties are not known, although 350 of them had been buried, but they were probably less than the British losses of 4,007 men, of whom 417 had been killed.

Tigris Corps was still below strength, and lamentably short of medical officers and equipment. Evacuation of the wounded was as distressing for these men as it had been for Townshend's, for neither the *Julnar* nor the few hospital tents were sufficient to hold the thousands of broken bodies that came back from the front. Men had to lie on the river bank cold and wet by night, plagued by flies in the heat of the day, and those unfortunates who were not evacuated for several days might find their wounds gangrenous. It was not the fault of the doctors or orderlies, who worked night and day, but of the system.

After the hammering his troops had received at Shaikh Saad, Aylmer would have liked to have halted his advance until reinforcements could reach him, but Townshend's telegrams made it clear his need was pressing. Khalil, who had succeeded Nur-ud-Din, and was probably responsible for halting the retirement the latter had ordered, had taken up a new defensive position on the right bank of the River Wadi.* This suited Aylmer, who reckoned he could defeat him in the open and gain possession of the narrow defile between the Tigris and the Suwaikiya Marsh.

What information was available indicated that the Turks had two divisions and a cavalry brigade on the left bank of the Tigris, but not much over 500 men on the right bank. Aylmer left only a strong column on that bank, moving the 28th Brigade across the river by his bridge of boats to join the main attack against the Wadi lines. This was to be another enveloping

---

*As Wadi denotes a dried watercourse, perhaps this river was usually dry.

movement by two brigades in an attempt to get between the Turkish lines and the defile, with one brigade (the 28th) initially to anchor the front, but later to join the assault.

The attacking force left the concentration area at 9.45 pm on 12 January, and marched north. They were to cross the Wadi for their right hook early on the 13th, but a mist delayed the start until 9 am Knowledge of the country to be crossed was extremely limited, for the maps were inaccurate, and although the infantry had no problem with the Wadi (which in places was dry), the steep banks held up the guns until 1 pm. This delay was the chief cause of the operation's failure, for the time lost enabled the Turks to reinforce their threatened left. Aylmer's plan nearly succeeded, but Khalil was a better tactician than Nur-ud-Din, and in order to block the sweeping movement he extended his line to his left, facing north and at right angles to the Wadi. In the late afternoon, when the 35th Brigade had come up on the right, there were three brigades in line and the Turks were being pushed back. But as the British advanced, they came under a punishing cross-fire and were halted. The 28th Brigade had by now gone forward in a frontal attack, but could make no headway against Turkish lines protected by the Wadi. By dusk the slender hope of encircling the enemy and gaining the defile was lost when the cavalry brigade on the right, where the ground was open, failed to act.

The Wadi had been captured, but it was a hollow victory, gained at the cost of 1,613 casualties. The Turks were thought to have lost rather more men, but they were now strongly entrenched in the mouth of the defile from which they would take some dislodging.

Meanwhile, in Kut, Townshend was not deceived by Aylmer's optimistic telegrams, and was not averse to telling that general how best to relieve him, for it seemed to Townshend that with the situation so critical, Aylmer could do with some first hand advice. Conditions in the town were naturally deteriorating under the heavy bombardment, and the weather was awful, with the trenches constantly flooded and deep mud everywhere. The garrison had now been under siege for six weeks. Even taking pot shots at von der Goltz, seen inspecting the lines (a sport not approved by Townshend who considered field marshals an endangered species), did nothing to relieve the tedium. There were still rations (now on a reduced scale) for 30 days, and Townshend's two principal worries were the shortage of hospital accommodation for the increasing sick, and the almost total lack of firewood. Nevertheless, with the help of men like General Melliss, whose nobility of character was a shining beacon to all, spirits were maintained at a fairly high level.

Aylmer was in a most unenviable position. He was the recipient of often conflicting communications from Townshend and Nixon, the former offering unsolicited advice and urging speed, the latter too sick to visit the front and therefore issuing orders for a situation with which he was not fully conversant. Aylmer knew he had too few troops, quite inadequate transport and insufficient medical services; and he was faced with a narrow frontal attack against a strongly held position. He suggested to Nixon that Townshend should break out on the right bank, and he would push a division across the river to meet him. Likely Turkish reinforcements, and deteriorating weather offered this last chance. But Nixon would have none of it. The garrison must stay in Kut. Aylmer must advance.

The attack went in at 7.45 am on 21 January after a (preliminary) very heavy bombardment, and was met with accurate and sustained fire; by midday, little progress had been made, and the rain was falling in torrents with a bitingly cold wind. Men floundered about often up to their knees in mud, bravely trying to break through the Turkish lines, but the task was hopeless and the day ended in total failure with 2,741 casualties that included 78 British officers. The 2nd Black Watch and 6th Jats, who had been in the forefront throughout the three battles, had almost ceased to exist, and in every brigade there were composite battalions.

There was now to be an interval of six weeks before Aylmer made his next move. Various considerations dictated this delay, the weather, the need for reinforcements (Aylmer had suffered a total of 8,700 casualties) and the fact that Townshend had discovered a quantity of barley which, together with his 3,000 animals, would provide food for 80 days. In the meanwhile, pressure was kept up against the Turkish entrenchments, but bombardment alone would never shift them. Reinforcements were constantly arriving at Basra, but there was insufficient transport to move them quickly to the front. Aylmer could not attack before receiving a new bridging train, and he wanted to wait until the three promised divisions had arrived. However, General Lake, who had succeeded the seriously ill Nixon, gave 15 March as an outside date, for thereafter the land could be flooded.

Eventually, 6 March was decided upon, but the state of the ground caused a 48-hour postponement. By now 3 Division had come up, and General Gorringe had been made chief-of-staff to Aylmer. The plan was simple, and the battle can be simply described. Younghusband with the 19th and 21st Brigades, a weak cavalry regiment and 24 guns was to hold the Turks on the left bank, while the rest of the corps advanced across ten miles of country to attack the position known as the Dujaila Redoubt, which stretched back north-westwards to the river. The force was divided into three columns; for the attack which was to go in south of the Redoubt, Kemball would have two columns comprising the 9th, 28th and 36th Brigades, while General D'Urban Keary, with the 7th, 8th and 37th Brigades, was to attack on a line a mile farther north. The cavalry brigade was to operate on the left flank, and had received no specific orders. Townshend was to make a sortie when the attack on the Redoubt got under way.

The troops were assembled at the Pools of Siloam, three miles south of the defile, for a seven-mile night march, so that the attack could go in at dawn on 8 March. Insufficient time was given for units to reach the assembly area, and so the march was delayed. But the staff's meticulous planning had allowed for this and the long, congested night march was a total success. Dawn came and it was soon clear that the Turks had been taken completely by surprise, with men standing about folding their bedding and the Redoubt trenches unoccupied. However, in the next few minutes, the battle, and very likely the relief of Kut, was lost through too rigid an adherence to the plan. Had Kemball, whose attack was to go in first, gone forward at once, the Turks would have been caught off balance, and Townshend would have taken them in rear. But Kemball telephoned back for orders and was told the plan, which stipulated an opening barrage, must stand. An ineffectual barrage came down, surprise was lost and the Turks immediately reoccupied the forward trenches.

Thereafter it was the same story as the other frontal attacks; great gallantry, heavy casualties and no progress. The only positive success did not come until 5.15 pm when the Manchesters, with great élan, broke through, and held two lines of the Redoubt trenches for a short time. Townshend's sortie never materialised, for he rightly judged the situation unfavourable. That night the battle was broken off, and the next day the troops retired to the assembly point. Aylmer's casualties were 3,474 men, including 123 British officers, and the Turks reported 1,200. Aylmer, who was sorely smitten by this third costly failure, lacked the confidence of the Commander-in-Chief and a few days later he handed over to General Gorringe.

Great hopes had been placed on this attack by those in Kut, and inevitably its failure brought depression, but the troops still placed their faith in Townshend. He must have known that the chances of relief were now very slender, nevertheless he withstood the constant disappointments with his customary calm, and took pains through a long, optimistic communiqué, to dispel the constant canards engendered by the Arab population. He also dismissed Khalil's politely worded letter suggesting surrender with a similarly courteous reply. However, by 13 March, which was the 100th day of the siege, the garrison's problems were grave enough to justify despondency.

The floods burst on the 14th, causing havoc in the trenches, which had to be constantly baled, and putting an end to any sorties that might relieve the boredom. But they did at least save Woolpress village from imminent attack, for the Turks were forced to withdraw to dry land. A new dimension now was aerial bombing, but this proved more irritating than damaging, although the hopelessly overcrowded hospital was hit. Townshend's ingenious sappers rigged up anti-aircraft mountings, but no aeroplane was brought down.

It cannot have been easy for the quartermaster's department to gauge the extent to which the rations would last, for it had to deal with a mélange of races and customs. By 8 March, the British troops were down to a 12-ounce loaf of bread, which ten days later was reduced to eight, and the Indians got ten ounces of flour meal. The animals were now being slaughtered, with inevitable sadness as old friends went to the butcher, and Townshend became very angry when the Indians refused to eat horsemeat. Special dispensation was hurriedly obtained from their religious leaders, but they still refused. For a while they were given extra flour, but when this stopped, and they had become almost too weak to take their turn in the trenches, most of them agreed to come on the meat ration. The unsatisfactory and somewhat meagre diet, together with rough living conditions, weakened men's resistance to disease, particularly to scurvy, which prompted the Sikhs to obtain permission to eat grass. At this time there were 1,500 men in hospital, and they got what few vegetables could still be grown.

Anyone who had money was willing to pay large prices for the smallest luxuries, and it is interesting – especially in these days of tobacco tantrums – to read of some prices obtained at auction for the possessions of a dead captain. A penny bar of chocolate went for half-a-crown, a pound of biscuits six shillings, his toothpaste fetched seven and sixpence, and 100 cigarettes went for ten pounds.* The British soldier felt the deprivation of tobacco almost more than he did food, and would resort to every type of leaf he could roll as a sad substitute for the balm of nicotine.

After Dujaila, Lake spent the month of March resting and reorganising his men. Composite battalions had to be formed in the hardly tried 7 Division, but a new division – the all-British 13th – was arriving with fresh troops drafted to replace heavy Gallipoli losses. This gave Gorringe three divisions and in all somewhere about 30,000 men and 130 guns with which to meet roughly the same number of Turks. Townshend remained unimpressed by this newly acquired strength. At the end of March he wired, 'If you do not arrive until nearly 15 April, remember my food will be entirely finished'. This slightly inaccurate forecast had the desired effect.

At the beginning of April, Tigris Corps had the 3rd Division on the right bank, and the 7th and 13th on the left bank. Gorringe had decided that even though the defences on the left bank were extremely strong, that was where he would attempt to break through. The weather was a major factor in this long drawn out battle which lasted from 5 to 23 April, because it dictated which ground could be fought over, it caused plans to be altered and timings changed. In the end, the mud and slime was so deep that the attacking troops were almost marking time.

*Braddon p211

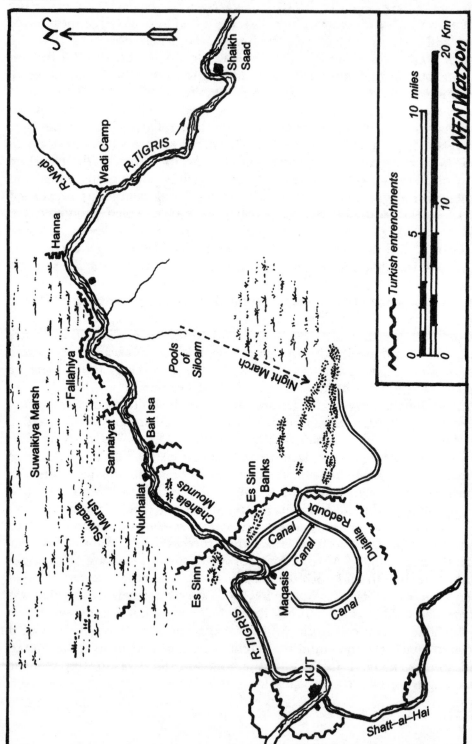

KUT: The Dujaila Redoubt attack 8 March 1916 and subsequent operations 5–24 April 1916

The first attack began in the early hours of 5 April when 13 Division advanced against the Hanna defences. This time there was to be no artillery barrage until the first line had been taken, for Gorringe was relying on surprise. In fact it was his own troops that were surprised, for the lines were empty. Khalil, well aware of the massive preparations for this attack, had withdrawn his forward troops to the stronger Fallahiya line, and here the newcomers were given their first taste of what their fellows had experienced in Gallipoli. All day they struggled, and by the end of it they had won the Fallahiya trenches, but it had cost them 1,868 casualties. So far the plan was working well, if expensively, and Gorringe now passed the 7th Division through to rush the Turks out of Sannaiyat, after which the 13th would go on to assault the Es Sinn line. But the Sannaiyat position was held by three lines of determined veteran soldiers, and the battle-scarred 7th lost 1,200 men with no impression made. Then, on 9 April, Gorringe sent the 13th forward again, but they too were beaten back adding 1,600 men to their first heavy casualty list.

The weather then held up operations. On 15 April, 3 Division attacked on the right bank of the river. Their objective was the Bait Isa lines on a fairly narrow front, for most of the ground was under water. Here the 7th and 9th Brigades, after a lot of hard fighting, met with success, the Bait Isa and Chahela Mounds positions being taken on the 17th with the Gurkhas doing great execution with their kukris in grim and deadly silence. But fresh waves of Turkish warriors were soon in counterattack, and pushed the two brigades back until the line was stabilised by the arrival of the 8th Brigade (a splendid amalgam of Manchesters, Rajputs and Sikhs). In subsequent suicidal attacks on this position, the Turks lost about 4,000 men until they realised that attacking was best left to the British. The 13th Division was then brought across to renew the offensive, but all attempts to advance in the succeeding days failed.

Khalil had reinforced the right bank from his troops in the Sannaiyat position, and this prompted Gorringe to try once more on that side. But the brave men of the 7th Division had little more to give. The first line of trenches was stormed and taken, but the Turks counterattacked and the battle came to a halt in deep squelching mud. After this, Gorringe told Lake his men could go on no longer. Tigris Corps had suffered too heavily to be, for the present, a viable offensive force against Turkish lines still held in great strength.

Aylmer and Gorringe had been driven to these terribly costly operations (in which the corps had had over 23,000 casualties) only because they knew that Townshend would have to surrender unless relieved by the middle of April. On the 16th, belated attempts were made to supply the garrison by air, but there were neither enough aeroplanes nor skilled pilots for this to be successful. The few machines available were not up to carrying heavy loads, and although some food found the target other containers went into the river.

Even less confidence could be placed in the *Julnar*, which left Amara on the night of 24 April with 270 tons of supplies. She had to run the gauntlet between banks lined with Turkish troops and guns. Nevertheless, her armour staved off the worst until she reached Maqasis, where the Turks had stretched a steel hawser across the river that fouled her rudder and held her fast. The next morning, after a sharp and bloody engagement, she was boarded and captured. The anxious garrison were able to see her a Turkish prize, and knew that that was the end.

While the last battle was being fought, Townshend had suggested that negotiations should be opened with Khalil who, since von der Goltz had died, now commanded the 6th Army. He had the quaint, old fashioned, idea that he and his troops might, on payment, be paroled to India, and on 26 April Lake telegraphed permission for Townshend to meet Khalil. At the meeting Khalil, knowing well the garrison's parlous condition, not surprisingly demanded unconditional surrender, but when a million (later two) in gold was mentioned the Turk demurred. However, his superior, the war minister Enver Pasha, was not interested in money, for British humiliation was what he wanted. There were to be no terms, and on 29 April the garrison destroyed their guns and ammunition.

The siege had lasted 143 days. During that time, the garrison had lost 1,025 men killed or died of wounds, 721 had died from diseases, 2,446 had been wounded, and there were still 1,450 in hospital. Over 8,000 British and Indian troops surrendered along with 3,248 Indian non-combatants. Townshend was to spend the rest of the war as a prisoner, enjoying considerable luxury, His officers too were well treated, for the Turks believed in privilege. But for his men it was a different story and, despite all the efforts of such caring officers as General Melliss, they became little better than helpless helots of monstrous masters. Of the 2,592 British other ranks that surrendered 68 per cent died in captivity, and one-third of the Indians also perished.

The surrender at Kut was on a scale even greater than that at Yorktown. It came as a tremendous shock to people in England, and inevitably it had serious repercussions throughout the Middle East. But at the beginning of almost every campaign that the British Army fights, the reputation of quite often good generals is sacrificed on the altar of inadequacy while later commanders, given all the troops and equipment they want succeed, and rightly win the recognition of posterity. So it was in the early days of Mesopotamia. Townshend, Nixon, Aylmer, Gorringe and Lake may not have been high flyers, but they were asked to fight battles with too few men, and far too little equipment.

Later in the summer of 1916 troops began to pour into Basra, and with them came field guns, howitzers, bridging material, river craft, medical stores, accurate maps and more modern aeroplanes. General Maude, who had arrived in command of the 13th Division, was promoted first to corps commander and then to commander-in-chief. In due course he was to march and fight victoriously into Baghdad and beyond, thereby redeeming the reputation of British arms among the peoples of the Great Rivers.

CHAPTER 14

The Alcázar of Toledo
July–September 1936

OF all forms of human conflict, none is so bitter as civil war and none so divisive of a country and its people. The Spanish Civil War of 1936 was no exception and was made all the more bitter by the involvement of elements from Germany, Italy and the Soviet Union, each seizing an opportunity to try out in war the equipment and troops with which it was preparing for the inevitable major war that was to come. But the story of the Siege of the Alcázar of Toledo pre-dates these foreign interventions and covers a period of ten weeks bitter fighting whilst General Franco and his Nationalist forces were assembling before coming to the relief of the beleaguered garrison.

The Alcázar, an old Moorish fort and the home of a military academy, was immensely strongly built and perched high above the ancient city of Toledo. Its defence is a truly remarkable tale of resolute courage. Despite being subject to continuous bombardment and machine-gun fire and repeated attacks seeking to gain a foothold, not one of the women or children in the fortress was even hurt, although the garrison was to suffer some 600 casualties including nearly 100 dead.

* * *

For many years before 1936 Spanish history had pursued a turbulent course. The First Republic ended in 1874 after slightly less than two disastrous years. The Bourbons were restored in the person of the young Alfonso XII, the son of Isabella II, who herself had come to the throne in extreme youth, the successful symbol of the first Carlist war. The monarchy survived until 1931 when Alfonso XIII abdicated in the hope of avoiding civil war. He might have gone earlier but for the seven years of comparatively beneficial military dictatorship (1923–1930) of Primo de Rivera, who kept the growing number of Anarchists, anti-monarchists and anti-clerical revolutionaries in some sort of control. The Socialist government, under Manuel Azana, that followed the abdication was briefly troubled by an attempted monarchist coup led by General Sanjurjo, but it was quickly suppressed and the general was lucky not to have been executed.

In 1933, a coalition of right wing parties came into power. Multi-partyism was responsible for much of Spain's troubles at this time. Monarchists, Carlists, Fascists, Socialists, Communists, Anarchists, and Militant Trade

Unionists all felt they should be at the centre of affairs. United in their dislike one for the other, individually they were capable of causing considerable trouble in support of their dogmas.

The elections in February 1936 returned a Popular Front government of the type supported, and to an extent controlled, by Moscow. The situation previous to this had been getting very ugly. A succession of right wing governments were faced with constant breakdowns in law and order instigated by parties of the left. There was an Anarchist insurrection in Cadiz, and Communist miners in Asturias marched in rebellion. The Church was a favourite target for left wing extremists. Violent riots in many towns usually ended in the burning of churches and the murder of monks and priests, with authority unable, or unwilling, to intervene. And governments had also to contend with Basque and Catalan Separatist agitations.

Casares Quiroga's Popular Front government proved quite incapable of controlling the men of violence among its own supporters, let alone the near two million Anarchists whose interests lay outside the Cortes. Political assassinations became commonplace, with reprisal by the bullet leaving behind its curse of vendetta. By the early summer of 1936, all was chaos and confusion as the country clattered into a war in which numerous factions would fight each other in furtherance of their own particular ideas and ideals.

For some time there had been unrest among senior officers of the Army over the general state of the country, and in particular over recent reforms that aimed at reducing the Army's power. Shortly after the February elections, some generals, whose loyalty to the Republic was suspect, were removed from the centre of affairs to distant commands. However, before they left Madrid, a few met to co-ordinate plans for a *coup d'état* should anarchy render the country ungovernable.

The men on whose shoulders the responsibility for an uprising would principally lie were Generals Sanjurjo, Mola, Franco, Orgaz and Varela. Sanjurjo, although in exile in Portugal had kept in close touch; Mola had recently been transferred from Morocco to be Military Governor of Pamplona; Franco had been banished from Madrid, where he had been Chief-of-Staff, to a command in the Canaries; Orgaz had retired after the army reforms, and never ceased to plot; and Varela had been involved (and subsequently imprisoned) in Sajurjo's attempted coup, and had recently been training the Carlist levies (*Requetés*).

There was no certainty as to how the garrison commanders would react when the signal to rise was given, but in general it was thought that the Army (and the *Guardia Civil*) would support the revolt. At any rate, Mola in the north could be certain of support from a large number of excellent *Requetés*, and Franco had few doubts about the Army of Africa. This comprised the tough, well-trained Spanish Foreign Legion commanded by General Yagüe*, and the almost equally excellent *Regulares*, Moorish troops.

The event that made the generals decide that the time had come to launch their *coup d'état*, which they firmly believed would quickly be successful, was the brutal mass murder, on 13 July, of Calvo Sotelo, the Monarchist leader in the Cortes. His was a revenge killing by the *Asaltos*† for the murder of one of their men by the Fascists. Sotelo was taken from his home in the early hours (although as a member of the Cortes and so immune from arrest) and shot in the car. It was clear proof, if such was needed, of the Government's inability to control their own agents. As a result of this crime the conspirators agreed that the uprising should begin in North Africa on 17 July.

They had not found it easy to co-ordinate the plot, for some supporters hung back, and there were a few senior officers who resisted persuasion. The possibility of a full-scale civil war could not be ruled out and, as a precaution, it had been ascertained that Portugal, Germany and Italy would give assistance, at any rate indirectly, should the need arise. It was very soon clear that the need would arise. Franco had been conveyed to Morocco in an aeroplane hired from an English company, and here matters went pretty well to plan, although there was some fighting (severe in places) before control was gained. But the greater part of the navy remained loyal to the Government, and almost all the aircraft (although not all of the pilots) were in Government control, and so crossing the Straits became a problem.

On the mainland, the rising had not been simultaneous, had it been so the *coup d'état* might possibly have succeeded. In those places where the garrison supported the revolt, the pattern was similar. The rebel soldiers were quickly joined by their Carlist and Falangist supporters, and usually by the *Guardia Civil*, but opposed by those officers loyal to the Republic, the *Asaltos* and various working-class militias. Seville fell to a very daring *coup de main* by General Queipo de Llano, but in most of the towns there was fighting which lasted several days before the issue was resolved one way or other. Fortunately for the Nationalists, as the rebels soon called themselves, the Government delayed arming the workers until the rebellion had taken a firm hold. By late July, Spain had settled into a civil war, with the Government holding most of the south, east and north-east, and the Nationalists the Caceres-Salamanca area in the west, and all the land north of Madrid except Asturias, the Basque provinces and Catalonia.

---

*The Legion was founded in the early 1920s, and was officered by Spaniards with almost entirely Spanish soldiers. In the Civil War it was divided into two *tercios* each of ten *banderas* (battalions) of approximately 600 soldiers.
†*Guardia de Asalto* (Assault Guards or *Asaltos*) were a well trained paramilitary constabulary force formed by the Popular Front as a counter-balance to the *Guardia Civil*.

Before the arrival of foreign troops, the Republicans relied mostly on the *Asaltos*, and the large number of working-class militiamen. Initially, these latter were untrained, undisciplined, and interested primarily in pillage and murder, but they could fight and had plenty of courage. They had a stiffening of some 200 army officers and 13 generals, but these were mostly valued for their technical advice, not leadership, which was often in the hands of a political committee. The Nationalists were well down numerically, but their army was much more professional. The Army of Africa had some 16,000 men operating on the mainland, and there were a further 40,000 (including 8,000 NCOs) of the Regular Army, and some 14,000 Carlist *Requetés*.

This then was the general situation before Toledo, a charming cathedral city lapped by the Tagus and just within Republican territory, became for a short time the epitome of the glamour, and the ghastliness, of war. In 1936 there were rather less than 30,000 inhabitants most of whom had supported the Right in the recent elections, although inevitably there were some left wing extremists. The city is built upon hills, and on the highest of these, perched in a dominating position like an eagle's eyrie, is the splendid Alcázar – once a Moorish fort, then a royal palace, and most recently a military academy. Originally the Academy of Infantry, it was later joined by the cavalry, although since the Republic the number of cadets had shrunk, and in 1936 there were no more than 130. In July these, with most of the staff, were on leave, but a handful remained in the vicinity.

The Alcázar was a massive rectangular building having at each corner a square tower surmounted by steeples. Its four walls – particularly the older east and west ones – which enclosed a courtyard and patio were extremely solid. The building stood on three different levels due to the nature of the ground, and this gave it additional strength when under bombardment. A wide underground passage circumscribed it, and beneath the courtyard were large cellars, which although almost airless and completely dark, provided excellent shelter for the women and children during the siege.

Just below the Alcázar were its dependency buildings, all of which played an important part in the siege. The headquarters of the military government, called the Gobierno, a strong, wedge-shaped, two-storey building with a basement used for stabling, lay below the North Terrace and connected with it by a road known as the Zig-Zag. The Gobierno itself was connected with the Esplanade (the parade ground on the east front of the Alcázar) by a footbridge leading from its second storey. Across the Calle del Carmen, and only a short stone thrown from the Gobierno, was the Santa Cruz (formerly a hospital) which, like the convent below it, was occupied by the Reds during the siege.

The other outbuildings were the Riding School, Dining Hall and Santiago Barracks (which housed the Academy's military contingent) below the Esplanade; and to the south of the Alcázar the Capuchinos, an old

MAP 14.1

The Spanish Civil War: areas held by the opposing forces in August 1936

monastery converted to cadet quarters. At the foot of the south-east tower was the Curved Passage, a very important covered way connecting the Alcázar with the outbuildings. There was an open space known as the Corralillo immediately south of the Dining Hall.

One further key factor of the defence was a passage running inside the west wall of the North Terrace, known from its length and Stygian darkness as the 'Simplon'. Off this passage were rooms from which the besieged, virtually immune from shell fire, were able to break up attacks coming from the Zocodover up the wide street (the Cuesta de Carlos V) which ran many feet below.

Besides the Military Academy there was, just outside the city, the Army's Central School of Physical Education (gym school), whose Director was

Colonel Jose Moscardó, an elderly unambitious soldier and devout Catholic. He had been apprised of the rising, for which he had much sympathy, and finding himself the senior officer in Toledo, for Colonel Abeilhé, the Director of the Academy, was in Madrid, he assumed the role of Military Governor of the Province*, and called those officers in the city to a conference. These included Captain Emilio Vela, a cavalry instructor at the Academy, just returned from Madrid where he had rounded up a few cadets, and Colonel Romero head of the *Guardia Civil* in the province. At this meeting when Moscardó explained the situation, and declared for the rebellion, the approval was virtually unanimous.

It was agreed by Moscardó's small junta that no public declaration of intention should be made until there were more troops available than those few members of the Academy and gym school not on leave. The principal source of reinforcement would come from the *Guardia Civil*, and Romero gave orders for his men to withdraw into Toledo. The figures given of his strength by Moscardó in his report are disputed by some authorities – particularly is this so in regard to the *Guardia Civil* – but assuming them to be more or less correct he had 1,200 men capable of bearing arms. These included 800 *Guardia Civil*, 200 Falangists, 100 officers (active, retired or on leave in the province), 200 young soldiers and a few cadets. In addition there were 328 women and 210 children†.

The first priority was to procure arms and ammunition from the Arms Factory that was situated some three kilometres north-west of the city, and commanded by Colonel Soto who was thought to be a Republican. This meant that Moscardó, while secretly arranging for an escorted convoy to take possession of the arms, had to employ delaying tactics and subterfuge both with Soto and the War Minister in Madrid, who repeatedly demanded immediate delivery of the Factory's contents. The operation was successfully concluded, although it was a near run thing, before the Red militia had reached Toledo in any numbers. The Alcázareños therefore started the siege with nearly a million rounds of small arms ammunition, two 70-mm mountain guns with 50 shells, 13 machine-guns, a 55-mm mortar with only a few bombs, and plenty of hand grenades. But foolishly, the Factory was left intact.

It was now time for Moscardó to nail his colours to the mast and so, while the arms were being collected, Captain Vela marched a detachment to the Zocodover, where the troops presented arms and the captain read a proclamation declaring a state of war, which was also broadcast over Toledo wireless.

---

*Many military governorships had been abolished by Republican governments, but duties continued to be performed by the senior officer of the province.
†These are the figures given in the official account now displayed in the new Alcázar. Most other authorities give them as 500 or 550 women and 50 children.

MAP 14.2

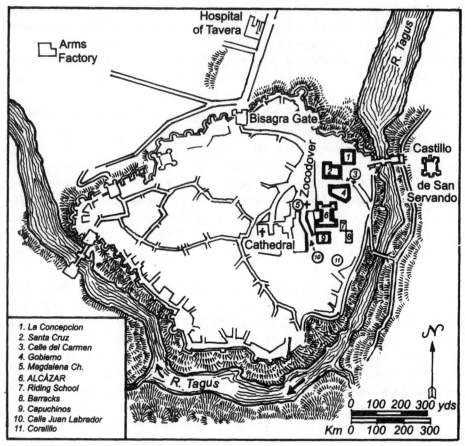

1. La Concepcion
2. Santa Cruz
3. Calle del Carmen
4. Gobierno
5. Magdalena Ch.
6. ALCÁZAR
7. Riding School
8. Barracks
9. Capuchinos
10. Calle Juan Labrador
11. Coralillo

The Siege of the Alcázar 1936: the City of Toledo

After demands for the ammunition came pleas and threats from Madrid for Moscardó to surrender, which were politely but firmly refused. Propaganda leaflets dropped from the air had a poor reception in the city, but with the arrival of the militia the war had come to Toledo. The Hospital of Tavera, just north of the city, was manned by a detachment of *Guardia Civil* with a machine-gun, and advancing militiamen in mob formation made a splendid target for this gun, and for other Nationalists in buildings flanking the road north of the Bisagra Gate. There was little discipline, and the Reds broke under fire, some were led to the Arms Factory, where fortunately the loading operation had just been completed, and others peeled away towards the city. The armoured cars' cannon made no impression on the solid walls of the Hospital and one was disabled by a well placed bomb. Artillery support from a 75-mm gun also proved ineffective.

On the next day (22 July), enemy aircraft made two bombing raids on the Alcázar and Tavera, but the damage was slight. It had been Moscardó's plan to hold the city, hence the detachments north of the Bisagra Gate, and at other key places, but once the militia were inside the walls, and among the narrow streets, the outlying detachments could be easily cut off. At first Moscardó refused to permit a withdrawal, and when the order was given it was almost too late. Major Villalba, commanding the Tavera post, had only half a mile to go, but because he had to make a difficult detour it took him six hours. Thirteen men, including two doctors and three senior NCOs, were lost in the process.

During the 23rd, the remaining outlying detachments, a number of refugees, and the Civil Governor and his family (willing hostages) made their way into the Alcázar, which with its dependencies now came under siege. The majority of the 1,200 defenders were stationed in the Alcázar itself, but details of varying size occupied the Gobierno, Riding School, Santiago Barracks and the Capuchinos.

The Republicans had hopes of starving the Alcázareños into surrender within a short time, and such hopes were not entirely ill-founded, for Moscardó, unwisely reckoning on a quick relief, had done nothing in the short time available to supplement the meagre supplies. In fact Captain Cuartero, acting quartermaster, reckoned the food could not last for more than ten days at most. There was a fair stock of vermin-infested oats and barley in the stables, and there were over 100 horses and about 27 mules representing a reserve stock of meat on the hoof. Water for drinking proved a lesser problem, for there were wells and cisterns, but it was of poor quality and the pumping machinery was smashed in an early bombing raid which meant that washing water from the Tagus was unobtainable. Medical facilities were totally inadequate. There was no surgeon, and of the three doctors one was a skin specialist and another an eye specialist. Five nuns, who had come as refugees, did what they could, but there was never enough of anything, and chloroform was soon finished.

The besiegers had no supply worries, for their line of communication was fairly short, and the city was well stocked with food: their task in this respect, which they carried out efficiently with one exception, was to ensure that forage raids by the besieged failed in their purpose. Initially their policy was simply to subject the defenders to occasional air-raids, and to constant and heavy artillery bombardment, while the 3,000 militiamen kept up an almost continuous *paqueo* (small arms fire) at targets of opportunity. In between whiles they amused themselves with murder, rape and loot, their butchery being particularly directed at priests, of whom it is said 107 died in Toledo. This was no worse than what was happening elsewhere in Spain, and merely in keeping with the appalling cruelty of the time.

On 23 July, when the siege was but a day old, there occurred the melodramatic event that symbolises the sacrifice and futility embodied in war, and which more than any other single act of this siege caught the imagination and stirred the hearts of all people. Luis Moscardó had fallen into the hands of the besiegers, and Candido Cabello – one of their leaders – saw what he thought was a certain way of obtaining the Alcázar's surrender. He telephoned Colonel Moscardó and informed him that unless he surrendered within ten minutes his son would be shot. To prove his word he brought Luis to the telephone: there followed the deeply moving valedictory exchanges. 'What is happening my boy?' to which Luis replied, 'They say they will shoot me if the Alcázar does not surrender' to this his father replied, 'If it be true, commend your soul to God, shout *Viva España* and die like a hero. Goodbye my son, a last kiss.' The fact that Luis was not executed until a month later would have been no consolation to Moscardó had he known it. His behaviour at this time of personal anguish entitles him to long renown, but it should not overshadow the heroic fortitude and constancy displayed by all the men and women in the Alcázar during their terrible ordeal.

The siege of the Alcázar lasted 68 days, and as soon as the Republicans realised it would not be surrendered easily, they stepped up their offensive action. Almost every day, the besieged suffered a few casualties, but there were some days when the fighting was exceptionally bitter and the damage greater than usual.

As early as 24 July, the besieged were made aware of what they would have to endure in the future. Republican batteries were established to the north of the city at Dehesa de Pinedo, and to the east across the Tagus at Alijares. Both places were beyond the range of the defenders' weapons, and with aerial spotting to help the 105-mm guns, considerable damage was done on this day to the northern facade of the Alcázar. This inevitably raised the question of the women and children. Moscardó would not allow the women to play any active part in the defence, although their presence and behaviour throughout contributed considerably to the general morale. They were constantly moved from one safe refuge to another, all of them below ground in chambers that were dark, damp and thoroughly obnoxious. There was nothing for them to do but gossip, and by the light of improvised candles (for the electricity supply was cut in the first bombardment) read 'The Alcázar', a daily news-sheet that throughout the siege never missed publication.

The first of a number of unsuccessful forays in search of food, and electricity cable or, later, to detect mine shafts, were launched on the second day of the siege. The militiamen, taken by surprise initially, for it was their dinner hour, quickly rallied and both sorties were driven back without the much needed food. A leading left wing extremist and his family were captured, but the Nationalists lost three men killed and nine wounded.

For some reason the shelling virtually ceased during the last days of

July, but with the coming of August it recommenced with greater intensity, supplemented by daily aerial bombing. On 1 August, the Riding School was practically demolished, and on the next day the guns switched their attention to the Capuchinos, and the all important Curved Passage which was badly damaged, but left still useable, provided that the crouch position was adopted. Two days later, the besieged were submitted to an almost round the clock bombardment, particular attention being paid to the Dining Hall, and nearby kitchen, at meal times. To avoid casualties, timings had to be changed, and meals were anyway now down from three to two a day. But on this day there was at least one piece of special good fortune for the besieged.

One of the civilians in the Alcázar suddenly recalled knowledge of a shack situated off the Calle del Carmen which probably still contained sacks of threshed wheat, deposited there by a bank as payment on loans. The shack stood perilously near enemy occupied buildings, nevertheless the truth of the story must be confirmed by reconnaissance. The moon was full, making movement hazardous, but 20 men stole silently out of the Alcázar, and on locating the building gained entrance by removing tiles from the roof. Inside were found sacks of wheat sufficient to feed the Alcázareños for a long time. That night 23 sacks were carried away, which was as much wheat as the improvised grinding machine could cope with. Further sorties were made as occasion demanded, and although these sometimes came under fire, the Republicans never discovered what was afoot.

As August progressed, life in the Alcázar settled into an uneasy routine. Moscardó, although by no means short of ammunition, forbade indiscriminate firing, not so the militia whose prodigal *paqueos* only slightly exceeded the expenditure of shells from the two batteries. The garrison, unable to retaliate, placed spotters who with glasses could see the Republican gunners approach their guns, and devised a 'Take Cover' signal which undoubtedly saved lives, but not of course damage, and this was becoming extensive, particularly to the north facade. Searchlights now played upon the building, and shelling would often continue into the night. This stopped the social gatherings in the courtyard for a chat and smoke enjoyed during the six hours off-duty spells which alternated with six hours on. Perhaps this mattered less now that tobacco was almost finished, and acacia leaves made an unsatisfactory substitute.

The daily trickle of casualties, although not serious, was beginning to mount with 25 killed, and over 100 men wounded by the middle of August. There had also been at least ten desertions, mostly young soldiers from the Academy staff. They probably gave information to the Reds, after which they would very likely be shot. It was not a wise course to desert, but for men lacking self-discipline it was perhaps understandable, for by now privations were beginning to bite. Meat was horse and mule stew, bread was baked wheat, coffee and rice were finished as were fresh vegetables.

The supply of salt had lasted only a few days. The daily ration had become very slender, nor was water holding out as well as expected, and the issue was three quarters of a litre a day per person. Sugar, too, was finished and some found the lack of sweetness so unbearable as to tempt them to unauthorised raids, which usually ended in disaster.

On 16 August, a wounded soldier, lying in one of the underground rooms, was frightened by strange subterranean sounds. It was soon established that what he had heard was the driving of a mine shaft. Thus a new and more frightening dimension was added to the siege. The rock on which the Alcázar stood was so hard, and materials available so inadequate, that countermining was impossible. The only hope lay in a successful raid to locate the source of the shaft and destroy it. This was a forlorn hope faced with a rabbit warren of streets and houses beyond the west wall, and although two patrols went out they were unsuccessful. There was nothing for it but to minimise casualties through evacuation of the danger area. The officer with most knowledge of these matters, a Lieutenant Barber, assured Moscardó that it would be some weeks before the mine exploded. But unknown to him, while progress with the tunnel would undoubtedly be slow, it would be very sure, for the expert service of Asturian miners had been procured and, to make certain of success, they dug parallel tunnels with a mine to explode under the south-west tower, and another beneath the west wall a little farther north. The long suspense was one of the worst ordeals the besieged had to bear.

On 20 August, the Republicans added nine 155-mm guns and seven 75s to their batteries, and the big guns soon did immense damage to the north wall of the Alcázar, causing large gaps that exposed the rooms. These could then be subjected to machine-gun fire from the nearby Magdalena Church. Indeed, the whole of this front was beginning to crumble away and, on 4 September, the north-east tower fell with an almighty crash on the Esplanade. Four days later, the north-west one crumpled on to the Cuesta, blocking the whole street. Damage elsewhere was only a little less; two 75-mm guns firing from San Servando Castle had put the kitchens out of action, made a mess of the east facade of the Alcázar, and further depleted the Curved Passage. Moreover, mortars had now been brought into action, lobbing bombs into the courtyards of the Gobierno and Alcázar; inevitably these caused casualties, for it was impossible to spot them and give a 'Take Cover' signal.

But on 22 August, the fortunes of the besieged took a well deserved upward turn when, after being subjected to one of the almost daily bombing raids, a Nationalist plane dropped four canisters crammed with what were to the besieged almost unbelievable delicacies, and a letter of greetings from Franco. The delicacies went nowhere among 1,700, but the morale effect was tremendous, for from the time when power was lost until almost the end of the siege, the improvised wireless could get only Radio Madrid, which constantly announced the surrender of the Alcázar. It was good therefore to know that Nationalist forces recognised this to be false.

However, a more insiduous form of propaganda, closer to hand, had serious results. The Republicans set up a broadcasting device, with loud speaker, just out of rifle range, with which they daily taunted the besieged. Vivid descriptions were given of the good life to be obtained by deserters – beer, cigarettes, plenty of food – and they even produced relatives of the besieged to say good-bye before execution. Not surprisingly, this had some effect. Deserters would then be made to broadcast. Even so, only 35 men deserted during the siege, although, towards the end, when pressure had become almost unbearable, there were three or four suicides.

During August and September, the militiamen (now considerably strengthened) made a number of minor attacks, three of which caused the garrison serious concern. The objective for almost all the smaller attacks was the Gobierno, and the defences at Stable Approach. These attacks were launched from the Santa Cruz, which was near enough for supporting incendiary bombs and hand grenades to be hurled from roof and windows. A favourite practice of trying to set fire to the Gobierno by spraying it with petrol and then rushing forward to ignite was never completely successful, although the laboratory at the wedge end was eventually destroyed. A hundred men, relieved every four days, held this building, which was a vital first line defence of the Alcázar, and when they were not fighting at the barricades and windows, they were busy reinforcing them. Support troops from the Alcázar were always ready to counterattack, and the one precious mortar had considerable success against the enemy forming up in the Calle del Carmen, but it suffered from having very few bombs.

On 29 August, the Reds had somehow contrived to manoeuvre a field-gun so as to fire through a hole in the massive gate of the convent La Concepcion. Its arc of fire was very limited, but it was quickly apparent that with firing at such short range, a section of the Gobierno large enough to pass, say, a thousand men into the assault, would soon lie open. There was little the defence could do but, for some reason, never properly explained, the gun became silent after firing only a few rounds. Had this not been so, the consequences might have been disastrous.

A week later, the Republicans mounted the first of their major attacks aimed at taking the Gobierno as a first step to assaulting the Alcázar. A large number of militiamen rushed the barricades at the west end of Stable Approach. The defenders were bombed out of the corner rooms, and the Reds swarmed down the whole length of Stable Approach, fighting their way into the Gobierno, and occupying it and Stable No 4. The Nationalists withdrew towards the Dining Hall under cover of the smoke billowing from the partially destroyed building. Here they could have been routed before fresh barricades were erected, but the hopelessly disorganised militiamen took to looting what they could find in the Gobierno. When fresh troops were sent from the Alcázar to counterattack, the Reds were quickly driven back to the Santa Cruz.

It could have ended very differently, and the Gobierno garrison realised that they must not be stampeded out of the building again. Another time, the retaking might not be so easy. Meanwhile, the Republicans, unsuccessful in assault, redoubled their bombardment on the Alcázar and, a few days later, sent in an emissary to offer terms. Major Rojo, a regular soldier who had been an instructor at the Academy, was blindfolded and led to Moscardó, whom he knew well, and offered to spare lives in return for surrender. The offer was not even considered. Two days later, he came again, this time to guarantee the safety of the women and children should they wish to leave. Their representatives were summoned, and all assured the Major that they would stay and – if need be – fight with their men folk. Rojo did, however, procure the services of a priest. Canon Vasquez Camarassa baptised a baby, visited the wounded and celebrated Mass at which he preached a most comminatory sermon. Later, the Republicans sent the Chilean ambassador to mediate, but he never got as far as the Alcázar.

By the middle of September the situation throughout the defence was becoming desperate. Nearly all the outbuildings had been reduced to rubble, but their defenders, with much courage and firmness of spirit, still held on. In the Alcázar, conditions were appalling. The north facade was completely down; the battered west wall still stood, but the mining was clearly getting nearer. Men on duty there realised that at any minute they could be blown sky high; nerves were taut; an officer and NCO committed suicide. Any form of sanitation or means of washing had long since ceased to exist, and the stench everywhere was ghastly.

The supply of horse and mule flesh was dwindling fast, but the wheat still held out, although men were now too weak to haul the sacks, and so the corn had to be transferred to pillowcases. Patrols were being sent to the shack almost nightly, for should the outer defences fall, it would be in Republican territory. On one such sortie (16 September) Lieutenant Fernando Barrientos slipped away in the darkness, and gave himself up. He was a young staff officer from the gym school with fighting experience in Morocco, but he had had enough. The Reds shot him on the last day of the siege. He was the only officer to desert.

It was later learnt that the mine shafts had been driven from two houses in the Calle de Juan Labrador, some 80 yards from the west wall of the Alcázar. By 16 September one of the tunnels had obviously been completed, and it could not be long before the other would be ready. Moscardó forbade anyone not on duty to enter the danger zone. The women and children were taken to the east side near the swimming bath, and the hospital was shifted to beneath the north facade. The once magnificent Alcázar waited, with what dignity and grace it could still command, the terrible explosion that might transform it into the cold splendour of a mausoleum. It came, at the end of an exceptionally heavy barrage, at 6.21 am on 18 September, and was witnessed by a carefully assembled squad of camera and newsreel men from Madrid.

The two mines exploded simultaneously, one under the south-west tower and the other midway along the west wall at the Waggon Entrance. Huge chunks of masonry, including the top of the tower in one piece, were hurled into the air and came crashing down on the houses in two nearby streets, which completely disappeared. The fine stained glass windows in the cathedral 300 yards away were smashed, but most of the city was undamaged. In the Alcázar, all was dark, and shrouded in thick dust, as the whole building shuddered under the impact of the enormous explosions. Much of the west side had been turned into vast slabs of rubble, but the south and east sides still held, and one tower, as yet unconquered, stood proud and lofty. Most of the inhabitants had been safely shepherded beyond the danger line, but an officer and four soldiers on sentry duty had been blown to smithereens. At the very moment of explosion, a baby girl was born.

About ten minutes after the explosions, when the drizzle of debris had cleared, some 2,500 militiamen and *Asaltos*, supported by two armoured cars and a tank, and backed by another thousand or so men in reserve, began their attack. The force was divided into two equal parts, which in turn were subdivided, so that the attack would be four-pronged. Major Madronero would lead a column against the northern face of the Alcázar, supported by a tank, Major Torres would command assaults on the south-west corner and the breach in the west wall by the Museum, while an independent attack by 500 militiamen was to go in across the Corralillo, supported by two armoured cars. Major Barceló, the overall commander, assured his officers they would be engaged only in a mopping-up operation. In the event, none of the four attacks was successful, although in every one of them the fighting was very severe.

It was a remarkable feat on the part of the garrison that in the space of little more than ten minutes, they had emerged shaken but resolute from the mess, and had taken up fire positions in time to meet the assaults. The situation was particularly dangerous on the west side of the building, where familiar rooms and loopholes had disappeared, floors had collapsed and stairways were just large chunks of rubble. There were open-ended rooms where some sort of barricade had to be hastily erected, and manned with machine-guns that took a lot of hauling into position by men weakened almost beyond endurance. But at least the mountains of masonry made any approach by the attackers slow, difficult and extremely hazardous.

The attack on the northern front went in marginally ahead of the others, because the distance was the shortest from the forming-up point – the Zocodover. In every instance, the attackers were taken off balance at finding that so many men had survived the explosions, and were ready

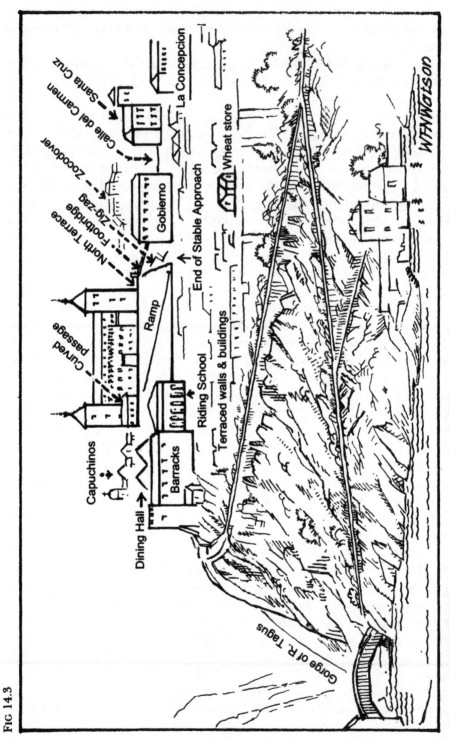

FIG 14.3

Sketch to indicate the approximate levels of various buildings in the immediate vicinity of the Alcázar as viewed from the East. (Not to scale).

to receive them. The first wave of militiamen was driven back by a withering fire, but reinforcements coming from the Zig-Zag below the terrace looked dangerous, and might have broken through if they had not been checked by accurate fire from the Gobierno. The Republicans had left that building out of their plan, which was a mistake, for although they tried to neutralise it by fire from the Santa Cruz, this was only partially successful. Support by the rather ancient tank achieved nothing. It waddled along the Calle del Carmen, and down Stable Approach brushing obstacles aside and, impervious to bullets and bombs, eventually reached the Zig-Zig, where it failed to negotiate the North Terrace rubble and gave up. Three determined assaults on this front all failed to gain their objective.

The approach to the west side of the building was the most difficult. Here, in both the attacks, the men emerged from a maze of wrecked streets into open ground, before having to flounder over obstacles which made them easy targets for the greatly outnumbered and sternly embattled Nationalists. In the south-west corner, all they could achieve was to hurl a few ineffective bombs; this assault never really materialised. Further along at the Museum breach, the *Asaltos* formed the first wave. Taken by surprise at the weight of lead that greeted their arrival at what they thought were empty rooms, they fell back, and adopted fire without movement. A charge before the few defenders had had time to complete their barricades, and receive reinforcements, could have succeeded, but loss of momentum was fatal.

On this front some *Asaltos* got into an upper room undetected and, shoving grenades through holes in the floor, killed and wounded nine *Guardia Civil.* They then caused casualties among men in the courtyard preparing to counterattack. These daring *Asaltos* were eventually outmanoeuvred by an equally daring act. Lieutenant Gómez and six men erected improvised ladders, and squeezed through the holes in the ceiling to take the *Asaltos* in rear while they were busily engaged at the far end of the room.

The attack which most nearly succeeded was the one from across the Corralillo. Here troops could advance in extended order, and the armoured cars had room to manoeuvre. The immediate objective was the Dining Hall, for when that was taken, fire could be brought to bear on the Alcázar and all the posts in that area would be cut off. Under cover of the cars, the militiamen were soon up to the buildings. They would have swept all before them, had they not been caught in a fierce enfilade fire from a previously unoccupied corner of the skeletal Capuchinos. Some *Guardia Civil*, seeing the danger, had hurriedly manned a machine-gun at the basement window of the laundry, and its devastating bursts from this unexpected quarter was too much for the untrained and undisciplined militiamen, who streaked back across the Corralillo, closely followed by the armoured cars.

There had been nearly four hours of fighting before the Republicans called off the attack at about 10.30 am. There was nothing to show for their great courage save large numbers of shapeless heaps upon the rubble. All the attacks had suffered from the ground being unstudied, and the plan unformed. The Nationalist casualties were surprisingly light with 18 killed and 62 wounded.

The besieged were justly proud of their stubborn defence in face of overwhelming odds, but by the evening of the 18th they were clinging to buildings that were all in ruins. It was now Autumn, and on their high, unprotected hill the nights were bitterly cold, adding another dimension to their discomfort, but their bodies, although dreadfully emaciated, were inured to hardship and fatigue. Perhaps more distressing was Madrid's constant broadcasting of reports that the Alcázar had fallen. Relief was thought to be near, but would the force commander, believing the broadcasts, by-pass Toledo and take the direct route to Madrid? The uncertainty made it more difficult to hold on, and there was fighting still to be done.

Once the attacking force had fallen back, the artillery bombardment was redoubled against the eastern defences. The Republicans were determined to take the Gobierno and Stable No 4, for with those lost, other garrisons would be isolated. Shells, bombs and every kind of incendiary device were hurled against the building, and the Asturian miners blasted away a large section of the stable with TNT. On the night of 19–20 September, militiamen gained entrance to the stable's long, subterranean tunnel. Although the defenders – mainly young soldiers – were harried by bomb and bullet, they fought with such stubbornness, sometimes amid flames, for the building above was burning, that the Reds withdrew, leaving their dead behind.

At about 9.30 am, while room-to-room fighting was still going on in what was left of the Gobierno, the Republicans launched another tank attack. It was only marginally more successful than the last one. After lumbering up the Zig-Zag, the cumbersome machine announced its arrival at the North Terrace with its klaxon, which was the signal for the waiting militiamen to go forward under cover of the tank's cannon. Three times the attempt was bravely made, and three times the tank found the rubble insurmountable, leaving the soldiers to breast the top unsupported. During its third rearward slide, it got badly worsted by Nationalist bombs, and withdrew from the battle. This left the militiamen exposed to the cold steel of a *Guardia Civil* bayonet charge, which they relished so little as to beat a hasty retreat.

The Alcázar had defied yet another attack, and the Gobierno was still held by a handful of battle-weary men. The field telephone had been destroyed, and contact with the outposts was now almost impossible. That night it was decided to withdraw them, and the operation was carried out efficiently and without loss. But, most unfortunately, an open rainwater conduit, large enough for a man to crawl through and running from Stable Approach to the east wall of the Alcázar, had been overlooked. It was a gift the Asturian miners did not intend to refuse.

The Alcázareños were now tightly trammelled in what was left of their fortress, although for three days the Reds did not realise the outbuildings had been abandoned. There were to be other attacks – one with a tank – and on the last day of the siege, the water-conduit mine was exploded leaving a vast crater in the Esplanade, but doing no other damage. All these attacks were held, but until the guns at Alijares were removed on 24 September, the shelling of the east front was constant and devastating. On 21 September, amid frenzied scenes of Republican joy, the last (south-east) tower came crashing down. Each day there were a few casualties, and conditions within the Alcázar became more dreadful than ever. The dead could no longer be buried*, and were placed in the Swimming Bath lockers, and loosely bricked up. They could be partly seen, and plainly smelt. Outside those of the Reds who had fallen in the attacks lay untouched, save by the swarms of rats that nibbled away. Only a very few horses and mules were left. But the gimcrack wireless had recently been receiving Portuguese broadcasts and, on about the 25th, these announced that the Nationalists had fought their way across the Guadarrama. This and the presence of Nationalist bombers clearly indicated relief was at hand.

A much more decisive event in this terrible civil war than the aid given to the Republicans by the Russians in November 1936 was that given earlier to Franco by the Germans and Italians. German JU 52s (officially on loan) enabled the Army of Africa to make a lodgement on the mainland in July. Not long afterwards, Italian fighters greatly contributed to Nationalist command of the Straits. The Army of Africa was therefore able to take Cadiz, Algeciras and La Linea, and to advance to Seville in support of General de Llano.

Franco arrived in Seville on 6 August to direct operations for the advance on Madrid. Command in the field was given to General Yagüe, and the army's route was via Mérida, Trujillo, Oropesa and Talavera. Mérida was reached virtually unopposed, but thereafter there was to be some fierce fighting. A diversion was made to reduce Badajos, once more seared by the flame of war, and the scene of a massacre even more dreadful than that of 1812. At Talavera, on 3 September, a large Republican force was drawn up in a strong defensive position, but showed little inclination to fight, and the Nationalists soon had the town. At Maqueda, which the Reds also abandoned after small resistance, the decision was taken to relieve the Alcázar rather than to press on to Madrid.

On 23 September the army, now commanded by General Varela, for Yagüe was sick, marched for the Alcázar. The Toledo-Madrid road was cut on the 26th, and as the Nationalists closed in on the town, many Republican troops, facing a desperate situation, fought bravely in isolated pockets, no longer supported by their guns nor, in some cases, by their officers. The

---

*Hitherto a corner of the Riding School had been used as a cemetery.

Republicans, like the Nationalists before them, made no attempt to destroy the Arms Factory which Varela's men took intact. In the late afternoon of 27 September, the Legion entered the city, and with it came the Moors – back again in Toledo after many centuries. There was little fighting in the streets, but plenty of killing, for the Nationalists had found the mutilated remains of two of their airmen. The militiamen made their escape as best they could, mostly over the rocky, barren hillsides towards Aranjuez.

The siege was over on this day, although it was not officially ended until the morning of the 28th when Varela climbed over the rubble and entered the Alcázar. Moscardó saluted him and delivered his well-known masterpiece of understatement, '*Sin novedad en Alcázar*' – 'Nothing new (to report) in the Alcázar'. There was certainly little left to report upon save dead, wounded and emaciated men and women, a little food and ammunition, a lot of rats, five mules and one horse – 'Cajon' – a thoroughbred belonging to an officer of the Academy, said to have been a member of the relieving force, and overjoyed to find him alive.

The next day, General Franco arrived in the city amid much acclamation. Spanish honour could never have let him leave the Alcázereños to their fate, but while it is easy to indulge in Sibylline pronouncements, had he done so, he might well have taken Madrid, and ended the war more quickly.

In the course of ten terrible weeks, the besieged had lost 92 men killed and 514 wounded (of whom ten were to die). There were no casualties among the women and children – indeed they increased their strength by two births. Losses among the besiegers, whose courage and determination deserves full recognition, are not known, but they were very heavy. The triumph of this great defence lay partly in the strength of the Alcázar, but mainly in the spirit of its defenders.

CHAPTER 15

Tobruk
April–December 1941

IN *the great battles of the Western Desert of Cyrenaica in the Second World War, the fortress of Tobruk was to play a crucial role. The only port between Benghazi and Alexandria, it was a vital link in the logistic support system of any forces operating in that area. Not only was it immensely valuable to the British but even more potentially valuable to the Germans, whose lines of communication stretched right back to the port of Tripoli. Thus, when General Rommel and his Afrika Korps swept the British back to the frontier and beyond, the security of the fortress and its denial to the Germans became a matter of critical importance.*

This chapter concerns itself with the defence of Tobruk during the first siege in 1941 in which, thanks to the stout fighting qualities of the Australian and British troops defending its perimeter and the heroic work of the Royal Navy and Royal Air Force, it was held and, ultimately, relieved. In 1942, when Rommel swept forward again and reached the Alamein position, a second siege ended in disaster.

* * *

'Our August and Powerful Sovereign profoundly loves his people, and charged me to bring prestige to this land, which shall be for ever Italian'. These words were spoken by Mussolini during his triumphal tour of Libya in the spring of 1926. Fifteen years later, General Wavell's Western Desert force was to sweep his pompous boasting into limbo.

When Italy declared war on 10 June 1940, Wavell, who was then General Officer Commander-in-Chief Middle East, had responsibilities stretching from Syria, where the French were undecided, and later hostile, through Palestine to Egypt, Libya and Cyrenaica. In East Africa, there was Italian Somaliland, Eritrea and the two long frontiers of Kenya and the Sudan bordering enemy occupied territory. Soon the Greek campaign would be added to his burden. After the fall of France, Marshal Graziani had an army of nearly a quarter of a million men in Tripolitania, Cyrenaica and Libya, and the Duke of Aosta in East Africa commanded a further 300,000. Against these legions Wavell had less than 100,000 troops widely scattered. His master strategy in successfully balancing, at any one moment, the requirements of a number of campaigns in distant theatres showed his genius. Wavell was, perhaps, the greatest general produced by any of the belligerents in the Second World War.

Two days before Italy declared war, General O'Connor had been given command of all British forces in the Western Desert. When Wavell began his triumphant campaign on 9 December 1940, the Western Desert Force, hopelessly outnumbered in troops and armour, was to roll the Italians back in a broadening tale of conquest that flowed across the barren desert of Libya and the greenery of Cyrenaica's Jebel Akhdar.

There had been some stiff fighting around Sidi Barrani and Bardia, but once the Italians broke, it was the fortress of Tobruk that gave most cause for concern. The coast has a number of small bays, and that of Tobruk was one of the larger, forming the only good harbour west of Alexandria for many miles. The Italians had developed the town on the northern shore of the bay, and had fortified an area of roughly the size of the Isle of Wight, which stretched from the sheltered beaches of white sand up a series of escarpments, each with its plateau of rocky earth and low, bushy scrub with the occasional elevated feature. The outer perimeter, which at its greatest depth was 11 miles from Tobruk, stretched in a semicircle from shore to shore with a frontage of 32 miles. The defences consisted of a double ring of about 140 individually protected concrete strongpoints behind a barbed wire entanglement. The wire was in need of repair, and the anti-tank ditch was incomplete and partially filled. However, the eastern and north-eastern sides of the perimeter were well protected by deep *wadis*.

Even though parts of the perimeter were weak, and there was no defence in depth, there were sufficient troops with a large number of guns and tanks to make its capture a formidable task. The 7th Armoured Division had isolated the fortress by 6 January, but it was not until the 22nd that 30,000 men laid down their arms, and 236 guns and 87 tanks were taken. After this the chase continued, and when O'Connor's corps reached Agheila, 175 miles south of Benghazi, there seemed nothing to stop it going on to Tripoli. The argument persists, but men and vehicles were at the end of their tether, and the line of communication was long, unprotected and unorganised – reasons enough for consolidation. In the space of 62 days, the Italian 10th Army and 5th Squadron of the Regia Aeronautica had been shattered. For less than 2,000 casualties, the corps had taken 133,000 prisoners, 1,200 guns and several hundred tanks.

Inevitably, Graziani was made the scapegoat for Italian incompetence and poltroonery, and command was given to General Gariboldi. For some time, the Germans had been anxiously watching the African situation, and although unwilling to become involved, by the end of January 1941, they had considered their presence essential if the Mediterranean was not to be entirely lost. Hitler therefore told Mussolini he would send an armoured and motorised division to ensure at least the safety of Tripolitania.

MAP 15.1

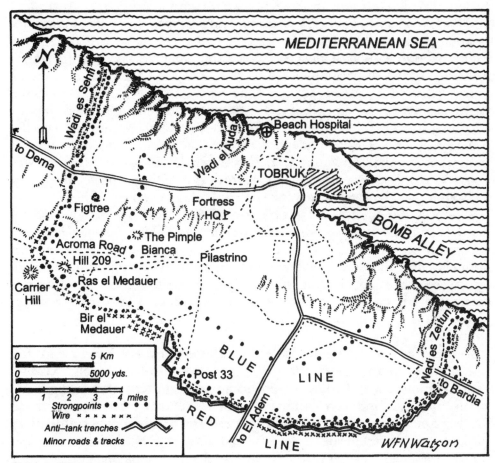

Tobruk: The Perimeter

The man chosen to command these divisions, who arrived on 16 February, was Erwin Rommel. He was to become something of a desert legend, a wily fox who could strike hard and swiftly at his enemies. His impulsive brilliance was the perfect foil to the stolid German soldier, producing a combination of the quicksand and the rock. But he was mistrusted, if not disliked, by many of his seniors.

The arrival of Rommel's Afrika Korps, and two fresh Italian divisions, virtually coincided with Wavell's small army being called upon to give aid to Greece. The rights and wrongs of aid to Greece cannot be entered into, but the dispatch of almost 60,000 troops in March, with their transport, made it nearly impossible for General Neame, who had recently succeeded O'Connor, to hold Cyrenaica. His was an unenviable task, for he was pitched into a desperate situation, arriving at Barce with no proper staff, no experience of desert warfare, with his two forward divisions (9th Australian and 2nd Armoured) badly fragmented, and a general shortage of anti-tank weapons and signal equipment.

On 16 March, Wavell flew to Barce, and what he saw horrified him. Neame's tactical dispositions were terrible and the Chief had no idea of 2nd Armoured Division's parlous state with its vitally important cruiser tanks mostly in the workshops. It was generally thought there would be no German offensive before May. Indeed, Rommel had had specific orders that he was not to advance before that month, and then only to undertake a limited operation to regain Cyrenaica. However, Rommel was a man perfectly prepared to disregard orders if an opportunity arose. On 24 March, he attacked the advanced British elements near Agheila.

This was intended as a reconnaissance in force, but as soon as he discovered the hopelessly weak opposition before him, he took immediate advantage of the situation, sweeping aside remonstrances from his nominal chief Gariboldi. In the course of the next fortnight, in a series of brilliant thrusting, feinting and flanking manoeuvres, he rolled up the outnumbered, out-gunned and out-tanked British to as far back as Sollum, with only Tobruk remaining a bastion of defiance and a fatal threat to his amibitions.

It had been a disastrous time for Western Desert Force, and for Wavell who, in the course of the retreat, lost three generals. Neame, with O'Connor, who had been sent to advise him, took the wrong track in their staff car and were captured, while General Gambier-Parry (whose predecessor in command of 2nd Armoured Division had died suddenly in January) was forced to surrender his headquarters at Machili. It is not easy for a commander-in-chief to lose four of his senior commanders in the space of three months, but Wavell bore these misfortunes with his customary calm. At least in Major General Morshead he had a first class fighting general. His 9th Australian Division had borne the brunt of the infantry battle, and fought splendidly although short of every kind of equipment. The division now fell back into Tobruk, where it was to man the perimeter for the next six months.

By 11 April, Tobruk was invested and, with a display of outrageous rodomontade, Rommel announced his immediate objective to be the Suez Canal. But while his 5th Panzer Regiment prepared to attack Tobruk, some of his other formations showed signs that the pace was too furious, and Brigadier Gott's Mobile Force was doing a good job in giving Lieutenant General Beresford-Peirse (recently appointed to command the reconstituted Western Desert Force) time to stabilise the line near the frontier. But the loss of Cyrenaica meant that the Australian General Laverack, whom Wavell had recently appointed to command all the troops there, was recalled to his division and this left Morshead in command of the Tobruk fortress.

There was a roaring sandstorm blowing on 9 April as the troops withdrew into the perimeter. It is difficult for those who have not experienced these sandstorms and dust devils to appreciate their fury. Sand gets everywhere, stinging the face, blinding the eyes, ruining the food, fouling the water, grounding aircraft and clogging machines. In battle, operations can be halted by whirling clouds of sand hideously mixed with the acrid smoke, reducing visibility to a few yards. In this instance, the storm was a blessing, for Morshead's weary, depressed and mystified men were not harried by the enemy. Now he told them what they most wanted to know. He would never beat the chamade, they would stay in Tobruk until relieved by the advancing army. Moreover, theirs would not be a passive defence, there would be constant sorties against the enemy. Morale was immediately restored.

At this time there were in Tobruk some 40,000 men, which was far too many for the food available. This figure included around 5,000 prisoners and a large number of British, Australian and Indian personnel who were not front-line troops and these were evacuated as soon as possible in ships bringing up stores and two badly needed regiments of Royal Horse Artillery (RHA). On 18 April, the official strength of the garrison was 1,363 officers and 33,944 other ranks, but by the end of June the total had been reduced to 24,000.

The 9th Division had four brigades, the 18th (recently with the 7th Division), the 20th, 24th and 26th; the Australians also provided the 2/12 Field Regiment, the 3rd Anti-tank Regiment, less a battery, a light anti-aircraft battery, a pioneer battalion, and four engineer field companies together with the 4th General Hospital, and a field ambulance unit. The British artillery regiments were the 1st, 104th (Essex Yeomanry), 107th (Notts Hussars) RHA firing 25-pounders; the 51st Field (18-pounders and 4.5 howitzers); 3rd Anti-tank RHA, 51st Heavy and 14th Light Anti-Aircraft, and a Searchlight Battery. In all there were 72 field weapons. The armoured forces were British and consisted of the 3rd Armoured Brigade, which included the 1st Royal Tank Regiment (RTR) and a squadron from the 7th RTR, and a composite regiment of Hussars and Dragoon Guards with light tanks and armoured cars respectively. There were 26 cruiser, 15 light and four Infantry ('I') tanks (later increased to 16). The 1st Royal Northumberland Fusiliers was a machine-gun battalion, and the 18th Indian Cavalry Regiment fought as infantry.

In January, the Italians had been winkled out of Tobruk largely by bluff, and not because the defences were inadequate but, in fact, they were incomplete, in a poor state of repair and, what had most worried Wavell on his visit, they lacked depth. It was decided to retain the existing outer line, which needed repairs to the wire, improvements to the anti-tank ditch and a new minefield. Depth would be obtain initially by each of the seven battalions manning the concrete posts having a company in a dug-in, wired position half a mile back. This first line of defence which became known as the 'Red Line' would make up for paucity of men by a bristling fire power to include anti-tank and machine-guns. Later a second line, the 'Blue Line', was constructed two miles in rear of the perimeter. This had a continuous minefield and a barbed wire entanglement covered by anti-tank and machine-guns. Those brigades allotted to the Red Line kept one battalion in the Blue Line.

In the centre of the perimeter there was a mobile reserve of tanks, armoured cars and Bren carriers ready to counterattack any breakthrough. There were no troops available to protect the coastline, which remained vulnerable to raids throughout the siege. The town and its harbour had to rely on the anti-aircraft gunners whose batteries formed the main defence against the almost continuous raids by dive-bombers, often escorted by fighters and accompanied by heavy bombers. It is true that at least 30 enemy planes were shot down by Hurricanes in the first fortnight of the siege, but it soon proved impossible to keep fighters in Tobruk, although throughout the siege the Desert squadrons maintained patrols over the town, and enemy airfields were constantly bombed. Nevertheless, the Stukas continued to come in noisy, restless flocks. In the first four months of the siege the anti-aircraft gunners shot down 83 enemy planes for certain, and probably a further 77, with many more damaged.

There was a great deal to be done and, although every man in the garrison gave of his best, it would be many weeks before the necessary repairs and improvements could be completed. Hence, when Rommel's soldiers made their first attack on 11 and 12 April, the defences were incomplete. This was in the nature of a probing attack by the 5th Panzer Regiment against the southern sector of the perimeter held by the 20th Brigade. Rommel had assumed that the presence of shipping in the harbour indicated evacuation of the garrison, and so it came as an unpleasant shock to find his troops blasted by artillery fire, and hustled out of the anti-tank ditch at bayonet point.

His next attempt was on a bigger scale and became known as the Easter Battle. On Easter Sunday, 13 April, large concentrations of Axis troops and tanks were sighted near the El Adem road and were attacked by two Blenheim squadrons. The battle began that night when, after a preliminary mortar bombardment, men of the 5th Light Motorised Division and a part of the Italian 132nd Ariete Armoured Division attacked the front held by the 2/17th Battalion of the 20th Brigade. The fighting was exceptionally fierce, especially round Post 33, where Corporal Edmonson won a post-humous VC, and by the small hours of the 14th the Germans had made a bridgehead sufficiently wide for the tanks to pass through.

The plan was for the armour to head north and divide at the El Adem crossroads some four miles inside the perimeter. But it was halted by the

MAP 15.2

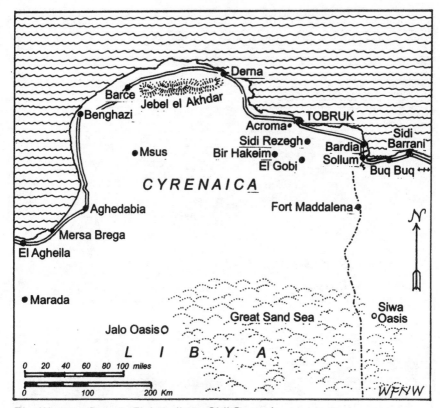

The Western Desert: El Agheila to Sidi Barrani

25-pounders, firing over open sights, and the anti-tank guns of the 3rd Australian regiment in position on the site of the future Blue Line. As the surviving tanks headed back for the perimeter they were knocked about by the British cruisers, while the Australian infantry had broken up all attempts by the German foot to advance. By the late morning of the 14th, the attack had been repulsed, and Rommel had lost 16 tanks and something like 80 per cent of his 8th Machine-gun battalion, for a garrison loss of 26 men killed, 64 wounded and two tanks disabled.

The axis losses were grievous but by no means irreparable, and Rommel simply had to have Tobruk if his advance into Egypt was to continue, or even be maintained. He was still loath to believe that a small garrison, with its defences incomplete, could resist him for long, and so he immediately planned a third attack. This would be under his personal direction, with Italian troops of the Ariete Division and the 62nd Infantry Brigade of the Trento Division, and against the western sector of the defences held by the 26th Brigade. It was scarcely likely that the Italians would succeed where the Germans had failed, and after the 62nd had been rudely handled by the

MAP 15.3

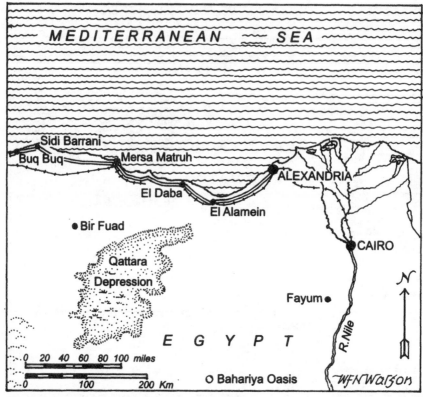

The Western Desert: Buq Buq to Alexandria

2/48th Australian Battalion, 26 officers and 777 men surrendered. The armoured division resumed the offensive on the morning of 17 April but, after losing five tanks and finding no infantry following, the division withdrew.

The Axis troops now dug themselves in at a little distance from the perimeter, while Rommel made preparations for yet another assault. The garrison was now given a fortnight's respite, during which important improvements were made to the defences, in between constant heavy air attacks which plastered the harbour area as well as the forward troops. But Morshead's defence was never intended to be passive and, at every opportunity, strong fighting patrols were sent out. The first of these met with considerable success when the enemy was still recovering from the effects of the Easter Battle. The 2/48th Battalion, together with a troop from 'M' Battery RHA and three 'I' tanks attacked an Italian battery position behind Carrier Hill, south-west of Ras el Medauar, destroying two guns and taking 370 prisoners.

Patrol activity became an important feature of the defence, for these operations promoted confidence, relieved boredom and kept the enemy (except in that part of the perimeter they were later to capture, where in places there was no more than 100 yards between trenches) at such a distance as to give comparative freedom to the front line soldiers. The patrols, which went out almost every night and on many days, were not usually on the scale of the one described above, but might consist of between ten and twenty men, often with carriers or mortars to cover their withdrawal, although a strong fighting patrol would be accompanied by tanks and preceded by a reconnaissance.

There was also that most trying of all patrols the standing - or more accurately lying - one, necessary for observing enemy movement, and later perfected by the Long Range Desert Group. It involved many motionless hours, lying in a cramped and camouflaged position at the mercy of every fly in the desert. Sappers had an important role to play in patrol work with their clearing and taping of minefields. To begin with, there was no special patrol equipment, and the men either covered their boots with socks or went out over the sharp desert ground in stockinged feet. Later, boots with soft rubber soles and special patrol suits were issued. This active patrolling against enemy strongpoints was carried out on an increasingly large scale, and often with most satisfying results. It was not unknown for a forward brigade to have 300 men out on a single night and, in one period of ten days, 26 Brigade took 1,700 prisoners.

At the end of April, Rommel made a much more determined attempt to take Tobruk. He was particularly keen to succeed, for the OKW (Oberkommando der Wehrmacht) were worried at his impulsiveness and had sent out General von Paulus (later to command the German Sixth Army in the siege of Stalingrad) as being 'perhaps the only man with enough influence to head off this soldier gone stark mad'. Both sides had received reinforcements; the Royal Navy, at the cost of two ships, having brought in a further 12 'I' tanks for 7 RTR (see pages 268/9) and some 25-pounders, while for Rommel, 15 Panzer Division had now arrived. The garrison had done much to improve the defences, in particular, unknown to the Germans, a minefield had recently been laid.

Rommel had learnt from the Easter Battle that a wide bridgehead must be made before passing through the armour. He planned the break-in to be made north and south of Hill 209, where there is a slight bulge in the perimeter. The 5th Light Division would be on the right and the 15th Panzers on the left. As soon as the breach was made, assault groups of the Ariete and Brescia Divisions would pass through to roll back the defences on both flanks. Depending on how the breakthrough went, a decision would be made either to press on for the harbour, or to hold the flanks preparatory to a fresh advance on D2 (May 1st).

The area chosen for the attack included 22 concrete posts held by the 2/24th Battalion of the 26th Australian Infantry Brigade. The battalion had a front of four and a half miles from post S11 (the posts north of Hill 209 were prefixed by the letter S, and those to the south of it by the letter R) through Hill 209 to R10. On the battalion's right, was the Brigade's 2/23rd Battalion, and on its left, the 2/15th of 20 Brigade. The 2/48th Battalion was in reserve. The forward troops were supported by the 51st Field Regiment, machine-guns of the 5th Fusiliers, and anti-tank guns of the 3rd RHA.

On the afternoon of 30 April, this sector was subjected to a heavy bombardment, and at about 7 pm 22 JU 87s (Stukas), making use of a setting sun, screamed in from the west, dropping their bombs, and roared away to the north, closely followed by another wave. Meanwhile, under cover of the barrage and increasing darkness, German sappers neutralised the mines, and blew gaps in the wire, on either side of Hill 209. The attack went in at 8 pm and soon there was chaos. The widely separated and shell-shattered defenders were unable to prevent an early penetration and, for some time, brigade headquarters had no knowledge of the battle, for the signal lines had been cut.

On 1 May, when the early morning mist had cleared, it was seen that the Germans had established a bridgehead about one and a half miles wide, had captured seven posts around Hill 209 and that their tanks were forming up to advance eastwards. But because the situation was so fluid, and the exact position of the troops unknown, the gunners could not fire. However, as these tanks moved towards the reserve company of the 2/24th, they were first engaged by an anti-tank gun unit and then they struck the new minefield. The gunners knocked out two of them before being put out of action themselves, and the mines brought 17 to a halt with broken tracks, but there were no anti-tank guns still in action to administer the *coup de grâce*. Under cover of their guns, the Germans brought up repair crews who salvaged all but five of their stricken tanks. A convenient dust storm then enabled the tanks to retire.

The tank thrust to the north had also failed to make much progress. Posts S5, 6 and 7 had been subdued, but the accompanying infantry had been halted well short of Bianca. South of Hill 209, posts R1 and R2 had been taken early in the morning, but R4 was not captured until midday, and the posts farther south were holding stubbornly. At this juncture, Paulus advised Rommel to abandon his plan to take Tobruk and to be content with Hill 209 and the positions around it. Rommel therefore decided to strike south-east towards Bir el Medauer. That afternoon, R3 and 5 were captured and there was very heavy fighting round R6, 7 and 8, with penetration as far as R12.

At about 4 pm, Morshead used some of his tanks in an attempt to regain the lost posts, but they were engaged by two greatly superior concentrations of armour and lost two cruisers and two 'I' tanks, with two more temporarily disabled. Morshead felt he could not risk concentrating his small amount of armour (for which he has been criticised) because, without proper air reconnaissance, he never knew where the next threat would come from, and so he used it in penny packets, relying greatly on his artillery. His gunners performed magnificently throughout the battle and, being well dug-in, survived constant counterbattery and Stuka poundings.

At the end of the first day's fighting, the Germans had captured 15 posts on a three-mile front. In the furious fighting for these posts it was not always possible to salvage LMGs and anti-tank weapons, and their loss was an embarrassment to the 'Q' Staff, for there were insufficient replacements in the fortress. However, a number of Italian weapons had been taken in January which helped to ease the shortage. The German gains had been made at considerable cost and, from then onwards, the enemy was content to consolidate them and to beat off two determined counterattacks. The first of these, by the 2/48th Battalion along the line of the Bianca-Acroma road, eventually petered out in a sandstorm, but the second, involving the reserve 18th Brigade, was more ambitious.

The plan was for one battalion to attack the German salient from the north against S6 and 7, and a second to come in from the south against R7 and 8. If these posts could be taken, the advanced German positions would be cut off. Enemy shelling was so intense that the attack had to be postponed until 9 pm, and then it soon developed into a series of independent, fierce close-quarter mêlées in which both sides suffered high casualities with little achieved. Before daylight, Morshead ordered a withdrawal, and the Battle of the Salient came to an end.

Rommel had penetrated the perimeter to a depth of rather less than two miles on a front of about three, for which he had suffered 1,150 casualties and lost a large proportion of his armour. But he had captured the important feature Hill 209. He was told by Paulus there were to be no more attacks on Tobruk unless the British were evacuating the port. The tremendous benefit to the desert campaign of the garrison's resolute and courageous defence in face of overwhelming odds was recognised by congratulatory telegrams to Morshead from Wavell and the Prime Minister.

It is now time to take a look at the problems of life that faced the garrison in this long siege. A close bond was quickly forged between the Diggers and the Pommies*; the former were grateful for the assistance of artillery, their own having been left in Palestine, and of armour; and the latter recognised with what courage and determination the perimeter was being held. Every man in the garrison came to appreciate the inspired leadership of Morshead, and the value of self-sacrifice and comradeship. Inevitably, morale had its periods of decline, but on the whole, and strangely, men were quite content and, at times, happy in their confinement.

Unlike most sieges, food was never a problem. It was monotonous, for

---

*Diggers and Pommies. Slang terms for Australians and British.

however many ways you treat bully beef it remains an unexciting pabulum, and constant canned fruit and army biscuits quickly pall. Moreover, the presence of Indians, Libyans, and later Poles put a strain on the Quartermaster's department. Lack of water was more serious - and there was no beer! The well in the Wadi Auda produced only brackish water, a limited amount could be obtained from the sea water distillery, and some was brought from Alexandria. At best, a man might get three pints a day for absolutely everything, but an anti-aircraft gunner who endured the siege told the author that for long periods his ration was only one mug a day, although a mug of tea was issued four times a day, and occasionally some of this was saved up for shaving.

Somewhat naturally, the men living in the town, where the Italians had had a number of substantial buildings, fared very much better than those on the plateau. Despite being bombed with great frequency, they could often find a place to sleep secure from all but a direct hit, and they had - when time and conditions permitted - the perpetually inviting sea in which to wash. Men manning the reserve lines lived almost permanently in dust churned up by many vehicles, although they were better off than those in the Red Line where to survive it was necessary to spend the daylight hours cooped up in cramped conditions. But no matter whether in desert or town, the fleas and flies were a living torment.

Front line troops rotated between the Red and Blue Lines and reserve, while the ack-ack gunners got one day off a week to relax, swim and wash. The padres held services in the Roman Catholic church, but gatherings were discouraged, and so there were no games or entertainments. Neither were there any women, and the sergeant-major was scarcely a surrogate sweetheart, and so men snug in wadi caves or dugouts spent hours writing letters or poring over the *Tobruk Truth*, one of the most comprehensive of newspapers in the history of siege warfare. Mail and tobacco were the great luxuries, boredom the great curse. But Morshead was well aware of the dangers of ennui, and kept those out of the line fully occupied in improving the defences.

On the whole, the health of the garrison remained remarkably good. The most serious problem was the unpleasant desert sores that could be very lowering and took time to heal. They came from poor hygiene and undernourishment, particularly lack of fresh fruit and vegetables for which Vitamin C pills were not a complete substitute. Nevertheless, these tough weather-stained warriors, who went about practically naked under a burning sun, knew that desert sores were a small price to pay for the skill and valour of those seamen who in great peril maintained their lifeline.

The ships that kept Tobruk supplied throughout the whole eight months of the siege came mostly from the Inshore Squadron, which had been established in December 1940 to assist the advance by shelling troop concentrations. It was composed of destroyers from the British and Australian navies, gunboats, sloops, minesweepers and landing craft known as 'A' Lighters. Admiral Cunningham's navy was very hard pressed, especially at the time of Greece, and these ships were supplemented by a variety of merchant vessels, trawlers, schooners and luggers. The smaller craft were used mainly for stores, and sailed from Mersa Matruh on a northerly course to avoid what became known as Bomb Alley.

The destroyers and lighters also carried stores, but they were responsible for transporting troops, tanks, weapons, ammunition and explosives. It was an exceedingly dangerous and unpleasant run for everybody, but especially for the soldiers, who were battened down below deck knowing that if the zig-zagging destroyers were hit, they were trapped. A typical convoy might consist of three destroyers and a minesweeper, which would leave Alexandria at 8.30 am, be off Bardia nine hours later and, if it was lucky, enter Tobruk's narrow, mine-swept channel shortly before midnight. A well trained work force of Indians would then speedily unload the stores, ready for the wounded and the enemy prisoners to come aboard. If all went well, and the harbour was not being heavily bombed, which it often was, the turn-round would be completed in time for the ships to be away well before daylight.

To give some idea of the magnitude of this work, in the month of June 1,900 troops were landed and 5,148 evacuated, while the daily average of stores landed was 97 tons. Needless to say, this fine performance was not achieved without losses, which were mainly suffered in the early months of the siege when there was little or no air cover, and the anti-aircraft gunners had not perfected their remarkably effective barrage shootings. In April, six ships were lost, and in May eight, but by June, when the RAF were able to give more support, it was often possible for the ships to be sufficiently clear of Tobruk to rendezvous with the fighters at daylight. Even so the 'Spud Run' as the sailors called it, remained one of the navy's most dangerous and unpleasant duties.

The main cause of the trouble was, of course, the Stukas and these were sometimes accompanied by high level bombers protected by fighters. In the first few weeks of the siege, the ack-ack gunners engaged (mostly in daylight raids) 1,550 aircraft, the town and harbour being raided by 807 dive-bombers. To begin with, the number of guns (3.7s and Bofors) was insufficient, and many of the gunners had had no experience of dive-bombing attacks, which were usually more terrifying than damaging. Nevertheless, they required great courage of the gunner to continue firing his gun in the face of unending attacks. The principal targets were the harbour installations, any shipping to be found and, later, gun sites. However, there was random bombing of the town. Two deliberate attacks on the plainly marked General Hospital caused heavy casualties among the medical staff and wounded. The hospital ship *Vita* was also attacked and sunk*.

Between the middle of June and October, rather less than 500 planes were engaged each month. This significant improvement in the number of attacks was the result of the tactical innovations introduced by Brigadier Slater (Commander Royal Artillery), and the substantial addition of light and heavy ack-ack guns ringing the harbour. With these guns Slater was able to organise a moving aerial barrage of varying thickness and height, which covered 3,000 feet of a Stuka dive. During the peak period of their attacks, this all-embracing barrage probably accounted for over a hundred planes. To make the enemy's task more difficult dummy gun sites were successfully interchanged with real ones, and each battery was allotted a light gun for protection. The loss to Rommel of so many machines was serious, but infinitely more so was the loss of his German pilots. Eventually shortage of these skilled airmen meant the virtual end of daylight bombing, for Italian replacements were unsatisfactory.

In May and June, Wavell made attempts to relieve the garrison. Operation 'Brevity' began on 15 May by which time a reinforcement of 50 'I' tanks had reached the desert. The object was to drive the enemy from Halfaya Pass and Sollum, and hope that he might fall back west of Tobruk, thereby making a relief possible. The garrison was to make a strong demonstration in order to bluff Rommel into thinking a break-out was to be made. Morshead only had two days' notice, nevertheless his attack mounted against the Salient, and other activities, caused Rommel to strengthen the investment. On the frontier the British had lost 30 tanks and six aircraft when the battle ended on 17 May, and gained the important Halfaya Pass, but unfortunately the Germans re-took it ten days later.

The second attempt at relief was Operation 'Battleaxe' which began on 15 June. By then 4th Indian Division was back from Eritrea, and 7th Armoured Division had been rebuilt. There were to be three days of very severe fighting before Beresford-Pierce's men were back on the frontier having suffered a little under 1,000 casualties, lost four guns and with two-thirds of their armour out of action. The two principal causes for the failure of 'Battleaxe' were the difficulties experienced in combining the ponderous 'I' tanks with the faster cruisers, and the powerful German 88-mm guns dug in and used to great effect as anti-tank guns.

Shortly after 'Battleaxe' Churchill decided to make a change in the Middle East Command. General Auchinleck, Commander-in-Chief in India, changed places with Wavell. From the beginning there had been a lack of empathy between Wavell and the Prime Minister which made a

---

*Rommel must have known of these atrocities. It is not always remembered that he was among the first to join the Hitler movement; skilful and courageous as he undoubtedly was, there was not much chivalry in his make up and plenty of Nazi arrogance and ruthlessness.

MAP 15.4

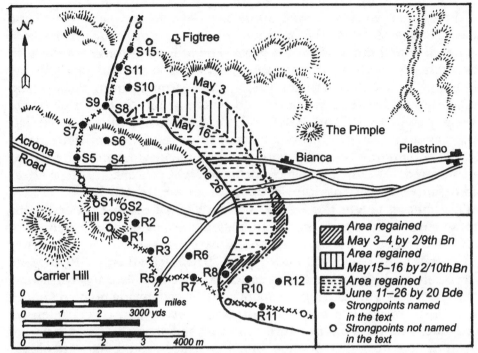

Tobruk: The Reduction of the Salient

complete understanding between the two men impossible. Wavell was the first to admit (to the Prime Minister) that the decision was entirely right, and that a fresh mind was needed, but his departure was widely regretted.

While the two attempts to relieve it were in progress, the garrison had also been on the attack, partly as a diversion but mainly in an attempt to push back the Salient. This important inroad into the defences was proving costly to both sides, for Rommel the possession of Hill 209 gave him an invaluable observation post, but to ensure its retention he had to use German troops which he badly needed to fight on the frontier; while Morshead had a greatly extended unfortified perimeter to hold that required five times as many troops as did the original one.

The 18th Brigade had recently taken over the western sector and Morshead ordered it to take offensive action as part of the demonstration to assist 'Brevity'. A sortie against the Italians west of S15 was entirely successful, but at the same time the Germans made an attempt to extend the northern side of the Salient to include the Fig Tree position which overlooked the Derna road. In the early hours of 16 May, under cover of a heavy barrage, they assaulted the three posts S8, 9 and 10 while the Italians tried to take S15. The Italian attack failed, but the Germans took S10 although they were stubbornly resisted at S8 and 9.

As soon as Morshead learnt that S8 and 9 had beaten off the attacks he ordered the 2/23rd Battalion to go for S6 and 7 and then on to S5 and 4. These latter posts were well inside the German occupied part of the Salient, and meant that the battalion would come under fire from both the new line and the old fortified posts. The fighting throughout the 17th was confused. With great élan, the Australians succeeded in capturing S4, 6 and 7, but the Germans fought back strongly from sangars and vantage points between the posts, and when, in the confusion of smoke screens put down by both sides and the continual dust, the tanks lost their way and retired, it proved impossible to retain two of these posts. Morshead therefore ordered a withdrawal to the original line. The 2/23rd had suffered 173 casualties which included eight officers, but their effort had definitely helped to withhold troops from the frontier battle.

This fighting taught the Germans that their Salient line needed to be strengthened. They gave up about half a mile of ground taken on 4 May, and started work on concrete emplacements ahead of which they had outposts. At the beginning of June, Brigadier Murray's 20 Brigade succeeded the 18th in this tough sector, and at once he moved forward across no man's land. During the month the brigade made no direct attack on the new enemy line but, by vigorous patrolling and a very intensive fire battle, first the outposts were captured and then the Germans were forced to take up a new position which, in places, was 1,000 yards back. It had been a gradual and rather costly business, for every position that the Germans abandoned had been thoroughly booby trapped, and mines had been liberally sown.

The enemy now boxed themselves in with more defence works and a deep minefield behind a line which ran in a semicircle for a little less than four miles. This was a mile and a half shorter than the first line, but even so it stretched Morshead's infantry resources, and he felt a continual need to win back the whole Salient. It would not be easy, for the defences were much stronger than on his previous attempts; the extensive minefields prevented the use of tanks, and any attack to succeed must be made at night. The 24th Brigade took over the sector at the beginning of July and its commander, Brigadier Godfrey, was ordered to carry out a double attack from north and south, and then fan out eastward. In the south, posts R5, 6 and 7 were to be taken first, and in the north S6 and 7; in both instances the line of advance would be approximately that of the old perimeter.

In the early hours of 3 August, after careful preparation and a barrage, a company of the 2/43rd Battalion opened the attack in the south against R7, which was held by units of the 115th Motorised Infantry Regiment. The 5th Fusiliers were in close support with their machine-guns, and under cover of their fire the sappers went forward to blow the wire. As the Bangalore torpedoes went off, flares went up and the leading troops were plastered by mortar fire, moreover when they did get through they found a minefield between the wire and the anti-tank ditch. Some men reached the ditch and started lobbing grenades, but most of the company were wiped out. A supporting attack on the right also failed, and a suicidal move forward by the reserve platoon had heavy casualties. Out of 129 men who made this abortive attack all but 23 had been killed, wounded or captured.

The simultaneous attack on the northern posts also failed, but after a more prolonged struggle. The enemy line was held by the 2nd Battalion of the 104th Motorised Infantry Regiment, and the attack on S6 was quickly repulsed with considerable loss to the men of the 2/28th Battalion. After some severe fighting, however, a few men survived to rootle the Germans out of S7 which they then held throughout 4 August. But heavy machine-guns, firing from the German reserve lines, made it impossible to reinforce the post, and on that night it was lost when the Germans mounted a strong attack. There had been 82 casualties, and some very hard fighting for no reward. The gunners had done their best in support of these two attacks, but the weight of artillery in Tobruk was insufficient to neutralise the enemy guns.

These two attacks were the last attempt to retake the Salient, but the Australians knew how to conduct an active defence, and by using every weapon in their armoury, including many captured ones, they kept the enemy fully alerted. In consequence, Rommel did not dare to remove his German troops. However, the time was approaching for the replacement of 9 Division. The Australian Government, backed by General Blamey, wanted their troops to fight as a corps. This had been thwarted principally by Greece, but now Churchill and the Chiefs of Staff found it impossible to resist the pressure, in spite of strong protests from Auchinleck, who feared that a change at this stage would prejudice the success of his forthcoming operation.

However, the Australians were adamant and between 19 and 29 August the 18th Australian Brigade was replaced by the 1st Polish Carpathian Brigade, and between 19th and 27th September the 16th Infantry Brigade Group of 70 Division, the 4th Royal Tank Regiment and headquarters 32nd Army Tank Brigade came in, and the 24th Australian Brigade was taken out. The final stage of the changeover took place between 12 and 25 October when nearly all the remaining Australians were taken off, and the remainder of 70 Division brought in.

These operations with their various code names had imposed a heavy additional burden on the Inshore Squadron and the Royal Air Force, for the former were already working round the clock to bring in stores and weapons to strengthen the garrison before Auchinleck's offensive. But the efficiency of Morshead's staff, and the extreme skill of the seamen ensured success. Taking advantage of a waning moon, and with the help of cruiser escorts and a substantial airforce presence, no fewer than 81,393 men were transported safely to and from Alexandria and Tobruk in the face of

Rommel's frantic attempts to sink them. Sadly the minelayer *Latona*, which had done great service to the Squadron, was sunk in the last operation. This meant that the men of the 2/13th Battalion and two companies of the 2/15th could not be taken off, but were to have the distinction of seeing the siege through from first to last.

On 23 October, General Morshead, who throughout the siege had shown immense personal force, and nerves of steel that no amount of danger or continual strain could affect, handed over command of the fortress to Major General Scobie, whose 70th Division comprised the 14th, 16th and 23rd Brigades together with Divisional troops, the Polish Infantry Brigade Group and the 32nd Army Tank Brigade.

The men of the new division had a little less than a month in which to accustom themselves to front line conditions in Tobruk and, like their predecessors, to carry out active patrolling before being involved in the hardest fighting so far in the desert. By the middle of November, both Rommel and Auchinleck were ready to launch a major offensive. Rommel against Tobruk, Auchinleck to destroy the Axis armour and to sweep its troops back to and out of Tripolitania - the relief of Tobruk being an important ancillary objective. Both sides had been substantially reinforced - the British in armour, the Axis in motorised units - but British tanks, anti-tank guns and tank recovery were still inferior to their German counterparts. However, as well as having air authority, Auchinleck also had the edge in manpower, for reinforcements were not readily available to Rommel.

The question as to which army would start operations was settled by General Cunningham, commanding what was now called 8th Army, beginning the battle on 18 November when his 30 Corps (General Norrie) crossed the frontier. This corps, which included the 7th Armoured Division, was to outflank the frontier defences in a broad southern sweep, and then strike north to Tobruk, while 13 Corps' (General Godwin-Austen) 4th Indian Division was to demonstrate against the frontier line, and its 2nd New Zealand Division was to skirt round the right flank of the enemy and make for Capuzzo and Bardia. It is not intended to attempt a description of the complicated manoeuvres of the fierce, and desperately confused, fighting of Operation 'Crusader' except in so far as they concern the relief of Tobruk, which was confidently expected to occur within a week.

Rommel was obsessed with the need to take Tobruk, partly to justify his gasconades to the OKW, and also because he knew he could never advance into Egypt while it held out behind him. The weather at the time was bad enough to prevent Axis aircraft taking off, and so Cunningham gained complete surprise, but Rommel was not worried, for he believed Auchinleck was only initiating another attempt to relieve Tobruk. He therefore did not immediately release troops and armour that were preparing to assault the perimeter. This enabled the British to gain some early success in that the Germans were forced to give ground in the first two days, but the deficiencies in British armour became quickly apparent.

The key position of the battle was the Sidi Rezegh ridge some 15 miles south-east of Tobruk. It was to change hands more than once, but on 20 November, 7 Armoured Brigade and Support Group captured it and the aerodrome. As part of the overall plan, 70 Division was to break out of Tobruk when Generals Cunningham and Norrie thought the time was right, and with the capture of Sidi Rezegh, Scobie was ordered to do so. His objective was El Duda, a point on the ridge some three miles north-west of Sidi Rezegh, and careful preparations were made on the night of the 20th with gaps in the wire and minefield marked, and bridges laid over the ditch prior to a dawn sortie.

The enemy had constructed a number of strongpoints in front of the perimeter, and the first of these to be taken was the one called Tiger. The fighting for this had been very severe, and the 1st and 4th Royal Tank Regiments had suffered serious losses, nevertheless a salient some 4,000 yards wide had been gained and nearly 1,000 prisoners taken. But soon after the order to break out had been given, the fighting round Sidi Rezegh had taken a turn for the worse, and 7 Armoured Division was unable to give Scobie the expected support. On the 22nd, when he learnt this, and in face of his own tank losses, he called a halt. This action was later confirmed by an order from Norrie not to press his sortie.

It was at this stage, with the outcome of the battle very much in the balance, that Rommel, who by now had realised the seriousness of the British attack, carried out one of those dashing and impulsive actions which caused such concern to friend and foe alike. He thought that if he could get behind the main battle he would not only relieve the pressure on his frontier troops, but also force the 7th Armoured Division to withdraw from the Sidi Rezegh area.

Accordingly at 10 am on the 24th, at the head of the 5th Panzer Regiment himself, he accompanied Major General Ravenstein's 21st Panzer Division, followed by the 15th Panzers, in an eastward dash to the frontier. The chaos caused by this foray was indescribable. Units were taken unawares, headquarters were upturned, and everyone was scrambling in all directions. Luckily, so great were the confusion and the dust clouds that a large British petrol, ammunition and water dump was never spotted by the raiders, for had this been taken the consequences would have been very serious indeed. As it was by the 26th the raid had spent its force, and failed in its purpose.

In the middle of all this brouhaha, Cunningham had asked Auchinleck to visit his headquarters, for he felt the situation was getting out of hand, and that 8th Army should pull back. Aucinleck rose to his greatest height; he realised that the initiative must be regained, and that there was an urgent need for risk-taking and forward engagement. Eighth Army would not fall

MAP 15.5

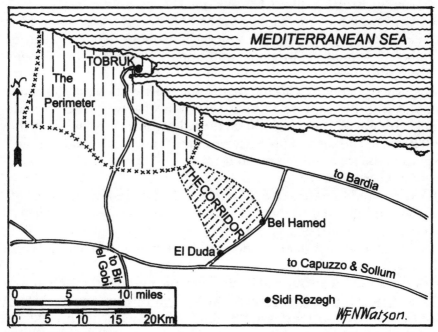

Tobruk: The Corridor

back, and indeed the New Zealanders would advance immediately towards
Tobruk. On his return to Cairo on the 25th, Auchinleck decided to replace
Cunningham with General Ritchie.

On the afternoon of 26 November men of the Essex Regiment, 5th
Fusiliers and 32nd Army Tank Brigade had fought their way through to
El Duda. All that night, they held on grimly until the 19th New Zealand
battalion, and some British 'I' tanks advancing from Sidi Rezegh joined
up with them early on the 27th. The corridor to Tobruk was now open,
and Godwin-Austen ended his signal reporting this fact with 'Tobruk and
I both relieved'. But, like so much in this battle, the report was premature,
for Rommel had regrouped his forces and was aiming another armoured
attack at the Sidi Rezegh, El Duda, Bel Hamed triangle.

On the 29th he made a double thrust at the triangle with the 15th and 21st
Panzer Divisions, and throughout that night the fighting was critical. On the
west flank of the corridor the Essex Regiment suffered numerous casualties
and was forced to give ground, and Scobie called upon the 2/13 Australian
Battalion to make one more effort in their long fight in defence of Tobruk.
That night the battalion left the perimeter and crossed the desert to El
Duda, where they attacked through the Essex positions. Supported by the
RHA and eleven 'I' tanks, the Australians succeeded in regaining the lost

ground, and El Duda was secured and stubbornly held. But before dark on the 30th, Rommel had retaken Sidi Rezegh, and Tobruk was again isolated.

There were to be four more days of desperate fighting before Rommel's troops weakened in the face of constant attack and stubborn defence. The battle continued to rage round Sidi Rezegh ridge, and against El Duda, where the newly arrived 4th Battalion The Border Regiment resisted all attacks. As German armour raced east to succour the frontier troops, Ritchie's South Africans in the north and Indians in the south struck west, while in the centre the 7th Armoured Division, the hard hitting, highly mobile 'Jock' Columns and the RAF punched the circling Axis armour.

By 5 December, the whole Afrika Korps, constantly harried from the air, was moving west. Two days later the Tobruk-El Gobi line was turned, and although the western face of the Tobruk perimeter was still in enemy hands the South Africans and 11th Hussars joined up with the garrison on the east side. On the night of 9/10 December, the Poles recaptured the bitterly contested Salient, and the siege of Tobruk was over. It had lasted 242 days, and was the longest siege in British military history.

Had Tobruk not been held as Rommel swept the Western Desert Force back to the frontier, there can be little doubt that he would have reached El Alamein, as he did when Tobruk fell a year later. However, in April 1941, when Tobruk was first invested, the political and military consequences would have been far greater. In the succeeding months, the presence of many Axis divisions before Tobruk gave Generals Wavell and Auchinleck time to receive a new flood of strength with which to replenish their forces and revive their fortunes.

CHAPTER 16

Leningrad
September 1941–January 1944

THE Siege of Leningrad, which lasted some two and a half years saw more misery and human suffering than any other similar operation in the Second World War. As we read of the privations and fortitude of its people, it is almost impossible for us to grasp the full measure of its horror. Yet despite the suffering and starvation (for many thousands died of malnutrition and cold), life in the beleaguered city went on. In the face of the worst that the Germans could do, the factories continued to turn out the weapons of war and ways and means were found of establishing some form of contact with the outside world so that supplies, however meagre, could get through – often across the ice of Lake Ladoga. Somehow, the Russians held on and their soldiers held the line against endless German attacks and ceaseless bombardment. Fortunately for the garrison, the winter and a serious lack of transport made the lot of the Germans little better than their own. Only in Stalingrad can conditions even have approached those in Leningrad. In the beautiful city which has now been re-born, it must be hard for the present generation to realise what their parents and grandparents went through and survived.

* * *

In terms of human suffering and misery the Siege of Leningrad was the worst of all those here described, and very probably the worst of any siege in history. Leningrad was (and is again) a beautiful city that had known greatness as the capital of Czardom, and renown as the cradle of the Revolution. But in 1941 the Germans set out to reduce it to rubble. This they virtually succeeded in doing, but its citizens, taking refuge from adversity in steadfastness and patriotism, showed a courage and sacrifice which irradiated the dark days and relumed the flames of victory. The price they had to pay was, perhaps, as many as a million people dead.

Ever since July 1940, when it was becoming increasingly obvious that the invasion of England could not succeed, Hitler had turned his eyes eastwards, and plans for the invasion of Russia in June 1941, Operation Barbarossa, were well forward by November. Three army groups were to advance on a very broad front with the ultimate object of occupying a line from Archangel to the Volga, destroying the Russian armed forces and taking over the country's rich agricultural, mineral and oil resources. Hitler had an obsession about Leningrad as the birthplace of Bolshevism, and not until it had been taken (and later razed to the ground) was the attack on Moscow to be pressed. Field Marshal von Leeb's Army Group North was to annihilate Russian forces in the Baltic area, occupy Kronstadt and the Balkan ports and take Leningrad by 21 July.

Stalin had consistently refused to believe in the possibility of a German attack, despite reliable information and even a warning, at great personal risk, from the German ambassador in Moscow. Right up to the moment of invasion, in the early hours of 22 June, and indeed in some places later, no provocative preparations were permitted. In consequence, Russian troops were quite unprepared, with many formations widely separated, giving the Germans complete strategic and tactical surprise and enabling them to concentrate numerical superiority in men, guns and armour at a given point. Matters were not made easier for General Kuznetsov, Commander of the Baltic Military District, as no fewer than 1,200 aircraft were destroyed (900 on the ground) in the first 24 hours*.

The German Army Group North consisted of the 16th and 18th Armies, and the 4th Panzer Group. The 18th Army advanced close to the Baltic coast, the Panzer Group was in the centre, and the 16th Army to the south. Lithuania and Latvia were soon occupied and, on 10 July, the Panzers broke through the Russian 11th Army south of Pskov. The next day, Marshal Voroshilov arrived to command the Northwestern Front, and it must have seemed to him – and indeed to von Leeb – that Leningrad was as good as lost. But the Leningraders had been working round the clock digging anti-tank ditches and erecting barricades, both in the immediate vicinity of Leningrad and on the line of the Luga river. Volunteers had rushed to take arms, and nine divisions of a 'people's army', known as the *Opolchenie*, were hastily raised. They were a mixed lot, poorly equipped and with little or no training, but on the Luga and in front of Leningrad they acted as a human shield to the city, showing enormous courage and resolution.

Hitler's target of 21 July was quite unrealistic, and by the middle of August the advance had slowed from a commendable 16 miles a day to a mere three. The Russians had even put the 4th Panzer Group into reverse in a fierce fight near Soltzy. The Luga line was held until 21 August, when the 16th German Army got round the flank to take Chudovo and Tosno, and nearly reached Mga, cutting off and capturing large numbers of Russians. On 28 August, Tallinn fell, and in the hasty evacuation to Kronstadt and Leningrad 25 transports were sunk. All this was bad enough for the Russians, but at the same time the Finns, who at first had been most reluctant to take any offensive action, advanced on

*The Air Commander Baltic District was summoned to Moscow and shot.

both sides of Lake Ladoga to recapture much of the ground they lost in the Winter War of November 1939–March 1940.

In September, the ring began to close as hard fighting raged south of, and in places only four miles from Leningrad. On 8 September, Schlusselburg was taken, and on the 10th, the important Duderhof Heights, from which German artillery posts had a good view of the city, were lost. Uritsk fell on the 12th and the Germans were soon on the Baltic coast at Peterhof. By then the outlying towns of Gatchina, Pulkova, Pushkin and Slutsk were also in German hands, and Leningrad had lost all land communication with what became known as the mainland. However, a German attempt to cross the Neva at Porogi failed, and von Leeb could make no further progress against the triple line of fortification with which the Leningraders had surrounded the city. His men had suffered very heavy casualties in the past two months, and he had been ordered to send two divisions to the Central Front. There were to be no more assaults and his men dug in, anticipating a long siege.

The front line was demarcated by three arcs, all of whose arms rested on water. To the west, Oranienbaum was encircled by a line 37 miles long with a depth (at its widest point) of 15 miles, and the other two arcs encompassed Leningrad to the north and south. The Russian defence and counterattacks on the Volkhov Front had prevented the Germans from linking up with the Finns, who had halted on the river Svir east of Lake Ladoga. So it was that a narrow strip of water was still open to the Leningraders, which was to prove their lifeline. Army Group North had advanced some 570 miles and conquered much land, and it was now within shelling distance of Leningrad, but to achieve complete strategic and tactical success it still needed to take the city, and this it intended to do by bombing and starvation. Meanwhile, the defenders tied down 300,000 of Germany's best troops, who faced some very unpleasant conditions at the end of a long and vulnerable line of communication.

Many Soviet Party members and generals played a prominent role for short or long periods during the siege, for throughout there was air communication with Moscow. Important military commanders such as Voroshilov and Zhukov came to advise, and prominent Party men, such as Molotov and Malenkov, visited the city with special instructions from Stalin. But the two men most responsible for the daily running of the city were Andrei Zhdanov, the Party chief of Leningrad, and Aleksei Kuznetsov, Secretary of the city Party Committee. From the Smolny – the seat of Revolution and formerly the scene of female elegance – these two men, and members of the Leningrad Front Military Council, presided over the city's destiny.

There had never been any shortage of volunteers either for civil defence or for the Army. The *Opolchenie* had performed prodigies of valour, but now their lack of training made them something of a liability, and it was thought best to disband them and draft the survivors into regular units of

MAP 16.1

Western Russia and the Baltic States

the Red Army that had withdrawn into the city defences. Leningrad proper was divided into seven military defence districts, each with three positions to be manned when needed by interior troops, the city militia (police) and volunteers. Much use was made of natural obstacles such as canals, and the sewage workers contrived an elaborate plan whereby the sewers could be used as communication trenches. Millions of sandbags protected vital places. They were used to construct barricades and to turn windows, and even stationary tramcars, into strongpoints.

The inner defence line followed the city's circular railway, but beyond this on the outskirts was a much more formidable line that included a multitude of concrete pillboxes, foxholes, bunkers, connecting trenches, miles of anti-tank ditches, and fields of anti-personnel and anti-tank mines. The work was tough, and time was short, therefore not surprisingly some of it was of poor quality. Later, when the city was less hard pressed, a new programme of fortification was carried out.

Civil defence was in the hands of the city militia, Komsomol (young Communists) guard units, and the NKGB (Intelligence Agency). Besides the usual duties of curfew enforcement, air raid precautions, blackout and fire-fighting, these men had an important security role, for although there was little overt disaffection (but plenty of grumbling!) among the Leningraders the city was crowded with refugees, some of whom, from the Baltic provinces, were German sympathisers.

Evacuation was always uppermost in the governing council's minds, and a target of a million - children, elderly people and refugees - was attempted early in the siege. In July and August 1941, 200,000 children left the city, but the operation was badly handled and some fell into German hands, while others returned to remain or be taken out again by a different route. By the end of August 636,203 people had been evacuated including 147,500 refugees, but in September, when the ring closed, no more than 70,000 could be got away. The target, therefore, was not achieved, and there were still two and a half million people left in the city. Besides carrying people, trains were earmarked for the removal to safety of more than half a million treasures from the Hermitage Museum, and thousands of valuable books from the Leningrad Library.

Leningrad was an important industrial city with about 520 factories, and some of these (one report says 86) were evacuated, along with certain institutions and academies; in others, key personnel who could not be risked, were transferred, which of course lowered production. More than 50 of these factories were converted to produce military hardware – twelve made tanks and armoured cars, five guns and mortars, while the others turned out flame-throwers, grenades and mines. There was no shortage of semi-skilled labour, but an increasing shortage of suitable material meant that never enough weapons could be produced.

On the night of 8 September, while von Leeb's men were hammering at the defences in their last major offensive, Leningrad had its first large-scale bombing raid. It was carried out in two waves when some 6,000 incendiary and about 50 high-explosive bombs were dropped, mainly in the south and south-west of the city. Many fires were started and the Badayev warehouses, a large complex of wooden buildings covering several acres, were burnt out. It has often been said that the fatal shortage of food in the first terrible winter of war was almost entirely due to the destruction of the city's principal supply in these warehouses. But in fact only 3,000 tons of flour, and 2,500 tons of lump sugar were lost, much of the latter being useable subsequently as confectionery. At the beginning of September, shortly after a further reduction of the bread ration, the consumption of flour was a little over 1,000 tons a day, so it can be seen that the Badayev fire was not all that catastrophic.

The real reason for shortage was an administrative muddle on the railways when the granaries of the Baltic states and Novgorod area were overrun. Large quantities of grain, which should have gone to Leningrad, were got away on time but disappeared in an easterly direction to be lost in the prevailing chaos. The large number of refugees, as well as the troops falling back on the city, had to be fed from rapidly diminishing stockpiles. As is always the way, no sooner was there a threat of siege than there was a rush of panic buying by every householder. Bread and sugar rationing began in August, and in October meats, fats, fish and cereals were added to the list. The bread ration was cut twice in September, and in that month restaurants were closed and the production of beer, ice-cream and pastries was forbidden. On 12 September, there was enough flour in the city for 35 days, meat 33, fats 45, cereals 30 and sugar 60 days*. The situation therefore was pretty desperate, for except for a precarious supply line across Lake Ladoga, for which there were no proper harbour facilities and a shortage of boats, the city was completely cut off.

All too soon, the chilling voice of the bitter northern winter was heard in Leningrad, heralding the frozen ground, the drifting snow and the deadly neutrality of a deepening cold that numbed the fingers on the pen and stiffened the clenched hand on the rifle. Life became harder every day, and – especially in the southern districts that were in range of enemy guns – more dangerous. By day and night, the Leningraders witnessed increasing damage to their city from shelling and aerial bombardment. The air defence consisted of a fast diminishing fighter force (which started with 400 planes), 160 anti-aircraft batteries and a number of barrage balloons. It proved quite inadequate to keep the bombers away.

In some districts, where the raids were heaviest, almost every window had been blown out, and as there were power shortages living conditions became very unpleasant indeed. Apart from the damage done to the power supplies by bombing, there was an acute shortage of every type of fuel, which meant that electricity had to be rationed quite early on. By the middle of November, householders were permitted only one hour's electricity every 24 hours and no electric appliances could be used. The telephone was cut from all private houses as early as 16 September, and with no power, most radio sets were defunct. Contemporary diaries and letters frequently mention the sense of emptiness this caused. Nevertheless, despite these and other tribulations, which became greater later on, men and women went about their duties with the unconscious pride of true patriots.

The ration situation, always critical, had to be kept under review daily. The only line of supply was the long and difficult one via Tikhvin, Volkhov, Novaya Ladoga then across the lake to Osinovets, where a new port was constructed. The whole route was vulnerable, but no part so much as the lake-crossing, which took 16 hours and, although carried out by night whenever possible, was subject to heavy bombing. The Ladoga Flotilla, under Captain V S Cherokov, did an exceptionally fine job in maintaining this vital lifeline. Ships were needed not only for food, but also to carry munitions, and their losses were virtually irreplaceable.

At one stage, in the critical winter of 1941–42, when there was less than a week's supply of flour, workers were getting ten very small pieces of bread a day, and non-working civilians only five. The troops always did better, for on them depended the safety of the city. An innovation for these times, even

*D V Pavlov in charge of food supplies in Leningrad.

in Russia, was the employment of women cooks who performed culinary miracles in front line kitchens. Tobacco was also issued to the forces at 10 grams per man per day. To preserve stocks, chocolates and candy were offered in lieu, but did not prove popular, although they might have been preferred (if still on offer) when hops and various leaves did duty for the no longer obtainable *nicotiana*. There was a flourishing black market, where prices were astronomical, and there was also ration card forgery and stealing, for when the ration was below subsistence level, extra cards could save lives. Forgery was eventually reduced through the tedious process of card registration, but theft was more difficult to eradicate.

In October, the great offensive against Moscow came near to success, and Marshal Zhukov, who had been sent to Leningrad in place of Voroshilov, was hastily recalled. Before he left, he was ordered to take steps to pin down the German troops in front of Leningrad, and so a joint operation with the Volkhov Front, whose commander was General Meretskov, was put into operation. Troops from Leningrad crossed the Neva and, with General Fedyuninsky's 54th Army, attacked the Germans in the Mga area. The fighting continued throughout October and into November, but without any notable success. It did, however, achieve the object of holding down German divisions, and at the same time a number of guns and mortars (which could ill be spared) were sent from these fronts to Moscow.

At about this time - the beginning of November - the Leningraders faced perhaps their most perilous days. The Ladoga boats had succeeded in preserving their existence only by the narrowest of margins, and now the ice was beginning to form on the lake, and there would be an agonising period when it impeded the passage of boats and yet was not thick enough to bear transport. The Leningrad Military Council made urgent preparations for an ice road to be opened between Osinovets and Kabona as soon as practicable. It was reckoned that a uniform depth of seven inches was needed for a loaded horse-drawn sleigh, and that eight to nine inches would bear a truck with a one ton load. A reconnaissance party was sent out to mark the route, and workers cleared the snow; by 22 November it was considered safe for the first convoy of trucks to make the crossing. This was successfully accomplished, but shortly afterwards a partial thaw set in, and in the last week of November less than two days' requirements were moved, and 40 trucks had disappeared through the ice.

Major General Shilov had been appointed to command this vital, but most hazardous, lifeline. He was a competent man and the heavy losses in boats and lorries were not his fault, but he incurred the wrath of Zhdanov and failure often meant the firing squad. He was, therefore, figuratively and literally on thin ice, with Leningrad reduced to only a few days of flour, and a perilous shortage of other commodities when, on 8 November, the Germans captured the railhead at Tikhvin. On the 16th, an air supply was organised to bring in 200 tons of food daily, which was anyway well short of requirement and, in the event, not achieved. Meanwhile, a huge labour force was set to work to hack a track, much of it across primeval bog and forest, from Zaborye station north and west to join with existing tracks that ran in a very circuitous route to Novaya Ladoga. Including the 18½ miles of ice road, the total distance from Zaborye to Leningrad was 237 miles, and it was hoped to move 2,000 tons a day. The new stretch of road, which was opened in the commendably short time of 15 days, was scarcely negotiable by vehicles, and passing places were few and far between. Inevitably, there was chaos, and nothing like the target could be achieved. Fortunately, Tikhvin was retaken on 9 December and the roundabout route was no longer needed.

With his railhead restored, Shilov's problem was greatly eased, but the ice road itself was never free from anxiety. To begin with, not until January was the ice permanently solid enough to support continuous convoys, and there was always the hazard of enemy bombing, and on one occasion, a German raid on skis. Blizzards were frequent. This involved clearance of snow and could result in trucks being lost. Even in January, cracks and crevices in the ice would appear that had to be marked and by-passed. Throughout December, the situation in Leningrad remained absolutely critical and rations needed to be constantly reduced. The city required a thousand tons of food to be delivered every 24 hours if the subsistence ration was to be maintained and there was also a need for munitions. It was difficult to get more than 800 tons a day through until, in January, the organisation began to work more smoothly. Even then, the road could only just meet the barest essential needs. Nevertheless, the ice road undoubtedly saved Leningrad and the recapture of Tikhvin was perhaps the deciding factor of the siege.

In their advance on Tikhvin, which, as already mentioned, the 39th Motorised Corps captured on 8 November, the Germans had hoped to join hands with the Finns striking south across the Svir and so to encircle the Russian 54th Army defending the south-east area of Lake Ladoga. The Finns were held up on the river through lack of ice, but the German double attack towards Volkhov and Voibokalo made progress. The Russian 4th Army had to give ground and Gostinopolye was taken. The fighting here became very fierce. Meretskov put the withdrawing 4th Army under General Fedyuninsky, who besides his own 54th Army had 3,000 officers and men recently flown from Leningrad to reinforce him, as well as Partisan detachments. These latter were students and young men operating by brigades behind the enemy lines in the Leningrad area. It is said that in the two and a half years in which they were effective, they killed at least 10,000 Germans, including eight generals, and destroyed numerous vehicles and tanks.

Fighting continued for a month without much change in the positions until Fedyuninsky's men broke through the German line on 4 December,

MAP 16.2

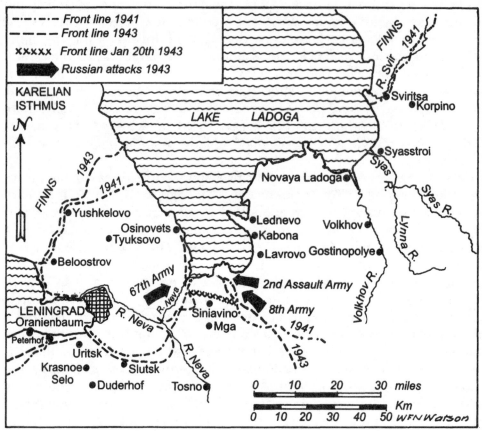

Legend:
- –··–··– Front line 1941
- – – – – Front line 1943
- xxxxx Front line Jan 20th 1943
- ➤ Russian attacks 1943

Leningrad: The Front Lines 1941 and 1943

retook Tikhvin on the 8th and drove the Germans back across the Volkhov to their October starting line. Their losses had been exceptionally heavy, chiefly from the appalling cold against which they were not protected. It was vitally important for Leningrad that Volkhov should not be lost, and although the Military Council ordered the removal to the interior of the hydroelectric plant and the demolition by Fedyuninsky of the dam, he refused to press the button until the Germans entered the town, which they never did. Thus, by the end of 1942, the plant was in working order again and supplying much needed electricity to Leningrad.

In the winter of 1941–42, the inhabitants of Leningrad suffered a torment that has no parallel in modern history. They lived in a city stinking of death, where only the frenzy of desperation saved the stronger from lying down with the weaker to die from hunger and the rigours of the northern winter. In their homes and at the factory men and women took inspiration and guidance from one and other, but there were many who faced the slow, cold fear of death from starvation alone and unknown. Nevertheless, in the emaciated and ravaged frames of the Leningraders there burnt an unquenchable fire, nurtured by a bitter hatred of the common foe.

A full catalogue of the horrors of these months would be wearisome and overly gruesome, but no description of the siege would be complete without reference to the worst of the woes that had to be endured. Hunger dominated everyone's thoughts and actions, and the bitter cold was an extra dimension in the continuing struggle for life. In November 11,089 people died of hunger, in December the total was 52,881, for January it had risen to around 120,000 and in February 10,000 died each day. First figures gave a death toll of 632,000 for the whole blockade, but later estimates made it nearer a million, the greatest proportion of which occurred in the first winter. Though obviously those on higher rations fared best, death was no respecter of persons, or indeed of time or place. Men and women might die alone in an attic bedroom, drop suddenly in the street never to rise again, or collapse at work in the factory or in the middle of a lecture or broadcast. Children at the age of 12 became very vulnerable, for then they lost their special children's ration, and the sudden transition often proved fatal.

This desperate gnawing hunger inevitably drove some to crime and violence, while others, more affluent, could be seen at the market bartering their jewels and furs quite literally for a crust of bread. Taking ration cards off the dead was perhaps a venial sin, but stealing them off the living with murder a viable option most certainly was not, and there were quite a few instances of this. By January cats and dogs had all been eaten, but rats abounded. Too skinny to be worth eating, even if people had the strength to catch them, they would infest houses, seemingly devoid of fear, trying to keep warm and hoping for humans to die. The militia attempted to keep crime off the streets, but in the central marketplace questions were seldom asked about the origins of certain meats. From contemporary accounts there seems no doubt that there was cannibalism; necro-butchery was definitely practised, and there are gruesome stories of well fed soldiers, sneaking into Leningrad late at night to see their families, being lured to their deaths and converted into cutlets and meat pies.

The temperature in January was 30 degrees below zero in the open, and in the offices (most of which were by now partially open) there was sometimes 14 degrees of frost freezing the ink in the bottle. In attempts to get some warmth, many householders had installed old-fashioned, poorly constructed and badly fitted stoves with a chimney through the roof. These *burzhuikis*, as they were called, would burn any rubbish to be found, and quite often the house as well. If pumping stations were out of fuel for short periods, the water and sewage systems in that district froze solid so that there was no water for fire-fighting - and precious few fire-fighters still strong enough to work. In consequence, some areas of the city often burnt for days, not from German incendiaries but from these infernal stoves. The heat from the fires might thaw the ice, but the people were too short of water for any to be used to quell the flames.

Until the spring, the city was largely free of disease, although dysentery combined with general inanition helped fill the hospitals, where doctors and nurses worked untiringly under unbelievably difficult conditions. The morgues were always choked with corpses waiting for the carts to convey them to the cemeteries, where occasionally Civil Defence squads might dynamite a hole in the iron-hard ground, but more often bodies were stacked to await the spring. Some attempt was made to register the dead in the morgues and cemeteries, but literally hundreds every day died unknown in the streets, from where working parties would do their best to shift them, but here again many bodies remained tucked away in corners until the spring. Occasional diary entries record women seen trudging over the uncleared snow dragging a sleigh to the cemetery on which was their dead child perhaps in a tiny coffin, but usually wrapped in a sheet. However, more often, the living were too weak to deal with their dead, whom they abandoned to the care of the hard pressed authorities, or the merciful covering of snow.

Work was therapeutic, and those fortunate enough to have something to do found it channelled the mind away from the daily round of death, and the rare opportunities for entertainment did the same. Almost all the theatre companies had been evacuated, but the operetta company remained and weak though artistes were, they bravely performed on occasions in theatres more suitable for cold storage than musical entertainment. Teachers kept their classes going, institutions of higher education remained open, and the intellectual fraternity would walk long distances to attend meetings and lectures. Vera Inber, the well-known poetess, whose husband, a doctor, was posted to Leningrad a few days before the siege began, made the journey across the ice and snow of Lake Ladoga to entertain the troops of General Fedyuninsky's army with talks and readings from her poetry. A gallant action for a lady not young, half starved and wholly unaccustomed to the rigours of camp life.

Exercise was considered important, and gym classes were organised for any who could muster a modicum of physical exertion. For soldiers, who anyway were in slightly better condition, this was most important, for they had to be ready to take the offensive at any time. Indeed, such a time was mid-January 1942 when another double attack was launched against the German fortified line, which ran for some 85 miles from Schlusselburg to Novgorod. The general plan was for the 54th Army (which was nominally part of the Leningrad Front) to join with Meretskov's Volkhov Front troops in an attempt to envelop and destroy the Germans in the Chudovo-Kirishi area by attacks from the north and south-east, centred on Lyuban. This achieved, the two forces would swing north against those troops of the German 18th Army still encircling Leningrad. There was to be simultaneously an offensive against the 16th Army in the Staraya Russa-Kholm-Demiansk region.

Little headway was made on the Leningrad front, either in the fighting on the Neva, or, later in the summer, in the subsidiary attacks directed against Uritsk on the south-western outskirts of the city. However, initially considerable success attended Meretskov's 2nd Shock Army which broke through the German lines midway between Novgorod and Chudovo. Fighting through appalling swamps, this army penetrated some 30 miles into German territory and almost reached Lyuban. But it had gone too far, and the Germans were able to cut it off and encircle it. In some very hard fighting, that lasted until mid-June, it made many attempts under its new commander, General Vlasov, to break out, and Meretskov sent the 59th Army to assist it. Eventually, a small corridor was opened through which, during the fortnight before it was closed, some 6,000 men escaped. Vlasov and the remainder were forced to surrender.

This was a serious blow; for although the fighting south of Lake Ilmen against the 16th Army went much better, with thousands of Germans besieged for several weeks in Demiansk and Kholm, where many died of cold, no permanent Russian advances were made. However, the long drawn out battle had succeeded in tying up so many German troops, and causing so many casualties, that the proposed attack on Leningrad was never made.

At the time these efforts to relieve Leningrad began, the city was still shrouded in snow and ice, and when the German guns were silent it assumed a ghost-like appearance. Vera Inber writes, 'At present our nights are indescribably quiet – not a hooter, nor the sound of a tram, nor the bark of a dog, nor the mew of a cat. There is no radio. The city falls asleep in dark icy flats, many never wake up.' However, in the important matter of food, the tide was very, very slowly beginning to turn. Shortly before this diary entry of 2 January, the bread ration had been increased by 100 grams for the forces and manual workers, and 75 grams for office workers and dependants. At last the delivery of provisions across the lake was exceeding the daily expenditure and, on 26 January, Zhdanov felt able to give a further increase in the ration of bread, fats, meat and vodka.

The air raids virtually ceased during the early months of 1942*, but the bombardment continued to be heavy with a total of 16,847 shells recorded as falling on the city between the first day of January and the last day of March. There were still shortages of fuel, water and power which continued to cripple industry, where less than 40 per cent of the factories had electricity. This also meant, and the Leningraders felt it acutely, that newspapers could not be printed, and as there were no radios in the home,

---

*The Leningrad Air Defence Army accounted for 322 German planes in 18 months during 1941–42.

people had to queue in the icy streets to listen to the public loud-speakers to know what was happening on their own and other fronts.

With the coming of spring, the ice road would disappear, and it was essential to ensure that the high loads it carried were maintained. Three major projects for the spring and summer were decided upon. A considerable shortening of the truck route; the evacuation of half a million people; and the laying of an underwater pipeline. Almost under the eyes of the enemy, a branch rail line 21 miles long was laid in the bitter February weather from Voibokalo station to Kabona, where warehouses were hastily built to store provisions. By greatly cutting the truck run, deliveries were speeded up and fuel consumption much reduced. It was a fine technical feat, successfully accomplished despite enemy air attacks and gunfire which caused many casualties.

Evacuation, which was begun in January 1943 under the direction of the Deputy Chairman of the Council of Ministers, A N Kosygin, who had come to Leningrad for the purpose, built up from 11,296 people in January to more than 163,000 in April. A total of 514,069 people were taken out in three months over the ice route, and nearly as many later in the summer by boat. The principal beneficiaries were women, children and the sick, but those who remained also benefited for there were now less than a million

MAP 16.3

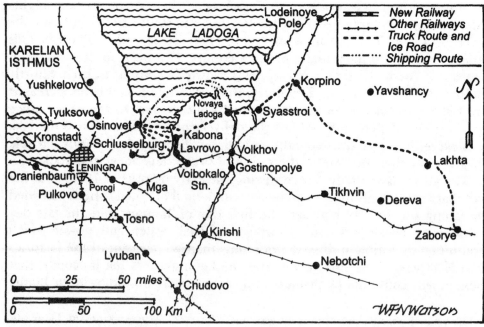

Supply Routes to Leningrad

mouths in Leningrad to be fed. The evacuation operation, like the railway line, attracted the full attention of the Germans, and again casualties were heavy, but there was never any thought of discontinuance.

A pipeline 19 miles long was laid under the lake by special underwater military units and, despite numerous difficulties, it was operating by the middle of June 1942. The amount of fuel that could be transmitted this way enabled a fair portion of Leningrad's industrial life to be reactivated. This was further stimulated when, in June, ships got an ice-free passage across the lake. Improvement to the harbours, and better construction of ships, resulted in over 100,000 tons of stores and materials being delivered to Leningrad in the last two months before the ice returned in November. The soldiers also received much needed supplies of military hardware that included tanks. On the whole it could now be said that while living conditions still remained very hard in the city, at least death from starvation was no more than a horrible memory, and light could be seen at the end of the tunnel for those who had the courage and patience to walk a little longer in the darkness.

Much had been done to ensure that the winter of 1942–43 would be nowhere near so dreadful as its predecessor, nevertheless the situation remained grave. The ice road was always a precarious means of supply, the Baltic Fleet was blockaded and the city continued in isolation. However, by the end of January, when a narrow corridor with the mainland had been opened, life became much easier and, by the summer, almost back to normal – in so far as normality can be achieved among wrecked buildings and a continuing bombardment.

The opening of the corridor was the result of yet another attempt by the Leningrad and Volkhov troops to break the blockade (Operation Iskra). General Meretskov was back in command of the Volkhov Front after a short absence in Moscow. In May, General Govorov had replaced General Khozin in command of the Leningrad Front and had been given a new army, the 67th, commanded by General Dukhanov. The outline plan for the joint offensive entailed the forcing of the Neva by the Leningrad troops on an eight mile front immediately south-west of Schlusselburg, while the reconstituted 2nd Shock Army from the Volkhov front made a strong thrust in the Sinyavino area to join up with Govorov's men.

The Soviet high command had assured the two commanders of a local superiority in men, tanks (sevenfold) and artillery (fivefold), and there was to be a high troop and artillery density. On the Leningrad front, the attack was to be in two echelons with four rifle divisions and a brigade of light tanks in the first, and 48 hours later a second echelon of three divisions and two brigades of tanks. Heavy tanks would cross the Neva in the first echelon. A density of one rifle division to three-quarters of a mile was laid down, and on the 67th Army's front the artillery concentration was 130 field guns and mortars to just over half a mile, and for the 2nd Army's sector 173 guns.

In all there would be some 4,500 field guns and mortars as well as massive fighter and bomber air support. Considerable skill on the part of the pilots and gunners was required to ensure that no damage was done to the ice on the Neva, which had already given some cause for concern*.

The assault on both fronts opened at 11.50 am on 12 January after an exceedingly heavy bombardment had plastered the German positions for two hours. An immediate breakthrough was made by both armies. At the end of the first day, after some very tough fighting, Govorov's troops had established a bridgehead up to three and a half miles wide on the east bank of the Neva, and the 2nd Army had penetrated almost two miles through enemy held territory towards the link-up. But once the Germans had recovered from the initial shock of the heavy pounding, and the devastating onslaught of the assault troops, they organised effective counterattacks. These, and the fact that in the marshy ground the tanks were not able to keep pace with the infantry, considerably slowed the advance. Nevertheless, late on the night of the 13th, the 86th Division of Dukhanov's army entered Schlusselburg. The old Swedish fortress town was much battered, and even more so was the little isolated fort at Oreshek which had held out for 500 days.

General Küchler, who had succeeded von Leeb in January 1942, had sent an urgent directive from his headquarters in Novgorod that Schusselburg was to be held at all costs, but it was not to be, and now the two Russian armies were steadily closing the gap between them. On the morning of 18 January, they joined up. The Germans had been thrown back rather more than six miles from the south shore of Lake Ladoga, and a corridor had been formed linking Leningrad with the mainland. At once, the Russians set about building a temporary rail line and dirt roads, and on the 526th day of the siege, a train crossed the new bridge at Schusselburg and steamed into the Finland station of Leningrad.

Total blockade was over, but there would be much more fighting and hardship before the city was relieved, for although the Germans had lost some 14,000 men in Operation Iskra, and been driven back in one important sector, they still hung on tenaciously to most parts of the city's perimeter. Further Russian attacks on both fronts made no progress, but defeats in the south and the need to withdraw some troops for North Africa caused the Germans to shorten their front by an overall 250 miles. Army Group North now had three fronts. The 18th Army held two sectors, one facing north against the Russian troops in the Oranienbaum enclave, and the other facing east along the Volkhov river down to Novgorod. The

---

*At the end of December, when preparations and rehearsals were being made for the attack, there was some doubt as to the thickness of the ice, and in the presence of Marshal Voroshilov and other senior officers a tank was launched to test it. The tank went through the ice almost at once, nearly taking Voroshilov with it!

16th Army held the line of the river Lovat from Staraya Russa to Kholm (Demiansk had been evacuated), and on from there until it joined Army Group Centre at Nevel, making a front of over 100 miles.

Physical contact with the outside world brought about by the recent fighting gave Leningraders, and the troops defending the city, many benefits. But these did not come all at once, and throughout 1943 there was an enormous amount of work to be done. One of the earliest signs of a revival came from the power stations, two of which in March were showing a three-fold increase in production over the previous month. This meant not only slightly improved domestic facilities, but that some street cars began to run again, and that by the end of April the presses were working and newspapers began to reappear. A high priority was given to the clearing up of the mess, which was indescribable. Not only were streets and buildings absolutely filthy, but so were the people, for during the winter there had been no baths or laundries in the city. Immediate steps were taken to mobilise all able-bodied men between the ages of 15 and 60 not engaged in essential work, and all women between 15 and 55 years, to work in shifting rubbish, snow and often bodies that lay under the snow.

It was a slow and painful business, for there was little or no mechanised equipment available, and in some cases the people were so weak they could hardly stand. With the opening of the corridor, the size of the ration began to improve, and within a few months was sufficient for a normal person. But the Leningraders were not normal people; they needed building-up and for that purpose the food was still insufficient. Moreover, with the coming of spring and warmer weather, typhus, spread on the wings of dirt and decomposing bodies, made some impact, but mass inoculations kept it within bounds. Living conditions remained basic for a long time, because there was more essential work than renovating houses. Indeed many wooden buildings were pulled down during the summer for much needed firewood, and their occupants crammed into temporary flats.

Party Secretary Kuznetsov, and his regional chiefs, had a difficult job in allotting priorities for the immense amount of work that had to be done. Preserving the life of the survivors, revitalising industry and cleaning the city gave little time for anything else. But as the summer of 1943 wore on, and men became stronger through better feeding (large quantities of vegetables were grown, and tinned food arrived from America and Australia), the important additional task of improving the defences could be undertaken. The fortifications required strengthening, new minefields needed laying and, in the city, new tank traps were made and the windows of lower floors were walled up. The civil defence organisation was over-hauled, air raid shelters were improved, and there was a most urgent need for firewood to be brought in from surrounding areas. In addition to all this volunteers from Party and Komsomol were trained in street fighting and formed into battalions for interior defence, if necessary.

At the coming of winter 1943-44, Leningrad was in a good position to resist any German offensive and, just as importantly, the trials and tribulations of another winter's siege. But the Germans had not let all these strenuous efforts at rehabilitation proceed unhindered. Throughout the summer and autumn they kept up a devastating programme of bombing and shelling. Six thousand Leningraders died on the streets, in the factories or in their houses and, once again, public places of entertainment and leisure, recently opened, had to be closed. Such destruction of life and industry stimulated the Soviet High Command to reinforce this front, so that it acquired superiority in numbers and fire power for a supreme effort to drive the Germans clean away from the city and its environs.

This major offensive was planned for the winter, a season in which the Russians had a natural advantage, but there had been a lot of fighting during the summer of 1943, and while the Russians had made considerable gains on other fronts, the 67th Army had failed to take the Sinyavino Heights. These, just south of the newly formed corridor, were strategically important for the coming battle. Once again, the two principal commanders were Govorov and Meretskov, and they were to receive considerable assistance from the Second Baltic Front. Two plans were drawn up because the Soviet High Command had received intelligence that German losses on various fronts had been so great that a withdrawal of troops from the Leningrad area was under consideration. This did not materialise, and so the plan known as Neva II was enacted.

It was an ambitious plan well thought out, but the success of the whole could be jeopardized by the failure of any one of the parts. There was to be a three-pronged thrust from the Oranienbaum enclave, from the troops holding the front south of Leningrad, and from Meretskov's Volkhov Front. The Leningrad troops had Gatchina as their objective, and Meretskov's men were to capture Novgorod. With these two places taken, the Germans in Mga and Tosno would be trapped if not withdrawn. As soon as the first phase had been accomplished, the general line of advance would be towards the Luga. The 3rd Shock Army and 10th Guards of the Second Baltic Front would assist by pinning down German reserves which might be sent to Leningrad, and large numbers of Partisans were to operate in rear of the enemy. The Oranienbaum troops and those from the Volkhov were to begin their attack on 14 January, but troops from the southern front – whose first objective was the Pulkovo Heights – would not move until the 15th. However, the Second Baltic Front would begin operations on 12 January, two days ahead of the main attack.

There had been a number of changes in armies and commanders since the 1943 offensive, and an even greater superiority in troops, armour and artillery had been achieved on both fronts. The 2nd Shock Army, now commanded by Fedyuninsky, was sent to reinforce the troops in Oranienbaum, and was moved through Leningrad and transported by the

Baltic Fleet in great secrecy beginning in early November, and concluding before the ice gripped the waters. The 42nd Army, commanded by General Maslennikov, was to spearhead the southern sector's attack, and Meretskov had the 54th and 59th Armies. The comparative figures* give some idea of the scale of the battle, and the Russian superiority in numbers. The combined Leningrad and Volkhov Fronts fielded 1,241,000 officers and men, 21,600 guns, 1,500 Katyusha rocket guns, 1,475 tanks and 1,500 aeroplanes. Against this formidable army, Küchler could muster from his two armies only 741,000 men, 10,070 guns, 385 tanks and 370 aeroplanes.

The attack began in extremely bad weather with heavy falls of snow and a certain amount of fog, which hindered the gunners and grounded the bombers. However, despite the conditions, the initial fighting went very well for the Russians. By 19 January, the 2nd Army had Krasnoe Selo and the 42nd had fought their way into Pulkovo and Pushkin. The Russian infantry then struggled up the ice-lined slopes of Duderhof (Crow's Mountain), to dislodge the Germans from that important position, and into Gatchina. Meanwhile, in the Volkhov area, the 59th and 54th Armies had some equally severe fighting in pushing the Germans back through a number of defensive positions to take Novgorod on 20 January. By then Küchler (recently made a Field Marshal) had withdrawn his troops from Mga and Tosno to the Luga. It was almost his last order, for at the end of the month Hitler replaced him with Field Marshal Model.

The fighting on the Luga was very savage throughout the first fortnight of February. The Soviet 42nd Army crossed the river in the Narva area and by 4 February had taken Gdov, but it was not until the 12th that the 59th Army, now joined by Leningrad's 67th, took Luga town. It was the 15th before the Luga and Narva lines were completely cleared. The Germans had been thrown back from Leningrad for almost 100 miles, and the advance was to continue up to the Velikaya river. The Volkhov Front was then disbanded and an augmented Leningrad Front, together with the Baltic troops, cleared the land around Lake Peipus and took the towns of Pskov and Ostrov.

However, the Leningraders were not prepared to wait upon these distant battles. At 8 pm on 27 January the sky was lit by a multitude of coloured rockets, and searchlights criss-crossing and pinpointing beautiful buildings untouched by the fury of bomb and shell, as well as those less fortunate whose battered walls still stood proud, bitter and silent. At the same time, the air was rent by 24 salvoes from 324 guns, General Govorov's 'Thunder of Victory'.

After 880 dark, dangerous and destructive days the city of Lenin had been liberated, and its citizens rightly showed joy that their long ordeal was

*Salisbury, pp561, 562.

over. But their joy was tempered with sadness, for so many had died and so much had gone that was lovely. In Leningrad as well as in places like Pushkin, Peterhof and Gatchina, marvellous palaces, pavilions and other buildings had been deliberately vandalised and destroyed by the Germans. The Russians, with infinite care and dedication, were to rebuild them. But somehow it is not quite the same thing.

CHAPTER 17

Dien Bien Phu 13 March–8 May 1954
and
Khe Sanh 20 January–1 April 1968

WE have seen in earlier chapters how the logistic factor has proved decisive throughout the history of siege warfare. While great leadership, the skilful husbanding of resources and the resolution and self-sacrifice of the besieged have always contributed enormously to survival, in the end, when stocks have finally dwindled to nothing or the fight against disease has been virtually lost, capitulation has become inevitable. In contrast, while stocks of food, water and ammunition have lasted, men and women have held out to the very limits of human endurance. In more recent times, the supply of ammunition has become much more critical and the garrison which is cut off from re-supply is ultimately doomed. The stories of the two sieges considered in this chapter illustrate to perfection how not only the existence of an adequate logistic system but also a proper understanding of the logistic factor proved decisive, with victory for the besiegers, albeit at great cost, in one case and defeat in the other. Of particular interest is the fact that the same general, Vo Nguyen Giap, was in command of the besieging force in both cases – despite the gap of 14 years between them. Many know that at Dien Bien Phu he won, but probably far fewer know how or why he lost at Khe Sanh.

* * *

When the Japanese surrendered in August 1945, the French, who had retained a presence in Indo-China throughout the war, hoped to revert to the *status quo ante* and resume the role of a colonial power. But this was not to be, for they immediately found themselves beset by internal and external problems that they were unable to overcome, and which were to lead them into a damaging and disastrous revolutionary war.

In 1930, a communist revolutionary, who was later to call himself Ho Chi Minh, formed the Indo-Chinese Communist Party. Banished by the French, he established himself in Kwangsi province of China, where in 1941 he formed a political party called the Viet Minh. In Kwangsi he was joined by another revolutionary, a schoolteacher from Hanoi called Vo Nguyen Giap, who was to become his lieutenant and, in due course, the commander of his army.

The Japanese take-over of Indo-China in March 1945 was a considerable help to the Viet Minh. By the end of August of that year, Ho Chi Minh, who had already formed a fairly efficient guerrilla force of some 5,000 men led by Giap, was established in Hanoi at the head of a puppet government, and in control of Tongking and northern Annam. For a short period he enjoyed the precarious protection of the Chinese Nationalists, who barred the way north at the 16th Parallel to General Le Clerc's French force that had landed in Saigon in November. But the Chinese (apart from the offer of some captured Japanese rifles) were a broken reed when it came to material assistance, and in May 1946 they left the country.

Ho Chi Minh knew very well that his guerrillas, although increasing in numbers daily, were in no position to take on the French, and so he decided to negotiate. Eventually an agreement, unsatisfactory to both sides and not likely to last long, was reached. Giap, who was busy training and expanding the guerrilla force at its base camp in the area of north-east Tongking, known as the Viet Bac, was eager for armed resistance. But Ho Chi Minh, a calm, deep and patient man, knew very well that peace, even an uneasy peace laced with cease-fires and truces, was important to him, and he continued to attend conferences and negotiate.

However, in the autumn of 1946, the French lost patience and made demands which Ho Chi Minh considered quite unacceptable. Now the Viet Minh must obtain independence by force. At the end of November, their war of resistance, which was to last eight years, began. But time spent in negotiation had not been wasted, and the two Viet leaders immediately embarked upon an elaborate plan of guerrilla warfare with a force now expanded to 30,000 and operating in a number of zones, each with an autonomous organisation, but subordinate to Giap's overall command.

The advent of Communist China in 1949, with its material aid, was a catalyst in the shaping of the Viet Minh and, by 1950, Giap had raised a regular force of four infantry divisions in the Viet Bac. His divisions had four regiments, each of three battalions, and their strength was around 10,000 combatants. The commissariat depended upon a huge force of locally recruited peasant porters.

In the autumn of that year, Giap felt himself strong enough to go over to the offensive against the French Expeditionary Force and their recently formed Vietnamese Nationalist army. At first, by skilful use of his superior numbers in a selected area, Giap met with great success. He swept the French clean out of northern Tongking and posed a serious threat to Hanoi and Haiphong. But with the arrival in December of their great soldier, General (later Marshal) de Lattre de Tassigny, French fortunes noticeably improved, and 1951 was a bad year for the Viets.

In January, a large-scale attack in the Red River delta, where de Lattre took personal command of the French troops, was a hard fought, close run affair in which Giap, with a superiority of at least three to one, lost

6,000 men killed in a three-day battle. Two further and extremely costly defeats that year decided him to revert to guerrilla warfare. But at the end of the year de Lattre, dying of cancer, returned to France and was succeeded in Vietnam by the much more cautious General Salan. Through this change in command, Giap got the breathing space he needed to regain the initiative. He not only replaced his heavy losses, but expanded his army to six divisions, one of which was the 351st Heavy Division, containing a regiment of engineers, two artillery regiments, a heavy weapons regiment, an anti-aircraft regiment and, later, a field rocket unit.

The raising of this division, and much else, was indirectly the result of a visit to Peking by Ho Chi Minh in April 1950, when he entered into an agreement with Red China for the supply of a wide range of arms and military instructors. Field guns, anti-aircraft guns, small arms and quantities of ammunition poured over the Yunnan border that year and later, save only for a short period during the Korean war, and even that break proved beneficial, for, when it ended, the Chinese were able to supply the Viets with captured modern American weapons. To what extent the Chinese participated in the actual fighting is not clear; there was a large military mission present to ensure the proper use of the arms supplied, and during the siege of Dien Bien Phu there was almost certainly at least one Chinese anti-aircraft regiment in action. But it would appear that Giap, the self-trained military prodigy so underrated by the French, was in sole command of all the major battles.

General Salan was replaced by General Navarre in May 1953. Navarre was a cavalry officer who had held important staff positions (chiefly on the intelligence side) and an armoured command. Normally self-confident, he was somewhat diffident in accepting the appointment, for he had no experience of high command and did not know Indo-China; but the politicians swept aside his disclaimers and sent him off with a directive to bring the war to a satisfactory stage from which the government could negotiate.

At the time of his arrival, the French forces in Indo-China were given as 189,000, comprising 54,000 French troops, 20,000 Legionnaires of varying nationalities (many Germans), 30,000 North African troops (Moroccans and Algerians), 10,000 Air Force, 5,000 Navy and the Vietnamese Army of 70,000*. However, the greater part of these troops were required for garrison duties in such places as the chain of defensive positions in the Red River delta known as the de Lattre Line, and elsewhere throughout the command. Giap, with six divisions and three independent regiments, had at lease 80,000 well-trained first-line troops, and a strong second-line militia of regional troops available for local operations. He also had a large reserve in varying stages of training. The Viet Minh were in control of

*O'Ballance p195.

the greater part of Tongking, held a commanding position in the 'waist' of Annam, and had a few strongpoints farther south.

It was not a very promising situation for Navarre, but he was quick to discern the weakness of his command and prepared a long-term plan based on a more mobile army, reinforcements and American aid. This he took back to Paris, where it was not particularly well received, and he returned with a promise of only ten more battalions, some American aid with strings attached and an order to get a move on. This he did with a successful operation in the north, a less successful one in the 'waist' of Annam, and the evacuation of the fortified camp at Na San.

Na San had been Salan's only successful operation. Three parachute battalions had been dropped well into enemy held country to construct a strongly entrenched camp against which Viet Minh troops could (and did) destroy themselves in a series of costly and pointless attacks. The successful evacuation of the garrison encouraged Navarre to think there was little danger in maintaining isolated bases in enemy territory. This, together with what he considered to be an obligation (though he had received no orders from his Government) to protect the friendly kingdom of Laos, decided him to form a similar, but larger, fortified camp at Dien Bien Phu, which straddled the only invasion routes to Laos from the north.

The village of Dien Bien Phu, which lies some 180 miles west of Hanoi, had been in Viet Minh hands since November 1952, and was a likely forward base for any Viet invasion of Laos. It is situated almost in the middle of a rich, fertile valley that measures some twelve miles in length and eight in breadth. The valley forms a basin completely rimmed by a series of jungle-clad hills whose peaks, in many places, rise to over 3,000 feet. It was not the easiest of places to defend, or to supply by air.

Navarre selected Major General René Cogny to be commander of the troops in Tongking, and from his base at Hanoi to direct the Dien Bien Phu operation. Cogny was a huge man physically with an excellent brain, who had been brought to Indo-China by de Lattre de Tassigny, whom he greatly admired. Ambitious, outspoken and prickly he would argue orders if he disapproved of them and, in making the choice, Navarre must have realised his worth, for there was no love lost between them. However, both were agreed that Colonel de Castries was the right man to take command of the garrison. Castries was a cavalryman and personally known to Navarre. He had recently commanded armour with success in the delta. Navarre anticipated mobile warfare in Dien Bien Phu, which was intended to be an offensive/defensive base, and felt that a cavalry officer in command would be most suitable. But Castries, unfortunately, had no experience of, or aptitude for, siege warfare.

On 20 November 1953, shortly after 10.30 am, the 6th Colonial Paratroop battalion and the 2nd Battalion of the 1st Paratroops were over the two dropping zones. Operation Castor had begun. The placid valley stretched

MAP 17.1

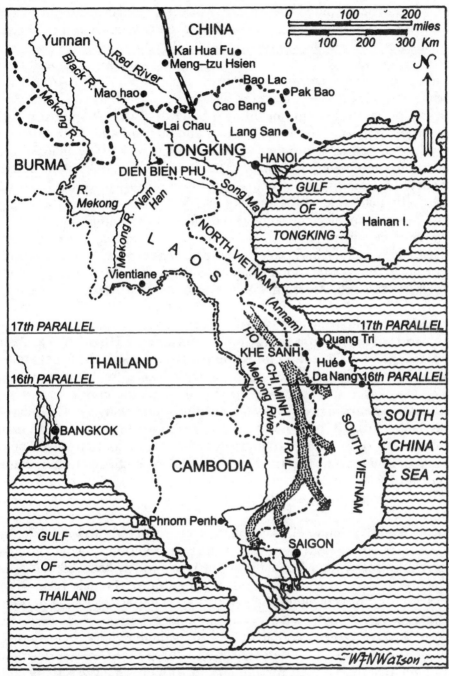

The Sieges of Dien Bien Phu 13 March–8 May 1954
and Khe Sanh 20 January–1 April 1968

itself in the sunshine, the peasants were at work in the fields and the Viet Minh troops were taken unawares. The battalions dropped a mile apart. The 1st Paratroops landed unopposed, but the Colonials, who came down just north-west of the village, met with spirited resistance and suffered a few casualties. Early in the afternoon, the 1st Battalion Colonial Paratroops, together with two batteries of 75-mm guns, a company of mortars and a surgical unit were dropped, and by 4 pm the Viet Minh troops had withdrawn from the valley, leaving 96 dead.

On D2, heavy equipment, including a bulldozer, was dropped and engineers began repairing the main airstrip and strengthening the 'fortress'. The valley contained a number of tiny hamlets and a few hillocks rose from the predominantly flat plain. The small river Nam Youm bisected the valley. In their previous occupation, the French had constructed two airstrips, the main one with a runway of 1,600 yards was near the village, and there was a smaller one some three miles to the south.

The defence was to be based on a number of bastions, each of which received a lady's name, and each was ringed by a series of (in theory) inter-supporting strongpoints. Somewhat isolated to the north was Gabrielle, manned by the 5th Algerian *tireilleurs*; to its south-east was Beatrice, held by the 3rd Battalion of the Foreign Legion's 13th Demi-Brigade; clustered round the principal airstrip was Hugette, with the 1/2nd Foreign Legion and a 155-mm gun troop; north and west of Huguette was Anne Marie, manned by Thais, and to its south Claudine, with the 1st Battalion Foreign Legion Demi-Brigade; east of the river were Dominique and Éliane, manned respectively by the 3/3rd Algerian *tirailleurs* and 4th Moroccan *tirailleurs*. Three miles to the south, and dangerously isolated, was Isabelle, strongly held by the 3/3rd Foreign Legion, 2/4th Algerian *tirailleurs*, a Moroccan *goum*,* a battery of 105-mm guns and a troop of tanks. Command headquarters and the Field Hospital were situated underground just north of Claudine, and here was centred the mobile striking force of infantry tanks and guns. At this stage, there were just under 5,000 troops in the valley.

During the following weeks, aeroplanes were constantly arriving bringing senior service visitors and ministers from Paris to listen to what Generals Navarre and Cogny hoped to achieve, for it was widely believed that upon the paddy fields of Dien Bien Phu, the destiny of French Indo-China turned. Most of these distinguished visitors were impressed by the position, which was being strengthened every day by entrenchments, wire and mines. General Navarre estimated that the enemy would require at least three full divisions to invest the perimeter and, if these could be tied down, an operation (Atlante) planned for January in Annam would greatly benefit. Should the enemy attempt a large-scale offensive, Navarre was confident

*Goum. A term used to signify a contingent of North African tribesmen or soldiers.

that the garrison's fire power would mow them down, and that this 'bristling hedgehog' would be the means of blunting the Viet Minh army.

However, not all the senior officers were so sanguine. Navarre, himself, while exuding confidence, did not neglect to order Cogny to make a secret withdrawal plan in case things went wrong. Cogny was nothing loath to undertake this, for he was one of the officers who had reservations, but the main opposition came from General Dechaux, the air force commander in North Vietnam. He pointed out the extreme vulnerability of the airstrips – the garrison's lifeline – and considered the whole venture misplaced. On the other hand, General Piroth, in command of the artillery, was dangerously optimistic. He was absolutely confident that his counterbattery plans would effectively knock out any guns the enemy might manage to haul through the jungle, and when asked whether he required any more guns himself, replied he already had more than he needed. In the event, the failure of the artillery was to be partly responsible for the French defeat.

In the three months following the occupation of the valley, the French carried out a number of sorties in strength. In early December, a force was sent to assist the evacuation of the Thai garrison of Lai Chau, and other strong raids of all arms, deep into enemy country, were undertaken in order to gain information, harass enemy movement and disrupt supply routes. Most of these raids and sorties had nugatory results, and many were costly failures either through air supply difficulties or enemy ambushes. Nor did an attempt to infiltrate guerrillas behind the enemy lines have any better results. By January, it had become obvious that Dien Bien Phu's role as a springboard for offensive operations had failed and belated attempts were made to improve the defence by bringing in more troops, artillery and tanks, for the enemy was closing the ring and clearly intended to take the bait with an all-out offensive.

Navarre and Cogny had not only hopelessly underestimated the number of first-line troops Giap would be able to put into the field, but also his ability to bring up heavy equipment over appalling terrain and, at the same time, to carry out mobile warfare. He quickly showed them how wrong they had been and ran rings round French attempts at similar tactics in the winter of 1953–54. Giap moved his divisions and regiments about without facing any serious resistance – he even succeeded in sending troops in and out of Laos. Marching long distances by day, and even longer ones by night to avoid enemy strafing, the winding divisional columns crept ever closer to the French camp. Besides his personal weapons, each man carried his waterbottle, his ration of 30 lbs of rice and a shovel with which he dug himself in at the end of a night's march.

By the time he was ready to open his attack on 13 March, Giap had three infantry divisions (the 308th, 312th and 316th), two independent regiments, and the 351st Heavy Division with its Engineer, Heavy Weapons and Artillery Regiments. A total of 49,000 combatants (and a further 10,000 would be thrown in as the siege went on) faced the French garrison, which, although reinforced by 12 battalions, still numbered only 13,200 of which no more than 7,000 were first-line troops.

The greatest surprise to the French was the performance of the 351st Heavy Division with its expertly handled fire power. The Viet Minh outgunned the French in heavy weapons by more than three to one. Moreoever, through prodigious efforts, the guns were hauled over steep jungle tracks, camouflaged when necessary by such ingenious methods as lashing tree tops together, and manhandled on to the forward slopes. Here they were dug-in and sited to bring direct fire on to vulnerable parts of the French camp, and in particular the airstrip. The guns at Isabelle could not reach them, and the counterbattery fire of those in the centre proved ineffective. If the French could have seized and held the high ground, the story would have been different.

The thunder of gunfire rolling down the valley was an ominous beginning to 13 March. Throughout the day, it continued unabated – and unaffected by the French riposte. The principal concentration was on the strongpoint Beatrice, with neutralising fire on the centre of the camp. Major Pégeaux, commanding the 3rd battalion of the Legion's 13th Demi-Brigade, was killed by a direct hit on his command post. Shortly afterwards, Colonel Gaucher, in command of the central sub-sector, was also killed. But it was not until 5.30 pm that Beatrice was assailed by an avalanche of men, stern and unflinching, who hurled themselves upon the wire and died in hundreds. Fresh battalions were poured in and by midnight the Legionnaires, who had fought with the utmost gallantry, were completely swamped, Beatrice was in Viet Minh hands. It was out on a limb and had been ripe for picking, but its loss meant that other parts of the camp now came under enemy fire.

The next evening, it was the turn of the isolated northern post, Gabrielle. The pattern was much the same, down to the consequences of a direct hit on the command post. Colonel Piroth was asked to silence the enemy batteries, but again his gunners were unable to do so. Once more, clouds of men stormed the position, once more they were mown down on the wire, and once again, numbers prevailed. The Algerians, having given a good account of themselves, fell back.

On 15 March, Anne Marie was attacked in force and the 3rd Thai Battalion (holding numbers one and two strongpoints) had no stomach for the fight, and who can blame them, for it was not their war and they knew the country well enough for them to slip away quietly in the dark, and disappear into the jungle or go over to the enemy. In the end, only one strongpoint held fast, and that was withdrawn to Hugette. And so it was that within forty-eight hours of the first attack, three of the main French bastions had fallen to the enemy. Furthermore, they had lost their artillery commander. Sadly disillusioned, and shamed by the worthlessness of his boasts, Piroth had held a grenade to his chest and pulled out the pin.

After this initial onslaught, there was a comparative lull in the fighting until the end of March, although there was always considerable activity both inside and outside the fortified camp. Giap needed this respite in order to bring up fresh troops to replace the enormous number he had lost in storming the three bastions. He also needed time for his slow, but exceedingly sure, commissariat to replenish ammunition stocks. Thousands of porters* and bicycle men busied themselves like a horde of ants over winding trails. Meanwhile Giap was tightening the ring of steel round the camp, sapping forward with trenches from which he proposed to launch his next attack.

The French had got themselves into an unenviable position. Even after this short time, it must have been obvious to their senior commanders that they could not win the battle, as the supply situation alone could have told them. The number of aircraft available was insufficient, even with both airstrips in use, and already they were virtually out of action. This latter proved a serious problem for the evacuation of the wounded. The occasional ambulance aeroplane managed to land (often under fire) until the end of March, and helicopters continued to make dangerous and difficult descents for a few more weeks, but it proved impossible to evacuate all the seriously wounded from a field hospital quite unable to cope with the high number of casualties.

Before the next round of serious fighting began, there was more trouble at garrison headquarters. Colonel Piroth was already dead, and now Castries' chief-of-staff broke down and had to be evacuated. Castries himself was nearing the end of his tether, and Lieutenant Colonel Langlais had to be brought into headquarters to assist in the command. General Cogny seriously considered dropping in to take charge of the battle, but was persuaded against it. It was a lost cause, and this was no time for a quixotic gesture by the commander of all the Tongking forces, even though it might have brought him fame immortal.

As both sides squared up for the coming second phase of the battle, the morale of the French troops remained high, despite their critical situation. The enemy batteries that ringed the heights became daily more deadly, but even so supplies continued to arrive – although some, dropped from too great a height, landed in enemy-held territory – and some guns and troops were also dropped. Among the latter were Major Bigeard's 6th Colonial Parachute Battalion, which had come in with the initial wave, and then been evacuated to fight elsewhere.

The second phase lasted from 30 March to 4 April. Langlais and Castries had done their best with the material available to strengthen the defence,

---

*At the beginning of the battle, Giap had 31,500 in close support, and almost as many strung out over his long lines of communication.

MAP 17.2

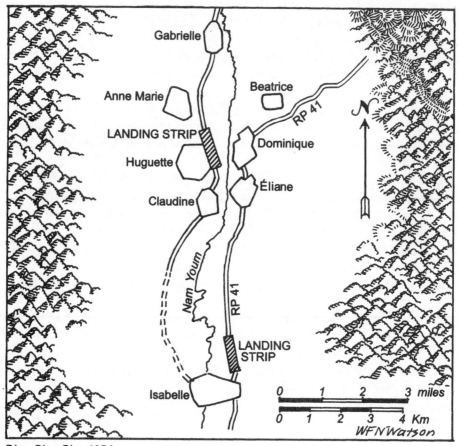

Dien Bien Phu 1954

and had placed a quota of reliable troops at all the vital strongpoints, concentrating on the defence of Dominique and Éliane east of the river. It was upon these two bastions that the Viet Minh barrage and assault was directed. Troops from the 312th Division, leaping from trenches pushed to within 300 yards of the forward Dominique strongpoints, surged forward, seemingly indifferent to minefields and wire. The terrified Algerians bent before the storm and departed for the rear.

What was to be called the battle for the Five Hills had made an unpromising start, with three of Dominique's six strongpoints soon captured. Two of these were briefly regained in a counterattack by Foreign Legion paratroopers. By the end of the second day's fighting, Giap's men were in possession of the north-east corner of the bastion and were preparing to deepen their penetration.

While possession of Dominique was being fiercely contested, Éliane came under heavy attack from the greater part of 316 Division. Here two companies of Moroccans, positioned in one of the strongpoints, followed the Algerian example and bolted. Every other position on this vital bastion had been softened up by concentrated artillery fire. But the defenders hung on grimly throughout the night, until, by daybreak, the fighting had subsided somewhat and the French made determined, but unsuccessful, attempts to regain the lost Dominique positions.

On the night of 1 April, one of Huguette's outlying strongpoints was attacked from the north-west by two regiments of 308 Division, and part of the airstrip was lost. The men of this bastion had to fend for themselves, because what troops were available for counterattacking were needed to save Dominique and Éliane. If they were lost, what happened at Huguette was academic. On 2 April, it was Isabelle's turn. A few days earlier, the 3/3rd Foreign Legion had been ordererd to join the battle at Dien Bien Phu, but they had been driven back and only their tanks averted a disaster. Then for the next three days the garrison was subjected to a series of fanatical attacks by the 57th Infantry Regiment of 304 Division, all of which they beat off.

During 2 and 3 April, savage fighting, much of it hand-to-hand, took place in all areas under attack. Early on the 4th, men of 308 Division made a determined attempt to gain more of the airstrip, but when this failed, with the customary heavy casualties, the fighting died down. The hopelessly outnumbered and severely embattled garrison had survived, although considerably dented, and Giap had lost literally thousands of men in an abortive attempt to break into the inner defences of the camp. His losses could be made good, but the French were not in the same enviable position. Early in the battle, the 2nd Battalion 1st Parachute Light Infantry Regiment and other details jumped in, but it was a desperate business in the face of heavy flak, and only a small offering. The garrison had been down to less than 4,500 infantrymen before this drop (of whom 1,600 were in Isabelle), and only one of the five paratroop battalions had more than 300 men. Tanks were reduced to four, and there had been serious artillery losses.

Giap's desperate and costly attacks on the Five Hills and northern Huguette positions had not brought him the victory he had wanted. The stubborn defence of the French had come as a surprise. However, the superb courage and complete disregard of death shown by the Viet Minh troops had brought some reward. By the time the fighting died down in early April, they had possession of part of the airstrip, two strongpoints on Dominique and one on Éliane. The loss to the French of the Dominique positions was particularly serious, for they barred the north-east entrance to the garrison's central position, which was now within a mile of Viet troops. The perimeter had become dangerously restricted, which narrowed the target for enemy artillery and seriously affected the dropping of supplies.

The decision to continue sending in reinforcements was not an easy one to take, for the battle was lost and the chances of a breakout were very slim. Nevertheless, Cogny felt that the losses suffered in the valiant defence of the Five Hills should be made good at least in part. The principal landings took place between 9 and 12 April with not particularly happy results. As well as the difficulties of restricted dropping zones the monsoon, which had recently begun, was exceptionally active on the night (9 April) that the 2nd Foreign Legion Parachute Battalion was to be dropped. Two companies and headquarters landed within the 'fortress', but they were more fortunate than some. On the night of 11/12 April 40 per cent of the 850 men dropped landed in Viet Minh hands. Most of those being dropped in this operation were volunteers from Legion infantry battalions, and some were making their first jump in these most inauspicious conditions with inevitable casualties.

For a short while, the fighting slackened, but conditions worsened. The monsoon, which the French had hoped would come as a friend, proved to be another enemy. Rain fell from leaden skies in sheets of water, turning the parched dust to rivers of mud. The Viets were well accustomed to such conditions, but the besieged floundered about in the slime and filth of unrevetted trenches, and the rain seeped through the flimsy roofs of the dug-outs. The plight of the wounded was appalling, operations were performed with the greatest difficulty and, in the foul conditions, gangrene began to affect wounds. Low cloud and mist hampered the air supply but not the Viet anti-aircraft gunners. The garrison was reduced, but it still had to be fed, and so did its prisoners. The future was dark indeed, and over Saigon and Hanoi there hovered a miasma of despair. It was decided to organise a relief force.

Giap spent the middle weeks of April sapping steadily forward to within a short distance of Castries' headquarters and the main French defences. Isolated Isabelle was surrounded, but remained defiant. Viet Minh units were withdrawn from Laos and other places, and reserves from training camps were summoned to make up numbers for the next major offensive. The Chinese were asked to provide 720 tons of ammunition and another anti-aircraft regiment. Giap reckoned to bring into the field 35,000 infantrymen and 12,000 gunners, sappers, signallers and details. The garrison of Dien Bien Plu dug themselves in and prepared to stem the tide as best they could.

The principal fighting in April, after the Viet's assault on the Five Hills had been largely resisted, was directed upon the three northern strongpoints of Huguette and what was still left of the airstrip (the chief dropping zone) in French hands. The initial attack had taken place during the Five Hills battle, and now after a comparative lull of nearly a month the fighting had flared up and become some of the fiercest seen so far. It was a desperate affair for the French against vastly superior odds, and although reinforcements arrived they were never enough; by 23 April, the three small, but important, Huguette strongpoints had been lost and the Viets had gained a further lodgement on the airstrip. The French suffered 500 casualties in this fight, including some of their best Legionnaire paratroopers, but the Viets had paid even more dearly for their gains, losing a large proportion of three regiments. It was only a temporary setback for Giap, but he required a full week to replenish ammunition and bring up more troops for what he hoped would be the final push.

Operation Condor had been under consideration for some time. Originally designed as a pursuit of Viet Minh troops after they had been broken up by the stubborn and active defence of Dien Bien Phu, it had to be changed in April to a desperate attempt to rescue the garrison. Colonel de Crévecoeur, who commanded the French troops in Laos, was in charge of the operation under Navarre, but it quickly ran into trouble through the contumacy of senior officers.

At the beginning of April, Cogny had agreed its usefulness if the force made haste, but Navarre procrastinated, for he was hesitant about compounding the Dien Bien Phu disaster with more troops. Cogny, who by now was hardly on speaking terms with Navarre, informed Castries on 14 April that the relief force was on the way, but this was not strictly true, because although a part of Crévecoeur's force was moving, Navarre did not give his final orders until the 27th, and then the airborne element was cancelled. Crévecoeur made what speed he could, but his North African and Laos troops were untrained in jungle warfare, and could not achieve a breakthrough in time. The familiar story of too little and too late.

Meanwhile, Giap was anxious to bring the battle to a swift and victorious conclusion. Not only was it proving extremely costly in manpower and materials, but the forthcoming international conference in Geneva would be considering the Indo-China situation. Accordingly, on 1 May, he hurled his men once more against the strongpoints. Encroachment tactics were over and he reverted to the mass attack. Because his trenches had been worked so close to the French perimeter, there was no opening barrage, but the wire was blasted by plastic charges, dug-outs were demolished, and the whole front came into close intense fire action. By the evening of 2 May, the Viets had made small gains on Éliane and Huguette and the outposts of Isabelle, but counter-attacking with the bayonet, the French drove them from some of these gains and showed that there was plenty of fight in them yet.

But the end was near, not because the morale and courage of the defenders was giving way, for they upheld both splendidly to the end, but because ammunition was running out. All along, supplies had been the key to this battle, and now the Viet Minh human chain was still standing up bravely to cannon, bomb and napalm rained on it whenever the weather allowed the French air force to fly, but there was nothing more for the French. It is true that on the night of 2/3 May part of a battalion of Colonial Paratroops, who had only arrived from France a few days earlier, were dropped. But they came far too late to be of any use and only added to the anguish, sacrifice and futility of the dying days of Dien Bien Phu. Someone had the sense to turn the remainder of the battalion back in flight.

During the last few days of the battle, the weather did its worst with low cloud and drenching rain. Conditions became appalling, but the French Air Force continued to drop supplies (196 tons were despatched on 6 May), but so small was the French perimeter by now that the Viets collected a great deal, and were soon rushing upon their enemy in an odd assortment of French uniforms and American helmets.

Gradually, inch by inch, the French in Huguette and Claudine were forced to give ground; the hand-to-hand fighting was being conducted by both sides with the utmost savagery; as a Viet Minh soldier fell, on came another and another. The perimeter kept shrinking; in the last two days the fighting was concentrated on the vital strongpoints of Éliane. On the morning of 7 May the last of these was caved in by fresh hordes of Viet troops, and by that afternoon Dien Bien Phu was disintegrating, with only isolated pockets of resistance still maintaining the fight. So as to save further bloodshed by another night of useless fighting, Castries announced that fighting would cease at 5.30 pm. At that time, only in Isabelle was there still some semblance of order.

Although at the receiving end of some very heavy bombardment, the garrison of Isabelle, until the last few days, had not been subjected to the punishing fighting of the main position. However, in most other ways its situation was the least enviable of all the bastions. Its principal role was to give flanking fire for the main position with its eleven 105-mm howitzers and, to do this, 1,166 men with guns and tanks were confined in a very small, rather boggy perimeter. Soon after the battle had begun, their small airstrip was out of action, the road to Dien Bien Phu was cut and the Viets had the position encircled. The garrison did not even have the morale-boosting pleasure of the two brothels, which a thoughtful command had installed farther north. Survival depended on airborne supplies and, on account of the very restricted dropping zone, Isabelle lost an even greater percentage than the main position.

On 1 May, the Viets had turned their full attention on this isolated bastion and the fighting for the next seven days was as fierce as any, with the artillery concentration on the small area devastating. Nevertheless, by the afternoon of 7 May, although some strongpoints had been swamped, the main position still held. At about 4 pm, Colonel Lalande, commanding the bastion, received a wireless communication from Castries to say that fighting would end that evening and that he (Lalande) was free to attempt Operation Albatross. This was a scheme for a fighting withdrawal worked out for the main garrison, which was to fall back through Isabelle, whose troops would act as rearguard. But events overtook the forward positions, and no breakout by them could be made. Lalande, for the sake of morale, had kept the scheme to himself and now attempted it without any rehearsal. At 10 pm, two companies disappeared into the darkness, but they were quickly cut off, overwhelmed and split up. Some men got back to Isabelle, and a handful escaped to the jungle. Fighting continued for a while, but further resistance was pointless. At 1 am on 8 May, Colonel Lalande surrendered. The siege of Dien Bien Phu was over.

It had been a victory for the Viet Minh, and there seems little doubt that it had been masterminded by Vo Nguyen Giap. It is true that he had the weight of numbers and a nearly homogeneous army, comprised of men dedicated to the cause of freedom. Nevertheless, Giap's fire and spirit, no less than his rapidly acquired tactical prowess, was the motivation behind the incredible exertions and endurance of his troops. He had paid very heavily for the glory; it is estimated that the Viet Minh suffered 23,000 casualties, of whom 8,000 were killed. The smaller French garrison, of which the Foreign Legion with seven battalions provided more than half the fighting men, also suffered grievously. In round figures there were 9,000 casualties of whom 2,000 were killed, and a further 7,000 were marched away as prisoners on 8 May.

There were a number of reasons why the French were defeated at Dien Bien Phu, but undoubtedly the deciding factor in the actual siege was logistics. With the exception of some food (a Viet Minh soldier subsisted on rice, lentils and dried fish), and later when French stores parachuted into their lines, all Viet Minh battle requirements came from China along a wide range of jungle tracks (there has never been any mention of the pre-Second World War Kunming-Lao Kai railway being used). Once across the border in the Lao Kai, Cao Bang, Lang Son areas, the Vietnamese Army Truck Regiment 16 was responsible for getting the supplies to Dien Bien Phu over more tracks, and one primary and one secondary truck road hacked from the jungle.

The French air force and navy pilots flew daring missions right up to the end of the siege in an attempt to disrupt these supply lines, but they had very little success. Every time roads or tracks were cut, the Viet engineers were quick to repair them or else to cut a by-pass. Supply depots and bridges across the Red River were well protected, and to approach these and the principal routes pilots had to brave a corridor of deadly flak. Whenever possible, supplies and troops were moved by night but, even in daylight, they were a difficult target. The Vietnamese needed no instruction in camouflage; depots, columns and gun positions were well concealed amid the impenetrable foliage, and when there was anything to cook, smokeless ovens betrayed no positions. These were just some of the factors that prevented successful interdiction.

The backbone of Giap's supply system was relays of porters, literally thousands being recruited from the peasantry, usually on a self-supplying basis. These men could not have supported an army manually, but it was made possible by the use of converted bicycles. Ever since 1951 the Viet Minh had been using bicycles manufactured in the Peugeot factories. The seat was removed and wooden struts were used to strengthen the frame, and bamboo poles extended the handlebars for ease in guidance when heavily loaded. These converted machines could carry split loads totalling up to 450lbs (as opposed to only 45lbs per man), and in the dry weather they were easily manoeuvred along jungle tracks. Thus if Giap had, say, 50,000 bicycles he was bringing up somewhere around 10,000 tons of ammunition, spare weapons, petrol and food.

During the last month of the siege, the monsoon had broken and bicycle transport had become difficult if not impossible. However, by then, the Viets were operating about 800 two and a half-ton Russian *Molotova* trucks over tracks and routes made passable by another huge conscription of coolie labour. Navarre had hoped that these roads would become impassible in the rains and make Giap's supply position as difficult as his own, but this did not happen. Moreover, the low cloud gave the Viet columns considerable protection against French aircraft, while seriously affecting the accuracy of their own drops.

As has been shown, the success or failure of the Viet Minh supply system depended, to a great extent, on porters. On the other hand, the French equivalent depended, entirely, on air support. Whereas the Viet Minh could recruit as many porters as they needed, at no time did the French have sufficient aircraft for their requirements. In its simplest form, that is why they lost the battle.

Matters might have been made easier for Navarre had he organised an adequate build-up of supplies during the weeks preceding the siege. But Giap had shown high qualities of generalship in forcing him, against his declared policy, to dissipate his resources by establishing small airheads for his mobile columns that were endeavouring to outmanoeuvre Viet Minh raids into northern Laos and the Mekong valley. In accomplishing this, Transport Command used up what reserves were available.

At the time of the siege, there were at most 100 transport aeroplanes, and only half that number of bombers (B-26s), with a shortage of crews. Nevertheless, between the first and last days of the siege, no fewer than 1,629 sorties were flown through very accurate flak from 37-mm anti-aircraft guns, which caused severe damage and losses – the French admitted to losing twenty-three aircraft. There was also a shortage of ground staff, and the Americans were chary of providing more aircraft if they could not be maintained. In the end, they did provide 1,200 maintenance men, which helped to shore up the supply situation but was far from solving it.

In the very short time in which it was possible to land Dakotas after the siege had begun, the garrison's daily minimum food requirement of 200 tons could usually be met, but once it came to parachuting, the problem became very acute. On two occasions in April, record drops of 217 and 229 tons were achieved but the figure was usually well below the minimum needed. There were two other complications to exercise the administrative staff. The allocation of priorities between medical requirements, munitions, reinforcements and food usually resulted in food having to come last, which could mean that fighting efficiency suffered when men were sometimes existing on survival rations. And anyway, food was a problem in itself. What was an acceptable diet for a European was not for a Mohammedan, nor for an African nor a Vietnamese. The requirements of each were different.

It was remarkable how well the French air force and navy pilots coped in the face of appallingly difficult and dangerous conditions. Troops and supplies were dropped round the clock up to the very last days of the siege on to a perimeter that was shrinking daily. The inevitable losses of valuable stores to the enemy was very seldom the pilots' fault, but just an unavoidable risk that had to be taken in a desperate calculation which, from the earliest days of the battle, could be seen to have gone wrong and to have become the one certain factor that ensured eventual defeat.

Dien Bien Phu was not the end of the first Vietnamese war: it had another three months to run. Both governments, French and Viet Minh, were war weary, but the Viets were prepared to hang on grimly to get what they could by negotiation. Giap now had some 90,000 first-line troops with which to confront the French, who in June decided upon a change of command, General Ely replacing Navarre. He conducted the last operation of the war, Auvergne, which petered out inconclusively. On 3 July 1954, French and Vietnamese representatives met at Trung Giao (just north of Hanoi) to discuss, among other things, an exchange of prisoners. On 23 July, the delegates at the Geneva Conference*, where a representative of the Viet Minh government was present, agreed a cease-fire. The Viet Minh received all the country north of the 17th Parallel. Laos, Cambodia and South Vietnam were to be independent.

* * *

Fourteen years after Dien Bien Phu there was another siege in Vietnam. This time it took place in the north-west corner of South Vietnam at a village called Khe Sanh. Here again, a comparatively small number of determined men defended for many weeks an improvised position against the challenge of thousands of dedicated Vietnamese Communists. There was some tough fighting, and great courage was shown on both sides, but the attention Khe Sanh received from the media was out of all proportion to its importance for, unlike Dien Bien Phu, the result at Khe Sanh was never really in serious doubt and the consequences of the siege were far less momentous.

*The Conference consisted of the Foreign Ministers of Britain, America, the Soviet Union and France, the Prime Minister of the Chinese Republic and the Delegates of North Korea and Associated States. The Viet Minh delegate was called Pham Van Dong.

The Geneva Accords of 1954 heralded a brief period of uneasy peace between North and South Vietnam. One of their stipulations was that there should be elections in 1956 to decide the question of reunification. But it was soon clear that the President of South Vietnam, Ngo Dinh Diem, who had inherited chaos, would never permit these to be held. For a while, Ho Chi Minh bided his time, for there were still many Communists in the South who he hoped might gain him eventual control of that country. However, by 1958, Diem had made remarkable progress in hunting these down and Ho had decided to give armed support to those who still survived. This resulted in the formation of the National Liberation Front, or Viet Cong, whose troops, by 1961, were strong enough to mount organised attacks against outposts of Diem's Army of the Republic of Vietnam (ARVN).

Successive Presidents of the United States viewed the rise of Communism in South-East Asia with deep concern. By 1954, America had more military advisers in South Vietnam than was permitted by the Geneva Agreement. By 1962, American helicopter companies were ferrying ARVN troops into action and when, two years later, the North Vietnamese Army (NVA) marched across the border, President Johnson sensationally reversed American policy of non-belligerency. By the middle of 1965, the United States was fully committed to a 'limited war' in South Vietnam and had some 80,000 troops in the country under Lieutenant General Westmoreland. These increased in succeeding years (by 1969 they had reached half a million) enabling Westmoreland to carry out a policy of attrition through the establishment of a wide network of fortified support bases from which to search out and destroy the NVA, while the ARVN concentrated on suppressing Viet Cong guerrilla activity.

The North Vietnam Politburo had developed a three-phase strategy of guerrilla war, guerrilla and conventional war combined, and total conventional war. The second and third phases were to be virtually consecutive, and had been reached by 1967. The most important part of these phases was to be the Tet* offensive, which included the siege of Khe Sanh. Giap at this time was Minister of Defence but, before the planning stage of Tet was reached, General Thanh, who had usurped Giap's post as field commander, had died, leaving Giap a free hand to plan and execute the operation.

Like the general strategy, this also was to be in three phases. The first followed the successful Dien Bien Phu strategy of attacks round the periphery to lure enemy forces away from the main target – in this case, the cities, which were to be simultaneously stormed by the Viet Cong. The final phase was to be a large-scale conventional battle, giving the North a prestigious knockout blow against the Americans that should strengthen subsequent political negotiations, as had happened at Dien Bien Phu. There were those who thought that Khe Sanh was the intended

*Tet was the Vietnamese Lunar New Year holiday.

MAP 17.3

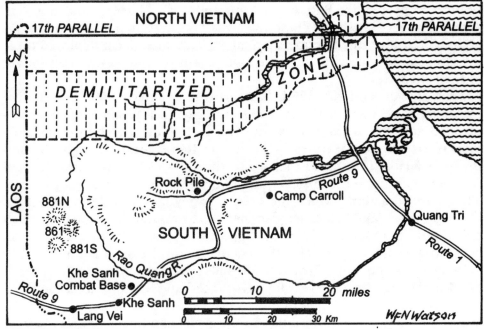

Khe Sanh 1968

set piece battle for phase three. The irony was that Giap, who was now to command in this battle, had always argued in council against a knockout blow in favour of a protracted war of raids and limited attacks, combined with political pressures.

The Khe Sanh Combat Base was situated in Quang Tri Province, just south of the Demilitarized Zone, and close to the Laos border. It sat atop a plateau and, to its immediate north-west, were three high and tactically important hill features. The river Rao supplied the Base with water. The principal importance of this base was that, along with other posts, it guarded Route 9, a vehicular track leading off the Ho Chi Minh Trail and used by the Northern guerrillas to infiltrate into Quang Tri.

There had been some fighting for the hills in April and May 1967. In this, US Marines had driven NVA troops off the two most important, 881 South and 861, but not until the end of that year, when it had become obvious that large NVA forces were assembling, was a serious attempt made to fortify the Combat Base. The 26th Marine Regiment, under Colonel Lownds, had then dug themselves in as the permanent garrison; the regiment had its own artillery but, in addition, the defended area could be supported by the 175-mm guns of the 94th Artillery in Camps Carroll and Rock Pile.

The small dirt airstrip was greatly improved and a suitable dropping zone was marked out at the edge of the perimeter. In due course, Lownds was reinforced by the 1st Battalion of 9th and 13th Marines, and the 37th ARVN Ranger Battalion. These five battalions and their supporting arms and services gave the defenders a total of 6,680 men. Giap deployed three divisions in the course of the siege, one of which - the 304th - had fought at Dien Bien Phu.

That division and the 325th had virtually encircled the Combat Base by 20 January, on which day a deserter gave information of an attack planned for that night against the troops holding the hills. This duly took place, but the Marines broke it up after some hard fighting, and this presumably forestalled the two further attacks that the deserter had foretold. Throughout the siege, these outposts were to prove invaluable. They were something which the French sorely lacked at Dien Bien Phu. The attack had taken place ten days before the assaults on the cities (which ended in a costly failure), lending support to that school of thought which believed Khe Sanh was to be a diversion and not the main battle.

In the early hours of 5 February, the hills were again subjected to a heavy attack and there was some very fierce hand-to-hand fighting. It was not until the afternoon, that the Communists were repulsed with the usual serious losses. Two days later, they attacked the American Special Forces base at Lang Vei. Here their armour could not be contained and the garrison had to be withdrawn, leaving Route 9 in Communist hands. Khe Sanh village was also attacked and it looked as though the 325th Division was poised to advance on the Combat Base from the west. However, Giap suddenly withdrew troops to support his men who were fighting at Hue and Da Nang, and there were no further assaults on the base until the end of the month, although pressure was kept up by a severe and continuing bombardment. This, and the closing in of the weather, made the air supply and parachute drops very hazardous and uncertain. Especially difficult was the supplying of that 20 per cent of the garrison who were holding the hills.

Giap's motives at Khe Sanh after 8 February are not easy to fathom. He seems to have given up his original intention of a prestigious sweeping of American troops from the Base. He had never been one to spoil the omelette for fear of breaking the eggs, and so even had he realised that he was playing Westmoreland's game, in giving the Americans the killing battle he wanted, this was unlikely to cause him to withdraw his troops. He never attempted to play the one important card he held – the water supply, which he could have poisoned at its source. Water was the Marines' Achilles heel, and had the river been fouled, they would have been in dire trouble. Be all that as it may, the fact is that on 29 February – 1 March, Giap put in what was to be his last major assault, and that by only one regiment of the 304th Division against the ARVN battalion. He may have thought it was a soft option, but if so he was wrong, for this was a good battalion and Giap's men were driven back in two attacks before they could breach even the outer wire.

Throughout March, ground activity was confined to patrols and raids for which, with the clearer weather, the Marines had the close support of fighter aircraft. The artillery of both sides was extremely active. On one day alone (23 March), the Base received 1,109 shells, but the only major encounter occurred on 30 March. On that day, B Company 1/26 Marines carried out a completely successful sweep to the south of the Base, routing their enemy from a number of fortified bunkers and trenches. Intelligence reports in the middle of the month indicated that Giap was withdrawing the 325th Division and other units towards Laos. Although it was not until April that, in Operation Pegasus, Route 9 was reopened and the area cleared of the NVA, the siege of Khe Sanh virtually ended with the successful battle at the end of March.

The Giap who fought the siege of Khe Sanh was not the same man who had triumphed at Dien Bien Phu. One wonders if he had been fully converted to the need for this type of battle in the present circumstances, for he certainly handled it badly. He moved troops from the battlefield in insufficient numbers to affect the issue at Hue, thereby weakening his power of attack, although he still had vastly superior numbers of which he made little use; he made virtually no effort to hinder the American air supply; and, above all, he threw away what was probably his only key to success by failing to strike at the water supply.

Opinions differ as to whether the North Vietnamese Politburo intended Khe Sanh to be a diversion in aid of phase two of the Tet plan, or to be the main battle of phase three. Two distinguished American historians (one of whom was on Westmoreland's staff) have marshalled a number of telling factors in support of their differing conclusions. It may be presumptuous for an outsider to venture an opinion, but it has to be said that the numbers of men he withheld from other important areas of battle, and the way he disposed them for attack, together with other considerations, both sentimental and practical, inclines one to believe that originally Giap intended the battle to be a set piece, and a show piece, in which eventual victory would have important military and political results. But halfway through the siege, original doubts on the whole concept of the set piece battle may have caused him to lose confidence in the outcome.

It is, indeed, difficult to understand how Giap could ever have had much confidence in victory knowing the limit of his resources and the strength of opposition. He may have based what confidence he possessed on what had happened at Dien Bien Phu. But there he had defeated French troops already battle weary, and who were dependent on an entirely inadequate air supply. Moreover, they were outgunned and fighting under a divided command, whereas at Khe Sanh, as Giap must have known, the fighting efficiency of the Americans was at its peak; they had a strong unified command; their supply base was comparatively close, and they had very considerable artillery and air support.

The Dien Bien Phu myth, which the North Vietnamese hoped to perpetuate, was that large numbers of valiant men, totally resigned to the demands of Fate, would prevail against all odds. It seems that Giap, good soldier that he was, did not at first appreciate that at Khe Sanh the myth was bound to be exploded.

Notes for Visitors to the Sites of the Sieges

These notes may be of use to people who happen to be in the vicinity of any one of those sieges recounted in this book where there is still something to be seen, or museums to be visited. There are some places such as Kut-el-Amara, Tobruk, Dien Bien Phu and Khe Sanh where a visit is likely to be unrewarding and at present uncertain, but more than half the sieges described still have something of interest to offer the visitor. Vienna is always worth a visit, but there is virtually nothing left of the 1683 siege that can be seen, and while the fortifications at Acre are very impressive they do not relate, except perhaps for one gate, to the siege of 1189. However, a visit to the following ten will help to add flesh to the bare bones of battle.

Constantinople

Here there is a great deal still to be seen. The land walls are sufficiently well preserved for the action to become realistic. It is possible to walk along a fair stretch of the top of the inner wall from the Romanus to the Adrianople Gates; the Tekfur Serai still stands at the junction of the double and single walls, and beyond it can be seen the Kerkoporta. From the top of the Golden Gate, a large stretch of the southern sector of the wall is visible, and the Rumeli Hisari fort is open to the public. The Military Museum has a section on Mehmet with such memorabilia as his sword and helmet. There is also the chain that blocked the Golden Horn.

Malta

Little now remains of the fortifications at the time of the siege, or indeed of the splendid auberges built subsequently by the Knights in Valletta. Forts St Elmo and St Angelo still stand, Forts Tigné and Ricasoli now crown Dragut and Gallows Points respectively, and Fort Manuel, guarding Marsamuscetto, was another later addition to the fortifications. The walls and bastions of Mdina can still be seen.

The original auberges were built between 1571 and 1590, and those of Aragon, Italy and Provence survive in part. The Auberge de Castile et Leon, built in the 18th century, is one of the finest buildings that now grace the lovely city of Valletta, where the founder's tomb can be seen in the crypt of St John's Cathedral.

Basing House

Basing House, once the largest private house in the country, is now a ruin, but a ruin which displays its history most vividly and wears its past with pride. Excavations are continuing, and much has already been revealed. The site is administered by the Hampshire County Council and is open to the public at certain times, and there is a guide book and other publications on sale, and a small exhibition. By following the guide book, it is possible to reconstruct the building and fortifications, and the course of the siege can be easily followed. Basing House can be reached by leaving the M3 at Junction 6 and following the signs.

Londonderry

A visit to Londonderry is very worthwhile, for there is still much to be seen. The wall is virtually intact, although, sadly, large parts have had to be wired off by the Army for security reasons. Nevertheless, enough can be seen of it to appreciate its importance, and from one place on the rampart, a good view of the undulating country can be obtained and also the extent of what was the bog. Windmill Hill to the south of the wall is a prominent feature, and still has its windmill. Long Tower church, where Brigadier Ramsey was buried, can also be seen from the top of the western wall.

Very few descriptions of this siege portray a true impression of the actual city in 1689, in particular how small it was, and how high perched. The walk from Shipquay Gate to the Diamond (the central part of the city) is decidedly steep.

The local authority put on an Exhibition to commemorate the three hundredth anniversary of the siege in 1989, and it remains open in the summer months. It is well worth visiting to see its excellent models, and other exhibits. St Columb's cathedral (inside the walls) has some extremely interesting siege memorabilia in the Chapter House, and memorials to one or two participants in the aisles.

Badajoz

The old part of Badajoz can scarcely have changed since the time of the siege. The narrow, twisting streets with their closely packed houses, and overhanging balconies must have been there in 1812, and no doubt they were just as squalid and dirty then.

It is possible to visit the Castle, and walk round a part of the battlements, from which a good view can be obtained of the country on both sides of what was the Rivillas stream, now a half empty canal. One can also see San Cristobal on its dominant feature across the river, commanding, as it did, the castle.

One can then walk over a particularly sordid area of gypsy encampments to get an extremely good impression of the deep ditch, the walls and, in one part, the fire step and covered way. Across a main road, which naturally breaks up the line, are the two important bastions of La Trinidad and Santa Maria. Standing on these, the visitor can get a fair impression of the scene at the time of the main assault, but it is not entirely clear in every aspect. By motoring round the walls, it is possible to fix the San Vicente bastion, but there does not appear to be any trace of the outworks, save for San Cristobal. Although outside the wall there is the Avenue de Pardeleras, which gives the visitor the position of that fort.

For a student of the siege, who happens to be in the area, the effort of walking the ramparts is rewarding, but there is not enough left to justify a special visit from any distance.

Lucknow

Anyone visiting India and being interested in the siege would be well advised to make a detour to Lucknow, for there is still much that has been preserved, a decent hotel in which to stay and pleasant gardens in which to walk.

The buildings most connected with the siege that still stand – at any rate in part – are the Residency, of which there is quite a bit left, the Machchi Bhawan, and the Kaiserbagh Palace, although here the gardens are now the main feature. The Baillie Guard Gate can still be seen, much as it was at the time, and also La Martinière school (near the Dilkusha bridge). The churchyard and graves have survived, but the church has gone. The tombs adjoining the Kaiserbagh – those of Nawab Ali Khan and Khurshed Begum – and the Shah Najaf (tomb of the first King of Oudh) are also well preserved. There is a small museum that is worth visiting, and from which guidance can be obtained as to certain other smaller buildings and points of interest.

Vicksburg

Like most of the important American battlefield sites, Vicksburg is beautifully, and intelligently, laid out in a National Military Park. The two battle lines were some eight miles in length and two thirds of the field can be covered by car over a route that stretches for 16 miles. Throughout this tour-route, the various important points of the battle are scheduled stopping places, and there are numerous plaques giving the story of that particular place, and the regiments that were defending or attacking there. These regimental markers extend throughout the lines so that one gets a complete picture of the layout.

The Visitors Center has some interesting memorabilia and a small audio-visual exhibition. It is important to take a route guide from the Center, for it is not easy to locate the positions without one. Some pre-knowledge of the battle is almost essential for full enjoyment, and only a visit to the site can give the student at this stage a proper understanding of the terrain.

Visitors to Vicksburg can find comfortable bed and breakfast accommodation in some of the charming antebellum houses in the city environs. The Court House (original building) Museum is well worth a visit, for Civil War memorabilia and other exhibits.

Ladysmith

The town has not grown greatly since the siege, and the visitor can still get a very good idea of what it might have been like at the beginning of the century. The features Caesar's Camp and Wagon Hill are much as they were at the time of the battle. Generally speaking, a visit to the site is very worthwhile. There is an excellent museum, with exhibits that explain the fighting very clearly.

The Alcázar

Those who wish to get the proper feel of the siege should certainly visit Toledo. The Spaniards have rebuilt the Alcázar from the total wreck it was after the siege as a replica, complete in every detail, of the former royal palace/military academy. Many of the rooms are now used to display weapons, uniforms and military history through the ages, but there is full information, and much memorabilia, of the siege. Moscardó's office is as it was during the siege complete with the telephone from which he received his son's last message. The underground chambers are still there, with explanatory plaques, so that every detail of the siege can be easily understood.

The splendid Santa Cruz stands just as it was. Although the Capuchinos can still be seen, it now has a very derelict appearance. The Curved Passage has not been rebuilt, for there is no longer a Riding School, Dining Hall or Santiago Barracks. A building of fairly similar dimensions to the old Gobierno stands on the same site, and the original zig-zag road to the North Terrace can be clearly traced. The battery sites to the north, and east across the river (Dehesa de Pinedo, and Alizares) cannot be seen from the Alcázar on account of new buildings, but San Servando Castle, which may also have been a battery site, stands out very clearly.

Toledo is only about 45 miles from Madrid over a very good road, and there is plenty of public transport. Besides the Alcázar it has, of course, much to offer, including the splendid El Greco Museum.

Leningrad

The city has been virtually rebuilt and most of the fine buildings that were destroyed, both in the city itself and its environs, have been restored to their former magnificence. There are therefore landmarks to be seen, but nothing of the actual fighting. However, there is the very good State Museum at 44 Krasnogo Flota Quay where there is a special exhibit illustrating the siege, and the Museum of the October Revolution (4 Kuibyshev) in the former Kshesinskaya Palace also has some exhibits illustrating the Second World War.

A visit to the very beautiful and well laid out Piskarevskoya Memorial Cemetery in Prospect Nepokorynnkh should certainly be included in any tour of the city.

Bibliography

Chapter 1: The Mechanics of a Siege
Bridge, Antony, *Suleiman the Magnificent*, Granada, 1983
Clausewitz, Carl von, ed. and trans. Michael Howard and Peter Paret, *On War*, Princeton University Press, 1984
Duffy, Christopher, *Fire and Stone*, David & Charles, 1975
Hoppen, Alison, *The Fortification of Malta by the Order of St John, 1530–1798*, Scottish Academic Press, Edinburgh, 1979
Oman, Charles, *A History of the Art of War in the Middle Ages*, Vols I and II, Methuen 1924
Vauban, Mr de, Marèchal de France, *De L'Attaque et De La Defense des Places*, 1738
Warner, Philip, *Sieges of the Middle Ages*, G Bell & Sons, 1968

Chapter 2: Acre 1189–91
Atiya, A S, *The Crusade in the Later Middle Ages*, Methuen, 1938
Beha ed-Din, *The Life of Saladin*, Palestine Pilgrims' Text Society, 1897
Hindley, Geoffrey, *Saladin*, Constable, 1976
Howarth, Stephen, *The Knights Templar*, Collins, 1982
Makhouly, N, *Guide to Acre*, Jerusalem, 1941
Newby, P H, *Saladin in His Time*, Faber and Faber, 1983
Oman, Charles, *A History of the Art of War in the Middle Ages*, Vol I, Methuen & Co Ltd, 1924
Perigrinorum et Gesta Regis Ricardi (1190–92), ed. William Stubbs, London, 1864
Porter, Whitworth, *A History of the Knights of Malta*, Vol I, Longman, Brown, Green, Longmans, & Roberts, 1858
Runciman, Steven, *A History of the Crusades*, Vol II, Cambridge University Press, 1957
Runciman, Steven, *A History of the Crusades*, Vol III, Cambridge University Press, 1954
Seymour, William, *Decisive Factors in Twenty Great Battles of the World*, Sidgwick & Jackson, 1989
Smail, R C, *Crusading Warfare*, Cambridge University Press, 1956
Stevenson, W B, *The Crusaders in the East*, Cambridge University Press, 1907
Sutherland, Alexander, *The Achievements of the Knights of Malta*, Vol I, Constable, 1830
Taaffe, John, *The History of St John of Jerusalem*, Vol II, Hope, 1852

Chapter 3: Constantinople 1453
Finlay, George, *History of the Byzantine and Greek Empires From 1057 to 1453*, Blackwood, 1854
Fuller, J F C, *The Decisive Battles of the Western World*, Vol I, Eyre & Spottiswoode, 1954
Gibbon, Edward, *The Decline and Fall of the Roman Empire*, Chatto and Windus Ltd, 1960
Guerdan, René, trans D L B Hartley, *Byzantium: Its Triumphs and Tragedy*, George Allen & Unwin, 1956
Oman, Charles, *The Byzantine Empire*, T Fisher Unwin, 1892
Oman, Charles, *A History of the Art of War in the Middle Ages*, Vol II, Methuen & Co Ltd, 1924

Pears, Edwin, *The Destruction of the Greek Empire*, Longmans, Green, 1903
Runciman, Steven, *The Fall of Constantinople 1453*, Cambridge University Press, 1965
Vasiliev, A A, *History of the Byzantine Empire, 324–1453*, Basil Blackwell, 1952

Chapter 4: Malta 1565

Balbi di Correggio, F, tr H A Balbi, *The Siege of Malta, 1565*, Copenhagen, 1961
Bradford, Ernle, *The Great Siege: Malta 1565*, Hodder and Stoughton, 1961
Bridge, Antony, *Suleiman the Magnificent*, Granada, 1983
Hoppen, Alison, *The Fortification of Malta by the Order of St John, 1530–1798*, Scottish Academic Press, Edinburgh, 1979
Hughes, Quentin, *Fortress: Architecture and Military History in Malta*, Lund Humphries, 1969
Porter, Whitworth, *A History of the Knights of Malta*, Vol II, Longman, Brown, Green, Longmans, & Roberts, 1858
Prescott, William H, ed J F Kirk, *History of the Reign of Philip the Second, King of Spain*, Vol II, George Routledge & Sons, Limited, London 1855
Schermerhorn, E W, *Malta of the Knights*, Heinemann, 1929
Sutherland, Alexander, *The Achievements of the Knights of Malta*, Vol II, Constable, 1831
Taaffe, John, *The History of the Holy, Military, Sovereign Order of St John of Jerusalem*, Vol IV, Hope & Co, 1852
Wood, A W, ed, *Cambridge Modern History*, Vol III, Cambridge University Press, 1904
Zammit, T, *Malta: The Islands and Their History*, Valetta, 1929

Chapter 5: Basing House 1643–45

Adair, John, *Cheriton 1644*, The Roundwood Press, 1973
Adair, John, *Roundhead General: A Military Biography of Sir William Waller*, Macdonald, 1969
Adair, John, ed., *They Saw it Happen: Contemporary Accounts of the Siege of Basing House*, Hampshire County Council, 1981
Clarendon, Edward Earl of, *The History of the Rebellion*, Books, VI, VII and VIII, Clarendon Press, 1826
Firth, C H, *Cromwell's Army*, Methuen, 1912
Fortescue, J W, *A History of the British Army*, Vol I, Macmillan, 1899
Gardiner, Samuel R, *History of the Great Civil War 1642–1649*, Vols I and II, Longmans, Green, 1886 and 1889
Godwin, G N, *The Civil War in Hampshire (1642–45) and the Story of Basing House*, London, 1904
Rogers, H C B, *Battles and Generals of the Civil Wars 1642–1651*, Seeley Service, 1968
Seymour, William, *Battles in Britain*, Vol II, Sidgwick & Jackson, 1975
Sprigge, Joshua, *Anglia Rediviva*, London, 1647

Chapter 6: Vienna 1683

Barker, Thomas M, *Double Eagle and Crescent*, State University of New York Press, 1967
Cacavelas, Jeremias, *The Siege of Vienna by the Turks in 1683*, ed. and trans. F H Marshall, Cambridge University Press, 1925
Leitsch, Walter, '1683, The Siege of Vienna', *History Today*, Vol XXXIII, July 1983
Morton, J B, *Sobieski, King of Poland*, Eyre & Spottiswoode, 1932
Salvandy, N A de, *Histoire du Roi Jean Sobieski et du Royaume de Pologne*, Vol II, Paris, 1876
Salvandy, N A de, *Lettres du Roi de Pologne Jean Sobiesky*, Paris, 1826
Stoye, John, *The Siege of Vienna*, Collins, 1964

Chapter 7: Londonderry 1689

Ash, Thomas, *A Circumstantial Journal of the Siege of Londonderry*, Londonderry, 1792
Beckett, J C, *The Making of Modern Ireland 1603–1928*, London, 1966
Graham, John, *History of the Siege of Derry and Defence of Enniskillen in 1688/9*, Dublin, 1829

Gray, Tony, *No Surrender! The Siege of Londonderry 1689*, London, 1975
Hargreaves, Reginald, *The Enemy at the Gate*, London, 1946
Kerr, W S, *Walker of Derry*, Londonderry, 1938
Macaulay, Lord, *The History of England from the Accession of James II*, Vol II, London, 1906
Mackenzie, John, *A Narrative of the Siege of Londonderry*, London, 1690
Macrory, Patrick, *The Siege of Derry*, London, 1980
Milligan, C D, *History of the Siege of Londonderry*, Belfast, 1951
Milligan, C D, *The Walls of Derry*, Part II, Londonderry, 1950
Walker, George, *A True Account of the Siege of Londonderry*, London, 1893
Witherow, Thomas, *Derry and Enniskillen in the Year 1689*, Belfast, 1873

Chapter 8: The Third Siege of Badajoz March–April 1812

Bryant, Arthur, *The Great Duke*, William Morrow, New York, 1972
Fortescue, J W, *A History of the British Army*, Vol VIII, London, 1917
Grattan, William, ed Charles Oman, *Adventures with the Connaught Rangers, 1809–1814*, London, 1902
Jones, Major General Sir John, Bt, *Journals of Sieges in Spain*, Vol I, London, 1846
Kincaid, J, *Adventures in the Rifle Brigade*, London, 1830
Knowles, Robert, *The War in the Peninsula: Some Letters of Lieutenant Robert Knowles*, Tillotson & Son, 1913
Longford, Elizabeth, *Wellington: The Years of the Sword*, Weidenfeld & Nicolson, 1969
Myatt, Frederick, *British Sieges of the Peninsular War*, Spellmount Ltd, 1987
Napier, W F P, *History of the War in the Peninsula*, Vol IV, London, 1834
Oman, Charles, *A History of the Peninsular War*, Vol V, Oxford, 1914

Chapter 9: Lucknow May–November 1857

Cass, A, *Day By Day at Lucknow*, London, 1858
Forbes-Mitchell, William, *The Relief of Lucknow*, The Folio Society, 1962
Forbes-Mitchell, William, *Reminiscences of the Great Mutiny 1857–59*, London, 1894
Fortescue, J W, *A History of the British Army, Vol XIII, 1852–1870*, Macmillan, 1930
Gubbins, M R, *An Account of the Mutinies in Oudh*, London, 1858
Harris, John, *The Indian Mutiny*, Hart-Davis MacGibbon, 1973
Hibbert, Christopher, *The Great Mutiny India 1857*, Allen Lane, 1978
Hilton, Richard, *The Indian Mutiny*, Hollis & Carter, 1957
Inglis, J S, *The Siege of Lucknow: A Diary*, London, 1892
Innes, J J McLeod, *Lucknow & Oude in the Mutiny*, London, 1895
Joyce, Michael, *Ordeal at Lucknow*, John Murray, 1938
Kaye, J W, *A History of the Sepoy War in India 1857–1858*, London, 1876
Morison, J L, *Lawrence of Lucknow 1806–1857*, G Bell and Sons, 1934
Verney, E H, *The Shannon's Brigade in India 1857–58*, London, 1867
Wilson, T F, *The Defence of Lucknow: A Diary*, London, 1858
Wolseley, Viscount, *The Story of a Soldier's Life*, London, 1903

Chapter 10: Vicksburg May–July 1863

Badeau, Adam, *Military History of Ulysses S Grant*, Vol I, London, 1881
Catton, Bruce, *The American Heritage: Short History of the Civil War*, Dell Publishing Co Inc, 1978
Catton, Bruce, *Never Call Retreat*, Victor Gollancz, 1966
Everhart, William C, *Vicksburg National Park Service Handbook*, 1961
Grant, U S, *The Papers of*, Vol 8, ed John Y Simon, Southern Illinois University Press, 1979
Grant, U S, *Personal Memoirs of*, Vol I, T. Fisher Unwin, 1895
Greene, F V, *The Mississippi*, New York, 1882
Johnson, R U, and Buel, C C, eds, *Battles and Leaders of the Civil War*, Vol III, New York, 1888

Livermore, W R, *The Story of the Civil War*, Book II, G P Putnams' Sons, New York, 1913
Mitchell, Joseph B, *Decisive Battles of the Civil War*, New York, 1955
Seymour, William, *Decisive Factors in Twenty Great Battles of the World*, Sidgwick & Jackson, 1989
Primary sources
War of the Rebellion, Series I, Vol XXIV, Parts 1, 2 and 3, 1860

Chapter 11: Ladysmith 1899–1900
Amery, L S, ed, *The Times History of the War in South Africa*, Vols 2, 3, and 4, London, 1906
Atkins, J B, *The Relief of Ladysmith*, London, 1900
Burleigh, Bennet, *The Natal Campaign*, London, 1900
Holt, Edgar, *The Boer War*, London, 1958
Maurice, Major General Sir Frederick, *History of the War in South Africa 1899–1902*, Vols I and II, London, 1906
McHugh, R J, *The Siege of Ladysmith*, London, 1900
Pakenham, Thomas, *The Boer War*, London, 1979
Reitz, Deneys, *Commando*, New York, 1930
Watkins-Pitchford, H, *Besieged in Ladysmith*, Pietermaritzburg, 1964
Wilson, C H, *The Relief of Ladysmith*, London, 1901

Chapter 12: Port Arthur 1904–05
Ashmead-Bartlett, Ellis, *Port Arthur: the Siege and Capitulation*, London, 1906
Connaughton, R M, *The War of the Rising Sun and Tumbling Bear*, Routledge, 1988
de Négrier, General, trans. E Louis Spiers, *Lessons of the Russo-Japanese War*, London, 1906
Hamilton, Ian, *A Staff Officer's Scrap Book*, Vols I and II, London, 1905
Hargreaves, Reginald, *Red Sun Rising: the Siege of Port Arthur*, Weidenfeld & Nicolson, 1962
James, D H, *The Siege of Port Arthur*, 1905
Kearsey, A, *A Study of the Strategy and Tactics of the Russo-Japanese War, 1904*, Aldershot, 1936
Nish, Ian, *The Origins of the Russo-Japanese War*, Longman, 1985
Nojine, E K, trans. and ed. Captain A B Lindsay and Major E D Swinton, *The Truth About Port Arthur*, John Murray, 1908
Norregaard, B W, *The Great Siege*, Methuen, 1906
Official History of the Russo-Japanese War, Parts II and III, prepared by the Historical Section of the Committee of Imperial Defence, HMSO, 1908 and 1909
Ross, Charles, *An Outline of the Russo-Japanese War*, Vol I, Macmillan, 1912
Russo-Japanese War, The, Part I, compiled by the General Staff, War Office, HMSO, 1906
Smith, W Richmond, *The Siege and Fall of Port Arthur*, London, 1905
Villiers, Frederick, *Three Months with the Besiegers*, (1905)

Chapter 13: Kut-el-Amara 1915–16
Barker, A J, *The Neglected War: Mesopotamia 1914–1918*, Faber & Faber, 1967
Braddon, Russell, *The Siege*, Jonathan Cape, 1969
Clark, A T, *To Baghdad with the British*, London, 1918
Moberly, Brigadier General F J, compiled by, *History of the Great War: the Campaign in Mesopotamia*, Vols I, II and III, HMSO, 1923–25
Neave, Dorina L, *Remembering Kut*, London, 1937
Townshend, Major General Sir Charles, *My Campaign in Mesopotamia*, London, 1920
Wilson, Lieutenant Colonel Sir Arnold, *Loyalties: Mesopotamia 1914–1917*, OUP, 1930

Chapter 14: The Alcázar of Toledo July–September 1936

Clough, James, *Spanish Fury*, Harrap, 1962
Eby, Cecil D, *The Siege of the Alcázar*, The Bodley Head, 1960
Kemp, Peter, *Mine Were of Trouble*, Cassells, 1957
Larrazabel, J S, *Air War Over Spain*, London, 1974
McNeill-Moss, G, *The Epic of the Alcázar*, London, 1937
Payne, Robert, *The Civil War in Spain*, Secker & Warburg, 1963
Richardson, R D, *Comintern Army*, University Press of Kentucky, 1962
Timmermans, Rodolphe, *Heroes of the Alcázar*, Eyre & Spottiswoode, 1937

Chapter 15: Tobruk April–December 1941

Carver, Michael, *Tobruk*, Batsford, 1964
Churchill, Winston, *The Second World War*, Vol III, Cassell, 1950
Connell, John, *Wavell*, Collins, 1964
Heckstall-Smith, Anthony, *Tobruk*, Anthony Blond, 1959
Moorehead, Alan, *The Desert War*, Hamish Hamilton, 1965
Playfair, Major General I S O, *The Mediterranean and Middle East*, Vols II and III, HMSO,
    1956 and 1960
Rankin, Kenneth, *Lest We Forget*, Odiham, 1989
Rankin, Kenneth, *Top Hats in Tobruk*, Odiham, 1983
Rosenthal, Eric, *Fortress on Sand*, Hutchinson & Co, 1943
Wilmot, Chester, *Tobruk, 1941*, London, 1944
Young, Desmond, *Rommel*, Collins, 1959
Public Record Office papers: CAB 106/630; CAB 106/812; CAB 106/834; CAB 106/838

Chapter 16: Leningrad September 1941–January 1944

Allen, W D, and Muratoff, Paul, *The Russian Campaigns, 1941–1943*, New York, 1944
Anders, Wladyslaw, *Hitler's Defeat in Russia*, Chicago, 1953
Clark, Alan, *Barbarossa*, Hutchinson, 1965
Fadeyev, A, *Leningrad in the Days of the Blockade*, Greenwood Press, 1946
Goure, Leon, *The Siege of Leningrad*, OUP, 1962
Inber, Vera, *Leningrad Diary*, Hutchinson, 1971
Karasev, A V, *The Leningraders During the Years of the Blockade*, 1957
Lavionov, V, Yeronin, N, Solovyov, B, Timokhovich, V, trans William Biley, *World War
    II, Decisive Battles of the Soviet Army*, Moscow, 1954
Pavlov, Dmitri V, *Leningrad 1941, the Blockade*, Chicago, 1965
Salisbury, Harrison E, *The 900 Days: The Siege of Leningrad*, Macmillan, 1969
Skomorovsky, Boris, and Morris, E G, *The Siege of Leningrad*, New York, 1944
Sokolovsky, V D, *Military Strategy*, 1963
Tikhonov, Nikolai, *The Defence of Leningrad: Eye-witness Accounts of the Siege*, New York,
    1944
Werth, Alexander, *Leningrad*, 1944

Chapter 17: Dien Bien Phu 13 March–8 May 1954 and Khe Sanh 20 January–1 April 1968

Beckett, Brian, *The Illustrated History of the Vietnam War*, London, 1985
Davidson, Phillip B, *Vietnam at War, the History: 1946–1975*, Sidgwick & Jackson, 1988
Fall, Bernard B, *Hell In a Very Small Place: The Siege of Dien Bien Phu*, Pall Mall Press,
    1967
Graham, Lieutenant Colonel Andrew, *Interval in Indo-China*, London, 1956
Hammel, Eric, *Khe Sanh: Siege in the Clouds*, New York, 1989
Hammer, Ellen J, *The Struggle for Indo-China*, Stanford University Press, 1954
Langlais, Colonel Pierre, *Dien Bien Phu*, Paris, 1963
O'Balance, Edgar, *The Indo-China War, 1945–54*, Faber & Faber, 1964
Roy, Jules, trans. Robert Baldick, *The Battle of Dienbienphu*, Faber & Faber, 1965
Seymour, William, *Decisive Factors in Twenty Great Battles of the World*, Sidgwick & Jackson,
    1989

Shore, Captain Moyers S, *The Battle for Khe Sanh*, Washington DC, 1969
Thompson, Willard Scott, and Frizzell, Donaldson D, *The Lessons of Vietnam*, Macdonald & Jane's, 1977
Turley, William S, *The Second Indochina War*, London, 1986

Index

331